Sociological Work

Sociological Work

Method and Substance

HOWARD S. BECKER

Northwestern University

ALDINE PUBLISHING COMPANY

Chicago

First published 1970 by
Aldine Publishing Company
529 South Wabash Avenue
Chicago, Illinois 60605

Library of Congress Catalog Card Number 77-115936
SBN 202-30096–X
Printed in the United States of America

Preface

The papers in this volume deal with several major areas of conventional sociological concern: problems of method, particularly the use of qualitative data; problems of educational organization and experience;[1] and social psychological theories, especially as they relate to the processes of deviance.[2] We ordinarily see these topics as separate, but, beneath the conventional differences, the papers are related by a distinctive way of thinking about society and how to study it. Let me say briefly what that way is.

I conceive of society as collective action and sociology as the study of the forms of collective action. I sometimes tell people that I arrived at this notion in graduate school, when I went out on the University of Chicago Midway and fasted for seven days, at which time the spirit of Robert E. Park appeared and revealed to me the kind of sociologist I was to become. The story is only metaphorically true. What actually happened was that I studied with Everett Hughes and Herbert Blumer and acquired that view from them, supposing that they had it from Park and George Herbert Mead and, through Park, from Simmel. In any case, it is not trivial to see society as collective action, for if you do you cannot see it as a structure, or a collection or organization of forces or factors, or a mechanism that produces rates, or in any of a number of other ways now common. When you think of society as collective action, you know that any talk of structures or factors in the end refer to some notion of people doing things together, which is what sociology studies. Any conception of society that doesn't have such a reference is to me suspect.

---

1. My other work in this area is reported in Howard S. Becker, Blanche Geer, Everett C. Hughes, and Anselm L. Strauss, *Boys in White: Student Culture in Medical School* (Chicago: University of Chicago Press, 1961); Howard S. Becker, Blanche Geer, and Everett C. Hughes, *Making the Grade: The Academic Side of College Life* (New York: John Wiley and Sons, 1968); and in the studies of non-college youth and their educational experiences which will be reported in Blanche Geer, editor, *Learning to Work,* forthcoming.

2. My other work in this area is reported in *Outsiders: Studies in the Sociology of Deviance* (New York: Free Press, 1963).

v

If you see society as people doing things together, then you see the necessity for studying social life at first hand. I don't know that there is any particular causal order involved. I have always preferred methods that gave the best chance of finding out what it was people were doing together—primarily lengthy periods of participant observation, and where that was not possible detailed unstructured interviewing. These methods have all kinds of problems, some because their logic has never been worked out in the detail characteristic of quantitative methodologies; others because you gather your data in the middle of the collective life you are studying. Over the years I have done a lot of research this way and worked with others who used these close-up methods; my natural desire to be orderly has led me to try to systematize the use of field techniques, the result being the papers in Part I.

If you study collective action, you cannot avoid the knowledge that everything—every person, every group, every action, every event—has a history. Nothing just pops into existence in some mysterious way we must not inquire into. Things get the way they are over some period of time, and to think this way leads inevitably to a conception of process. The idea of process appears most prominently here in the papers on personal change, but it also informs those on education in their emphasis on the development of careers.

Likewise, you cannot avoid the knowledge that events are transactional or interactional, that you understand what one person does by knowing the network of interaction he operates in and what all those other people are doing and how that conditions and is conditioned by what he does. This approach has led me, for instance, to raise the kinds of questions about deviance the papers in Part IV speak to.

To recommend that we study process and focus on interaction hardly seems revolutionary. I have tried in my own work to take those ideas seriously, accepting and following through on their implications even when that requires doing violence to accepted notions of how the world is or how sociologists ought to study it. I am a naturalist, in the sense that David Matza has given to that term,[3] and an occupational sociologist, as opposed to a professional, in the typology proposed by Irving Louis Horowitz.[4] These are well-established, even respectable, positions in sociology, but their implications can lead to unusual, even unrespectable, conclusions.

3. See David Matza, *Becoming Deviant* (Englewood Cliffs: Prentice-Hall, Inc., 1969), especially pp. 3–10.
4. See Irving Louis Horowitz, "Mainliners and Marginals: The Human Shape of Sociological Theory," in his *Professing Sociology: Studies in the Life Cycle of the Social Sciences* (Chicago: Aldine Publishing Co., 1968), pp. 195–220.

There is also something of a historical connection among these papers. Over the years I have engaged in many large research projects, some reported here, some published elsewhere in works on education and deviance. In the course of trying to gather and make sense of a body of data, I often found myself improvising techniques and using ideas I later realized I did not fully understand. Having done things a certain way, I tried to understand what I had done and make its logic clear; having used a certain concept in an uninspected way, I tried to work out what it might mean in some extended theoretical context. I call attention, without going into the matter in detail, to how this differs from approaches that develop "correct" methods *a priori* and choose concepts by seeing what will "fit" with already established theory. The best example of this conceptual development is perhaps the way I became aware that Carper and I (in the research reported in chapters 12–14) had used the concept of commitment without thinking much beyond its commonsense meaning, which led me to the analysis in chapter 18. In this way, every project has generated theoretical and methodological by-products, which then found their use in later projects. I suppose that set of historical links is why I see rather more continuity than others may in the papers in this volume.

The papers, then, are most of my work of the past twenty years that has not appeared in book form. I have made minor stylistic changes but otherwise reproduce them without change. I am grateful to James Carper and Anselm Strauss for allowing me to reprint work done jointly with them, and to the original publishers for allowing me to use papers that originally appeared elsewhere.

San Francisco, September 1969

Contents

PART IV   DEVIANCE

PART I

Problems
of
Sociological
Method

CHAPTER ONE

On Methodology

Methodology is too important to be left to methodologists.

By that trite paraphrase of a cliché I mean a distinction that will be clearer when I define the terms. Methodology is the study of method. For sociologists, it is presumably studying the methods of doing sociological research, analyzing what can be found out by them and how reliable is the knowledge so gained, and attempting to improve these methods through reasoned investigation and criticism of their properties.

One might say that methodology so defined is every sociologist's business insofar as he participates in doing research or in reading, criticizing, and teaching its results. That is surely true. Yet we have courses in methodology that some, but not all, sociologists teach. We have an official Section on Methodology of the American Sociological Association, to which some, but not all, sociologists belong. In short, some sociologists are methodologists while others are not, which is to say that in some institutional sense methodology is not every sociologist's business, whether it ought to be or not, whether in fact it is or not. The question then arises as to whether methodologists—the institutionally accepted guardians of methodology—deal with the full range of methodological questions relevant for sociology, or whether they deal with a non-randomly selected subset (as they might say) of those questions.

Obviously, I raise that question because I believe methodologists do *not* deal with the full range of questions they ought to. Instead, they attempt to influence other sociologists to adopt certain kinds of methods; in so doing they leave practitioners of other methods without needed methodological advice and fail to make an appropriately full analysis of the methods they do consider. I do not make that harsh judgment in a quarrelsome way. I am

3

less concerned with proving that methodologists have done wrong than with improving methodological practice by removing some of the presently un-inspected barriers between methodology and research.

I first take up the question of the limits of conventional methodology, demonstrating (what may be obvious) its predominantly proselytizing character. Then I consider alternative modes of methodological discourse, including some that were they more commonly used might improve our over-all methodological prowess. Finally, I discuss some important questions of method that now suffer from the lack of sustained methodological inquiry.

Methodology as a Proselytizing Specialty

Although some distinguished methodologists and philosophers of sicence believe that methodology should devote itself to explicating and improving contemporary sociological practice, conventional methodology does not or-dinarily do so. Rather, it devotes itself to telling sociologists what they should be doing, what kinds of methods they should be using, and suggests that they either study what can be studied by those methods or busy them-selves figuring out how what they want to study can be turned into what can be studied by those methods. I call methodology a proselytizing specialty because of this very strong propensity of methodologists to preach a "right way" to do things, because of their desire to convert others to proper styles of work, because of their relative intolerance of "error"—all these exhibiting the same self-righteous assurance that "God is on our side" that we associate with proselytizing religions.

What brand of salvation does methodology sell? What do they propose as the proper path to better science? The details vary and indeed show a tremendous amount of faddishness. At one moment we may be assured that only through the use of strict experimental designs in controlled laboratory conditions can we achieve rigorously tested scientific propositions. A year later, someone else enjoins us to pay more careful attention to our sampling procedures, lest our conclusions turn out to be inapplicable to any larger universe. Some bemoan the failure of sociologists to replicate earlier studies, and others recommend more extensive use of statistical models of causal inference, path analysis, mathematical models, computer techniques—each has its champions.

Beneath this surface diversity, one can easily discern a common pattern: a concern for quantitative methods, for the a priori design of research, for techniques that minimize the chance of getting unreliable findings due to uncontrolled variability in our procedures. Is it too extreme to say that methodologists would like to turn sociological research into something a machine could do? I think not, for the procedures they recommend all have in common the reduction of the area in which human judgment can operate, substituting for that judgment the inflexible application of some procedural rule.

That substitution clearly has much to recommend it, for you cannot have a science when propositions can be asserted with no more warrant than "it looks that way to me." Such assertions are notoriously subject to all sorts of extraneous influences, especially wishful thinking. And propositions generated by more scientific procedures may still be subject to those influences at every point where what is to be done is left unspecified. Thus, a fully specified sampling procedure, machinelike, is better than quota sampling, which leaves the choice of which middle-aged white males to interview to the interviewer, and thus to whatever nonrandom biases might affect what the interviewer does, with the danger that those biases are correlated with the attitudes under study. If an interviewer, fearing rejection, picks "nice" people and that "niceness" is correlated with liberal political attitudes, for instance, then the unspecified sampling procedure can produce distorted results in a way true probability sampling does not allow.

So science-as-machine-activity has much to recommend it, ruling out all sorts of uncontrolled biases. But, as is well known, it is difficult to reduce science to such strict procedures and fully worked out algorithms. Confronted with this difficulty, we can take one of at least two courses. Rather than insisting on mechanical procedures that minimize human judgment, we can try to make the bases of these judgments as explicit as possible so that others may arrive at their own conclusions. Or we can transform our problems into problems that can be handled by machinelike procedures. Or we can decide not to study problems that cannot be so transformed, on the ground that we had best apply our limited resources to problems that can be handled scientifically. Contemporary methodologists have by and large chosen the latter course.[1]

We might think their choice reasonable, if it were not that most working sociologists do not accept it. The people who do sociological research often accept, even champion, the methodologist's general tendency to push for more "rigorous" methods. But they will not accept his implicit recommendation not to do what cannot be done in that rigorous way. Though they respect the methodologist's achievements, they respect other achievements

1. See the perhaps unduly pessimistic description of the current scene in Herbert Blumer, "The Methodological Position of Symbolic Interactionism," in his *Symbolic Interactionism: Perspective and Method* (Englewood Cliffs, N.J.: Prentice-Hall, 1969), 1–60. For the kind of approach that makes Blumer pessimistic, see H. M. Blalock, Jr., "On Graduate Methodology Training," *The American Sociologist* 4 (February 1969), 5–6; but this is only one of dozens of examples available.

as well. And these other achievements are accomplished by methods that conventional methodology, not particularly approving of them, has had little to do with formulating, criticizing, or improving.

Let me propose a simple test of what Richard Hill has spoken of as the "relevance of methodology."[2] We can take the chairmen of the ASA Section of Methodology to represent those sociologists whose methodological work is especially respected, the true carriers of the methodological tradition. And we can take those books that have received one of the three major prizes awarded in sociology—the MacIver, Sorokin, and Mills awards—to represent kinds of sociological analysis generally thought worthwhile. How many of the methods used to produce prize-winning books could one have learned by studying the methods associated with the chairmen of the Section?

Tables 1.1 and 1.2 list the chairmen of the section since its founding in 1961 and the winners of the major awards since their founding dates. Without characterizing the work of the section chairmen in individual detail, we can safely say that they have all been associated with methodological work of the restricted kind I have described: methods of survey research, statistical analysis, sampling, and the use of mathematical models. By studying such methods one could clearly have learned to produce some of the prize winners: Blau and Duncan's *American Occupational Structure,* Hirschi and Selvin's *Delinquency Research,* the Hollingshead-Redlich study of *Social Class and Mental Illness,* showing that methodologists are not entirely without honor in their own country. But many more of the prizewinners used methods our most honored methodologists have spent little time on. The point is not that methods recommended by methodologists are bad because they have produced relatively few prizewinners. (A persistent rumor suggests that prejudice has operated to keep the number low.) I mean only to say that some methods they do not ordinarily discuss or recommend also produce high quality work.

Methodologists particularly slight three methods used by prizewinners. They seldom write on participant observation, the method that produced Skolnick's *Justice Without Trial* and Goffman's *Asylums.* They seldom write on historical analysis, the method that produced Erikson's *Wayward Puritans* and Bendix's *Work and Authority in Industry.* And they seldom write on what few of us even perceive as a method—the knitting together of diverse kinds of research and publicly available materials which produced Frazier's *Black Bourgeoisie.* All three methods allow human judgment to operate, unhampered by algorithmic procedures, though they all allow the

2. Richard J. Hill, "On the Relevance of Methodology," *Et Al.* 2 (Summer 1969), 26–29.

Table 1.1   Winners of Major Sociological Awards

MacIver Award

  1968 Barrington Moore, Jr., *The Social Origins of Dictatorship and Democracy*
  1967 Kai T. Erikson, *Wayward Puritans*
  1966 John Porter, *The Vertical Mosaic*
  1965 William J. Goode, *World Revolution and Family Patterns*
  1964 Samuel N. Eisenstadt, *The Political Systems of Empires*
  1963 Wilbert E. Moore, *The Conduct of the Corporation*
  1962 Seymour Martin Lipset, *Political Man*
  1961 Erving Goffman, *Asylums*
  1960 A. B. Hollingshead and F. C. Redlich, *Social Class and Mental Illness*
  1959 Reinhard Bendix, *Work and Authority in Industry*
  1958 E. Franklin Frazier, *Black Bourgeoisie*

Sorokin Award

  1968 Peter Blau and Otis Dudley Duncan, Jr., with Andrea Tyree, *The American Occupational Structure*

Mills Award

  1968 Elliot Lebow, *Tally's Corner*
        Travis Hirschi and Hanan C. Selvin, *Delinquency Research*
  1967 Jerome H. Skolnick, *Justice Without Trial*
  1966 David Matza, *Delinquency and Drift*
        Robert Boguslaw, *The New Utopians*

---

full presentation of the bases of those judgments that satisfies scientific requirements.

I propose, then, that methodologists have failed us because in their effort to reduce human sources of error they have ignored what a great many sociologists do and think worth doing. They have thus ignored extremely important methodological problems, problems that affect even the methods they recommend. When methodologists apply their talents to the full range of problems that afflict us, making use of a full range of analytic techniques, then methodology will achieve that usefulness to working sociologists it ought to have had all along.

Table 1.2   Chairmen of the Section on Methodology, American Sociological Association

---

1968–69 Hanan C. Selvin	1964–65 Peter H. Rossi
1967–68 H. M. Blalock, Jr.	1963–64 Sanford Dornbusch
1966–67 Richard J. Hill	1962–63 Herbert Hyman
1965–66 Robert McGinnis	1961–62 Leslie Kish

Modes of Methodological Discourse

Sheer technical description constitutes the first and most primitive form of methodological writing in sociology. Such writings are really no more than "how to do it" treatises, describing what practical men in our discipline have found to be useful ways to do research. They may be more or less logically described, but the ways described do not arise out of any particularly profound analyses of the problem at hand. The problem has, rather, been viewed as a practical one about which something needs to be done so that research can go forward. The writer describes something he tried and found to "work," whatever that may be taken to mean.

What I include in this category will be clear enough shortly, when I describe the other kinds of methodological writing it is not. But some examples may be helpful. They are found in writing about all the varieties of methods used by sociologists. For example, the technical innovations in handling qualitative field notes proposed by Geer and myself represent a tentative solution to a problem that had annoyed field workers for some time and for which most of them had already devised schemes of their own.[3] Similarly, many techniques of survey analysis or of getting surveys done in the field are described in works of this kind.

It may, perhaps, mean something that technical description does not often appear in the published literature, but rather is handed on by word of mouth, as a kind of oral tradition. Since this kind of technical material frequently has little or no logical or theoretical basis, it somehow seems too crude to publish. Professors tell their graduate students how to handle the problem, considering the whole thing part of the "art of sociology." Or colleagues working in the same area may pass on tips about useful ways to proceed. When these materials do find their way into print, they are often denigrated as "mere cookbook" stuff.

I mention technical description because this earthy form of knowledge is probably the precursor of a more systematic approach to methodology we can call *analytic*. Analytic writing attempts to discover the logic inherent in conventional practice, in order to reduce that practice to a defensible set of rules of procedure. The analytic methodologist assumes, in effect, that if some sizable number of sociologists do something in some particular way they probably have, by some means or another, blundered on to an essentially correct method, which now needs to have its logical structure laid bare. By uncovering that structure, we can sort out what is logically inherent in the method and what is only attached to it by circum-

---

3. Howard S. Becker and Blanche Geer, "Participant Observation: The Analysis of Qualitative Field Data," in R. N. Adams and J. J. Preiss, *Human Organization Research: Field Relations and Techniques* (Homewood, Ill.: Dorsey Press, 1960), 267–89.

stance or custom and can safely be ignored or, better, be done in a more useful and sensible way.

Analytical methodology arises out of dissatisfaction. A sociologist may feel it beneath his dignity as a scientist to work by conventional rules of thumb. His methods may not work as well as he would like them to. He may begin to explore the underlying logic of what he is doing from simple intellectual curiosity or because someone has attacked it.

In any event, analytic methodology characteristically takes the form of asking what real sociologists do when they do research and then tries to see what logical connection can be made among the various steps in the research process. Asking why things are done in a certain way, it develops a logically defensible description of what had perhaps before been only a collection of customary practices. We can then improve everyday practice by designing research activities according to what they should be in order to play their proper role in the method as it has been analyzed.

For instance, the dissatisfaction of the "Columbia school" with the conventional use of statistical tests of significance provoked a profound reevaluation of what those tests were supposed to be accomplishing and of how that same end might better be accomplished. Following those discussions, sociologists developed a number of new and potentially more useful tests specifically designed to deal with the data available for sociological research. Instead of using tests developed for data with quite different characteristics—because there was nothing better available and one was supposed to use *some* test—sociologists now have a wide array of logically defensible tests and measures. This advance has come about because analysts have gone very deeply into the question of what a test is supposed to do and have then designed tests likely to accomplish the job.[4]

Similarly, Lazarsfeld, Hyman, and others have systematized and rationalized the art of survey analysis, by developing out of what had been common practice the several ways a third variable influences the relation be-

4. The chief documents in the significance test controversy are Hanan C. Selvin, "A Critique of Tests of Significance in Survey Research," *American Sociological Review* 22 (October 1957), 519–527; Robert McGinnis, "Randomization and Inference in Sociological Research," *ibid.*, 23 (August 1958), 408–414; Leslie Kish, "Some Statistical Problems in Research Design," *ibid.*, 24 (June 1959), 328–338; and Santo F. Camilleri, "Theory, Probability, and Induction in Social Research," *ibid.*, 27 (April 1962), 170–178. See also Johan Galtung, *Theory and Methods of Social Research* (New York: Columbia University Press, 1967), 358–388; Thomas J. Duggan and Charles W. Deane, "Common Misinterpretations of Significance Levels in Sociological Journals," *The American Sociologist* 3 (February 1968), 45–46; Robert F. Winch and Donald T. Campbell, "Proof? No. Evidence? Yes. The Significance of Tests of Significance," *The American Sociologist* 4 (May 1969), 140–143; and Denton E. Morrison and Ramon E. Henkel, *The Significance Test Controversy: A Reader* (Chicago: Aldine Publishing Co., 1970). Leo Goodman, Herbert L. Costner, Robert J. Somers, and Robert K. Leik have been particularly active in developing new measures of association and ways of testing their significance.

tween two variables and explicating the conclusions one can plausibly draw in the several cases so distinguished. This increased self-consciousness allows the development of further methods as an extension of the logic that has been created to account for what has been done in the past.[5]

The last phrase sounds a little awkward, but I want to make clear that the logic eventually "uncovered" in such an analytic search may not have been present all along, but may have been *read into* what was done in the *past*. In the development of sociology, it probably makes no difference whether the analytic rendering of a method is faithful to what it proposes to render or whether that subject has been used simply as a springboard for a more imaginative production. The more serious test is whether what it produces is of greater use to working sociologists than what went before.

There is some virtue, however, in having an analytic account of a method remain faithful. It may be that in the course of the analysis the analyst, in order to simplify and achieve logical closure, does away with some features of the older method that he cannot fit into his logic but that are nevertheless of great practical importance. In fact, many of the problems sociologists face in their research may arise because thorny difficulties have been brushed aside in the search for analytic closure and elegance. It is certainly true, as we shall see, that many important problems are really not dealt with in current writing on methodology. This condition may come about because analytic methodologists are too eager for logical elegance and too willing to sacrifice for it details of what sociologists habitually do. (Anyone who buys a secondhand sailboat should never throw away any piece of junk he finds therein—a nail or a bit of wood or whatever—because it will undoubtedly turn out that it was there for a reason, that the former owner used it to do something important. It may not have been the best way to get the job done, and a manufactured device could probably be bought to do it better (or as well), but the job needs to be done, and you dare not throw anything away until you know what jobs it was called on to do and devise another way to do those jobs. The analogy to analytic methodology here may be quite strict.)

The analytic dissection of methods, however, typically focuses on only a few steps in the actual implementation of a method, those that can best be assimilated to the mechanical, algorithmic model. What are the various ways to relate three variables contained in a survey questionnaire? What is the best way to pick survey respondents to obtain an optimum degree of generalizability? But other problems arise in the implementation of these methods that cannot be so reduced, problems involving the very interaction of the researcher and those he studies, or the researcher and his

5. A systematic presentation of these techniques can be found in Herbert Hyman, *Survey Design and Analysis* (New York: Free Press, 1955).

peers and assistants, which arise out of the social context in which every research operation takes place. These problems are likewise amenable to analysis, but the analysis must rely on more than the logic of variable analysis or probability theory or similar approaches. It must instead incorporate the findings of sociology itself, making the sociological and interactional aspects of the method part of the material subjected to analytical and logical revision. We can call such an approach to methodology *sociological*. A few examples may make the point clearer.

The problem of interviewer cheating has plagued directors of survey research organizations from their beginning. The logical analysis that accompanies survey research simply takes for granted that the interviews specified in the sample design will be conducted and that their findings will be returned to the organization. It is known, however, that a certain number of interviewers will fake some interviews, filling out schedules and interview guides with imaginary answers from interviews that have never been conducted. As practical men of affairs, survey directors have devised rules of thumb for defining the problem and practical methods of dealing with it. For instance, one can reinterview a certain proportion of the sample, or at least check back with them to see if an interview has actually been conducted. Journals and organizations in this field occasionally publish or hold symposia about how to deal with the problem, and the answers given are practical and untheoretical. They do not get their justification from any logical analysis of the problem.[6]

A logical analysis is not likely to be very helpful. A more direct approach to the problem, embodying a sociological methodology, has been proposed by Julius Roth.[7] He suggests that we see the problem of the cheating interviewer as an example of a well-known sociological phenomenon, usually called "the restriction of production." When skilled technicians or professionals use relatively unskilled workers to do the ordinary work of an organization, the workers are often more concerned with generating the appearance of having done what they are expected to do than with actually accomplishing whatever goals the professionals set up for them. Thus factory workers are less concerned with the organization's overall goals of profit and efficiency than with maximizing their own autonomy. They therefore manipulate their work to make it appear to inspectors and supervisors

---

6. See the roundtable, "Survey on Problems of Interviewer Cheating," *International Journal of Opinion and Attitude Research* 1 (1947), 93–106; Herbert H. Hyman *et al.*, *Interviewing in Social Research* (Chicago: University of Chicago Press, 1954), 241–242; and Franklin B. Evans, "On Interviewer Cheating," *Public Opinion Quarterly* 25 (Spring 1961), 126–127. A more theoretical early effort is Leo Crespi, "The Cheater Problem in Polling," *ibid.*, 9 (Fall 1946), 431–445.

7. Julius A. Roth, "Hired Hand Research," *The American Sociologist* 1 (August 1966), 190–196.

as though they are working as hard as they can all the time, even though they are accumulating substantial amounts of "free time" for their own uses. Nothing in their work situation makes it important to them that the organization should be profitable and efficient; everything conspires to make it to their interest to maximize their own area of discretionary activity.[8]

Roth argues that the interviewers who do the leg work of the ordinary survey operate just this way. They neither gain nor lose if the survey is less accurate or less scientific than it is supposed to be; they gain if they get the maximum amount of income for the minimum amount of work. They gain, further, when they avoid tasks that seem to them, whatever rationale may have been developed by their superiors, foolish or pointless. Thus they will avoid conducting interviews when it is difficult to get respondents to agree to be interviewed, when the questions they must ask seem to them meaningless, and so on.

In short, Roth suggests that the problem of interviewer cheating is essentially a problem common to most hierarchical organizations, the attempt of the lower echelons of the organization to maximize their own autonomy and discretion. The solution to the problem, in this view, is not tighter supervision but rather to attach the motivation of workers to the goals of the organization, insofar as this is possible. Roth suggests several innovations in the organization of research that might accomplish this goal and thus presumably lower the rate of cheating.

This example shows the essential features of a sociological methodological analysis. We analyze the system of interaction in which the problem arises just as we would analyze any other system of interaction. We ask what categories of participants are involved in the interaction, what their expectations of one another are, what sanctions are available to each category of participant to be used in attempting to control the behavior of others. We locate the methodological problem in the behavior of the people participating in this system, asking what in the recurrent patterns of interaction causes people to do the things that give us difficulties as scientists.

Roth actually deals with only a portion of the entire system of interaction involved in interviewer cheating. We might go on to ask, for example, what the characteristics of the typical survey organization are such that interviewers can cheat without the results being apparent in the document they produce. Why can't supervisors tell a phony interview simply by looking at it? Why must they instead rely on checking back with respondents? Such an inquiry would lead us into questions about the hierarchical nature of survey organizations and would lead us to ask, for instance, as Roth has elsewhere,

8. The classic study of this phenomenon in industry is Donald F. Roy, "Quota Restriction and Goldbricking in a Machine Shop," *American Journal of Sociology* 57 (April 1952), 427–442.

why basic scientific work is regarded as something that can be done by un-trained persons.[9] A host of interesting questions about the organization of research arises here and, indeed, we can see that a full exploration of the problem of interviewer cheating would lead to a profound inquiry into the sociology of survey research, a task I will not undertake here.

The example also shows that we can, at least sometimes, rely on findings about social organization already present in the sociological literature. We have only to use our sociological imaginations to see that the problem we are concerned with, however narrowly technical it may appear, actually belongs to a class well known in sociological research, in this case the class of actions undertaken by subordinates to preserve their autonomy.

Sometimes the analysis of a methodological problem helps us to see general features of organizations not already available in the sociological literature. For instance, in considering the perennial problem of bias in re-search, I found it useful to introduce a feature of stratificatory structures that, to my knowledge, has not before been pointed out in the literature.[10]

Social scientists usually view the problem of bias as a technical difficulty, to be overcome by stricter and more rigorous methods of research. But it seems apparent that even though we are more and more careful about sam-pling procedures, about questionnaire construction, about methods of ob-servation and recording of field data, the problem of bias remains with us. Let us approach it as a problem of the social organization of researchers and those they study, instead of seeing it as a matter to be solved by in-creasingly rigorous and disciplined technique.

When does the accusation of bias arise? If we take as one instance of the problem organizational studies that have provoked such accusations, we typically find that the accusation is made by the people who run the orga-nization studied and that it reflects their dissatisfaction with a research report that gives substantial credence to the view of the organization taken by sub-ordinates in it. The people who run the organization usually phrase their complaint this way: "You have been listening to the gripes of these people lower down in the organization and you seem to take them seriously. You don't seem to understand that they do not know the whole story and that there are good reasons why we do the things they complain about. You make it sound as though they were right and we are wrong."

The complaints of the people who run organizations, properly under-stood, reveal the essential sociology of bias and in particular make clear that bias will never be eliminated by increasing methodological rigor. For

9. Julius A. Roth, "The Status of Interviewing," *Midwest Sociologist* 19 (December 1956), 8–11.
10. I discuss the problem at greater length in "Whose Side Are We On?" in this volume.

the essential complaint has nothing to do with the rigor with which we gathered our facts but rather with the point of view we seem to be taking. To state a complicated matter briefly, it is part of the structure of any stratified organization that ordinary participants in the society routinely assign greater credibility to the story told about the organization by those who run it than they do to the stories told by participants lower in the hierarchy. This *hierarchy of credibility* seems to me a characteristic feature of all hierarchical organizations. The sociologist provokes the charge of bias whenever he says something that denies the legitimacy of the hierarchy of credibility. He can avoid that kind of charge only by taking the viewpoint of superiors in the organization as given, clearly an equally serious form of bias, and one that will be so regarded by subordinates. Nor can he avoid the charge by being neutral and presenting both sides of the story, for when he undertakes to tell the story from the point of view of subordinates, he violates the hierarchy of credibility and thus will necessarily be accused of bias.

This analysis tells us how to avoid taking one side or the other unconsciously. In that we know what we are doing instead of just doing it haphazardly, we might be said to avoid the problem. But insofar as the problem arises because we worry about the accusations made by the people studied, we shall never avoid it.

The salient point about this example is that by undertaking a sociological analysis of a methodological problem we can make a small discovery in the theory of stratification. In this case no ready-made theory was available to handle the problem, but it was possible to devise a theoretical class of phenomena of social interaction into which we could place the problem of bias in order to get a greater understanding of it.

The basic strategy of a sociological analysis of a methodological problem, then, consists of viewing the scientific activity whose methodological features are under investigation just as we would view any other kind of organized human activity. This strategy leads, of course, to a very direct connection with the sociology of science, but differs from the sociology of science in focusing on problems of method, as they arise either in the practical activities of sociologists or in the logical analyses of what they do. Many problems of method, now seldom subjected to methodological inquiry, can perhaps best be approached in this fashion.

Some Neglected Problems of Method

A most striking feature of the specialty of methodology to a nonmethodologist is its focus on a relatively small number of problems, chosen from among all the problems of method that sociologists in fact have to contend with. While sociologists at work in the field occasionally write articles about particular problems of method that have come up in their own work, the great bulk of specialized work in methodology deals with problems of sampling, methods of statistical inference, scale construction, and the like. By virtue of the restricted set of questions on which this work has focused, it has implicitly urged sociologists to consider these the important questions of method and the solutions proposed the approved styles of work.

This has been an unfortunate development, for it has very often kept people with a gift for methodological work from concentrating on other problems whose solutions are equally vital to our common enterprise. It has further strengthened the hardly conscious belief of most sociologists that some problems can be approached in a "scientific" way while other problems, no matter how interesting or important, must either be ignored for the time being, until we devise sufficiently rigorous methods, or dealt with in ways that rely on intuition and other non-communicable gifts. If no strict set of approved rules and procedures exists, then either don't do it or anything goes.

We need not be stuck with these unpalatable alternatives. In what follows, I suggest some problems methodologists ought to deal with, give a few examples of how these have on occasion been gone into, and in particular suggest that the application of sociological methodology may be advantageous in approaching a great many of them. The list is neither exhaustive nor systematic; it deals with problems for which my indictment is only partly true, for I would not have become aware of them if they had not already been made the object of some attention. I offer these as suggestions of the kind of thing we ought to be examining.[11]

Getting In. A problem that afflicts almost all researchers—at the least, all those who attempt to study, by whatever method, organizations, groups, and communities in the real world—is getting in: getting permission to study the thing you want to study, getting access to the people you want to observe, interview, or give questionnaires to. The problem is perennial for practitioners of participant observation, who ordinarily have to negotiate the matter anew each time they enter an organization, for it will be the first time any sociologist has done so.[12] Until recently it has not been so pressing for those who use survey methods, largely because they have dealt with aggregates rather than groups, and so had only the problem of individual refusals rather than group refusal, or because they habitually used

11. Gideon Sjoberg and Roger Nett have recently published *A Methodology for Social Research* (New York: Harper and Row, 1968), which takes much the point of view suggested here, as does Norman K. Denzin's *The Research Act* (Chicago: Aldine Publishing Co., 1970).

12. A number of accounts of this process and its problems can be found in Philip Hammond, editor, *Sociologists at Work* (New York: Basic Books, 1964) and in Arthur J. Vidich, Joseph Bensman and Maurice R. Stein, editors, *Reflections on Community Studies* (New York: John Wiley, 1964). A pioneering discussion of the problem is Burleigh Gardner and William F. Whyte, "Methods for the Study of Human Relations in Industry," *American Sociological Review* 11 (August 1946), 506–512.

the same settings to administer their questionnaires (usually schools, and often schools where they taught) so that they had direct and privileged access to respondents.

The problem has recently been brought into the open again for survey researchers by a renewed interest by a variety of groups in the possible effects of allowing questionnaires to be administered indiscriminately to students and other captive populations. Some conservatives (including some in the Congress) have become offended by the practice of asking students personal questions about their feelings toward their parents, their own religious and sexual attitudes and experiences, and other material that laymen usually regard as personal. An occasional school system has refused entry to a researcher as the result of conservative pressure on the school board. Similarly, such groups as Students for a Democratic Society and the National Student Association have echoed the concerns of a few social scientists that data may not always be kept as confidential as we promise, or that they will be used for ends the students who provide them would not approve; and the use of deceptive experimental techniques has created the problem of the "wise" subject who deliberately acts to disconfirm what he understands to be the hypothesis under test. We may yet experience difficulties in financing research; what we have already is a heightened awareness among groups and individuals that, after all, one need not cooperate in social science research.[13] The problem of getting in thus has a new and increased saliency.

In any event, getting permission to conduct a study has had little serious methodological discussion. What can be found in the literature deals largely with the question of ethics, of what promises it is proper to make to the people you propose to study in order to get access and to what degree you are bound by those promises.[14] Hughes,[15] for instance, has contributed

13. On school systems refusing entry, see Harwin L. Voss, "Pitfalls in Social Research: A Case Study," *The American Sociologist* 1 (May 1966), 136–140. Problems of confidentiality in studies of students are described in John Walsh, "ACE Study on Campus Unrest: Questions for Behavioral Scientists," *Science* 165 (11 July 1969), 157–160 and Judith Coburn, "Confidentiality is not the Only Issue Causing Unrest Among Student Critics of the Effort to Study Protests," *ibid.*, 160–161. The "wise" subject is described in Martin T. Orne, "On the Social Psychology of the Psychological Experiment: With Particular Reference to Demand Characteristics and Their Implications," *American Psychologist* 17 (October 1962), 776–783.

14. See, for example, Arthur J. Vidich and Joseph Bensman, "The Springdale Case: Academic Bureaucrats and Sensitive Townspeople," in Vidich, Bensman, and Stein *op. cit.*, 313–349; Joseph R. Gusfield, "Field Work Reciprocities in Studying a Social Movement," in Adams and Preiss, *op. cit.*, 99–108; Kai T. Erikson, "A Comment on Disguised Observation in Sociology," *Social Problems* 14 (Spring 1967), 366–373; and the articles by Fred H. Goldner, Joan W. Moore, Richard Colvard, and Pierre L. van den Berghe in Gideon Sjoberg, *Ethics, Politics and Social Research* (Cambridge: Schenkman Publishing Co., 1967).

15. Everett C. Hughes, "The Relation of Industrial to General Sociology," *Sociology and Social Research* 41 (March-April 1957), 251–256.

some insightful discussions of the research bargain, and several people have given us rather detailed narratives of how they went about "getting in" in particular cases.[16] The raw material for the beginnings of a serious analysis of the question is at hand.

This seem to me preeminently a problem for a sociological methodology. We need to investigate those cases in which access has been achieved easily and those where it proves difficult or impossible. We need to know what conceptions members of organizations have of the work of social scientists and its effects, how the question of whether to allow social science investigations to be done gets involved in the distribution of power in an organization, and so on. We may find it interesting, too, to estimate the effect on our theories of the fact that by and large we study only those organizations that allow us in and do not study those organizations that can be studied only by "sneaking in." This sampling error, and it is properly called that, may have distorted many of our theories; for instance, it may contribute to the substantial predilection of social scientists for theories of consensus rather than conflict.

Once we have some sociological understanding of the relation between researchers and potential subjects of study, we may be able to work out analytically appropriate methods of gaining access. In the meantime, the first order of business probably is to continue to accumulate narratives of success and failure, searching them for the clues to a comprehensive theoretical understanding.

Avoiding Error. Sociologists have for a long time diligently searched out sources of error in their work. Following the lead provided by Morgenstern's classic work *On the Accuracy of Economic Observations,*[17] David Gold and I have compiled a long list of known safeguards against known kinds of error. Sociologists have discovered many sources of error in their data and analyses and have either devised ways to avoid them or cautioned other practitioners to take account of these errors in presenting their findings. It is instructive to look through current journals with a list of such errors before you and see in how many cases the known safeguard has not been used and the known error committed when it could have been avoided.

As an example, it seems to me now to have been shown beyond doubt that response sets—tendencies to give a certain style of response (acquiescent, socially desirable, and so on) without regard for the content of the attitude item—account for some of the variance in scores on attitude scales that do not specifically use devices designed to guarantee against their operation. Yet sociologists continue to use attitude scales that do not take those

16. Cf. Vidich, Bensman, and Stein, *op. cit.,* and Hammond, *op. cit.*
17. Oskar Morgenstern, *On The Accuracy of Economic Observations* (Princeton: Princeton University Press, 1950).

relatively simple precautions, even though their absence means that all the findings of such studies are in doubt, because some of the variance may be accounted for by response set variables rather than by those posited in the study itself.[18] Such examples could be multiplied greatly. Morgenstern's book provides a list of errors any reader can check through and compare with current practice in sociology.

The interesting question, of course, is why sociologists do not use available methodological safeguards. This question is clearly a topic in the sociology of science, for to answer it we would also have to know why those who take advantage of the precautions methodologists have invented do so, and thus what we are really after is the system of social control in science as it directly affects day-to-day scientific work itself. What kinds of sanctions operate to make those who use such techniques use them, and how do they fail to operate where the techniques are not used? How does science, supposedly a self-correcting operation, get organized institutionally so that the corrections are systematically not made?[19]

Institutional studies of scientific organizations are of course necessary here. But in addition some basic features of social organizations make the operation of science as a self-correcting mechanism problematic. Garfinkel[20] has suggested that the countless decisions a scientist must make in creating and organizing his data are in principle subject to a kind of uncertainty. The rules that are supposed to govern the making of those decisions—and I refer here to such simple decisions as what category to code a given piece of data in—cannot be drawn so precisely that there will not always be some case undecidable by them, which therefore must be decided on an *ad hoc* basis. Some of the variation in our data will therefore not be a consequence of the character of the thing it is supposed to measure, but rather a reflection of our inability to apply our definitions and rules as precisely and automatically as we claim to be able to do. The working scientist, who knows all along that he engages in such *ad hoc* decision-making, may generalize that attitude to many other problems he confronts. If we ask sociologists why they do not make more use of the methodological safeguards available to

18. See B. M. Bass, "Authoritarianism or Acquiescence?", *Journal of Abnormal and Social Psychology* 51 (1955), 616–623; and A. Couch and K. Keniston, "Yea-sayers and Naysayers: Agreeing Response Set as a Personality Variable," *ibid.*, 60 (1960), 151–174.

19. Cf. Thomas S. Kuhn, *The Structure of Scientific Revolutions* (Chicago: University of Chicago Press, 1962); Warren Hagstrom, *The Scientific Community* (New York: Basic Books, 1965); and Charles S. Fisher, "The Death of a Mathematical Theory: a Study in the Sociology of Knowledge," *Archive for History of Exact Sciences* 3 (1966), 137–159, and "The Last Invariant Theorists: a Sociological Study of the Collective Biographies of Mathematical Specialists," *European Journal of Sociology* 8 (1967), 216–244.

20. Harold Garfinkel, *Studies in Ethnomethodology* (Englewood Cliffs, N.J.: Prentice-Hall, 1967).

them in the literature, we may be told that it is too much trouble and, any-way, it really does not make much difference in the long run, because the errors are either too small to matter or they all cancel out.

Morgenstern has shown that these latter assertions are untrue for eco-nomic data[21] and I see no reason to believe that sociological data are any different in that respect. But the notion that it is too much trouble to under-take all these safeguards deserves further inspection. Clearly, everyone agrees that there is some amount of "trouble" worth taking with one's data, but likewise that there is some point beyond which the research will never get done for the taking of safeguards. As practical men, sociologists know that they must get their work done, and they do. What are the social supports for such a belief?

One possibility is that sociology, compared to some other disciplines, is quite polite. Compare the rather gentle controversies found in the letters to the editor of the *American Sociological Reveiw* with the bare-knuckle brawls that occasionally take place in the pages of *The American Anthro-pologist*. (It may also be that American social scientists are overly polite, as compared, for instance, to the British, and so sociology is polite because it is dominated by Americans.) I do not know why we are so polite, but we are and in consequence we are loath to say that someone has ignored an important safeguard. (As an example, I think it true that although many were shocked by the refusal of the "Columbia school" to use significance tests, this sense of outrage found its way into print only after long years of complaining over drinks at conventions.)

Another source of sociologists' reluctance to bother with methodological safeguards may be the difficulty of replicating sociological research. No one can ever study exactly the same group another person has studied, for at the least it will have changed in the interim between the studies and any differences may be attributable to that. Or, when people study two orga-nizations of the same kind (as for instance two medical schools)[22] the differences in the resulting characterizations may come from any of a great variety of factors, of which the question of technical safeguards is only one. In any event, it becomes quite difficult to show in substantive studies that the failure to take the advised precautions has made any difference. (Thus, what are we to make of the difference in the characterizations of Tepoztlán by Oscar Lewis and Robert Redfield?[23] Is it a difference between the men? Between their theories? Between details of their technique?)

21. Morgenstern, *op. cit.*

22. See the discussion in Samuel W. Bloom, "The Sociology of Medical Education: Some Comments on the State of a Field," *Milbank Memorial Fund Quarterly* 43 (April 1965), 143–184.

23. Robert Redfield, *Tepoztlán* (Chicago: University of Chicago Press, 1930) and Oscar Lewis, *Life in a Mexican Village: Tepoztlán Restudied* (Urbana: University of Illinois Press, 1951).

In any event, sociologists' reluctance to use methodological safeguards is another prime subject for a sociologically oriented methodologist.

Choice of Frameworks. A serious problem that confronts any sociological investigator who wishes to study a group or community is the choice of a theoretical framework with which to approach it. A naturally occurring group or organization can be viewed in many different ways; none of them are right, none of them are wrong, they are simply alternative and perhaps complementary. How does one go about making this choice? At present, we rely on personal taste; we choose the framework that seems most congenial to us and who's to argue? Occasionally someone will suggest that the choice ought to be made with an eye to the accumulation of research results in one area or on one topic, but such suggestions usually go unheeded. No one chooses his framework just because it will add to a growing body of knowledge, however desirable that might be.

The classic reference on this problem, and the only one I know that goes into it seriously as a methodological problem, is *The Little Community*.[24] In this book, Redfield shows us many viewpoints from which we may study the small peasant community: the ecological, the biographical, and so on. He describes with great perception and wisdom what we gain from each choice and what we lose by making each choice. Probably this kind of analytic work is what is most necessary at this time. It would be of interest, too, to know what actually influences the choices made, but it seems to me more important for us, as working sociologists, to know what we are choosing when we do choose.

Hidden Assumptions. I have under this heading, at the present, only an example, which, however, seems to be an important one. Some years ago, Sterling[25] showed that experimental journals in psychology never published negative results (that is, results where there was no difference between an experimental and a control group) and hardly ever published replications of earlier studies. He used these two facts to make the following demonstration. Suppose that a scientist gets an idea for a hypothesis to test. He designs an experiment to test it and his findings are negative; he does not publish the article. Subsequent scientists get the same idea and go through the same procedure with the same result. However, once out of every twenty trials, positive results will occur at the .05 level of significance by chance alone. The twentieth scientist, who has achieved these chance positive results, publishes his work. Since hardly anyone ever replicates published findings,

---

24. Robert Redfield, *The Little Community* (Chicago: University of Chicago Press, 1955).

25. Theodore D. Sterling, "Publication Decisions and their Possible Effects on Inferences Drawn from Tests of Significance—or Vice Versa," *Journal of the American Statistical Association* 54 (March 1959), 30–34.

what he reports goes unchallenged. Thus, Sterling argues, the entire literature of experimental psychology may well be filled with results that have occurred by chance alone. Or, at least, such findings are present in the literature in some now unknown proportion.

Other factors, as a number of psychologists have argued to me, may well be at work that prevent this unseemly outcome. Nevertheless, Sterling's analysis makes clear an important assumption made by those who use standard significance tests, an assumption that requires for its justification a sociological approach to the methodological problem. The assumption, of course, is that every study testing a hypothesis has an equal probability of being published and appearing in the literature. You will not find this assumption among those listed when a statistics text explains what we assume when we compute a Chi square, but it is an assumption that we make and an important one.

The assumption of equal probability of publication is important precisely because, as Sterling's figures showed, it is systematically violated. Whatever other factors may facilitate or hinder the publication of an article, whether its findings are negative or positive is clearly a crucial characteristic that affects its publication fate. Probabilities of publication in these two categories, far from being equal, are zero for one category and some figure discoverable from editorial records for the other.[26] In any case, the statistical calculation of the probability of getting a given result depends, for its utility in making inferences about the validity of a hypothesis, on the social structure surrounding the submission and choice of articles for publication.

I do not immediately see what the analogue of this hidden assumption by users of significance tests is in other kinds of methodological strategies, but it seems clear that here is an area where much useful work can be done.

Developing Hypotheses. Most books on research methods begin by suggesting that we already have a hypothesis. The question before us is how that hypothesis may be best and most efficiently tested. Such a presentation of problems of method leaves out one crucial step in the development of any piece of research: the process by which we acquire the hypothesis to be tested. This unfortunate omission makes it appear either that the step is quite easy to accomplish and therefore need not be worried about or that it is done by some mystical procedure not subject to analysis.

Neither of these is true. Developing hypotheses is a complex procedure, but one that can be explained so that others can carry it out as well. Gen-

---

26. Erwin Smigel and H. Laurence Ross present some data on this point in an as yet unpublished article analyzing data on the editorial practices of *Social Problems*. See also the mathematical model proposed in Arthur L. Stinchcombe and Richard Ofshe, "On Journal Editing as a Probabilistic Process," *The American Sociologist* 4 (May 1969), 116–117.

erations of sociologists somehow manage to develop the hypotheses they eventually test. How do they do it?

Scientific mythology says that hypotheses should be arrived at deductively, from a body of axioms, theorems, and corollaries. To say this does not change the problem very much, for we can always deduce a great many hypotheses from any set of axioms and theorems. We still have to choose from among the possible deductions the particular ones to be tested.

The procedure by which sociologists develop hypotheses is now pretty much in the realm of technical lore, learned through casual conversation and the like. It has been discussed most openly with respect to participant observation studies, for in participant observation one has both the chance and the necessity to develop hypotheses after one has begun to gather data. Most other techniques require the researcher at least to pretend to have some fairly well-formulated hypotheses before he starts (although it is common knowledge that most hypotheses in research papers were developed during the analysis, rather than before it). Insofar as field workers have made it a tenet of their method that hypotheses are to be developed in the course of the work itself, they have become self-conscious about the problem and have attempted to say something about it. It is from that background that Glaser and Strauss developed their account of theoretical discovery.[27]

The development of hypotheses is a methodological problem that clearly calls for an analytic approach. We need to go over the folklore, the gimmicks and tricks that people have used successfully, the personal narratives available, and see what logical structure we can fashion that will allow us to develop more systematic procedures. An example of the kind of analysis I have in mind can be found in the works of George Polya, who has developed several methods for getting good ideas and discovering ways to prove them out of his own experience in mathematical research.[28] Perhaps some of these will be equally useful in sociology, but I expect that the subject matter of sociology is sufficiently different that perhaps other methods will be found as well.

In particular, it seems to me that, since the subject matter of sociology is the social life in which we are all involved, the ability to make imaginative use of personal experience and the very quality of one's personal experience will be important contributors to one's technical skill. How do we go about

---

27. Barney G. Glaser and Anselm L. Strauss, *The Discovery of Grounded Theory: Strategies for Qualitative Research* (Chicago: Aldine Publishing Co., 1967). For a more formal approach to the same problem, see Robert Dubin, *Theory Building* (New York: Free Press, 1969) and Arthur L. Stinchcombe, *Constructing Social Theory* (New York: Harcourt, Brace and World, 1968).

28. George Polya, *Mathematics and Plausible Reasoning* (Princeton: Princeton University Press, 1954). Blumer, *op cit.*, also suggests the necessity of considering these early steps in the research process as part of our methodology.

translating personal experience into hypotheses or, to put it another way, how do we use that experience to give shape to hypotheses developed in other ways? Many sociologists advise their students to read novels, not so much for their literary value as for the "ethnographic" reporting on various aspects of society thay often contain. Some sociologists (often the same ones) advise their students to "get around" in their society, to enter many parts of it and get to know many different kinds of people in many different social settings. Probably one or the other of these is sufficient for the purpose. And what is the purpose? In part, it is to help us avoid framing foolish hypotheses; Galtung argues that Latin American sociologists often entertain patently false hypotheses about other social groups, largely because the social structure of Latin American society is such that they have never had any personal contact with members of those groups and thus are able to entertain outlandish notions about them.[29] Another virtue of wide personal experience (whether gathered by reading or direct participation) is that it makes available to us a large store of possible analogies. The role of reasoning by analogy as a means of suggesting hypotheses requires explication, which might bring to consciousness a number of replicable procedures many now use without quite knowing what they are doing.

Another problem we can look into is the criteria by which we distinguish "good" hypotheses from "bad" ones. Most sociologists have an intuitive sense that some hypotheses are better than others in vaguely defined ways, and they certainly act on that intuition in choosing hypotheses to pursue. They believe that some hypotheses will "work" and that others will not, whatever they take that term to mean. Among the criteria of a good hypothesis that come to mind immediately: A good hypothesis is one whose variables are present in the situation under study, or, if this is what is sought, they vary enough so that the influence of the differing values they may take is sufficient to show an effect. A good hypothesis, again, is one that seems to organize a lot of data, one to which we can attach other subhypotheses that make use of other parts of our data, in this way agglutinating the various hypotheses we entertain into a larger whole. A good hypothesis is one that does not run afoul of any facts we have available to us.

Conclusion

I have not attempted a complete catalog of ignored methodological problems. We might attempt one by a logical analysis of the steps involved in sociological research, an analysis that would however be based on the steps sociologists actually go through as those can be derived from the experience

29. Johan Galtung, "Los Factores Socioculturales y el Desarollo de la Sociología en America Latina," *Revista Latinoamericana de Sociología* 1 (1965), 72–102.

of practicing researchers.[30] We might simultaneously address ourselves to those difficulties experienced by researchers as practical problems, attempting to find their generic character and their place in some logical scheme.

We need, in any event, to continue to add to that inventory of problems, no longer ignoring those that cannot conveniently be dealt with in conventionally "rigorous" ways. We do not solve or dispose of a problem by ignoring it; we only leave its effects to operate unobserved and to create unknown difficulties in our common scientific enterprise. If we confront our problems of method and technique with a combination of logically rigorous analysis and a sociological understanding of research as a collective enterprise, we may finally create a viable science.

30. See Blumer, *op. cit.*

CHAPTER TWO

Problems of Inference
and Proof
in Participant Observation

The participant observer gathers data by participating in the daily life of the group or organization he studies.[1] He watches the people he is studying to see what situations they ordinarily meet and how they behave in them. He enters into conversation with some or all of the participants in these situations and discovers their interpretations of the events he has observed.

Let me describe, as one specific instance of observational technique, what my colleagues and I have done in studying a medical school. We went to lectures with students taking their first two years of basic science and frequented the laboratories in which they spend most of their time, watching them and engaging in casual conversation as they dissected cadavers or examined pathology specimens. We followed these students to their fra-

1. This paper grew out of my experience in the research reported in Howard S. Becker, Blanche Geer, Everett C. Hughes, and Anselm L. Strauss, *Boys in White: Student Culture in Medical School* (Chicago: University of Chicago Press, 1961). I worked out the basic approach in partnership with Blanche Geer and we then applied it in writing up our study of medical education and in the research reported in Becker, Geer, and Hughes, *Making the Grade: The Academic Side of College Life* (New York: John Wiley and Sons, 1968). Our own experience has been largely with the role Gold terms "participant as observer," but the methods discussed here should be relevant to other field situations. Cf. Raymond L. Gold, "Roles in Sociological Field Observations," *Social Forces* 36 (March 1958), pp. 217–223.

ternity houses and sat around while they discussed their school experiences. We accompanied students in the clinical years on rounds with attending physicians, watched them examine patients on the wards and in the clinics, sat in on discussion groups and oral exams. We ate with the students and took night call with them. We pursued internes and residents through their crowded schedules of teaching and medical work. We stayed with one small group of students on each service for periods ranging from a week to two months, spending many full days with them. The observational situations allowed time for conversation and we took advantage of this to interview students about things that had happened and were about to happen, and about their own backgrounds and aspirations.

Sociologists usually use this method when they are especially interested in understanding a particular organization or substantive problem rather than demonstrating relations between abstractly defined variables. They attempt to make their research theoretically meaningful, but they assume that they do not know enough about the organization *a priori* to identify relevant problems and hypotheses and that they must discover these in the course of the research. Though participant observation can be used to test *a priori* hypotheses, and therefore need not be as unstructured as the example I have given above, this is typically not the case. My discussion refers to the kind of participant observation study which seeks to discover hypotheses as well as to test them.

Observational research produces an immense amount of detailed description; our files contain approximately five thousand single-spaced pages of such material. Faced with such a quantity of "rich" but varied data, the researcher faces the problem of how to analyze it systematically and then to present his conclusions so as to convince other scientists of their validity. Participant observation (indeed, qualitative analysis generally) has not done well with this problem, and the full weight of evidence for conclusions and the processes by which they were reached are usually not presented, so that the reader finds it difficult to make his own assessment of them and must rely on his faith in the researcher.

In what follows I try to pull out and describe *the basic analytic operations carried on in participant observation,* for three reasons: to make these operations clear to those unfamiliar with the method; by attempting a more explicit and systematic description, to aid those working with the method in organizing their own research; and, most importantly, in order to propose some changes in analytic procedures and particularly in reporting results which will make the processes by which conclusions are reached and substantiated more accessible to the reader.

The first thing we note about participant observation research is that analysis is carried on *sequentially*,[2] important parts of the analysis being made while the researcher is still gathering his data. This has two obvious consequences: further data gathering takes its direction from provisional analyses; and the amount and kind of provisional analysis carried on is limited by the exigencies of the field work situation, so that final comprehensive analyses may not be possible until the field work is completed.

We can distinguish three distinct stages of analysis conducted in the field itself, and a fourth stage, carried on after completion of the field work. These stages are differentiated, first, by their logical sequence: each succeeding stage depends on some analysis in the preceding stage. They are further differentiated by the fact that different kinds of conclusions are arrived at in each stage and that these conclusions are put to different uses in the continuing research. Finally, they are differentiated by the different criteria that are used to assess evidence and to reach conclusions in each stage. The three stages of field analysis are: the selection and definition of problems, concepts, and indices; the check on the frequency and distribution of phenomena; and the incorporation of individual findings into a model of the organization under study.[3] The fourth stage of final analysis involves problems of presentation of evidence and proof.

Selection and Definition of Problems, Concepts, and Indices

In this stage, the observer looks for problems and concepts that give promise of yielding the greatest understanding of the organization he is studying, and for items which may serve as useful indicators of facts which are harder to observe. The typical conclusion that his data yield is the simple one that a given phenomenon exists, that a certain event occurred once, or that two phenomena were observed to be related in one instance; the conclusion says nothing about the frequency or distribution of the observed phenomenon.

By placing such an observation in the context of a sociological theory, the observer selects concepts and defines problems for further investigation. He constructs a theoretical model to account for that one case, intending to refine it in the light of subsequent findings. For instance, he might find

2. In this respect, the analytic methods I discuss bear a family resemblance to the technique of *analytic induction*. Cf. Alfred Lindesmith, *Opiate Addiction* (Bloomington: Principia Press, 1947), especially pp. 5–20, and the subsequent literature cited in Ralph H. Turner, "The Quest for Universals in Sociological Research," *American Sociological Review* 18 (December 1953), pp. 604–611.

3. My discussion of these stages is abstract and simplified and does not attempt to deal with practical and technical problems of participant observation study. The reader should keep in mind that in practice the research will involve all these operations simultaneously with reference to different particular problems.

the following: "Medical student X referred to one of his patients as a 'crock' today."[4] He may then connect this finding with a sociological theory suggesting that occupants of one social category in an institution classify members of other categories by criteria derived from the kinds of problems these other persons raise in the relationship. This combination of observed fact and theory directs him to look for the problems in student-patient inter-action indicated by the term "crock." By discovering specifically what students have in mind in using the term, through questioning and continued observation, he may develop specific hypotheses about the nature of these interactional problems.

Conclusions about a single event also lead the observer to decide on specific items which might be used as indicators[5] of less easily observed phenomena. Noting that in at least one instance a given item is closely related to something less easily observable, the researcher discovers possible short-cuts easily enabling him to observe abstractly defined variables. For example, he may decide to investigate the hypothesis that medical freshmen feel they have more work to do than can possibly be managed in the time allowed them. One student, in discussing this problem, says he faces so much work that, in contrast to his undergraduate days, he is forced to study many hours over the weekend and finds that even this is insufficient. The observer decides, on the basis of this one instance, that he may be able to use complaints about weekend work as an indicator of student perspectives on the amount of work they have to do. The selection of indicators for more abstract variables occurs in two ways: the observer may become aware of some very specific phenomenon first and later see that it may be used as an indicator of some larger class of phenomena; or he may have the larger problem in mind and search for specific indicators to use in studying it.

Whether he is defining problems or selecting concepts and indicators, the researcher at this stage is using his data only to speculate about possibilities. Further operations at later stages may force him to discard most of the provisional hypotheses. Nevertheless, problems of evidence arise even at this point, for the researcher must assess the individual items on which his speculations are based in order not to waste time tracking down false leads.

4. The examples of which our hypothetical observer makes use are drawn from *Boys in White*.
5. The problem of indicators is discussed by Paul F. Lazarsfeld and Allen Barton, "Qualitative Measurement in the Social Sciences: Classification, Typologies, and Indices," in Daniel Lerner and Harold D. Lasswell, editors, *The Policy Sciences: Recent Developments in Scope and Method* (Stanford: Stanford University Press, 1951), pp. 155–192; "Some Functions of Qualitative Analysis in Sociological Research," *Sociologica* 1 (1955), pp. 324–361 (this important paper parallels the present discussion in many places); and Patricia L. Kendall and Paul F. Lazarsfeld, "Problems of Survey Analysis," in R. K. Merton and P. F. Lazarsfeld, editors, *Continuities in Social Research* (Glencoe: Free Press, 1950), pp. 183–186.

We shall eventually need a systematic statement of canons to be applied to individual items of evidence. Lacking such a statement, let us consider some commonly used tests. (The observer typically applies these tests as seems reasonable to him during this and the succeeding stage in the field. In the final stage, they are used more systematically in an overall assessment of the total evidence for a given conclusion.)

THE CREDIBILITY OF INFORMANTS

Many items of evidence consist of statements by members of the group under study about some event which has occurred or is in process. Thus, medical students make statements about faculty behavior which form part of the basis for conclusions about faculty-student relations. These cannot be taken at face value; nor can they be dismissed as valueless. In the first place, the observer can use the statement as evidence *about the event,* if he takes care to evaluate it by the criteria an historian uses in examining a personal document.[6] Does the informant have reason to lie or conceal some of what he sees as the truth? Does vanity or expediency lead him to mis-state his own role in an event or his attitude toward it? Did he actually have an opportunity to witness the occurrence he describes or is hearsay the source of his knowledge? Do his feelings about the issues or persons under discussion lead him to alter his story in some way?

Secondly, even when a statement examined in this way proves to be seriously defective as an accurate report of an event, it may still provide useful evidence for a different kind of conclusion. Accepting the sociological proposition that an individual's statements and descriptions of events are made from a perspective which is a function of his position in the group, the observer can interpret such statements and descriptions as indications of the individual's perspective on the point involved.

VOLUNTEERED OR DIRECTED STATEMENTS

Many items of evidence consist of informants' remarks to the observer about themselves or others or about something which has happened to them; these statements range from those which are a part of the running casual conversation of the group to those arising in a long intimate tête-à-tête between observer and informant. The researcher assesses the evidential value of such statements quite differently, depending on whether they have been made independently of the observer (volunteered) or have been directed by a question from the observer. A freshman medical student might remark to the observer or to another student that he has more material to study than

6. Cf. Louis Gottschalk, Clyde Kluckhohn, and Robert Angell, *The Use of Personal Documents in History, Anthropology, and Sociology* (New York: Social Science Research Council, 1945), pp. 15–17, 38–47.

he has time to master; or the observer might ask, "Do you think you are being given more work than you can handle?," and receive an affirmative answer.

This raises an important question: to what degree is the informant's statement the same one he might give, either spontaneously or in answer to a question, in the absence of the observer? The volunteered statement seems likely to reflect the observer's preoccupations and possible biases less than one which is made in response to some action of the observer, for the observer's very question may direct the informant into giving an answer which might never occur to him otherwise. Thus, in the example above, we are more sure that the students are concerned about the amount of work given them when they mention this of their own accord than we are when the idea may have been stimulated by the observer asking the question.

THE OBSERVER-INFORMANT-GROUP EQUATION

Let us take two extremes to set the problem. A person may say or do something when alone with the observer or when other members of the group are also present. The evidential value of an observation of this behavior depends on the observer's judgment as to whether the behavior is equally likely to occur in both situations. On the one hand, an informant may say and do things when alone with the observer that accurately reflect his perspective but which would be inhibited by the presence of the group. On the other hand, the presence of others may call forth behavior which reveals more accurately the person's perspective but would not be enacted in the presence of the observer alone. Thus, students in their clinical years may express deeply "idealistic" sentiments about medicine when alone with the observer, but behave and talk in a very "cynical" way when surrounded by fellow students. An alternative to judging one or the other of these situations as more reliable is to view each datum as valuable in itself, but with respect to different conclusions. In the example above, we might conclude that students have "idealistic" sentiments but that group norms may not sanction their expression.[7]

In assessing the value of items of evidence, we must also take into account the observer's role in the group. For the way the subjects of his study define that role affects what they will tell him or let him see. If the observer carries on his research incognito, participating as a full-fledged member of the group, he will be privy to knowledge that would normally be shared by such a member and might be hidden from an outsider. He could properly interpret his own experience as that of a hypothetical "typical" group mem-

7. See this volume, pp. 49–51.

ber. On the other hand, if he is known to be a researcher, he must learn how group members define him and in particular whether or not they believe that certain kinds of information and events should be kept hidden from him. He can interpret evidence more accurately when the answers to these questions are known.

Checking the Frequency and Distribution of Phenomena

The observer, possessing many provisional problems, concepts, and indicators, now wishes to know which of these are worth pursuing as major foci of his study. He does this, in part, by discovering if the events that prompted their development are typical and widespread, and by seeing how these events are distributed among categories of people and organizational sub-units. He reaches conclusions that are essentially quantitative, using them to describe the organization he is studying.

Participant observations have occasionally been gathered in standardized form capable of being transformed into legitimate statistical data.[8] But the exigencies of the field usually prevent the collection of data in such a form as to meet the assumptions of statistical tests, so that the observer deals in what have been called "quasi-statistics."[9] His conclusions, while implicitly numerical, do not require precise quantification. For instance, he may conclude that members of freshmen medical fraternities typically sit together during lectures while other students sit in less stable smaller groupings. His observations may indicate such a wide disparity between the two groups in this respect that the inference is warranted without a standardized counting operation. Occasionally, the field situation may permit him to make similar observations or ask similar questions of many people, systematically searching for quasi-statistical support for a conclusion about frequency or distribution.

In assessing the evidence for such a conclusion the observer takes a cue from his statistical colleagues. Instead of arguing that a conclusion is either totally true or false, he decides, if possible, how *likely* it is that his conclusion about the frequency or distribution of some phenomenon is an accurate quasi-statistic, just as the statistician decides, on the basis of the varying values of a correlation coefficient or a significance figure, that his conclusion is more or less likely to be accurate. The kind of evidence may vary considerably and the degree of the observer's confidence in the conclusion will vary accordingly. In arriving at this assessment, he makes use

8. See Peter M. Blau, "Co-operation and Competition in a Bureaucracy," *American Journal of Sociology* 59 (May 1954), pp. 530–535.
9. See the discussion of quasi-statistics in Lazarsfeld and Barton, "Some Functions of Qualitative Analysis . . .," *op. cit.,* pp. 346–348.

of some of the criteria described above, as well as those adopted from quantitative techniques.

Suppose, for example, that the observer concludes that medical students share the perspective that their school should provide them with the clinical experience and the practice in techniques necessary for a general practitioner. His confidence in the conclusion would vary according to the nature of the evidence, which might take any of the following forms: (1) *Every* members of the group said, *in response to a direct question,* that this was the way he looked at the matter. (2) *Every* member of the group *volunteered* to an observer that this was how he viewed the matter. (3) *Some given proportion* of the group's members either *answered* a direct question or *volunteered* the information that he shared this perspective, but none of the others was asked or volunteered information on the subject. (4) Every member of the group was asked or volunteered information, but *some given proportion said* they viewed the matter from the differing perspective of a prospective specialist. (5) No one was asked questions or volunteered information on the subject, but *all members were observed to engage in behavior* or to make other statements from which the analyst *inferred* that the general practitioner perspective was being used by them as a basic, though unstated, premise. For example, all students might have been observed to complain that the University Hospital received too many cases of rare diseases that general practitioners rarely see. (6) *Some given proportion* of the group *was observed* using the general practitioner perspective as a basic premise in their activities, but *the rest of the group* was not observed engaging in such activities. (7) *Some proportion* of the group *was observed* engaged in activities implying the general practitioner perspective while *the remainder* of the group was observed engaged in activities implying the perspective of the prospective specialist.

The researcher also takes account of the possibility that his observations may give him evidence of different kinds on the point under consideration. Just as he is more convinced if he has many items of evidence than if he has a few, so he is more convinced of a conclusion's validity if he has *many kinds* of evidence.[10] For instance, he may be especially persuaded that a particular norm exists and affects group behavior if the norm is not only described by group members but also if he observes events in which the norm can be "seen" to operate—if, for example, students tell him that they are thinking of becoming general practitioners and he also observes their complaints about the lack of cases of common diseases in University Hospital.

The conclusiveness which comes from the convergence of several kinds of evidence reflects the fact that separate varieties of evidence can be recon-

10. See Alvin W. Gouldner, *Patterns of Industrial Bureaucracy* (Glencoe, Ill.: Free Press, 1954), pp. 247–269.

ceptualized as deductions from a basic proposition which have now been verified in the field. In the above case, the observer might have deduced the desire to have experience with cases like those the general practitioner treats from the desire to practice that style of medicine. Even though the deduction is made after the fact, confirmation of it buttresses the argument that the general practitioner perspective is a group norm.

It should be remembered that these operations, when carried out in the field, may be so interrupted because of imperatives of the field situation that they are not carried on as systematically as they might be. Where this is the case, the overall assessment can be postponed until the final stage of postfield work analysis.

Construction of Social System Models

The final stage of analysis in the field consists of incorporating individual findings into a generalized model of the social system or organization under study or some part of that organization.[11] The concept of social system is a basic intellectual tool of modern sociology. The kind of participant observation discussed here is related directly to this concept, explaining particular social facts by explicit reference to their involvement in a complex of interconnected variables that the observer constructs as a theoretical model of the organization. In this final stage, the observer designs a descriptive model which best explains the data he has assembled.

The typical conclusion of this stage of the research is a statement about a set of complicated interrelations among many variables. Although some progress is being made in formalizing this operation through use of factor analysis and the relational analysis of survey data,[12] observers usually view currently available statistical techniques as inadequate to express their conceptions and find it necessary to use words. The most common kinds of conclusions at this level include:

(1) Complex statements of the necessary and sufficient conditions for the existence of some phenomenon. The observer may conclude, for example, that medical students develop consensus about limiting the amount of work

11. The relation between theories based on the concept of social system and participant observation was pointed out to me by Alvin W. Gouldner. See his "Some Observations on Systematic Theory, 1945–55," in Hans L. Zetterberg, editor, *Sociology in the United States of America* (Paris: UNESCO, 1956) pp. 34–42; and "Theoretical Requirements of the Applied Social Sciences," *American Sociological Review* 22 (February 1957), pp. 92–102.

12. See Alvin W. Gouldner, "Cosmopolitans and Locals: Toward an Analysis of Latent Social Roles," *Administrative Science Quarterly* 2 (December 1957), pp. 281–306, and 3 (March 1958), pp. 444–480; and James Coleman, "Relational Analysis: The Study of Social Structure with Survey Methods," *Human Organization* 17, pp. 28–36.

they will do because (a) they are faced with a large amount of work, (b) they engage in activities which create communication channels between all members of the class, and (c) they face immediate dangers in the form of examinations set by the faculty.

(2) Statements that some phenomenon is an "important" or "basic" element in the organization. Such conclusions, when elaborated, usually point to the fact that this phenomenon exercises a persistent and continuing influence on diverse events. The observer might conclude that the ambition to become a general practitioner is "important" in the medical school under study, meaning that many particular judgments and choices are made by students in terms of this ambition and many features of the school's organization are arranged to take account of it.

(3) Statements identifying a situation as an instance of some process or phenomenon described more abstractly in sociological theory. Theories posit relations between many abstractly defined phenomena, and conclusions of this kind imply that relationships posited in generalized form hold in this particular instance. The observer, for example, may state that a cultural norm of the medical students is to express a desire to become a general practitioner; in so doing, he in effect asserts that the sociological theory about the functions of norms and the processes by which they are maintained which he holds to be true in general is true in this case.

In reaching such types of conclusions, the observer characteristically begins by constructing models of parts of the organization as he comes in contact with them, discovers concepts and problems, and the frequency and distribution of the phenomena these call to his attention. After constructing a model specifying the relationships among various elements of this part of the organization, the observer seeks greater accuracy by successively refining the model to take account of evidence which does not fit his previous formulation;[13] by searching for negative cases (items of evidence which run counter to the relationships hypothesized in the model) which might force such revision; and by searching intensively for the interconnections *in vivo* of the various elements he has conceptualized from his data. While a provisional model may be shown to be defective by a negative instance which crops up unexpectedly in the course of the field work, the observer may infer what kinds of evidence would be likely to support or to refute his model and may make an intensive search for such evidence.[14]

After the observer has accumulated several partial-models of this kind,

13. Note again the resemblance to analytic induction.
14. See Alfred Lindesmith's discussion of this principle in "Comment on W. S. Robinson's 'The Logical Structure of Analytic Induction,' " *American Sociological Review* 17 (August 1952), pp. 492–493.

he seeks connections between them and thus begins to construct an overall model of the entire organization. An example from our study shows how this operation is carried on during the period of field work. (The reader will note, in this example, how use is made of findings typical of earlier stages of analysis.)

When we first heard medical students apply the term "crock" to patients we made an effort to learn precisely what they meant by it. We found, through interviewing students about cases both they and the observer had seen, that the term referred in a derogatory way to patients with many subjective symptoms but no discernible physical pathology. Subsequent observations indicated that this usage was a regular feature of student behavior and thus that we should attempt to incorporate this fact into our model of student-patient behavior. The derogatory character of the term suggested in particular that we investigate the reasons students disliked these patients. We found that this dislike was related to what we discovered to be the students' perspective on medical school: the view that they were in school to get experience in recognizing and treating those common diseases most likely to be encountered in general practice. "Crocks," presumably having no disease, could furnish no such experience. We were thus led to specify connections between the student-patient relationship and the student's view of the purpose of his professional education. Questions concerning the genesis of this perspective led to discoveries about the organization of the student body and communication among students, phenomena which we had been assigning to another part-model. Since "crocks" were also disliked because they gave the student no opportunity to assume medical responsibility, we were able to connect this aspect to the student-patient relationship with still another tentative model of the value system and hierarchical organization of the school, in which medical responsibility plays an important role.

Again, it should be noted that analysis of this kind is carried on in the field as time permits. Since the construction of a model is the analytic operation most closely related to the observer's techniques and interests he usually spends a great deal of time thinking about these problems. But he is usually unable to be as systematic as he would like until he reaches the final stage of analysis.

Final Analysis and the Presentation of Results

The final systematic analysis, carried on after the field work is completed, consists of rechecking and rebuilding models as carefully and with as many safeguards as the data will allow. For instance, in checking the accuracy of statements about the frequency and distribution of events, the researcher can index and arrange his material so that every item of information is accessible and taken account of in assessing the accuracy of any given conclusion. He can profit from the observation of Lazarsfeld and Barton that the "analysis of 'quasi-statistical data' can probably be made more systematic than it has been in the past, if the logical structure of quantitative research at least is kept in mind to give general warnings and directions to the qualitative observer."[15]

An additional criterion for the assessment of this kind of evidence is the state of the observer's conceptualization of the problem at the time the item of evidence was gathered. The observer may have his problem well worked out and be actively looking for evidence to test an hypothesis, or he may not be as yet aware of the problem. The evidential value of items in his field notes will vary accordingly, the basis of consideration being the likelihood of discovering negative cases of the proposition he eventually uses the material to establish. The best evidence may be that gathered in the most unthinking fashion, when the observer has simply recorded the item although it has no place in the system of concepts and hypotheses he is working with at the time, for there might be less bias produced by the wish to substantiate or repudiate a particular idea. On the other hand, a well-formulated hypothesis makes possible a deliberate search for negative cases, particularly when other knowledge suggests likely areas in which to look for such evidence. This kind of search requires advanced conceptualization of the problem, and evidence gathered in this way might carry greater weight for certain kinds of conclusions. Both procedures are relevant at different stages of the research.

In the post field work stage of analysis, the observer carries on the model building operation more systematically. He considers the character of his conclusions and decides on the kind of evidence that might cause their rejection, deriving further tests by deducing logical consequences and ascertaining whether or not the data support the deductions. He considers reasonable alternative hypotheses and whether or not the evidence refutes them.[16] Finally, he completes the job of establishing interconnections between partial models so as to achieve an overall synthesis incorporating all conclusions.

15. "Some Functions of Qualitative Analysis . . .," *op. cit.,* p. 348.
16. One method of doing this, particularly adapted to testing discrete hypotheses about change in individuals or small social units (though not in principle limited to this application), is "The Technique of Discerning," described by Mirra Komarovsky in Paul F. Lazarfeld and Morris Rosenberg, editors, *The Language of Social Research* (Glencoe, Ill.: Free Press, 1955), pp. 449–457. See also the careful discussion of alternative hypotheses and the use of deduced consequences as further proof in Lindesmith, *Opiate Addiction, passim.*

After completing the analysis, the observer faces the knotty problem of how to present his conclusions and the evidence for them. Readers of qualitative research reports commonly and justifiably complain that they are told little or nothing about the evidence for conclusions or the operations by which the evidence has been assessed. A more adequate presentation of the data, of the research operations, and of the researcher's inferences may help to meet this problem.

But qualitative data and analytic procedures, in contrast to quantitative ones, are difficult to present adequately. Statistical data can be summarized in tables, and descriptive measures of various kinds and the methods by which they are handled can often be accurately reported in the space required to print a formula. This is so in part because the methods have been systematized so that they can be referred to in this shorthand fashion and in part because the data have been collected for a fixed, usually small, number of categories—the presentation of data need be nothing more than a report of the number of cases to be found in each category.

The data of participant observation do not lend themselves to such ready summary. They frequently consist of many different kinds of observations which cannot be simply categorized and counted without losing some of their value as evidence—for, as we have seen, many points need to be taken into account in putting each datum to use. Yet it is clearly out of the question to publish all the evidence. Nor is it any solution, as Kluckhohn has suggested for the similar problem of presenting life history materials,[17] to publish a short version and to make available the entire set of materials on microfilm or in some other inexpensive way; this ignores the problem of how to present *proof*.

In working over the material on the medical school study a possible solution to this problem, with which we are experimenting, is a description of the natural history of our conclusions, presenting the evidence as it came to the attention of the observer during the successive stages of his conceptualization of the problem. The term "natural history" implies not the presentation of every datum, but only the characteristic forms data took at each stage of the research. This involves description of the form that data took and any significant exceptions, taking account of the canons discussed above, in presenting the various statements of findings and the inferences and conclusions drawn from them. In this way, evidence is assessed as the substantive analysis is presented. The reader would be able, if this method were used, to follow the details of the analysis and to see how and on what basis any conclusion was reached. This would give the

17. *Gottschalk et al., op. cit.,* pp. 150–156.

reader, as do present modes of statistical presentation, opportunity to make his own judgment as to the adequacy of the proof and the degree of confidence to be assigned the conclusion.

Conclusion

I have tried to describe the analytic field work characteristic of participant observation, first, in order to bring out the fact that the technique consists of something more than merely immersing oneself in data and "having insights." The discussion may also serve to stimulate those who work with this and similar techniques to attempt greater formalization and systematization of the various operations they use, in order that qualitative research may become more a "scientific" and less an "artistic" kind of endeavor. Finally, I have proposed that new modes of reporting results be introduced, so that the reader is given greater access to the data and procedures on which conclusions are based.

CHAPTER THREE

Field Work Evidence

How credible are the conclusions derived from data gathered by field work? If we enter to some degree into the lives of the people we study, take part in their daily round of activity and observe the scenes and sites where it occurs; if we talk with them both informally and in relatively organized interviews; if we inspect organization records, official documents, public media, letters, diaries, and any other records and artifacts we can find; if we record systematically all the information we acquire in these ways; and if, finally, we assess that information systematically to see what evidence it provides for what conclusions—if we do all that, should people take our conclusions to be highly credible? Or should they find it risky to give much evidentiary value to conclusions so arrived at?[1]

Anthropologists might find the question foolish, because they do so much of their work this way and because so many of their classics depend on such evidence; but a minority among them, possibly a growing minority, might see some sense in the question, feeling that anthropological field work techniques are too unstructured to produce reliable knowledge. Psychologists, on the other hand, find the question meaningful and, indeed, are forever raising

1. Problems of the validity of field work data have been discussed in Arthur J. Vidich, "Participant Observation and the Collection and Interpretation of Data," *American Journal of Sociology* 60 (1955), 354–360; Morris Zelditch, Jr., "Some Methodological Problems of Field Studies," *ibid.*, 67 (1962), 566–576; Arthur J. Vidich and Joseph Bensman, "The Validity of Field Data," *Human Organization* 13 (1954), 20–27; and Lois R. Dean, "Interaction, Reported and Observed: The Case of One Local Union," *ibid.*, 17 (1954), 36–44.

it about sociological research. "It sounds very interesting, even plausible," they say, "but is it true? How can we be sure?" Sociologists waver. Many of our acknowledged classics—*Street Corner Society, The Polish Peasant, The Urban Villagers*—rely on such methods. But we whore after the gods of rigor and precision, and the apparently undisciplined procedures of field work scarcely meet the requirements of that religion.

One reason people worry that the conclusions of field studies are untrustworthy is that field workers sometimes come up with quite different characterizations of the same or presumably similar institutions, organizations, or communities. If the methods are reliable, shouldn't two studies of the same thing yield a similar description? But Oscar Lewis' Tepoztlán looked very different from Robert Redfield's, the medical school my colleagues and I studied seemed very different from the one studied by Merton *et al.,* and these are not the only cases.[2]

These disparities may occur simply because the organizations are in fact not the same. The passage of time may have changed Tepoztlán substantially; it would not be surprising. The University of Kansas Medical School we studied differs from the Cornell Medical School that Merton *et al.,* studied in location, the recruitment of faculty and students, the sources of support, and dozens of other ways that might easily account for the differences in our descriptions. We should never assume that two institutions are alike simply because they belong to the same conventionally defined social category: some elementary schools may resemble prisons, others country clubs, while still others do indeed look like ordinary schools. If two studies uncover such differences the result is anomalous only if we insist that things called by the same name therefore *are* the same.

But suppose even that two researchers study the identical organization and yet describe it quite differently. In laboratory research, we think it very unlikely that people would give very different descriptions of what took place in the same experiment. The experimenter did this, the subjects did that; one may argue the interpretation, but one seldom disputes the description. So varying descriptions of the same organization distress people used to research modeled on the experimental paradigm.

But their distress may rest on an unwarranted assumption: that the two field workers in question set out to study the same thing, answer the same questions. People often study the same or similar organizations using field methods but have different theories and different questions in mind. When

2. See Robert Redfield, *Tepoztlán* (Chicago: University of Chicago Press, 1930), and Oscar Lewis, *Tepoztlán Revisited* (Urbana: University of Illinois, 1951); and Howard S. Becker, Blanche Geer, Everett C. Hughes, and Anselm L. Strauss, *Boys in White* (Chicago: University of Chicago Press, 1961), and Robert K. Merton, George Reader, and Patricia L. Kendall, eds., *The Student-Physician* (Cambridge: Harvard University Press, 1957).

they ask different questions, they get different answers. The data in the two studies will indeed be different, but the difference does not indicate that the information is untrustworthy. It shows only that the observer is observing something different.

We mistakenly assume that observers must be studying the same thing because we suppose that only one social structure is present in an organization or community. That is true in some general sense. All the people who occupy a given geographical area or a particular building that houses a given organization do in some sense constitute one large social structure. But the overall structure contains smaller units and the difference between two field studies of the same thing may lie in their differential emphasis on one or another of these smaller units. Whyte and Gans described essentially similar low-income Italian districts in Boston, but their descriptions are vastly different. Whyte describes the characteristic activities of a group of young unmarried men and explores their relation to the poltical structure of the community and to a settlement house located there. Gans describes what seems to be a quite different society made up of married people and their families and containing, in addition to the settlement house, a host of other institutions.[3]

But no one would argue seriously that the difference between Gans' description and Whyte's shows that one or the other or both are implausible or that their data are untrustworthy. They focused on different parts of the total community, and they asked different questions about them. There is no reason for their descriptions to be similar.

In the same way, two observers might study the same organization or organizational part, but with reference to different problems. When Renée Fox studied medical freshmen, she wanted to know how the social structure of the medical school trained them in qualities likely to be important for successful performance as physicians; when Blanche Geer studied medical freshmen, she wanted to know how they organized themselves to deal with the everyday problems of being medical students. They studied the same thing, but they studied different aspects of it, and we should not expect their descriptions of the social structure of the freshman year of medical school to be identical.[4]

In general, we should not expect identical results when two observers study the same organization from different points of view or when they study different substructures within a larger organization. What we have a right to expect is that the two descriptions be *compatible,* that the con-

3. See William Foote Whyte, *Street Corner Society* (Chicago: University of Chicago Press, 1955), and Herbert J. Gans, *The Urban Villagers* (New York: Free Press, 1962).
4. See Merton *et al., op. cit.,* and Becker *et al., op. cit.*

clusions of one study do not implicitly or explicitly contradict those of the other. Thus, we can see that Whyte and Gans described essentially the same kind of community, for Whyte's description of the corner boys meshes perfectly with Gans' description of the family units in the community; the families Gans describes are just the families we expect the corner boys to come from and to create themselves when they have the chance.

We now approach the heart of the question, which has to do with the lack of strict procedural rules to guide a field worker's data-gathering activities. Suppose that two observers ask the same question of the field situation they observe and also use similar modes of analysis. Isn't it possible, even likely, that the lack of formalization in data-gathering techniques will allow whatever biases the investigator has to mold the data he gets? Won't he then, in effect, simply be studying his own prejudices, the data so perverted by his (probably unconscious) influence that we cannot use it as scientific evidence?

The question has often been raised about field work data but has added force because of the studies showing the effect of the investigator's bias in much more controlled situations. Studies by the staff of NORC and others demonstrate that the characteristics and biases of survey interviewers exert a considerable effect on the answers they get from respondents.[5] Even more shocking, Rosenthal's studies of experimenter bias have shown that the experimenter's knowledge of the hypothesis he is testing and of the conclusion he expects to arrive at affect the responses of the subjects of social-psychological experiments. Rosenthal even reports that the experimenter's bias affects the outcome of animal experiments.[6] If the researcher's bias can affect the data gathered in these more controlled styles of research, is it not much more likely in the unformalized techniques of field work, where the observer has infinitely more opportunity to emit cues that affect those he studies and to pick from all that is happening only the evidence that suits him?

There are good reasons to believe that the opposite is true. Field observation is less likely than the more controlled methods of laboratory experiment and survey interview to allow the researcher to bias the results he gets

5. See Herbert H. Hyman *et al., Interviewing in Social Research* (Chicago: University of Chicago Press, 1954); and Mark Benney, David Riesman, and Shirley A. Star, "Age and Sex in the Interview," *American Journal of Sociology* 62 (1956), 143–152.

6. Robert Rosenthal, *Experimenter Effects in Behavioral Research* (New York: Appleton-Century-Crofts, 1966). Some controversy has arisen over the generality of Rosenthal's conclusions, but I do not find the arguments against him convincing. See T. X. Barber and M. J. Silver, "Fact, Fiction, and the Experimenter Bias Effect," *Psychological Bulletin Monograph Supplement* 70 (1968), 1–29; Robert Rosenthal, "Experimenter Expectancy and the Reassuring Nature of the Null Hypothesis Decision Procedure," *ibid.,* 30–47; and Barber and Silver, "Pitfalls in Data Analysis and Interpretation: A Reply to Rosenthal," *ibid.,* 48–62.

in directions suggested by his own expectations, beliefs, or desires. Almost every field worker believes that proposition, ordinarily because he has often had to sacrifice pet ideas and hypotheses to the recalcitrant facts in his field notes. Before I discuss the characteristics of data gathering in the field that produce those recalcitrant facts, I want to introduce the personal experience that convinced me on this score.

My dissertation dealt with the career patterns of Chicago public school teachers.[7] I knew, before I started to interview teachers, that most teachers began their careers in Negro and slum schools and made strenuous, and usually successful, efforts to escape into middle-class schools. One of my major problems was why they did so. My advisor, Everett C. Hughes, had a theory about it. He expected that I would find what he and his students had found in other professions: that the highest professional prestige went to those who had clients of the highest social status. Teachers would prefer middle-class schools because they regarded them as the most prestigeful places a teacher could work. I firmly believed Professor Hughes' theory correct; even if I had not, the wily wisdom of graduate students dictated that I pretend to believe it and make every effort to prove it. When I interviewed teachers, however, they refused to support my expectation. They gave a good many reasons for not liking Negro and slum schools, in answer to my more or less nondirective questions, but none of the reasons had anything to do with professional prestige. Even when at the end of the interview (where it could do no harm) I pursued teachers with direct and leading questions, they simply denied that prestige had anything to do with their actions. My expectation, firmly grounded in theory, belief, and what I took to be my own self-interest, had no effect on my data. (When, with some trepidation, I reported my results to Professor Hughes, he turned out to be much more ready than graduate-student culture had led me to believe to embrace the new findings and revise his theory; so much for the wily wisdom of graduate students. That my vision of my self-interest was incorrect, however, did not in the least moderate its influence on what I hoped to find, or the inability of my hopes to influence reality.)

But the firmest convictions of field workers, based on just such anecdotes, neither convince doubters nor explain analytically the reasons we should take field work data seriously as evidence. Those reasons fall into two categories, which I now propose to examine. First, the people the field worker observes are ordinarily constrained to act as they would have in his absence, by the very social constraints whose effects interest him; he therefore has little chance, compared to practitioners of other methods, to influence what they do, for more potent forces are operating. Second, the field worker in-

---

7. The findings of that research are reported in Chapters 9–11 of this volume.

evitably, by his continuous presence, gathers much more data and, in a sense to be explained, makes and can make many more tests of his hypotheses than researchers who use more formal methods.

Constraints

Rosenthal, Friedman, Orne, Rosenberg, and others have shown, in my judgment quite conclusively, that the subjects of carefully controlled psychological experiments respond not only to the stimuli specified in the experimental design, but also to a variety of other stimuli found in their relationship to the experimenter. Believing in science and wanting to help the scientist, subjects respond to the "demand characteristics" of the experiment and do things they would not otherwise do—like giving the experimenter's stooges apparently lethal electric shocks—because that seems to be what they are "supposed" to do.[8] Believing that psychologists can tell things about you from seemingly innocent bits of behavior and not wanting to appear "sick," "unintelligent" or whatever other bad thing a psychologist might be able to discern, they respond in ways they think will cause a psychologist to think well of them.[9] For reasons not quite so clear, they alter their behavior so as to confirm the hypothesis the experimenter expects to be confirmed.[10]

Since experimenters attempt to influence subjects only in the ways specified in their design, the findings from this research indiciate that subjects respond to very slight cues, which not only are not intended to have an effect, but which no one even conceived as possibly having an effect. Minor variations in the wording of instructions, changes in the name of the organization allegedly sponsoring the research or in the name of the tests administered, differences in the number of times the experimenter smiled—it is trivia of this kind that confounded experimental results.

8. See M. T. Orne, "On the Social Psychology of the Psychological Experiment: With Particular Reference to Demand Characteristics and Their Implications," *American Psychologist* 17 (1962), 776–783; M. T. Orne and K. E. Scheibe, "The Contribution of Nonprivation factors in the Production of Sensory Deprivation Effects: The Psychology of the 'Panic Button,' " *Journal of Abnormal and Social Psychology* 68 (1964), 3–12; and Stanley Milgram, "Group Pressure and Action Against a Person," *ibid.*, 69 (1964), 137–143.

9. See Milton J. Rosenberg, "When Dissonance Fails: On Eliminating Evaluation Apprehension from Attitude Measurement," *Journal of Personality and Social Psychology* 1 (1965), 28–42, and "The Conditions and Consequences of Evaluation Apprehension," in R. Rosenthal and R. Rosnow, eds., *Sources of Artifact in Social Research* (New York: Academic Press, 1970).

10. See Rosenthal, *Experimenter Effects in Behavioral Research, op. cit.*, Neil Friedman, *The Social Nature of Psychological Research* (New York: Basic Books, 1967), and Susan Roth Sherman, "Demand Characteristics in an Experiment on Attitude Change," *Sociometry* 30 (1967), 246–261.

Similarly, survey researchers have discovered that the social attributes and the attitudes and beliefs of survey interviewers affect the answers their respondents give. People answer questions about race differently when interviewers are of one color or another, and they similarly vary their answers on questions about sex and mental illness depending on the age and sex of the interviewer. Interviewers get the answers they expect, just as experimenters get the responses they expect.[11]

It is not so clear that the influences on survey responses come from the trivial stimuli that influence experiments. For one thing, interviewers work in a less supervised situation; we cannot observe them going about their business and ordinarily rely on their own reports of what went on. So they are freer than experimenters to deviate from their instructions, and they might do so in grosser ways. Some of the variation may come from interviewer cheating. Still, interviewers' actions are constrained by their instructions and by the fixed wording and question order of the schedules they administer, so that their effect on responses must result from relatively small variations in behavior.

Field workers have a great deal more freedom than either experimenters or survey interviewers. They can ask anyone anything they want to ask, can use the most outrageously leading questions and the most biased wordings; they can take actions of all kinds, not just the minor variation in number of smiles that affects an experiment's results but much bolder interventions in an organization's workings; they can indicate not only an indirect and muted evaluation of another's actions but also the most direct kind of positive evaluation, as when they join in some controversial group activity. They can, in short, produce stimuli of a grossly biasing kind, much grosser than those that have been demonstrated to have serious effects in more controlled styles of research. How can we put any weight in conclusions based on data so produced?

So far, I have focused on the freedom of the researcher, in various techniques, to engage in potentially biasing forms of behavior vis-à-vis the people he studies. But to suppose that the subjects of field research are affected by the bias of the observer, and mold their acts and words to what they think he wants, supposes not only that they are willing to do so but that they are free to. It supposes that they are under no other constraints and so can follow their disposition to be pleasing, if they have such a disposition. But this freedom is found most characteristically in the laboratory experiment, where the ideal of control is precisely to remove all influences other than those the experimenter wants to operate. Experimenters neutralize external constraints by isolating the subjects of their experiments from their usual surroundings, by experimenting on topics unconnected with any strong be-

11. See the items cited in footnote 5, *supra*.

liefs held by the subject, and by assuring the subject that his behavior in the experiment, however he performs, will have no influence on his life outside the experimental laboratory. To precisely the degree that these aims are achieved, subjects are free to shape their words and deeds in accordance with cues unwittingly given off by a biased experimenter.

Somewhat the same freedom is available to the respondent in a survey interview. He is approached by someone he has never seen before and never expects to see again who asks him a series of questions about his attitudes on a variety of topics, none of which he has any direct control over or responsibility for. His answers will not have the slightest effect (and so he is assured by the well-trained interviewer) on anything in his real life. Since he is not constrained by anything but the pressures arising in the immediate face-to-face situation of the interview, these pressures are most likely to have a biasing effect on what he says. Hence the findings of the studies on interviewer bias. Are whites embarrassed to admit prejudiced feelings to the black interviewer? Do women hesitate to discuss sex with a young male interviewer? They are free to indulge these embarrassments and hesitations, for they are guaranteed that the frankness of their answers (or the lack thereof) will have no consequence beyond the immediate situation. Why not avoid embarrassment, since what you say makes no other difference?

Consider, in contrast, the people a field worker studies. They are enmeshed in social relationships important to them, at work, in community life, wherever. The events they participate in matter to them. The opinions and actions of the people they interact with must be taken into account, because they affect those events. All the constraints that affect them in their ordinary lives continue to operate while the observer observes.

Whether or not the person being observed knows what the observer expects of him, he dare not respond to that expectation. What he is involved in at the moment of observation is as a rule much more important to him than the observer is. If I observe a college student responding to a teacher in the classroom, I observe a person to whom my reactions are much less important than those of the teacher, who may give him a low grade, and even of other students, whose opinion of him has consequences long after he has seen the last of me. He may not care to have me think him stupid, naïve, or deceitful; but better I should think so than those whose opinions are more fateful than mine.[12] Similarly, when Skolnick observed police officers, they were busy doing things to earn them promotions (or at least prevent reprimands) from their superiors, things to maintain their position in the department and vis-à-vis lawbreakers, such as prostitutes, with whom they had repeated contact. They might like to have Skolnick think well of them, but they want much more to have their officers think well of

12. See Howard S. Becker, Blanche Geer, and Everett C. Hughes, *Making the Grade* (New York: John Wiley, 1968), 63–79.

them, to have whores respect them enough to do what they are told and so on.[13]

In short, the presence in the observational situation of the very social constraints the sociologist ordinarily studies makes it difficult for the people he observes to tailor their behavior to what they think he might want or expect. However much they want to, the real consequences of deviating from what they might otherwise have done are great enough—loss of a promotion or of reputation in the eyes of stable members of their community —that they cannot.

Two further remarks are in order. First, the analysis above does not apply, of course, when the people observed regard the observer in fact as important enough to constitute a threat and thus act as a real-life constraint on what they do. When they believe that, they will put on a show for him quite like the one they may for different reasons put on for an experimenter or survey interviewer. Industrial managers, for example, may suspect that a sociologist's findings presented to and interpreted by their superiors will uncover matters they would prefer kept secret and thus have untoward consequences for their immediate situations and future careers. Dalton suggests that a good many researchers have been led down the garden path by wary managers.[14] Schoolteachers and their pupils often collaborate to put on demonstrations of efficiency, industry, and harmony for a visitor because they fear that he may give a bad report to the principal and cause them all grief. Any situation where participants may cast the observer in the role of Inspector General contains this difficulty.

One cure for the ill consists of convincing people that you are not important, that those who control their fate don't know you or, if they do, don't care much what you say. Miller recounts an amusing instance in which the medical interns he was studying lost their fear that he was spying for hospital administrators when one of those administrators indirectly accused him of being the intern who was allegedly stealing food from patient's trays. Miller earned the accusation by being of a size that made the accusation plausible, and the incident convinced interns that none of their superiors knew him and that he was therefore harmless.[15] (I consider a second cure later.)

When a field worker convinces the people he studies that what he sees will have no further consequences, it paradoxically has the opposite effect

13. Jerome H. Skolnick, *Justice Without Trial* (New York: John Wiley, 1966).

14. See Melville Dalton, *Men Who Manage* (New York: John Wiley, 1959), and "Preconceptions and Methods in *Men Who Manage*," in Philip Hammond, ed., *Sociologists at Work* (New York: Basic Books, 1964), 50–95.

15. Stephan J. Miller, *Prescription for Leadership* (Chicago: Aldine Publishing Co., 1970). Morris Zelditch, Jr., has pointed out to me that this is a special instance of a more general situation in which different groups or participants keep things secret from one another, so that secrets are kept from the researcher not because he may inform the outside world but because he may inform other factions or segments.

that the same success has in more controlled research situation. There, the more that people believe it makes no difference what the observer sees them do or say, the more open they are to being influenced by him; in field work, the more that people believe the researcher is unimportant, the freer they are to respond to the other pressing constraints that surround them.

The general principle, then, is that research subjects respond most to the things in the research situation that seem most important to them. If you, the researcher, are most important—either because you have carefully insured that nothing more important will intrude or because they fear that your findings will become known to people who can affect their fate—your data will reflect that importance, as subjects politely shape their response to the cues you give them of what you need to be told or shown. If you are less important or not important at all from their point of view, they will do what they might have done were you not there. Field work data tend to approach the latter pole, experimental and survey data the former; but those connections, while not accidental, are not uniform, so that field workers need to be cautious while users of more structured methods can take advantage of the comparison to devise appropriate safeguards.

My second remark concerns the differences between data secured from people in the field when they are in the company of others and when they are alone with the field worker. Observers report that people say one thing and do another, or say one thing in one setting and something else in another. In particular, they may voice a "public" opinion in public, whether they act on it or not, and quite another opinion when they speak privately to the researcher and indicate a disbelief in the common culture. Gorden, for example, showed that the attitudes toward Russia of the members of a cooperative college living unit varied depending on whether they were expressed in group discussions with other members, in private interviews, or in a supposedly anonymous questionnaire; the more public the situation, the more the person conformed to the house "line."[16]

We would err if we interpreted one or the other of these expressions as the "real" one, dismissing the other as mere cover-up. I take the liberty of reproducing here an earlier discussion of this point, which arose from my experience studying medical students. It indicates when and how the observer can note or even provoke these variations, and how they may be interpreted.[17]

16. Raymond L. Gorden, "Interaction Between Attitude and the Definition of the Situation in the Expression of Opinion," *America Sociological Review* 17 (1952), 50–58.

17. The following material first appeared, in slightly different form, as Howard S. Becker, "Interviewing Medical Students," *American Journal of Sociology* 62 (1956), 199–201. The study of medical students referred to was eventually reported in Becker *et al., Boys in White, op cit.*

The values of any social group are an ideal actual behavior may sometimes approximate but seldom fully embodies. To deal with the tension between ideal and reality conceptually, there are two possible polar attitudes toward values. Individuals may be *idealistic,* accepting the values warmly and wholeheartedly, feeling that everyone can and should live up to them and that they are both "right" and "practical." Or they may be *cynical,* conceiving the values as impossibly impractical and incapable of being lived up to; they may feel that anyone who accepts these values wholeheartedly deceives himself and that one must compromise in meeting the exigencies of daily life.

Probably most commonly, individuals feel both ways about the values of their group at the same time; or one way in some situations, the other way in others. In which of these moods do they respond to the interviewer seeking sociological information? Or to turn attention to the interviewer himself: Which of these is he looking for in the people he talks to? Which response does he want to elicit?

Sociologists have had a penchant for the exposé since the days of muckraking. The interviewer is typically out to get "the real story" he conceives to be lying hidden beneath the platitudes of any group and discounts heavily any expressions of the "official" ideology. The search for the informal organization of a group reflects this, and Merton's dictum that sociology's distinctive contribution lies in the discovery and analysis of latent rather than manifest functions is a theoretical statement of this position.[18]

The interviewer must always remember that cynicism may underlie a perfunctory idealism. In many situations, interviewees perceive him as a potentially dangerous person and, fearing he will discover secrets better kept from the outside world, resort to the "official line" to keep his inquisitiveness politely at bay. The interviewer may circumvent such tactics by affecting cynicism himself, so that the interviewee is lulled into believing that the former accepts his own publicly disreputable view of things, or by confronting him with the evidence of his own words or reported deeds which do not jibe with the views he has presented. There may, perhaps, be other ways, for this area has not been well explored.

Convinced that idealistic talk is probably not sincere but merely a cover-up for less respectable cynicism, the interviewer strives to get beneath it to the "real thing." If he is using a schedule, he may be instructed or feel it necessary to use a "probe." An interview is frequently judged successful precisely to the degree that it elicits cynical rather than idealistic attitudes. A person interviewing married couples with an eye to assessing their adjustment would probably place less credence in an interview in which both partners insisted that theirs was the perfect marriage than he would in one in which he was told "the honeymoon is over."

Important and justified as is the interviewer's preoccupation with the prob-

18. Robert K. Merton, *Social Theory and Social Structure* (Glencoe: Free Press, 1949), 68.

lem, it creates the possibility that he will either misinterpret idealism sincerely presented to him or, by his manner of questioning, fashion a role for himself in the interview that encourages cynicism while discouraging idealism. For the observer's manner and role can strongly affect what people choose to tell him, as can the situation in which the interview is conducted.

In talking to medical students, I had no difficulty in eliciting cynical attitudes; such statements are likely to be made without much help from the interviewer. The real problem is quite different—that of making sure that one does not prevent the expression of more idealistic attitudes but helps the interviewee to say such things if he has them to say. Using the semicynical approach I had found useful in piercing the institutional idealism of school-teachers,[19] in interviewing the students informally and casually in the midst of the student groups I was observing, I failed to allow them much opportunity to vent their hidden personal idealism.

By being warm and permissive, by expressing idealistic notions one's self, and subtly encouraging their expression on the part of the student, one might well gather a set of data which would picture the student as wanting to "help humanity," uninterested in the financial rewards of medical practice, intrigued by the mysteries of science, bedeviled by doubts about his ability to make sound judgments in matters of life and death—a set of data, in short, which would draw heavily on this part of the student's repertoire of mixed emotions. If one saw students alone and was not with them as they went through their daily routine, he would be even more likely to get such an impression. The student cannot well express such thoughts to his fellows or in front of them, for they are almost ritualistically cynical and, more important perhaps, their attention is focused on immediate problems of studenthood rather than on problems which will be forced into immediate awareness only when, as young doctors, they assume full medical responsibility. By playing his role properly, the interviewer can help the student express this submerged part of his medical self and become a sounding board for his repressed better half.

As I began my field work, I fell into a relationship with students which would have inhibited their expressing idealistic sentiments to me, even had I been operating with an "idealistic" frame of reference rather than the "realistic" one I in fact used. I was with them most of the time, attending classes with them, accompanying them on teaching rounds, standing by while they assisted at operations and in delivering babies, having lunch with them, playing pool and cards with them, and so on. This meant that I was with them mainly in larger groups where cynicism was the dominant language and idealism would have been laughed down; this fact colored more intimate and private situations. More subtly, in being around them so much, day after day, I was likely to see the inevitable compromises and violations of lofty ideals entailed by the student role. Could a student expect me to believe his statement that the patient's welfare should be a primary consideration for him (to take a hypothetical example) when he knew that I had seen him give less than his full time to his patients because of an impending examination?

19. I describe this procedure below.

My data give a quite different picture from that arrived at by our hypothetical "idealist" researcher. I finally became aware that I had been systematically underestimating the idealism of the men I was studying by finding evidences of it in my own field notes. Some men made almost continual implicit reference, in their comments about practicing physicians they had seen at work, to an extremely high and "impractical" standard of medical practice best typified by their clinical teachers. Others went to great lengths to acquire knowledge on specific topics required neither by their immediate practical interests as students nor by the more long-range material interests related to their medical futures. Particular patients seen on the hospital wards typified certain difficult dilemmas of medical idealism, and, faced with a concrete example, some students brought up their own heavily idealistic worries about what they might do if confronted with a similar dilemma when they became doctors.

Seeing this, I began deliberately encouraging the expression of such thoughts. I spent more time with students engaged in activities carried out alone, raising questions in a sympathetic fashion quite different from the manner I used in groups. I kidded them less, asked interestedly about topics in which they had an "impractical" interest, and so on. Not every student displayed strong "idealism"; a few, indeed, did not respond idealistically at all, no matter how hard I searched or what situations I attempted to search in. But I had now looked; if I missed it where it was in fact present, it was not because my own actions suppressed its expression.

In the long run, I got both kinds of data on students. I had long enough contact with them to get by another means the idealism I missed at first and so ended with a picture of them which included both aspects of their selves. The technical moral to be drawn is perhaps that one should assume that people have both varieties of feelings about the values underlying the social relationships under study and be aware of and consciously manipulate those elements of role and situation which give promise of eliciting one sentiment or the other.

The technical moral forces a theoretical moral as well. We may assume too readily that the people we study will be easily classified as "attitude types" and that they will be more or less consistent in their view of things germane to our study. It is, after all, such a theoretical assumption that accounts for the exposé, with its emphasis on uncovering the "real" attitudes, as well as for the opposite "Pollyanna" attitude, with its unquestioning belief that people are as good as they say they are. It may be more useful to start with the hypothesis that people may entertain each attitude, at one time or another, and let this notion inform a more flexible interviewing style.

Rich Data

We often say that field work data are "rich," meaning thereby to find some saving grace in our failure to gather them systematically or use precise measurements. We think of rich data as containing great detail and specificity about the events studied, as much as a historian might want were he interested in the same events. The adjective also suggests that, like a sauce, it may be too much of a good thing, more than anyone needs or can put to good use.

But the rich detailed data produced by field work have an important use. They counter the twin dangers of respondent duplicity and observer bias by making it difficult for respondents to produce data that uniformly support a mistaken conclusion, just as they make it difficult for the observer to restrict his observations so that he sees only what supports his prejudices and expectations. I have already suggested that ordinarily we observe people subject to all the structural constraints of everyday life, so that they cannot mold their actions to please us. But suppose now that an occasion arises in the field, as it sometimes does, in which people are momentarily freed from those constraints. And suppose that at just such a moment the observer appears, makes his observations, and departs before things get back to normal. Observer bias could then influence what the observer sees, for the subjects of his study would be free to respond to his cues. If the observer observed only on such occasions, or on a few occasions that happened to be of this kind, he would be in the position of the experimenter who makes a limited series of observations when his subjects are free of external constraint.

But the field worker typically gathers his data over an extended period of time, in a variety of situations, using several ways of getting at the questions he is interested in, all of these reducing the danger of bias. Because he observes over a long time, he finds it hard to ignore the mass of information supporting an appropriate hypothesis he may neither have expected or desired, just as the people he studies would find it hard, if they wanted to deceive him, to manipulate such a mass of impressions in order to affect his assessment of the situation. Because he does not constrain himself with inflexible and detailed procedural rules, he can use a variety of devices to elicit talk and action from his subjects.

In short, the very large number of observations and kinds of data an observer can collect, and the resulting possibility of experimenting with a variety of procedures for collecting them, means that his final conclusions can be tested more often and in more ways than is common in other forms of research. We therefore act correctly when we place great reliance on field work evidence.

Numerous Observations. Field workers ordinarily spend a long time gathering their data. Students of a community usually reckon their stay in years: Whyte spent four years in Cornerville, Gans spent two years in Levittown, Suttles three years on Chicago's Near West Side, all of them living in the area so that their observations went on twenty-four hours a day.[20]

Students of organizations spend somewhat less time, the decrease often resulting from the simple fact that people do not live in a factory or school, from the use of multiple observers, or both. Still, Dalton[21] spent several years collecting material on industrial organization; my colleagues and I spent three-plus man-years studying a medical school and more than seven man-years studying an undergraduate college.[22] Field work reports sometimes attempts to convey the bulk of the data gathered by announcing the number of pages of field notes eventually subjected to analysis; in large studies the figure can run well into the thousands.

All these numbers serve simply to indicate that there is a sufficiency of data gathered over a substantial period of time. Any conclusion based on these data has therefore been subjected to hundreds and thousands of tests. Not only has the observer seen many actions and heard many statements that support his conclusion, but he has seen and heard many, many more actions and statements that serve as evidence negating alternative likely hypotheses. Thus, we not only heard college students talk about the importance of grades and saw them do things that reflected that importance, we also saw and heard things that indicated that they did not use other likely alternative perspectives, such as a liberal arts or a vocational perspective. Perhaps more important, we failed to hear and failed to see those things that would have signaled the existence and importance of alternative perspectives—all the variety of interconnected ideas and actions that might have constituted a liberal arts perspective, for instance—and that failure occurred over and over, day in and day out, through our entire time in the field. (The failure finds its evidentiary use in the field worker's consideration of the number and explanation of items of negative evidence.)[23]

Insofar as many items in those data support the same conclusion, one can dismiss some other important objections to research results. For example, a college student might say, in a moment of pique, that he did not care what happened in any of his courses or what his grades would be. If we have only one expression of his perspective, the one expressed during that moment, we would properly worry about how accurately it represented the perspective he used day in and day out through the school year. If we have thirty expressions of varying kinds—talk, actions, things done or said privately, things done and said in the company of others—that reveal the same perspective, we worry less about this threat to the validity of our conclusion.

20. See Whyte, *op. cit.;* Herbert J. Gans, *The Levittowners* (New York: Pantheon Books, 1967); and Gerald D. Suttles, *The Social Order of the Slum* (Chicago; University of Chicago Press, 1968).

21. Melville Dalton, *Men Who Manage* (New York: John Wiley, 1959).

22. Becker *et al., Boys in White, op. cit.;* and *Making the Grade, op. cit.*

23. The example is based on *Making the Grade, op. cit.,* especially pages 76–79 and 121–128.

In general, multiple observations convince us that our conclusion is not base on some momentary or fleeting expression of the people we study, subject to ephemeral and unusual circumstances.

Similarly, the circumstances surrounding people's actions sometimes change according to a regular temporal schedule: college students take examinations at the end of the quarter or semester, industries have busy times and slow times, and so on. People may not be aware of the temporality of their behavior, but the researcher must be, for data gathered at different times reflect different realities. The nursing students Davis and Olesen[24] studied had a new notion about school, their profession, and their careers after they returned from their first vacation, which revealed to them just how isolated from the world of men and marriage they now were. If one used pre-vacation data only, he would implicitly assume that student perspectives did not vary meaningfully over time; having both allows you to avoid that error and develop a more sophisticated analysis of student experience. In general, if one observes over a long period of time, we believe that he has not mistaken a temporally restricted phenomenon for one that does not change and that he has had a chance to observe processes of change that may be occurring.[25]

Most important, a characteristic feature of social organization combines with a common feature of everyday civility to make it unlikely both that the people the researcher studies will dissemble successfully and that he will be able to ignore contradictory evidence. The organizational characteristic is the interconnectedness of organizational life. The tenet of everyday civility is the unwillingness of people to lie or dissemble when there is a danger of being caught. Because the various aspects of activity in a social organization are connected, it becomes difficult for people to tell a coherent lie and even more difficult for them to act on it. Because they are unwilling to be caught in a lie or in incoherence, they eventually reveal their true beliefs and act as they would were the observer not present.

Life in an organization or community is all of a piece. What you do in one area of action depends on and has consequences for other areas. College students worry about their course grades not just because they want to know whether they have learned what they are supposed to, but also because their grades affect their fraternity membership, their campus political careers, their postgraduate success, and their social lives. Campus organizations, be-

24. Fred Davis and Virginia L. Olesen, "Initiation into a Woman's Profession," *Sociometry* 26 (1963), 89–101.
25. For a discussion of the utility of observations over a period of time, see Zachary Gussow, "The Observer-Observed Relationship as Information About Structure in Small-Group Research," *Psychiatry* 27 (August 1964), 230–247.

cause of eligibility rules and other factors, likewise take student grades into account in making decisions about their own activities. Each aspect of the collective action that makes up the life of a college campus has connections to the other parts, and an emphasis on grades usually forms one of the major connections.

Suppose that, for whatever reason, some students wish to make a field worker believe that they do not place much importance on grades, although in fact they do. They tell him they don't care about grades and even spend the evening they might otherwise have spent studying drinking beer with him as though they hadn't anything else to do. If he talks with them casually over several hours, they will find it necessary to lie about many other things: how they recruit members of their fraternity, what they do with their time, how active they have been in campus politics, and all the other matters where they base their day-to-day activity on the premise they now wish to deny, that grades are in fact important to them. They can lie about all these things, but it is a difficult job requiring a quick mind and intense concentration; one must see the possible ramifications of every remark and tailor what is said to take account of them.

If the students know that the observer has not come just for the evening but proposes to spend the next year observing them and their kind, they can easily see that he will soon discover that they have been lying to him. Say what they will, he will come by some night to drink beer only to be told that they must study for an exam; if he asks why, they will have to say that they need better grades to stay in school (or because they want to get into campus politics or law school or whatever). Furthermore, other people will probably describe to him a system in which their position will seem bizarre and unusual, so that he will be back with more questions. Eventually, he will uncover their lies, in their further words, in their deeds, and in the words and deeds of others.

People can, of course, construct Potemkin Villages for inspection by outsiders such as sociologists, in which all these problems have been analyzed and social life so arranged that exactly the desired impression emanates from it and nothing else. But Potemkin Village must have for its primary business fooling outsiders, for everything that would belie the intended impression must be suppressed at the risk of defeating the goal of the entire enterprise. The communities, schools, and factories we study, however, always have some other primary business. They are places to live, places where people try to teach other people something, places where goods are supposed to be produced. That other business creates the external constraints—the necessity of adjusting to other members of the community or organization and to important others elsewhere—that make it impossible for our subjects to put on a continual show for us. Though fooling us may, on occasion, become quite important, it is never the first and only order of business.

If, then, we make numerous and lengthy observations over a long period of time, we will see, if not everything, most things, and will be able to make some pretty good guesses about the rest. Furthermore, as our intention to do this becomes known, people will see they cannot hide things from us forever without paying some very large price in organizational and personal efficiency. They foresee that they will eventually be found out and then be revealed as having been uncivil enough to have lied or dissembled earlier. Some people will not mind being thought uncivil, but very many people do mind. We may say, in general, that (given an interconnectedness of activities of the kind described and a sensitivity to notions of civility) numerous observations give us good reason to suppose that little will have been hidden from the observer; and therefore that his conclusions are warranted.

For much the same reasons, many observations made over a substantial period of time helps the observer guard against his own conscious or unconscious biases, against "seeing only what he wants to see." For it is equally difficult to lie to yourself. Contradictory evidence appears and it appears not in subtle forms but in very gross ways. The more observations one makes and the more different kinds of observations one makes, the more difficult it becomes to ignore or explain away evidence that runs counter to one's expectation or bias. One has the same problem of making a coherent picture of what he sees that the person studied has when he confronts the observer.

We often conceive of observer bias as a subtle process, involving a failure to attend to subtle cues, an unconscious ignoring of unemphasized remarks and events, an unintentional distortion of ambiguous or equivocal stimuli. But the major features of a social organization, and their ramifications and interconnections, have no such subtle and equivocal character. The college students we observed did not remark casually and ambiguously on their interest in grades; they talked about it much of the time, placed great emphasis on the point, explained much of what they did with reference to the grading system, and in general kept it before us constantly. Had we observed and talked with them only a few times we might have been able to ignore the point. But one could not ignore or fail to record a matter students paraded so incessantly and even obsessively without consciously cheating. (Cheating, however, is a problem that affects the validity of data gathered by all research methods and I do not consider it here.)

In addition, the interconnectedness of an organization's parts already referred to means that our attempt to understand any particular aspect of what we see probably requires us to have some grasp of its other major aspects. The observations we record require us to attend to other observables, however unexpected or distasteful to us, in order to make sense of them.

In general, then, by making numerous observations we confront ourselves with the major features of the collective activity we study in a gross and repeated way such that it is unlikely that we will unconsciously avoid recording some important matters. For this reason, we correctly place confidence in the field worker's evidence.

Flexible procedures. The field worker, because he has continuing contact with those he studies, can gather data from them by multiple procedures, in several settings and in many moods. This variety allows him to crosscheck his conclusions and retest them repeatedly, so that he may be sure his data are not an artifact of some one way of proceeding or some one situation or relationship. He is not limited to what can be gathered in one interview (even if it is eight hours long!)[26] nor is he limited in what he asks about by his knowledge and understanding as of that time; since he can interview repeatedly, he can inquire about different matters on different occasions. He can change his relation to people, dealing with them differently as they come to know one another better. He can take chances with words and actions that may annoy or anger people, because he knows he will probably have a chance to repair the damage.

I want to comment on three of the possibilities created by this flexibility of procedures for gathering evidence to test research conclusions: (1) using unconventional measures suggested by experience in the situation; (2) making evidentiary use of one's own experience; and (3) using aggressive and deceitful styles of interviewing to provoke people into saying things they might otherwise keep to themselves. The availability of such procedures gives us further reason to trust conclusions based in field work.

(1) Sociologists treat concrete items of data as instances of general theoretical classes, as an embodiment of some abstractly conceived variable most conveniently measured in that way. When we use standardized items of data to measure those abstract variables, we assume that the specific concrete datum we measure will serve as an adequate embodiment across a variety of times, places, and people. If we ask for father's occupation, intending the datum to indicate something about parental social class, we assume that it has roughly the same relation to social class in one time and place as in another, and that the people we ask will all understand roughly the same thing by the question. Naturally, these assumptions sometimes fail, but we put faith in them anyway, as a way of achieving convenience and

26. See Neal Gross and Ward Mason, "Some Methodological Problems of Eight-Hour Interviews," *American Journal of Sociology* 59 (November 1953), 197–204.

comparability. Our faith accounts for the persistent use of the variety of scales and items that form the standard tools of research.[27]

We can, however, take another approach to the problem of finding embodiments of our theoretically defined variables. We can look for the specific local variants, the way that variable finds expression under all the local and peculiar characteristics of the immediate situation. This procedure makes comparability somewhat more complicated to achieve, but it maximizes the fit between concept and datum. Roth, for example, wanted to study how people complied with institutional rules. Instead of using some general measure of compliance, or some measure specific to the medical settings he was particularly interested in, he noted that in the tuberculosis hospital he was observing people sometimes obeyed and sometimes violated strictly formulated rules about wearing protective masks and gowns. He counted the occasions on which various categories of hospital personnel wore or did not wear protective garb and thus found evidence that compliance is inversely related to rank: doctors conformed least, aides most.[28]

The field work literature contains many examples of such locally restricted measures of abstract variables. Thus Blau measured patterns of influence and deference by observing the frequency with which coworkers asked advice of each other.[29] Whyte used seating patterns as a measure of clique structure.[30] My colleagues and I used a variety of items to demonstrate the existence among college students of a "grade point average" perspective on their academic work: the kinds of questions students asked in class, their methods of studying (both individual and collective), patterns of residential group prestige, and so on.[31]

Each such newly proposed measure must be explained and justified, a bother compared with the ease of using well-known standardized measures. But an ingenious field worker can usually invent several useful ones and thus make it easy to adopt multimethod triangulation as a way of warranting his conclusions, a substantial gain well worth the bother.[32]

27. See the attack on this kind of "measurement by fiat" in Aaron V. Cicourel, *Method and Measurment in Sociology* (New York: Free Press, 1964).
28. Julius A. Roth, "Ritual and Magic in the Control of Contagion," *American Sociological Review* 22 (1957), 310–314.
29. Peter Blau, *The Dynamics of Bureaucracy* (Chicago: University of Chicago Press, 1955).
30. Whyte, *op. cit.* See also Becker *et al., Boys in White, op. cit.*
31. Becker *et al., Making the Grade, op. cit.*
32. See the description in D. T. Campbell and D. W. Fiske, "Convergent and Discriminant Validation by the Multitrait-Multimethod Matrix," *Psychological Bulletin* 56 (1959), 81–105, and the direct application to sociological problems in Norman Denzin, *The Research Act* (Chicago: Aldine Publishing Company, 1970). See also Paul Diesing, *Studies in the Methods of the Social Sciences* (Chicago: Aldine Publishing Co., 1970), Chapter 12.

(2) The field worker can sometimes take advantage of his presence in the situation to produce evidence based on his own experiences. Most obviously, we can make a datum of the way the people we study respond to us as observers. Gussow reports using his varying reception in several schools as a way of understanding their structure. Teachers in a traditional school, for example, were less aware of which child he was observing than teachers in a modern school (the difference reflecting their relative indifference to children's individuality) and more interested in using the researcher as an authority aide (the difference reflecting their greater concern over hierarchy and control).[33]

We can also, if we actually engage in the same activities as the people we study, make use of our responses to the events, tasks, and troubles of that style of life. In a remarkable table, Roy used his own production record in a machine shop to demonstrate the amount workers restricted production, and the degree to which they lowered their own earnings in the process.[34]

(3) Interviewers frequently inhibit themselves by adopting a bland, polite style of conversation designed to create rapport with their respondents and to avoid "leading" them. A more flexible procedure often elicits much fuller data, as the interviewer himself takes positions on some issues and as he uses more aggressive conversational tactics. This flexibility can also characterize the one-shot interview, but it is probably true that you feel freer to use it when you are working with people over a period of time and can make use of their knowing that you know a good deal about what is going on. (On the other hand, field workers sometimes worry more over souring a relationship that must persist than do interviewers who will not see their respondent again.)

I once again take the liberty of reproducing, as an extended example of this point, an earlier discussion based on my own study of schoolteachers.[35]

Arnold Rose once proposed that sociological interviewers be more experimental in dealing with their informants. He pointed out that use of the questionnaire or schedule is appropriate only in certain research situations, particularly where information as to the prevalence of a given attitude in a defined population is desired. However, where information as to the nature of a given attitude is desired, "where the subject's attitude must be fully known . . . ," the interviewer must take an active role.[36] The interviewer

33. Gussow, *op. cit.*

34. Donald Roy, "Quota Restriction and Goldbricking in a Machine Shop," *American Journal of Sociology* 57 (March 1957), 427–442.

35. The following material first appeared, in slightly different form, as Howard S. Becker, "A Note on Interviewing Tactics," *Human Organization* 12 (Winter 1954), 31–32.

36. Arnold M. Rose, "A Research Note on Interviewing," *American Journal of Sociology* 51 (September 1945), 143–144.

must experiment, using those tactics which seem most likely to elicit the desired kind of information. This note presents tactics that proved successful in a study designed to get information about the role problems of Chicago public school teachers.[37]

Chicago public school teachers, like functionaries of many institutions, feel that they have a good deal to hide from what they regard as a prying, misunderstanding, and potentially dangerous public. They have certain problems whose existence, if admitted, would provoke unfavorable public comment. Further, they are afraid to make statements about their superiors and colleagues which might get them into trouble with and provoke retaliation from those people. This makes interviewing around the basic relationships of a teacher's role difficult. Fear prevents them from being frank and giving an undistorted picture of the reality as they know it. To overcome this, I developed certain techniques in the course of the research which enabled me to get franker statements than would normally be forthcoming. These can best be described in the context of particular problems in connection with which they were used.

The interview ordinarily started with questions at a high level of generality: "What are the problems of being a schoolteacher? What kinds of things can make your work tough or unpleasant?" Most teachers could talk about these relationships at this abstract level of discussion; they could say that a principal might make their work difficult by being too "bossy" and interfering, that parents might get "out of their place" in a variety of ways, things they would have been reluctant to state at the outset about specific persons. When a number of such statements had been made and we were well launched on our conversation, I would assume a skeptical air and ask the teacher if she could give me any evidence for these statements, in the form of examples from her own experience. (Obviously, one cannot build up a description of a social structure from such general statements alone; material of a more specific nature is needed to check the way these general attitudes are expressed in behavior.) This somewhat suddenly put the interviewee in the position of having to put up or shut up, substantiate what she said or admit that it was only hearsay. In most cases these abstract statements were generalizations from experiences the teacher had had and, in the face of a direct challenge, she ordinarily came across with descriptions of specific situations in which these generalities were embodied.

Once the interview area had been shifted in this way to personal experience, I used another strategy to elicit further information that was being withheld. I played dumb and pretended not to understand certain relationships and attitudes which were implicit in the description the teacher gave, but which she preferred not to state openly. In so doing, I forced her to state these things in order to present a coherent description. For example, these teachers ordinarily differentiate students, among themselves and to themselves, according to racial and social-class criteria, on the basis of observed

37. The research is reported in Chapters 9–11 of this volume.

differences in the way children of each type act in school. They prefer not to say this in any public way, particularly to a person coming from the University of Chicago as I did,[38] for fear of being accused of discriminatory and undemocratic thinking and activity. I was extremely interested in getting attitudes around just this point. To take a particular instance, in describing a given experience with a principal, the notion of such differences would be implicit in what was being said, and it was part of the unspoken etiquette of the situation that I was to accept this implication without stating it. I would refuse to do this, however, and play dumb. If, for instance, I was told that she had taught in a "colored" school where the principal wasn't tough enough with the children, I was meant to understand that such children needed firmer treatment than others. But I refused to understand this and would say, "Why did he have to be tough? What do you mean?" To make her judgment of the principal's action plausible and reasonable, the teacher then had to explain to me that it was unfortunately true that colored children seemed to misbehave more than the other varieties. The same tactic was used in a variety of contexts.

By continually moving the area of discussion to the level of concrete personal experience, and by playing dumb about the implied descriptions of relationships involved in accounts of such experiences, I coerced many interviewees into being considerably more frank than they had originally intended. I was quite aggressive, often expressing open disbelief in the face of statements that seemed evasive, implausible, or inconsistent with what had already been said or with my general knowledge of the particular topic, and equally open curiosity about the things that were left out. It is certain that such tactics, used in just this way, would not work with all kinds of people. Some of the success attained with schoolteachers must be attributed to the professional politeness and courtesy they felt obliged to extend to me. Once the interview had gotten under way and the teacher had committed herself to accepting me and my questions, she found it difficult to be so insulting as abruptly to refuse to discuss certain issues or to make statements she knew would appear implausible or inconsistent to me. Where failure to tell the truth about her feelings made her statements obviously false or evasive she found it necessary, in the logic of the developing situation, to tell the truth in order to avoid being unpleasant to me.[39]

Such tactics will not prove effective in all situations, nor would one want to use them indiscriminately. Where, for example, your research places you in continuous contact with those being studied, as in a long-term community study, it might be wisest to avoid the possibility of antagonizing informants which lies in this stratagem, especially since the information which might be elicited could undoubtedly be picked up more tactfully in the course of an

38. This research constituted my dissertation at the University of Chicago and I identified myself to teachers as a graduate student at the University and an employee of its Committee on Race Relations.
39. I relied here on the tenet of everyday civility described earlier, according to which it is uncivil to be openly implausible or evasive.

extended series of interviews and observations. Further, not all interviewer-informant relationships carry such a ready-made bond of courtesy as the one here described, and many informants would undoubtedly simply ignore the situational pressure to be consistent plausible. I believe, however, that similar pressures to which informants of diverse kinds will be sensitive can be built up if the interviewer is willing to experiment. Finally, the situation can be complicated, and often is, by the fact of the informant being of higher social-class position that the interviewer. The unspoken etiquette of such a relationship leaves the informant free to be rude through evasiveness or implausibility, free to ignore the demands of a questioner who is stepping out of the confines of his deference role.[40]

Field workers experimenting with this device may find ways to adapt it for use in the more difficult situations, ways of creating a bond between interviewer and informant of such a character that the informant can be coerced into stating things he would otherwise leave unsaid.

Conclusion

We ought not to decide that only field work can provide trustworthy evidence for sociological conclusions. Many people have argued cogently that we should use methods appropriate to the form of our problem and to the character of the world we are studying.[41] Where field work is the appropriate method, however, the burden of my argument has been that we can use the evidence it produces without undue worry. Because it gives us information on people acting under the very social constraints whose operation we are interested in, and because its numerous items of information and flexible procedures allow us to test our conclusions repeatedly and in a variety of ways, we need not fear that its unsystematic character will distort our findings in ways that we, our readers, or the people we study find convenient, congenial, or expectable.

40. Erving Goffman pointed out this possibility to me.
41. See, especially, Morris Zelditch, Jr., "Some Methodological Problems of Field Studies," *American Journal of Sociology* 67 (1962), 566–576.

CHAPTER FOUR

The Life History
and the Scientific Mosaic

Thomas and Znaniecki published the first sociological life history docu-
ment to receive wide attention in The Polish Peasant.[1] *Clifford Shaw and his*
associates published several others in the years following: The Jack-Roller,
The Natural History of a Delinquent Career, *and* Brothers in Crime. *During*
the same period Edwin Sutherland published the still popular Professional
Thief. *And similar documents have appeared occasionally since, most*
recently The Fantastic Lodge *and* Hustler![2] *When* The Jack-Roller *was*
reissued a few years ago, I was asked to write an introduction and made
that the occasion for some thoughts on the place of the life history in con-
temporary sociology.

The life history is not conventional social science "data," although it
has some of the features of that kind of fact, being an attempt to gather
material useful in the formulation of general sociological theory. Nor is it
a conventional autobiography, although it shares with autobiography its
narrative form, its first-person point of view and its frankly subjective

1. W. I. Thomas and Florian Znaniecki, *The Polish Peasant in Europe and Amer-ica* (2d ed., New York, 1927), II, 1931–2244.
2. Clifford R. Shaw, *The Jack-Roller* (Chicago, 1930), *The Natural History of a Delinquent Career* (Chicago, 1931), and *Brothers in Crime* (Chicago, 1936); Chic Conwell and Edwin H. Sutherland, *The Professional Thief* (Chicago, 1937); Helen MacGill Hughes (ed.), *The Fantastic Lodge* (Boston, 1961); Henry Williamson, *Hustler,* edited by R. Lincoln Keiser (Garden City, N.Y., 1965).

stance. It is certainly not fiction, although the best life history documents have a sensitivity and pace, a dramatic urgency, that any novelist would be glad to achieve.

The differences between these forms lie both in the perspective from which the work is undertaken and in the methods used. The writer of fiction is not, of course, concerned with fact at all, but rather with dramatic and emotional impact, with form and imagery, with the creation of a symbolic and artistically unified world. Fidelity to the world as it exists is only one of many problems for him, and for many authors it is of little importance.

The autobiographer proposes to explain his life to us and thus commits himself to maintaining a close connection between the story he tells and what an objective investigation might discover. When we read autobiography, however, we are always aware that the author is telling us only part of the story, that he has selected his material so as to present us with the picture of himself he would prefer us to have and that he may have ignored what would be trivial or distasteful to him, though of great interest to us.

As opposed to these more imaginative and humanistic forms, the life history is more down to earth, more devoted to our purposes than those of the author, less concerned with artistic values than with a faithful rendering of the subject's experience and interpretation of the world he lives in. The sociologist who gathers a life history takes steps to ensure that it covers everything we want to know, that no important fact or event is slighted, that what purports to be factual squares with other available evidence and that the subject's interpretations are honestly given. The sociologist keeps the subject oriented to the questions sociology is interested in, asks him about events that require amplification, tries to make the story told jibe with matters of official record and with material furnished by others familiar with the person, event, or place being described. He keeps the game honest for us.

In so doing, he pursues the job from his own perspective, a perspective which emphasizes the value of the person's "own story." This perspective differs from that of some other social scientists in assigning major importance to the interpretations people place on their experience as an explanation for behavior. To understand why someone behaves as he does you must understand how it looked to him, what he thought he had to contend with, what alternatives he saw open to him; you can understand the effects of opportunity structures, delinquent subcultures, social norms, and other commonly invoked explanations of behavior only by seeing them from the actor's point of view.

The University of Chicago sociology department promoted this perspective vigorously during the 1920's. Almost every study made some use of personal documents. Theoretically grounded in Mead's social psychology, its practicality in research attested by *The Polish Peasant,* and its use persuasively urged by Ernest W. Burgess, the life history enjoyed great popularity. It was one of the many research devices that found a place in the research scheme of the department.

The research scheme did not grow out of a well-developed axiomatic theory, but rather from a vision of the character of cities and city life which permeated much of the research done at Chicago in the exciting period after the arrival of Robert E. Park in 1916. *The Ghetto, The Gold Coast and the Slum, The Gang*[3]—all these were part of the research scheme. And so were the ecological studies of the succession of ethnic groups in Chicago and of the distribution of juvenile delinquency, mental illness, and other forms of pathology. Park enunciated the general scheme, as it developed, in occasional papers on the nature of the city and the role of communication in social life, and in introductions to the books his students produced. Everything was material for the developing theory. And studies of all kinds, done by a variety of methods, contributed to its development.[4] The contribution of any study could thus be evaluated in the context of the total enterprise, not as though it stood alone.

When I first went to San Francisco several years ago and began to think about doing research there, I automatically began looking for the Local Community Fact Book, the demographic studies, the analyses of neighborhoods and institutions, and all the other kinds of background material I had come to take for granted when I worked in Chicago. But they were not there; no one had done them. Perhaps it is because no one group of researchers had ever existed there as well organized as the group that got its start under Park during the twenties. That group saw connections among all the various problems they were working on. Above all, they saw that the things they were studying had close and intimate connections with the city, considered in the abstract, and with Chicago itself, the particular city they were working in. For the Chicago group, whatever the particular subject matter under study, the researcher assumed that it took its character in part from the unique character and form of the city it occurred in. He relied, implicitly and explicitly, on the knowledge that had already been gathered, as he contributed his own small piece to the mosaic of the theory of the city and knowledge of Chicago that Park was building.

The image of the mosaic is useful in thinking about such a scientific enterprise. Each piece added to a mosaic adds a little to our understanding of the

3. Louis Wirth, *The Ghetto* (Chicago, 1928); Harvey W. Zorbaugh, *The Gold Coast and the Slum: A Sociological Study of Chicago's Near North Side* (Chicago, 1929); Frederic M. Thrasher, *The Gang: A Study of 1,313 Gangs in Chicago* (Chicago, 1928).
4. See Everett C. Hughes' account of this "great movement of social investigation" in "Robert Park," *New Society* (December 31, 1964), 18–19; and Robert E. Park, *Human Communities* (Glencoe, Ill., 1952).

total picture. When many pieces have been placed we can see, more or less clearly, the objects and the people in the picture and their relation to one another. Different pieces contribute different things to our understanding: some are useful because of their color, others because they make clear the outline of an object. No one piece has any great job to do; if we do not have its contribution, there are still other ways to come to an understanding of the whole.

Individual studies can be like pieces of mosaic and were so in Park's day. Since the picture in the mosaic was Chicago, the research had an ethnographic, "case history" flavor, even though Chicago itself was seen as somehow representative of all cities. Whether its data were census figures or interviews, questionnaire results or life histories, the research took into account local peculiarities, exploring those things that were distinctively true of Chicago in the 1920's. In so doing, they partially completed a mosaic of great complexity and detail, with the city itself the subject, a "case" which could be used to test a great variety of theories and in which the interconnections of a host of seemingly unrelated phenomena could be seen, however imperfectly.

Our attention today is turned away from local ethnography, from the massing of knowledge about a single place, its parts, and their connections. We emphasize abstract theory-building more than we used to. The national survey is frequently used as a basic mode of data collection. Above all, researchers are increasingly mobile, moving from city to city and university to university every few years, building no fund of specialized local knowledge and passing none on to their students. The trend is away from the community study—there will be no more elaborate programs of coordinated study such as those that produced the *Yankee City Series*[5] or *Black Metropolis*.[6] And a great loss it will be.

In any case, the scientific contribution of such a life history as *The Jack-Roller* can be assessed properly only by seeing it in relation to all the studies done under Park's direction, for it drew on and depended on all of them, just as all the later studies of that Golden Age of Chicago sociology depended, a little, on it. Much of the background that any single study would either have to provide in itself or, even worse, about which it would have to make unchecked assumptions, was already at hand for the reader of *The Jack-Roller*. When Stanley, its protagonist, speaks of the boyish games of stealing he and his pals engaged in, we know that we can find an extensive and penetrating description of that phenomenon in Thrasher's *The Gang*. And when he speaks of the time he spent on West Madison Street, we know that we can turn to Nels Anderson's *The Hobo*[7] for an

5. Published in several volumes by W. Lloyd Warner and his collaborators.
6. St. Clair Drake and Horace Cayton, *Black Metropolis* (New York, 1945).

understanding of the milieu Stanley then found himself in. If we are concerned about the representativeness of Stanley's case, we have only to turn to the ecological studies carried on by Shaw and McKay[8] to see the same story told on a grand scale in mass statistics. And, similarly, if one wanted to understand the maps and correlations contained in ecological studies of delinquency, one could then turn to *The Jack-Roller* and similar documents for that understanding.

I am not sure what the criteria are by which one judges the contribution of a piece of scientific work considered in its total context, but I know that they are not such currently fashionable criteria as are implied by the model of the controlled experiment. We do not expect, in a large and differentiated program of research, that any one piece of work will give us all the answers or, indeed, all of any one answer. What must be judged is the entire research enterprise in all its parts. (One can, of course, assess life histories by such criteria as those suggested by Kluckhohn, Angell and Dollard.)[9] Criteria have yet to be established for determining how much one piece of a mosaic contributes to the conclusions that are warranted by consideration of the whole, but these are just the kind of criteria that are needed. In their place, we can temporarily install a sympathetic appreciation of some of the functions performed by life history documents, taking *The Jack-Roller* as a representative case.

What are those functions? In the first place, *The Jack-Roller* can serve as a touchstone to evaluate theories that purport to deal with phenomena like those of Stanley's delinquent career. Whether it is a theory of the psychological origins of delinquent behavior, a theory of the roots of delinquency in juvenile gangs, or an attempt to explain the distribution of delinquency throughout a city, any theory of delinquency must, if it is to be considered valid, explain or at least be consistent with the facts of Stanley's case as they are reported here. Thus, even though the life history does not in itself provide definitive proof of a proposition, it can be a negative case that forces us to decide a proposed theory is inadequate.

To say this is to take an approach to scientific generalization that deserves some comment. We may decide to accept a theory if it explains, let us say, 95 per cent of the cases that fall in its jurisdiction. Many reputable scientists do. In contrast, one can argue that any theory that does not ex-

7. Nels Anderson, *The Hobo* (Chicago, 1923).

8. Clifford R. Shaw and Henry D. MacKay, *Juvenile Delinquency and Urban Areas* (Chicago, 1942).

9. Clyde Kluckhohn, "The Personal Document in Anthropological Science," in Louis Gottschalk *et al., The Use of Personal Documents in History, Anthropology, and Sociology* (New York, 1945), pp. 79–173; Robert Angell, "A Critical Review of the Development of the Personal Document Method in Sociology 1920–1940," *ibid.,* pp. 177–232; John Dollard, *Criteria for the Life History* (New Haven, 1932).

plain all cases is inadequate, that other factors than those the theory specifies must be operating to produce the result we want to explain. It is primarily a question of strategy. If we assume that exceptions to any rule are a normal occurrence, we will perhaps not search as hard for further explanatory factors as we otherwise might. But if we regard exceptions as potential negations of our theory, we will be spurred to search for them.[10]

More importantly, the negative case will respond to careful analysis by suggesting the direction the search should take.[11] Inspection of its features will reveal attributes which differ from those of otherwise similar cases, or processes at work whose steps have not all been fully understood. If we know the case in some detail, as a life history document allows us to know it, our search is more likely to be successful; it is in this sense that the life history is a useful theoretical touchstone.

The life history also helps us in areas of research that touch on it only tangentially. Every piece of research crosses frontiers into new terrain it does not explore thoroughly, areas important to its main concern in which it proceeds more by assumption than investigation.[12] A study of a college, for instance, may make assumptions (indeed, must make them) about the character of the city, state, and region it is located in, about the social class background and experience of its students, and about a host of other matters likely to influence the operation of the school and the way it affects students. A study of a mental hospital or prison will make similarly unchecked assumptions about the character of the families whose members end up in the institution. A life history—although it is not the only kind of information that can do this—provides a basis on which those assumptions can be realistically made, a rough approximation of the direction in which the truth lies.

In addition to these matters of neighboring fact, so to speak, the life history can be particularly useful in giving us insight into the subjective side of much-studied institutional processes, about which unverified assumptions are also often made. Sociologists have lately been concerned with processes of adult socialization and, to take an instance to which Stanley's case is directly relevant, with the processes of degradation and "stripping" associated with socialization into rehabilitative institutions such as prisons and

10. See, for instance, George H. Mead, "Scientific Method and Individual Thinker," in John Dewey *et al., Creative Intelligence* (New York, 1917), pp. 176–227, and Alfred Lindesmith, *Opiate Addiction* (Bloomington, 1947), pp. 5–20. Lindesmith turns the strategy into a systematic method of inquiry usually referred to as analytic induction.

11. See, for a similar view growing out of the tradition of survey research, Patricia L. Kendall and Katherine M. Wolf, "The Analysis of Deviant Cases in Communications Research," in Paul F. Lazarsfeld and Frank Stanton (eds.), *Communications Research 1948–1949* (New York, 1949), pp. 152–79.

12. See Max Gluckman (ed.), *Closed Systems and Open Minds* (Chicago, 1964).

mental hospitals.[13] Although the theories concern themselves with institutional action rather than individual experience, they either assume something about the way people experience such processes or at least raise a question about the nature of that experience. Although Stanley's prison experiences do not, of course, provide fully warranted knowledge of these matters, they give us some basis for making a judgment.

The life history, by virtue again of its wealth of detail, can be important at those times when an area of study has grown stagnant, has pursued the investigation of a few variables with ever-increasing precision but has received dwindling increments of knowledge from the pursuit. When this occurs, investigators might well proceed by gathering personal documents which suggest new variables, new questions, and new processes, using the rich though unsystematic data to provide a needed reorientation of the field.

Beneath these specific contributions which the life history is capable of making lies one more fundamental. The life history, more than any other technique except perhaps participant observation, can give meaning to the overworked notion of *process.* Sociologists like to speak of "ongoing processes" and the like, but their methods usually prevent them from seeing the processes they talk about so glibly.

George Herbert Mead, if we take him seriously, tells us that the reality of social life is a conversation of significant symbols, in the course of which people make tentative moves and then adjust and reorient their activity in the light of the responses (real and imagined) others make to those moves. The formation of the individual act is a process in which conduct is continually reshaped to take account of the expectations of others, as these are expressed in the immediate situation and as the actor supposes they may come to be expressed. Collective activity, of the kind pointed to by concepts like "organization" or "social structure," arises out of a continuous process of mutual adjustment of the actions of all the actors involved. Social process, then, is not an imagined interplay of invisible forces or a vector made up of the interaction of multiple social factors, but an observable process of symbolically mediated interaction.[14]

Observable, yes; but not easily observable, at least not for scientific purposes. To observe social process as Mead described it takes a great deal of time. It poses knotty problems of comparability and objectivity in data gathering. It requires an intimate understanding of the lives of others. So

13. Harold Garfinkel, "Conditions of Successful Degradation Ceremonies," *American Journal of Sociology* 61 (1956): 420–24; and Erving Goffman, *Asylums* (Garden City, N.Y., 1961), pp. 127–69.

14. See George Herbert Mead, *Mind, Self, and Society* (Chicago, 1934); Herbert Blumer, "Society as Symbolic Interaction," in Arnold Rose (ed.), *Human Behavior and Social Processes* (Boston, 1962), pp. 179–92; and Anselm L. Strauss *et al., Psychiatric Ideologies and Institutions* (New York, 1964), pp. 292–315.

social scientists have, most often, settled for less demanding techniques such as the interview and the questionnaire.

These techniques can, I think, tell us much, but only as we are able to relate them to a vision of the underlying Meadian social process we would know had we more adequate data. We can, for instance, give people a questionnaire at two periods in their life and infer an underlying process of change from the differences in their answers. But our interpretation has significance only if our imagery of the underlying process is accurate. And this accuracy of imagery—this congruence of theoretically posited process with what we could observe if we took the necessary time and trouble—can be partially achieved by the use of life history documents. For the life history, if it is done well, will give us the details of that process whose character we would otherwise only be able to speculate about, the process to which our data must ultimately be referred if they are to have theoretical and not just an operational and predictive significance. It will describe those crucial interactive episodes in which new lines of individual and collective activity are forged, in which new aspects of the self are brought into being. It is by thus giving a realistic basis to our imagery of the underlying process that the life history serves the purposes of checking assumptions, illuminating organization, and reorienting stagnant fields.

But perhaps the most important service performed for sociology by a document like *The Jack-Roller* is one that it also performs for those who are not sociologists. David Riesman has described social science as, in part, a "conversation between the classes."[15] It describes to people the way of life of segments of their society with which they would never otherwise come in contact. The life history, because it is the actor's "own story," is a live and vibrant message from "down there," telling us what it means to be a kind of person we have never met face to face. The United States is fortunate in having fewer barriers, in the form of closed social circles and rules against interaction outside of them, than most societies. Nevertheless, the distances between social classes, between ethnic groups, and between age groups are such that it is hard for most sociologists (let alone others whose work does not push them toward this knowledge) to comprehend what it means to live the life of a Negro junkie or a Polish delinquent.

Johan Galtung suggests the function of this kind of knowledge in the scientific process in his discussion of the causes of the excessive abstractness and formality of Latin American sociology. He argues that Latin American society is more rigidly stratified, both horizontally and vertically, than the societies of northern Europe and North America. This means that the Latin American, when he comes to sociology, will never have had the informal

15. David Riesman, *Abundance for What?* (Garden City, 1965), pp. 493–4.

interaction with members of other classes and social segments that young people in other societies gain through travel, through summer employment, and in similar ways. As a result, Galtung says, preconceived ideas of the character of other members of the society are never put to the test of direct confrontation with social reality:

> Sociologists who would never accept the idea that the only thing which has motivated them has been the desire to make money have no difficulty in perceiving the capitalist as interested only in the most money for the least work, or the worker as motivated in a similar manner. A more intimate knowledge of them would invariably reveal shadings, greater identification, greater variety in motives, but the paucity of interaction protects the sociologist from this knowledge. From this comes the great interest in the alienation of the lower classes: without denying its reality, a factor which maintains the image of the alienation of the working class is the alienation of the intellectual himself, with respect to his society in general and certainly with respect to the working class.[16]

By providing this kind of voice from a culture and situation that are ordinarily not known to intellectuals generally, and to sociologists in particular, *The Jack-Roller* enables us to improve our theories at the most profound level: by putting ourselves in Stanley's skin, we can feel and become aware of the deep biases about such people that ordinarily permeate our thinking and shape the kinds of problems we investigate. By truly entering into Stanley's life, we can begin to see what we take for granted (and ought not to) in designing our research—what kinds of assumptions about delinquents, slums, and Poles are embedded in the way we set the questions we study. Stanley's story allows us, if we want to take advantage of it, to begin to ask questions about delinquency from the point of view of the delinquent. If we take Stanley seriously, as his story must impel us to do, we might well raise a series of questions that have been relatively little studied —questions about the people who deal with delinquents, the tactics they use, their suppositions about the world, and the constraints and pressures they are subject to. Such studies are only now beginning to be done. Close study of *The Jack-Roller* and similar documents might provide us with a wide range of questions to put as we begin to look at the dealings of policemen, judges, and jailers with delinquents.

Given the variety of scientific uses to which the life history may be put, one must wonder at the relative neglect into which it has fallen. Sociologists, it is true, have never given it up altogether. But neither have they made it one of their standard research tools. They read the documents available and

16. Johan Galtung, "Los factores socioculturales y el desarrollo de la sociología en América latina," *Revista Latinoamericana de Sociología* 1 (March, 1965): 87.

assign them for their students to read. But they do not ordinarily think of gathering life history documents themselves or of making the technique part of their research approach.

A number of simultaneous changes probably contributed to the increasing disuse of the life history method. Sociologists became more concerned with the development of abstract theory and correspondingly less interested in full and detailed accounts of specific organizations and communities. They wanted data formulated in the abstract categories of their own theories rather than in the categories that seemed most relevant to the people they studied. The life history was well suited to the latter task, but of little immediately apparent use in the former.

At the same time, sociologists began to separate the field of social psychology from that of sociology proper, creating two specialties in place of two emphases within one field, and focused more on "structural" variables and synchronic functional analyses than on those factors that manifested themselves in the life and experience of the person. Again, the life history made a clear contribution to the latter task but seemed unrelated to studies that emphasized group attributes and their interconnections.

But perhaps the major reason for the relatively infrequent use of the technique is that it does not produce the kind of "findings" that sociologists now expect research to produce. As sociology increasingly rigidifies and "professionalizes," more and more emphasis has come to be placed on what we may, for simplicity's sake, call the *single study*. I use the term to refer to research projects that are conceived of as self-sufficient and self-contained, which provide all the evidence one needs to accept or reject the conclusions they proffer, whose findings are to be used as another brick in the growing wall of science—a metaphor quite different than that of the mosaic. The single study is integrated with the main body of knowledge in the following way: it derives its hypotheses from an inspection of what is already known; then, after the research is completed, if those hypotheses have been demonstrated, they are added to the wall of what is already scientifically known and used as the basis for further studies. The important point is that the researcher's hypothesis is either proved or disproved on the basis of what he has discovered in doing that one piece of research.

The customs, traditions, and organizational practices of contemporary sociology conspire to make us take this view of research. The journal article of standard length, the most common means of scientific communication, is made to order for the presentation of findings that confirm or refute hypotheses. The Ph.D. thesis virtually demands that its author have a set of findings, warranted by his own operations, which yield conclusions he can defend before a faculty committee. The research grant proposal, another ubiquitous sociological literary form, pushes its author to state what his project will have proved when the money has been spent.

If we take the single study as the model of scientific work, we will then use, when we judge research and make decisions about how to organize our research, criteria designed to assure us that the findings of our single study do indeed provide a sound basis on which to accept or reject hypotheses. The canons of inference and proof now in vogue reflect this emphasis. Such methodologists as Stouffer, and others who followed him, developed techniques for assessing hypotheses based on the model of the controlled experiment.[17] Compare two groups, those who have been exposed to the effects of a variable and those who have not, before and after the exposure. The multiple comparisons made possible by this technique allow you to test not only your original hypothesis, but also some of the likely alternative explanations of the same results, should they be what you have predicted. This is the approved model. If we cannot achieve it, our study is deficient unless we can devise workable substitutes. If we do achieve it, we can say with assurance that we have produced scientific findings strong enough to bear the weight of still further studies.

Criteria drawn from the experimental model and used to evaluate single studies in isolation, however useful they may be in a variety of contexts, have had one bad by-product. They have led people to ignore the other functions of research and, particularly, to ignore the contribution made by one study to an overall research enterprise even when the study, considered in isolation, produced no definitive results of its own. Since, by these criteria, the life history did not produce definitive results, people have been at a loss to make anything of it and by and large have declined to invest the time and effort necessary to acquire life history documents.

We can perhaps hope that a fuller understanding of the complexity of the scientific enterprise will restore sociologists' sense of the versatility and worth of the life history. A new series of personal documents, like those produced by the Chicago School more than a generation ago, might help us in all the ways I have earlier suggested and in ways, too, that we do not now anticipate.

17. See the very influential paper by Samuel A. Stouffer, "Some Observations on Study Design," *American Journal of Sociology* 55 (January 1950): 355–61, and any of a large number of books and articles on method which take essentially the same position.

CHAPTER FIVE

Social Observation
and Social Case Studies

The term "case study" comes from the tradition of medical and psychological research, where it refers to a detailed analysis of an individual case that explicates the dynamics and pathology of a given disease; the method supposes that one can properly acquire knowledge of the phenomenon from intense exploration of a single case. Adapted from the medical tradition, the case study has become one of the major modes of social science analysis.

The case studied in social science is typically not an individual but an organization or community. Case studies have been done of such widely varying phenomena as industrial towns,[1] urban neighborhoods,[2] factories,[3] mental hospitals,[4] and the interconnections of slums, politics, and rackets.[5] Case studies of individuals are, of course, also undertaken by social scientists, especially in the form of the life history; but such studies, although often made by an earlier generation of sociologists and psychologists[6] are now relatively rare.[7]

Reprinted with permission of the publisher from the *International Encyclopedia of the Social Sciences,* David L. Sills, ed. Volume 14, pages 232–238. Copyright © 1968 by Crowell Collier and Macmillan, Inc.

1. Everett C. Hughes, *French Canada in Transition* (Chicago: University of Chicago Press, 1943).
2. Herbert J. Gans, *The Urban Villagers* (New York: Free Press, 1962).
3. Melville Dalton, *Men Who Manage* (New York: John Wiley and Sons, 1959).
4. Erving Goffman, *Asylums* (Chicago: Aldine Publishing Co., 1961).
5. William F. Whyte, *Street Corner Society* (Chicago: University of Chicago Press, 1943).
6. See William I. Thomas and Florian Znaniecki, *The Polish Peasant in Europe and America,* 2d ed., (New York: Alfred A. Knopf, 1927), pp. 1931–2244; Clifford R. Shaw, ed., *The Jack-Roller* (Chicago: University of Chicago Press, 1930); and Chic Conwell, *The Professional Thief* (Chicago: University of Chicago Press, 1937).
7. But see Helen M. Hughes, ed., *The Fantastic Lodge* (Boston: Houghton Mifflin Co., 1961); and Henry Williamson, *Hustler!* (Garden City, N.Y.: Doubleday and Co., 1965).

The social scientist making a case study of a community or organization typically makes use of the method of participant observation in one of its many variations, often in connection with other, more structured methods such as interviewing. Observation gives access to a wide range of data, including kinds of data whose existence the investigator may not have anticipated at the time he began his study, and thus is a method well suited to the purposes of the case study.

Aims of the Case Study

The case study usually has a double purpose. On the one hand, it attempts to arrive at a comprehensive understanding of the group under study: who are its members? what are their stable and recurring modes of activity and interaction? how are they related to one another and how is the group related to the rest of the world? At the same time, the case study also attempts to develop more general theoretical statements about regularities in social structure and process.

Because it aims to understand all of the group's behavior, the case study cannot be designed single-mindedly to test general propositions. In contrast to the laboratory experiment, which is designed to test one or a few closely related propositions as rigorously and precisely as possible, the case study must be prepared to deal with a great variety of descriptive and theoretical problems. The various phenomena uncovered by the investigator's observations must all be incorporated into his account of the group and then be given theoretical relevance.

So stated, the aims of the case study can scarcely be realized; it is utopian to suppose that one can see, describe, and find the theoretical relevance of *everything*. Investigators typically end up by focusing on a few problems that appear to be of major importance in the group studied—problems that touch on many aspects of the group's life and structure. Thus a community study[8] may come to focus on the problems of industrialization and cultural contact, or a study of an urban neighborhood may focus on the relation between ethnicity and social class.[9]

The comprehensive goal of the case study, however, even though it is not reached, has important and useful consequences. It prepares the investigator to deal with unexpected findings and, indeed, requires him to reorient his study in the light of such developments. It forces him to consider, however crudely, the multiple interrelations of the particular phenomena he observes. And it saves him from making assumptions that may turn out to be incorrect about matters that are relevant, though tangential, to his main

8. Hughes, *op. cit.*
9. Gans, *op. cit.*

concerns. This is because a case study will nearly always provide some facts to guide those assumptions, while studies with more limited data-gathering procedures are forced to assume what the observer making a case study can check on.

The aims of the case study and the kinds of problems it ordinarily poses for study suggest particular techniques of data gathering and analysis. After describing these, we will consider the uses, scientific and otherwise, which may be made of observational case studies.

Techniques of Observation

In gathering data, the participant-observer engages in a number of different activities. One can distinguish several possible modes of proceeding, depending on the degree to which one is a participant as well as an observer.[10] At one extreme, the observer may not participate at all, as when he hides behind a one-way screen in an experimental room; at the other, he may be a full-fledged participant, living in the community under study or holding a full-time job in the organization he studies and subject to the same life chances as any other member of the group. The particular techniques he uses are shaped by the demands of playing these different roles; a hidden observer cannot openly interview other participants, while a known observer may find that certain group secrets are systematically kept from him.

The observer places himself in the life of the community so that he can see, over a period of time, what people ordinarily do as they go about their daily round of activity. He records his observations as soon as possible after making them. He notes the kinds of people who interact with one another, the content and consequences of the interaction, and how it is talked about and evaluated by the participants and others after the event. He tries to record this material as completely as possible by means of detailed accounts of actions, maps of the location of people as they act[11] and, of course, verbatim transcriptions of conversation.

THE PROBLEM OF BIAS

The observer has the problem of trying to avoid seeing only those things which accord with his explicit or implicit hypotheses.[12] This kind of bias can occur in several ways. The observer, interacting with those he studies on a long-term basis, comes to know them as fellow human beings as well

10. Raymond L. Gold, "Roles in Sociological Field Observations," *Social Forces* 36 (March 1958), pp. 217–223.

11. See Whyte, *op. cit.*

12. See the discussion of biases in Morris Zelditch, Jr., "Some Methodological Problems of Field Studies," *American Journal of Sociology* 67 (March 1962), pp. 566–576.

as research subjects; thus, he can hardly help acquiring feelings of friendship, loyalty, and obligation, which may make him wish to protect some members of the group by not seeing those events which would render them liable to criticism. Some persons or factions may see his research as dangerous and try to keep him from seeing certain aspects of group activity.[13] Finally, he may feel that certain events are so distasteful or personally dangerous (for example, the activities of homosexual networks or violent gang conflict) that he is unwilling or afraid to remain close enough to the participants to see what actually happens.

Bias can be avoided by carefully rendering a complete account of *all* events observed; by seeking to cover all *varieties* of events by some kind of primitive sampling device (making observations at different times of the day or year, deliberately seeking out members of different groups in the community or organization, and so forth); and by formulating *tentative hypotheses* as the field work proceeds and then deliberately searching for negative cases.[14] These topics are more fully treated below.

TYPES OF DATA

The observer is especially alert for incidents of anything defined as conflict or "trouble" by the community or organization being studied. Such incidents enable him most quickly to discover the expectations that guide interaction; when expectations are violated, trouble follows. By seeing what kinds of actions produce conflict, the observer can infer the existence of implicit expectations, which then become part of his analytic model of the group under study.

He is also alert to nuances of language, such as special meanings given to ordinary words, for these signal the existence of situations, events, and persons the members of the group think distinctive enough to merit being singled out linguistically and thus give a clue to the characteristic problems and responses of the group. By inquiring into the meaning and usage of an unusual term, by investigating instances of its use and seeing when it applies and when it does not, he adds to his analytic model.[15]

The observer does not confine himself to observation alone. He may also interview members of the group, either alone or in groups. In the first case, he can inquire into the social background and earlier experiences of a participant as well as into his private opinions about current affairs. In the latter, he is in effect "tapping" the ordinary kinds of communications cur-

13. See Dalton, *op. cit.*

14. This is a generalized description of the method of analytic description embodied in Lindesmith, *op. cit.*, and discussed in Ralph H. Turner, "The Quest for Universals in Sociological Research," *American Sociological Review* 18 (December 1953), pp. 604–611.

15. See Howard S. Becker and Blanche Geer, "Participant Observation and Interviewing: A Comparison," *Human Organization* 16 (Fall 1957), pp. 28–32.

rent in a group, seeing what members will say when in the company of other members. The difference between private opinion and public communication may provide important clues to group norms.[16]

The observer will also find it useful to collect documents and statistics (minutes of meetings, annual reports, budgets, newspaper clippings) generated by the community or organization. These can furnish useful historical background, necessary documentation of the conditions of action for a group (as in a codified set of rules), or a convenient record of events for analysis (as, for instance, when a college newspaper reports the marriages of students, specifying their position in the campus social structure). In every case, the observer must inquire carefully into how the documents he works with are created: by whom, following what procedures, and for what purposes? For it is clear that documents cannot be taken at face value but must be interpreted in the light of such considerations.[17]

The observer may also create his own statistics for the solution of particular problems. Thus, one may observe the number of times people in an office ask one another for advice,[18] or one may keep accurate records of one's own piecework production in a machine shop, to be used as an indication of what is possible for the average group member.[19]

Techniques of Analysis

It is a truism to say that procedures of analysis and proof take their form from the problem one is trying to solve. It is more important to indicate the variety of problems typically encountered in analysis of observational material and the means by which they may be solved.

Observational materials, since they are usually gathered over a long period of time, can be analyzed sequentially. That is, analysis need not await completion of data gathering but can go on concurrently with it; results of early analyses may be used to direct further data-gathering operations. Different problems arise at different stages of the research.

CHOICE OF PROBLEM

In the beginning the researcher may not be sure what problem is most deserving of study in the community or organization he is working in; he

16. An instructive use of such data is contained in Raymond L. Gorden, "Interaction Between Attitude and the Definition of the Situation in the Expression of Opinion," *American Sociological Review* 17 (February 1952), pp. 50–58.

17. For further discussion, see John I. Kitsuse and Aaron V. Cicourel, "A Note on the Uses of Official Statistics," *Social Problems* 11 (Fall 1963), pp. 131–139.

18. As Peter Blau did in *The Dynamics of Bureaucracy* (Chicago: University of Chicago Press, 1955), pp. 99–130.

19. As did Donald Roy in "Quota Restriction and Goldbricking in a Machine Shop," *American Journal of Sociology* 57 (March 1952), pp. 427–442.

devotes his first analytic efforts to uncovering worthwhile problems and hypotheses that will prove most useful in attacking them.[20] Researchers frequently discover that the problem they set out to study is not as important as, or cannot be studied except in the context of, some other problem they had not anticipated studying. Thus, Vidich and Bensman found that the problem of the relationships between the rural communities and the various agencies and institutions of American mass society that affect rural life could be understood only if one also investigated how the community and its members were able to function in spite of the fact that their immediate social environment demonstrably negated their basic beliefs.[21]

In selecting problems, hypotheses, and concepts, the investigator works from concrete findings made early in the research. Typically, he discovers that a given event has occurred, perhaps only once, and asks what the significance of such an event might be. It may be an incident of conflict or the kind of linguistic nuance already referred to. Whatever it is, the investigator must first ascertain that the event actually is what it seems to be and then trace out its possible theoretical implications. The first problem requires him to consider whether people may have been consciously or unconsciously deceiving him; this can be checked by an assessment of whether the event that arouses his curiosity is one that was concocted for his benefit or whether it would have occurred in the same way even if he had not been there. For instance, a statement volunteered by an informant who does not know what the observer is after may be given more weight than one that has been influenced by the observer's leading questions. Similarly, an event that occurs in an ordinary institutional context, subject to all the constraints of that context, can be given more weight than one that occurs without being observed by other members of the group.

The observer then traces the possible theoretical implications of his finding by considering what class of events it might be representative of, utilizing such theory as is available about that class of events to deduce further propositions. For instance, if one hears a worker in a service profession categorize members of his clientele, he may apply the proposition that such a categorization will be based on the problems clients of various kinds pose for the worker in trying to realize his occupational goals. (Teachers, for example, distinguish pupils according to how hard they are to teach and discipline; doctors distinguish patients according to how easily they can be

20. A detailed exploration of this process is contained in Blanche Geer, "First Days in the Field," in Phillip E. Hammond, ed., *Sociologists at Work* (New York: Basic Books, 1964), pp. 322–334.
21. Arthur J. Vidich and Joseph Bensman, *Small Town in Mass Society* (Princeton: Princeton University Press, 1958).

cured, whether they pay on time, and so on.) Working from this, the observer begins to look for the basic problems implied by the set of categories and the way the problems impinge on workers at different career stages. Obviously, a large number of theories may be applied to discrete observations in order to draw out their implications and use them to direct further observations.

QUASI-STATISTICAL METHOD

At a later stage, the observer, having decided, at least provisionally, what he will study in the situation at hand and what theoretical apparatus he will use, is concerned with whether his initial findings hold for the entire community or organization. His data will usually not, unless expressly gathered for the purpose, be sufficiently systematic to be amenable to statistical manipulation. But he can generate what have been called "quasi statistics," [22] that is, such imprecisely sampled and enumerated figures as his data contain. Such data are often quite adequate for the points he wishes to make.

In particular, quasi statistics may allow the investigator to dispose of certain troublesome null hypotheses. A simple frequency count of the number of times a given phenomenon appears may make untenable the null hypothesis that the phenomenon is infrequent. A comparison of the number of such instances with the number of negative cases—instances in which some alternative phenomenon that would not be predicted by his theory appears—may make possible a stronger conclusion, especially if the theory was developed early enough in the observational period to allow a systematic search for negative cases. Similarly, an inspection of the range of situations covered by the investigator's data may allow him to negate the hypothesis that his conclusion is restricted to only a few situations, time periods, or types of people in the organization or community.

The technical problem in creating quasi statistics lies in making sure that one has in fact inspected all the relevant cases. A number of workers have devised schemes for doing this.[23] The common feature of these schemes is the reduction of the body of data by making an abstract of the field notes that have been accumulated, breaking them down into small units, and classifying each unit under all the analytic categories to which it might be relevant. When the investigator desires to analyze all the material on a given

---

22. See Allen H. Barton and Paul F. Lazarsfeld, "Some Functions of Qualitative Analysis in Social Research," in S. M. Lipset and Neil J. Smelser, eds., *Sociology: The Progress of a Decade* (Englewood Cliffs, N.J.: Prentice-Hall, 1961), pp. 95–122.

23. A representative scheme is described in Howard S. Becker and Blanche Geer, "Participant Observation: The Analysis of Qualitative Field Data," in Richard N. Adams and Jack J. Preiss, eds., *Human Organization Research: Field Relations and Techniques* (Homewood, Ill.: Dorsey Press, 1960), pp. 267–289.

point, he sorts his units (which may be reproduced on keysort cards, for convenience), takes out those items which are irrelevant, and frames a conclusion that takes account of all the relevant evidence remaining.

One of the greatest faults in most observational case studies has been their failure to make explicit the quasi-statistical basis of their conclusions. Even though the investigator uses faulty sampling and enumeration procedures, his evidence may nevertheless be sufficient to warrant the conclusions he draws if he explicitly states what the evidence is and shows his conclusions are related to it. In particular, the conclusions may appear extremely plausible[24] if they are supported by several kinds of evidence at once. Thus, the conclusion that medical students make use of a perspective based on the values of clinical experience and medical responsibility gains great plausibility when it is shown not only that use of the perspective is frequent and appears in a wide range of situations but also that students' characterizations of patients depend heavily on the same criteria.[25]

CONSTRUCTION OF MODELS

As a result of the early stages of analysis, the researcher acquires a number of limited models of parts of the organization or community, propositions which describe one kind of interaction between one pair of statuses in one kind of situation. The final stage of a case study consists in a progressive refinement of these part-models (accomplished by continual checking against evidence already available in the field notes or newly gathered in the field) and their integration into a *model* of the entire organization or community. The model provides answers to the theoretical questions of the study and shows the contribution of each part of the analyzed structure to the explanation of the phenomenon in question.

Models of the community or organization that result from case studies are not to be confused with mathematical models. Rather, they have the same relation to the group studied that the *natural history* of a process (such as the race-relations cycle or the process of becoming a drug addict) has to any specific set of events said to embody it. In a natural-history analysis of the process we strip away the historical uniqueness of a number of instances of the same phenomenon, leaving as our result the generic steps in the process—those steps that would always occur if the same result were to be found. Similarly, in a csae study of social structure we strip away what is historically unique and concentrate on the generic properties of the

24. See the analysis of plausibility in George Polya, *Mathematics and Plausible Reasoning* vol. 2, "Patterns of Plausible Inference" (Princeton: Princeton University Press, 1954).

25. The example comes from Howard S. Becker *et al.*, *Boys in White: Student Culture in Medical School* (Chicago: University of Chicago Press, 1961), pp. 338–340.

group, viewed as an example of a particular kind of structure. Relations between the essential characteristics of that kind of structure are stated by verbal generalizations. For instance, one might study a prison or school with a view to discovering what the characteristic statuses and forms of interaction are in an institution in which one class of participants is present involuntarily. The result would be a model that might also be applied to other institutions having that characteristic, such as mental hospitals.

THE PROBLEM OF RELIABILITY

The reliability of such an analysis is sometimes questioned in an equivocal way that plays on the meaning of "reliability." The question is put thus: would another observer produce, with the same analysis, the same total model, were he to repeat the study? The answer is of course that he would —but only if he used the same theoretical framework and became interested in the same general problems, for neither the theoretical framework nor the major problem chosen for study is inherent in the group studied. Nevertheless, given the same basic framework—for instance, a sociology based on conceptions of social structure, culture, and symbolic interaction—the same fundamental parts of the group studied would be found in a second study, even if the major problems chosen for study were quite different. For instance, one might study a medical school to discover how the students are changed by their experience in it; this would be a problem in the theory of adult socialization. Or one might, with equal justice, choose to use the medical school as the arena for a study of how specialists cooperate in a common task, a problem in the "politics" of complex organiaztions. In either case, a complete study would necessarily describe the same basic relationships among students, among faculty, between students and faculty, between both and patients, and so on. Admittedly, the theoretical use to which the analysis was to be put would shape the kind of structural model built, and a model built for one purpose might slight or ignore important elements in the other; but the two could be combined, so that neither would contain any element denied in the other.

The Use of Observational Studies

Every case study allows us to make generalizations about the relations of the various phenomena studied. But, as has often been pointed out, one case is after all only one case. Suppose that some of the most important factors involved in understanding the particular theoretical problems posed by the case are so invariant in it that we are unaware of their importance. How is one to discover their importance?

The problem can be handled (or can in principle be handled) by gather-

ing a large number of cases and "partialing out" the effects of various influences. In any case, the problem is not a real one if we take a long-term
view of the development of theory. Each study can develop the role of a
different set of conditions or variables as these are found to vary in the
setting of the study. Over a series of studies, the comparison of variations
in conditions and consequences can provide a highly differential theory of
the phenomenon under study. As a simple example, a community study
might locate six social classes in a community. A later study, in a somewhat different community, discloses only five, the upper class failing to
divide between "old" and "new" wealth; comparison of the two may show
variations in the histories or ecological positions of the communities that
might account for the difference, and the hypothesis can be checked out
in yet another study.

COMPARATIVE ANALYSIS: AN EXAMPLE

To take another example, some studies of prisons[26] have revealed elaborate organizations of inmates around matters of deprivation; wherever
inmates were deprived of something—material possessions, sex, autonomy—they developed social units and practices designed to deal with the
deprivation as best they could under prison conditions. Because these early
studies were all of men's prisons, they could not discover what a later study
of a women's prison revealed: that the informal organization of the prison
varied according to the kind of people recruited, because deprivations differ
according to what it is one values and, therefore, misses when deprived of
it. Women apparently set far less store by autonomy than men, do not
miss it, and do not develop a *sub rosa* government; they are, however, very
dependent on intimate affectional ties, miss their families intensely, and
develop homosexual liaisons as their form of informal organization.[27] Other
studies might show the influence of age, region, and other factors on the
organization of prison life. A series of comparisons, based on variations in
the phenomenon, show the influence of each factor; each succeeding study
can be built on the contributions of its predecessors.

Developing theory by comparative analysis is necessarily a protracted
process. Comparative findings take many years to establish, for each study,
by itself, may take several years and, for maximum effect, studies should

26. See Gresham M. Sykes, *The Society of Captives* (Princeton: Princeton University Press, 1958) and Donald R. Cressey, ed., *The Prison* (New York: Holt, Rinehart
and Winston, 1961).

27. See David A. Ward and Gene G. Kassebaum, *Women's Prison: Sex and Social
Structure* (Chicago: Aldine Publishing Co., 1965) and Rose Giallombardo, *Society of
Women* (New York: John Wiley and Sons, 1966).

be built on one another rather than being done simultaneously. The result can be a detailed understanding of the operation of a large number of factors and conditions as they interact to produce different results.

One useful strategy is to state the findings of each study as universal propositions, even though it is obvious that they are provisional. By doing so, the investigator makes it possible to identify exceptions to his propositions and to proceed most efficiently with fruitful comparisons.[28]

PRACTICAL USE OF RESEARCH FINDINGS

The observational study of an institution or community can be (and often is) used by various people in various ways, depending on their position in, or relation to, the group and their interest in its functioning. It does not differ in this from other kinds of research, but it does differ, typically, in the range and number of variables considered and the distance beneath the surface of events that the research reaches. Studies are often undertaken with the subsidiary—if not primary—purpose of providing guidance to administrators and others who may wish to intervene in the organization or community in order to change some condition thought to be inefficient, distasteful, or inimical to group welfare. The observational study is useful in identifying and specifying such problems and in finding their origins and consequences at various levels and in various parts of the group.

Clues to Intervention. The observational study also makes it possible to go beyond the problem as originally conceived by those group members who wanted help and to discover other problems that, from some viewpoint other than theirs, require or warrant intervention. For instance, the officers of an autocratically governed trade union may not think the absence of organizational democracy a problem, but some of the members or an outside observer might take a different view. The farther beneath the surface the study penetrates, the more likely it is to discover problems that have not been labeled as such by the leaders of the group.

Whatever the problems identified, the wide range of the case study makes it likely that it will contain hints or suggestions as to the crucial points of possible intervention. Many studies diagnose the "causes" of a problem and yet are not useful for social action, because the causes discovered are not accessible to manipulation by the people involved. Thus, even though the generalization that the cause of teen-age vandalism lies in the early childhood experiences of the vandal might be true, knowing this is of little value. It is more useful to know, through close observation, that (as might be the case) vandalism takes place more frequently in unlit and unwatched places

28. See Lindesmith, *op. cit.,* and Turner, *op. cit.*

or becomes more frequent as the certainty of apprehension declines, for these matters are more subject to remedial action by police and other agents of social control.

Ethical Problems of the Researcher

The published report of an observational study may be used, either by members or outsiders, to embarrass or even endanger the organization or community studied or, at least, its leaders. Every group maintains fictions about itself—they may, perhaps, be necessary for the continued existence of the group—which present it as better in some ways than unprejudiced research will reveal it to be. A town may feel that its government is more broadly representative than it is; a hospital may think its treatment of patients more successful than it is. A case study is bound to reveal the discrepancy between the operating reality and the image believed in and presented to the rest of the world by members. When the results of the study are published, the discrepancy is publicly attested to in a way that members cannot ignore. Their enemies may make use of the opportunity to embarrass or attack them. The members may ask that the findings be withheld or may attempt to coerce the researcher into suppressing them.

The investigator therefore faces an ethical dilemma. Science requires frank and unfettered reporting, and the matters group members complain of may be important aspects of group functioning, whose suppression would emasculate the report and strip it of scientific significance. On the other hand, the investigator surely has some obligation not to bring harm to those who have allowed themselves to be studied; he may, indeed, have promised them that they will not be harmed. In making the promise, he may have meant merely that he would not expose any *individual* to ridicule or retribution—most sociologists probably regard this as a fixed ethical principle— but he now finds that he is being asked to respect the same niceties in the case of a group.

The solution to the dilemma depends in part on the investigator's own ethical commitments. However, he can avoid some of the difficulties inherent in the research relationship by striking a clear bargain with those he studies before he begins his work, taking care to alert them to the full range of unpleasant possibilities they may be exposing themselves to. He can also attempt to educate those most likely to take offense at the final report, explaining to them as the study proceeds what its consequences are likely to be and helping them to find a workable way of living with the published study.[29]

29. See Howard S. Becker, "Problems in the Publication of Field Studies" and "Whose Side Are We On?", in this volume.

CHAPTER SIX

The Nature
of a Profession

The Debate

The question, "What is a profession?" is an old one. Many definitions have been proposed by students of the professions. Still other definitions are implicit in everyday speech. Members of the accepted professions, interested laymen, and social scientists each use the word in their own way. Those interested in the question tend to disagree over fine points, and no agreement has been reached as to what the term specifies.

Abraham Flexner set the tone of discussion for years to come in his classic paper, "Is Social Work a Profession?"[1] He noted that "The term profession, strictly used, as opposed to business or handicraft, is a title of peculiar distinction, coveted by many activities. Thus far it has been pretty indiscriminately used." He pointed out that not only doctors, lawyers, and preachers but trapeze and dancing masters, equestrians, and chiropodists as well lay claim to the title and that many of these groups indeed gave degrees in support of their claim. He proposed to formulate basic standards: "In this narrower and eulogistic sense, what are the earmarks of a profession?"[2]

Reprinted by permission from *Education for the Professions,* Sixty-first Yearbook of the National Society for the Study of Education, Part II, pp. 27–46. Distributed by The University of Chicago Press. Copyright © 1962 National Society for the Study of Education.

1. Abraham Flexner, "Is Social Work a Profession?" in *Proceedings of the National Conference of Charities and Correction* (Chicago: Hildmann Printing Co., 1915), pp. 576–90.
2. *Ibid.,* p. 577.

Flexner set forth six criteria for distinguishing professions from other kinds of work. (Many of these criteria recur in various permutations in later definitions.) In his view, professional activitiy was basically *intellectual,* carrying with it great personal responsibility; it was *learned,* being based on great knowledge and not merely routine; it was *practical,* rather than academic or theoretic; its *technique* could be taught, this being the basis of professional education; it was strongly *organized* internally; and it was motivated by *altruism,* the professionals viewing themselves as working for some aspect of the good of society.[3]

He used these criteria to classify various occupations and found that medicine, law, engineering, literature, painting, and music were definitely professions, but that plumbing was not a profession, being unintellectual and having no social end. Banking had insufficient science and too much profit motive. Pharmacy had no primary responsibility, but only carried out the physician's orders. Social work had no technique of its own, and only mediated between people with problems and those who could help them.[4]

But Flexner perhaps felt his analysis becoming too rigid, too mechanical, for he ended with the following drastic qualification of his objective criteria:

> What matters most is professional spirit. All activities may be prosecuted in the genuine professional spirit. In so far as accepted professions are pros-ecuted at a mercenary or selfish level, law and medicine are ethically no better than trades. In so far as trades are honestly carried on, they tend to rise toward the professional level. . . . The unselfish devotion of those who have chosen to give themselves to making the world a fitter place to live in can fill social work with the professional spirit and thus to some extent lift it above all the distinctions which I have been at such pains to make.[5]

Flexner's attempt at definition was not the last. Looking back on the successive refinements of differentiating criteria, one is hard put to under-stand why anyone should want to alter Flexner's original statement, for the similarities between it and those that followed are more striking than the differences.

A few examples will illustrate the point. Carr-Saunders and Wilson, constructing an ideal-typical model, conclude that "The application of an intellectual technique to the ordinary business of life, acquired as the result of prolonged and specialized training, is the chief distinguishing characteristic of the profession."[6] Tyler found the two essential character-

3. *Ibid.,* pp. 578–81.
4. *Ibid.,* pp. 583–88.
5. *Ibid.,* p. 590.
6. A. M. Carr-Saunders and P. A. Wilson, *The Professions* (Oxford: Clarendon Press, 1933), p. 491.

istics of a true profession to be the existence of a generally recognized code of ethics supported by group discipline and the basing of technical operations on general principles, rather than rules-of-thumb or routine skills.[7] Lloyd E. Blauch lists these earmarks of the profession: specialized skills requiring long study and training; success measured by the quality of service rendered rather than by any financial standard; the organization of a professional association to maintain and improve service and also enforce a code of ethics.[8]

Goode has pointed out[9] that although there is a great deal of unanimity in these definitions, there has also been continuing disagreement. Cogan, after a careful and lengthy review of the literature, concluded that "No broad acceptance of any 'authoritative' definition has been observed."[10] Why, with such a high degree of consensus, should it be impossible for students of the problem to agree on a definition?

We can find the answer to this question by considering certain crucial ambiguities in Flexner's original statement. First, Flexner is unclear as to whether professions are to be defined by objective features of organization and activity or by the praiseworthy moral stance of their practitioners. He presents a list of objective criteria to which any occupation may be compared. But he ends by denying the usefulness of these criteria and depending instead on the presence or absence of a "genuine professional spirit" of unselfish devotion. Similarly, what is the relation between those kinds of work usually recognized as professions—medicine, law, and perhaps engineering—and the objective criteria specified in the definition? Are these professions the benchmark against which others are to be measured, their own "professionalism" being taken for granted? Or are these occupations simply relatively good, though still imperfect, embodiments of an ideal contained in the definition? (Flexner apparently tended to the latter view, but also felt that progress would soon wipe out the disparity between the actual and the ideal in the case of the historic professions. Speaking of "routineers," who are not really intellectual in their professional activity, he said: "They are already obsolete, mere survivals destined soon to pass away.")[11]

These ambiguities are not accidental. They arise because one term is

7. Ralph W. Tyler, "Distinctive Attributes of Education for the Professions," *Social Work Journal* XXIII (April 1952), 52–62, 94.

8. *Education for the Professions,* pp. 1–8. Organized and edited by Lloyd E. Blauch. United States Department of Health, Education and Welfare, Washington: Government Printing Office, 1955.

9. William J. Goode, "Encroachment, Charlatanism, and the Emerging Profession: Psychology, Sociology, and Medicine," *American Sociological Review* XXV (December 1960), 903.

10. Morris L. Cogan, "Toward a Definition of Profession," *Harvard Educational Review* XXIII (Winter 1953), 33–50.

11. Flexner, *op. cit.,* p. 584.

being made to do two quite different jobs. On the one hand, we use *pro-fession* as a scientific concept. Carefully defined, with a precise ·list of differentia, we mean the term to point to an abstract and objectively dis-criminable class of human phenomena. It is a verbal tool with which the social scientist isolates a particular kind of occupational organization for further analysis and investigation, just as physical and biological scientists use such terms as *carbon* or *mammal* to isolate particular phenomena for study. In using this term, the social scientist means it to be as neutral and descriptive as other concepts he uses, like *bureaucracy* or *Crow kinship system*. He wants to be able to distinguish professions as one of the several forms of occupational organization to be found in society. This was Flex-ner's original intention.

But *profession* is not the sole property of the social scientist. Members of some occupations use it to describe themselves. Members of other oc-cupations would like to use it to describe themselves but find that no one else takes their claim seriously. Laymen habitually use it to refer to certain kinds of work and not to others, which they describe variously as "busi-ness," "sciences," "trades," "rackets," and the like. Used in this way in the ordinary intercourse of our society, the term has another kind of mean-ing. Instead of describing and pointing to an abstract classification of kinds of work, it portrays a morally desirable kind of work. Instead of resembling the biologist's conception of a mammal, it more nearly resembles the phi-losopher's or theologian's conception of a good man. It is a term of individ-ious comparison and moral evaluation;[12] in applying it to a particular occu-pation people mean to say that the occupation is morally praiseworthy just as, in refusing to apply it to another occupation, they mean to say that it is not morally worthy of the honor. Clearly, this meaning of the term, as used by members of the professions and laymen, was in Flexner's mind when he abandoned his original list of criteria and turned to the "genuine pro-fessional spirit" of unselfish devotion as the key criterion.

It is not difficult to combine these two ways of using the term in theory; there is no reason why one cannot use morally evaluative criteria to create an objectively discriminable class of phenomena. Flexner did just this when he specified altruism as one of the distinguishing marks of a profes-sion. In practice, however, substantial difficulties arise.

People conventionally apply the term *profession,* in the morally evalu-ative sense, to certain occupations, medicine and law being the most com-mon. By doing this, they implicitly affirm that medicine and law have in fact achieved this morally desirable kind of organization. Similarly, people conventionally refuse, as Flexner did, to think of certain other occupations

12. See, for instance, Oliver Garceau, *The Political Life of the AMA* (Cambridge: Harvard Press, 1941), p. 186, cited in Goode, *op. cit.*

as professions; plumbing, to use Flexner's example, is a case in point. In so doing, they implicitly affirm that plumbing has not achieved this morally desirable kind of organization. Yet to some people, both those within the professions in question and laymen, it is not so clear that medicine and law are necessarily morally praiseworthy and plumbing not.

The arguments over definition express in part the disparity that some people feel between the conventional use of the term *profession* and the results that might be produced by a strict application of moral criteria to existing occupational groups. Such a strict application would probably lead to the kind of conclusion Flexner reached: that any kind of work may be professional, and that many kinds of work conventionally called professional may not deserve the title. Attempts at refining the definition are intended to bring conventional usage and a strictly applied set of moral criteria together in such a way as to produce a scientifically useful concept. But they almost inevitably fail, because popular usage changes and becomes uncertain under the impact of concerted efforts by occupational groups to win the honorific label of *profession* for themselves.

Because the title of profession expresses a positive moral evaluation, many work groups seek it. The arguments over definition also express disagreement between members of different occupations and within the general public over whether particular groups have achieved this honored state. Attempts at definition, as Cogan pointed out, must deal with the "complexities they encounter when faced with the necessity of discriminating among the hosts of vocations laying claim to the title."[13] They must deal with the difficult cases which arise when some people think a particular work group is a profession and others do not; and with the equally difficult cases that arise because almost any definition will include some work groups no one thinks are professions. (Thus, Cogan notes that Carr-Saunders and Wilson, following their own definition, are forced to include as professionals or near-professionals patent agents, midwives, and masseurs.)[14] It must cope with the "efforts of many persons and groups to secure to themselves the values clustering around it by simply pre-empting the title."[15]

This is a specific instance of a perennial problem. Social-science concepts refer to matters of concern to the people they are applied to and to the general public. In the effort to make concepts abstract and scientific, we tend to lose touch with the conceptions of laymen. Yet, if we try to incorporate their concerns into our concepts, we are faced with ambiguities like those surrounding *profession*.

13. Cogan, *op. cit.*, p. 34.
14. *Ibid.*
15. *Ibid.*, p. 47.

One way out of this dilemma is to give up the attempt to construct a definition which will, at the same time, be objectively specific and still accurately describe the layman's sense of which occupations are "really" professions. We can, instead, take a radically sociological view, regarding professions simply as those occupations which have been fortunate enough in the politics of today's work world to gain and maintain possession of that honorific title.[16] On this view, there is no "true" profession and no set of characteristics necessarily associated with the title. There are only those work groups commonly regarded as professions and those which are not.

Such a definition takes as central that "profession" is an honorific title, a term of approbation. It recognizes that "profession" is a collective symbol[17] and one that is highly valued. It insists that "profession" is not a neutral and scientific concept but, rather, what Turner has called a *folk concept,*[18] a part of the apparatus of the society we study, to be studied by noting how it is used and what role it plays in the operations of that society.

If we accept this kind of definition, two questions present themselves for consideration. First, what are the characteristics of the folk concept and how is it used? What are commonly agreed to be the features of a work group that can legitimately be called professional? Second, what are in fact the characteristics of those work groups now regarded as professional? More particularly, in what respects does the reality differ from the symbol?

The Symbol

Earlier attempts to define *profession* were intended to describe accurately those features of work organization and activity which were characteristic of occupations commonly accepted as professions and only of those occupations, thus differentiating them from other occupations. Such definitions, as we have seen, ran afoul of the tension between an objective listing of differentia and the necessity of taking account of the layman's subjective sense that certain occupations are morally worthy of the title of professions while others are not. So, instead of trying to improve on these earlier efforts,

16. I have put forward this same view more briefly in an earlier paper: Howard S. Becker, "Some Problems of Professionalization," *Adult Education* VI (Winter 1956), 101–5.

17. See Emile Durkheim, *Sociology and Philosophy,* trans. by J. G. Peristiany (London: Cohen and West, 1953) pp. 1–34; *The Elementary Forms of the Religious Life,* trans. by Joseph Ward Swain (Glencoe: Free Press, 1947) pp. 431–44. The term is translated in these works as "collective representation."

18. Ralph H. Turner, "The Normative Coherence of Folk Concepts," *Research Studies of the State College of Washington* XXV (June 1957), 127–36.

I have suggested that we view *profession* as an honorific symbol in use in our society and analyze the characteristics of that symbol.

In making this analysis we are not concerned with the characteristics of existing occupational organizations themselves but with conventional beliefs as to what those characteristics ought to be. In other words, we want to know what people have in mind when they say an occupation is a profession, or that it is becoming more professional, or that it is not a profession. Although people disagree as to what occupations are "really" professions and quibble over just which characteristics are "really" professional, I shall argue that beneath these surface disagreements we can find substantial agreement on a set of interconnected characteristics which symbolize a morally praiseworthy kind of occupational organization.

This symbol is used in many ways, by different kinds of people for different purposes. Members of those occupations accepted as true professions have this set of ideal characteristics in mind when they speak of their professional responsibilities. Members of occupations which are not ordinarily thought of as true professions have this same set of characteristics in mind when they try to claim professional status for themselves. Laymen have their eye on the same symbol of the ideal when they condemn members of the established professions for not being truly professional. No matter the purpose for which it is used, the symbol has essentially the same elements.

This symbol of the ideal profession consists of a set of ideas about the kind of work done by a real profession, its relations with members of other professions, the internal relations of its own members, its relations with clients and the general public, the character of its own members' motivations, and the kind of recruitment and training necessary for its perpetuation. These characteristics have, in the symbol, a necessary kind of relationship. The kind of work determines the relations of the members of the professions with other persons and groups, and these in turn require a certain kind of recruitment and training. This is not to say that in fact these relationships hold true, but rather that both members of professions and laymen believe that they must be made to hold true if the occupation is to be a real profession and its work is to be done in a morally praiseworthy manner.

The best data for an analysis of this symbol would be the findings of research on the meaning of "profession" to people in our society. In lieu of such research, I have used as the basis of my analysis of the symbol the definitions constructed by earlier students of the problem.[19] Since these

---

19. The most complete list of characteristics can be found in Goode, *op. cit.*

definitions tried to take account of popular conceptions, they furnish an adequate source of characteristics out of which to construct the symbol of the profession in our society. In describing the symbol, I have tried at the same time to indicate the kinds of relationships thought to be morally necessary. It should be clear, however, that when I say, "The profession must, therefore, do such-and-such . . . ," the *must* comes from the conventional beliefs associated with the symbol and does not express my own opinion.

Professions, as commonly conceived, are occupations which possess a monopoly of some esoteric and difficult body of knowledge. Further, this knowledge is considered to be necessary for the continuing functioning of the society. What the members of the profession know and can do is tremendously important, but no one else knows or can do these things. The archetype in this respect is medicine, which is supposed to have an absolute monopoly of the knowledge necessary to heal the sick. Healing the sick and maintaining the health of the society is seen as one of the important functions which must be preformed if the society is to maintain its equilibrium.[20]

The body of knowledge over which the profession holds a monopoly consists not of technical skills and the fruits of practical experience but, rather, of abstract principles arrived at by scientific research and logical analysis. This knowledge cannot be applied routinely but must be applied wisely and judiciously to each case. This has several consequences.

In the first place, it is supposed that only the most able people will have the mental ability and the proper temperament to absorb and use such knowledge. Therefore, recruitment must be strictly controlled, to ensure that those who are not qualified do not become members of the profession. Recruitment is controlled, first, by careful weeding out of prospective candidates, and, then, by a lengthy and difficult educational process which eliminates those who were mistakenly selected. Lengthy training is considered necessary anyway, because the body of knowledge is supposed to be so complex that it cannot be acquired in any shorter time.

Secondly, it is felt that entrance into professional practice must be strictly controlled, and that this control must ultimately lie in the hands of members of the profession itself. Difficult obstacles, in the form of examinations of all kinds, must be surmounted by candidates for practice, and no one must be allowed to practice who has not so demonstrated his competence. This means that the police power of the state must be utilized, through the

20. See Talcott Parsons, *The Social System* (Glencoe: Free Press, 1951). ". . . health is included in the functional needs of the individual member of society so that, from the point of view of functioning of the social system, too low a general level of health, too high an incidence of illness, is dysfunctional," p. 430.

device of licensure procedures, to control entrance into practice. But if the knowledge monopolized by the profession is so difficult to acquire, it follows that no layman can fully acquire it and, therefore, that the governmental bodies which grant licenses must be controlled by members of the profession itself. Similarly, the approval and accreditation of educational institutions and procedures must also be done by members of the profession. In short, the professional, by virtue of the esoteric character of his professional knowledge, is free of lay control.

Finally, since recruitment, training, and entrance into practice are all carefully controlled, any member of the professional group can be thought of as fully competent to supply the professional service.

Any profession which so monopolizes some socially important body of knowledge is likely to be considered potentially dangerous. It might use its monopoly to enrich itself or enlarge its power rather than in the best interests of its clients. The symbol of the profession, however, portrays a group whose members have altruistic motivations and whose professional activities are governed by a code of ethics which heavily emphasizes devotion to service and the good of the client and condemns misuse of professional skills for selfish purposes. This code of ethics, furthermore, is sternly enforced by appropriate disciplinary bodies. Professional associations have as their major purpose the enforcement of such ethical codes.

The client, therefore, is supposed to be able to count on the professional whose services he retains to have his best interests at heart. He rests comfortable in the knowledge that this is one relationship in which the rule of the market place does not apply. He need not beware but can give his full trust and confidence to the professional who is handling his problems; the service given him will be competent and unselfish. This is conceived as necessary if the professional is to perform his work successfully. If the patient cannot trust the physician completely, he will withhold facts that might be vital in successful treatment; the lawyer cannot protect his client's interests without full knowledge of his client's affairs, and this might be withheld if the client could not trust him.[21]

If the client is to trust the professional completely he must feel that there are no other interests which will be put before his in the performance of the professional activity. Among the other interests which might intrude are the interests related to institutions within which the professional makes his career. Thus, the ideal professional is a *private* practitioner, in business for himself, so to speak. He has no ties to a superior officer or bureaucratic

21. *Ibid.* ". . . the collectivity-orientation of the physician, and its universalism, neutrality, and specificity, make it possible for the things he has to do to be made acceptable to the patient and his family. These include validation of his professional authority and justification of the 'privileges' he must be accorded," p. 475.

system of rules; he receives his income directly from fees paid by the client, not from any third party.

A final element in the symbol of the profession is not so often mentioned in the attempts to define the term. This is the image of the profession and the professional as occupying an esteemed position in the society.[22] Members of the professions are usually thought of, as they often in fact are, as people of sizable income and high community prestige.[23] They are considered to be entitled to an important voice in community affairs. Professional associations are thought of as important public institutions, similarly entitled to a voice in public affairs, particularly (although not exclusively) with respect to those issues which touch on their professional concerns or competence.

The features above are the essential components of the symbol "profession." To risk repetition, this symbol does not describe any actual occupation. Rather, it is a symbol that people in our society use in thinking about occupations, a standard to which they compare occupations in deciding their moral worth. It represents consensus in the society about what certain kinds of work groups *ought* to be like, though it is not an accurate picture of any reality.[24]

What role does this symbol play in the operation of our society and in the functioning of work groups? In the first place, the symbol can be seen as containing an ideology which provides a justification and rationale for one very important aspect of the work situation of those groups possessing the title. Professionals, in contrast to members of other occupations, claim and are often accorded complete autonomy in their work. Since they are presumed to be the only judges of how good their work is, no layman or other outsider can make any judgment of what they do. If their activities are unsuccessful, only another professional can say whether this was due to incompetence or to the inevitable workings of nature or society by which even the most competent practitioner would have been stymied.[25] This image of the professional justifies his demand for complete autonomy

22. Cogan, *op. cit.*, p. 38, indicates that the profession is often thought of as an elite.

23. See Everett C. Hughes, *Men and Their Work* (Glencoe: Free Press, 1958), pp. 102–15. Hughes points out that every status, including occupational statuses, has both specifically determining traits and "auxiliary traits which come to be expected of its incumbents" (p. 103). Thus, the specifically determining trait of the physician is a license to practice medicine; but in this country, people ordinarily expect the physician to be male, white, Protestant and of Old American stock as well. What I am suggesting is that among the auxiliary traits associated with the status of "professional" are high income and community prestige.

24. Turner, *op. cit.*, pp. 132–33.

25. Cf. Becker, *op. cit.;* and Hughes, *op. cit.*, pp. 88–101.

and his demand that the client give up his own judgment and responsibility, leaving everything in the hands of the professional.

This analysis may lead some people to conclude that I am saying that the symbol of the profession is used simply as a device by which the self-interest of the work group can be furthered. This would be incorrect. Professional autonomy may be used strictly in the interests of the client; in fact, it is likely that without some measure of autonomy the client's interests cannot be well served. If a doctor is not free to make the diagnosis he thinks correct and prescribe the course of treatment he thinks most efficacious rather than the one the patient finds most palatable, the patient's health may indeed suffer.[26] In short, the symbol of the profession is not merely selfish propaganda; many of the propositions contained in it are in large part true. Nevertheless, we must not forget that it is a symbol, rather than an exact description of reality, and that it may be used for political purposes.

Because the symbol legitimates the autonomy of the worker, occupations that are trying to rise in the world want very much to possess it, to be known as professions rather than businesses or sciences (or any of the other alternative stereotypes available to describe kinds of work).[27] These emerging professions feel strongly that their work is hampered by the interference of laymen who do not fully understand all the problems involved, the proper standards to be used, or the proper goals to be aimed for. These emerging professions, in addition, often feel that their prestige will be raised if they can become "real" professions.

So we find many occupations trying hard to become professions and using the symbol of the profession in an attempt to increase their autonomy and raise their prestige. Optometrists, nurses, librarians, social workers— these are only a few of the many occupations engaged in this kind of activity.[28] They attempt to appropriate the symbol by taking on as many of its features as practical. They subsidize research, they adopt codes of ethics, they lengthen the period of required training, and so on. They

26. The fact of professional autonomy can be viewed as having both good and bad consequences. For a discerning discussion, see Ruth Kornhauser, "Parents and School: Clients' Expectations and Demands." Unpublished Master's thesis, University of Chicago, 1957. See also Howard S. Becker, "Schools and Systems of Social Status," in this volume.

27. Hughes, *op. cit.,* pp. 139–44.

28. A number of authors have noted this phenomenon. See, for instance, Goode, *op. cit.;* Hughes, *op. cit.,* pp. 131–38; Everett C. Hughes. "The Professions in Society," *Canadian Journal of Economics and Political Science* XXVI (February 1960), 57–59; and A. M. Carr-Saunders, "Metropolitan Conditions and Traditional Professional Relationships," in *The Metropolis in Modern Life,* ed. by R. M. Fisher, (Garden City: Doubleday & Co., 1955), pp. 279–88.

succeed in varying degrees, both in adopting the proper characteristics and in achieving public recognition of their claim. (This varying success leads to such distinctions as that made by Carr-Saunders between'professions, new professions, near-professions, and would-be professions.[29])

Having looked at the symbol of the profession, we can now turn to a consideration of the realities of occupational life. In what ways do the occupations commonly called professions differ from the symbol?

The Reality

In comparing the realities of professional organization and practice to the symbol they strive to embody, I do not mean to assume a debunking attitude. People often assume that the historic professions of medicine and law, particularly, have already achieved a complete identity with this morally praiseworthy symbol. They take for granted that this is what medicine and law are really like and that occupations striving to become professions have only to work hard enough, become more and more like this symbol until they finally achieve professional status themselves. If one says that not even the historic professions are like this symbol, he may be accused of criticism or muckraking.

But it is necessary to look at this matter in an unsentimental way, neither praising the professions for coming so close to the ideal as they do nor chastising them for failing to met the requirements completely. Without such an unsentimental analysis, we cannot understand the nature of modern professions; and without such understanding we cannot properly assess professional education. If we do not know what the work situation of the professional is, we cannot really know what kind of training he needs.

If deviations from the symbol of the profession were simply the result of natural human orneriness—of Original Sin, so to speak—the sociologist would indeed be nothing but a muckraker in drawing attention to them. But the fact is that deviations from the ideal are neither random nor idiosyncratic. They do not occur because a few professionals are bad men or weak men. They occur systematically and and are created by the operation of social forces. In other words, they are integral parts of the social structure of occupational life and are regarded as deviations because they are considered morally unworthy. (Not all the deviations I will speak of are so heavily morally toned, although some are.) I confine myself to a consideration of medicine and law, because these occupations most closely approach the symbol. Also, medicine and law have been much studied by sociologists, so that we have some accurate descriptions to compare the symbol to.

29. Carr-Saunders, "Metropolitan Conditions . . . ," *op. cit.*, p. 281.

Medicine and law fail to match the symbol in that neither actually holds a monopoly over its esoteric knowledge or functions. Lawyers do a great many things, but hardly any of them are not done on occasion, or, often, as full-time work, by people who are not lawyers. In fact, many lawyers suffer greatly because of the competition of nonlawyers in many fields of legal work. Lawyers do tax work and draw up wills; but accountants also do tax work, and officers of banks are quite willing and able to draw up wills. The lawyer does maintain a monopoly over one area: appearing in court to defend clients; but this represents a small part of the lawyer's work.[30] Similarly, doctors perform the function of healing the sick. But they share this function with members of many other occupations: osteopaths, chiropractors, chiropodists, faith healers, and so on.[31] Nor is their knowledge restricted to the circle of those who are fully trained and licensed physicians, for much of it is created by and known by nonphysicians who are scientists.

The reality differs from the symbol in another respect. All members of a profession are not equally competent to supply the *core service*—"the most characteristic professional act."[32] This is true because of the great internal differentiation and specialization which characterize present-day professions. It is not only that there is a technical division of labor among the various specialties, although this is certainly so much the case that the services provided can only be provided by a member of a particular specialty. But beyond this we find that the specialties differ so in ideology, sense of mission, work activities, and work situation that they can most profitably be thought of as distinct occupations rather than as specialized aspects of one occupation.[33] In medicine, it has been argued that even the specialties are so internally divided that we cannot think of, let us say, radiologists as constituting a homogeneous group with a distinctive set of skills all members share. Some radiologists spend their work day in diagnostic activities, interpreting and evaluating x-ray pictures, while others are primarily therapists, who spend their time trying to extirpate tumors with radiation.[34]

The relations of clients and professionals, in fact, differ greatly from those specified in the symbol. Ideally, the client puts his full faith and trust in the professional whose services he uses. But clients do not behave that way. They continually make judgments about the work and capabilities of

30. Evidence for these assertions can be found in Jerome E. Carlin, "The Lawyer as Individual Practioner: A Study in the Professions." Unpublished Ph.D. dissertation, University of Chicago, 1959.

31. See Beatrix Cobb, "Why Do People Detour to Quacks?", in *Patients, Physicians and Illness,* ed. by E. Gartly Jaco (Glencoe, Ill.: Free Press, 1958), pp. 283–87.

32. Rue Bucher and Anselm Strauss, "Professions in Process," *American Journal of Sociology* LXVI (January 1961), 328.

33. *Ibid.*

34. *Ibid.*

the professionals they use. Medical patients often change doctors, and they do this because they have decided for themselves, on the basis of their own knowledge and experience or, frequently, on the advice of friends, relatives, and neighbors, that another doctor will do a better job for them. Research has shown that patients distinguish between diseases which are ordinary and everyday and therefore can be treated by any doctor (so long as he is convenient and inexpensive) and those diseases which are dramatically out of the ordinary and require the services of a doctor who can convince them, in one way or another, that he is specially good.[35] The clients of professionals, in short, characteristically reserve a right of judgment denied to them by the symbol.

Similarly, the symbol of a work group bound by a code of ethics designed to protect the client is in some ways not a realistic description. Every profession contains unethical practitioners. This would be of small importance, as I have said, if it were simply a matter of human frailty, of weak men succumbing to temptation. But it appears that this is a chronic feature of the social structure of prestigeful occupations, another aspect of their differentiation and specialization (although in this case the differentiation takes place with respect to ethicality rather than technique). Hughes points out that lawyers deal with human quarrels:

> A lawyer may be asked whether he and his client come into court with clean hands; when he answers, "yes," it may mean that someone else's hands are of necessity a bit grubby. For not only are some quarrels more respectable, more clean, than others; but also some kinds of work involved in the whole system (gathering evidence, getting clients, bringing people to court, enforcing judgments, making the compromises that keep cases out of court) are more respected and removed from temptation and suspicion than others. In fact, the division of labor among lawyers is as much one of respectability (hence of self concept and role) as of specialized knowledge and skills. One might even call it a moral division of labor, if one keeps in mind that the term means not simply that some lawyers are more moral than others; but that the very demand for highly scrupulous and respectable lawyers depends in various ways upon the availability of less scrupulous people to attend to the less respectable legal problems of even the best people.[36]

Very little is known about the social systems in which unethical practice is embedded; this is one of the most neglected areas in the study of professions, partly because of the pratical difficulties involved and partly, I fear,

35. Eliot Freidson, *Views of Professional Practice* (New York: Russell Sage Foundation, 1961).
36. Hughes, *Men and Their Work, op. cit.,* p. 71.

because to study such problems calls attention to the disparity between symbol and reality.

Finally, professional practitioners are typically not as autonomous as the symbol would have us believe. The constraints which belie the symbol have several different sources. In the traditional pattern of private practice for a fee, professionals may be constrained by the wishes of their clients. In so far as a professional depends on his reputation among laymen for his practice, there is a continuing pressure for him to give the kind of service that, in the layman's eyes, is satisfactory. Freidson has noted that the general medical practitioner, of all physicians, is most in this position and is most likely to defer to his patients' wishes with respect to methods of treatment.[37] Depending essentially on other laymen for his referrals (standing, as Freidson says, at the apex of the "lay referral structure" which also includes friends, neighbors, relatives, and the corner druggist),[38] the general practitioner tends to be sensitive to the demands of clients for new drugs, for instance, and to avoid procedures which may seem unnecessary and unpleasant to his patients.[39]

A professional may escape the constraints imposed by his clients by becoming part of an organization which insulates him, economically and otherwise, against their demands. Thus, Hall describes the kind of medical career in which success depends on acceptance by the "inner fraternity" of the colleague group as one in which relationships with patients are impersonal:

> Patients have access to the doctor by appointment only; there are no "office hours." There are few house calls; patients who are sufficiently ill are admitted to the hospital and seen there. Telephone calls are also discouraged. Frequently doctors charge for all advice given by telephone, which tends to reduce the number of calls and to limit them to those which are really urgent.[40]

These doctors, typically specialists, have freed themselves from the demands of their patients. But, as a consequence, they are "responsive to the

37. Eliot Freidson, "Client Control and Medical Practice," *American Journal of Sociology* LXV (January 1960), 374–82.

38. *Ibid.*, pp. 376–80. My classification of barriers to professional autonomy closely parallels Freidson's typology of "independent" and "dependent" professional practices, (pp. 380–82).

39. A recent study, for instance, found that sizable percentages of a sample of general practitioners in North Carolina failed to perform rectal examinations and palpation of the breasts as a routine part of every physical examination. See Osler L. Peterson *et al.*, "An Analytical Study of North Carolina General Practice, 1953–1954," *Journal of Medical Education* XXXI, Part II (December 1956), 32.

40. Oswald Hall, "Types of Medical Careers," *American Journal of Sociology* LV (November 1949), 248.

demands and benefits of the informal organization of medicine in the community,"[41] for it is through this organization that they get patients. They are now part of the "professional referral structure"[42] and practice the professional etiquette of referral (which serves to minimize competition and thus reduce hostility between colleagues).[43] What they gain in autonomy vis-à-vis patients they lose in autonomy vis-à-vis their professional colleagues.

Finally, many professionals now have what Freidson refers to as "organizational practices."[44] That is, they work in bureaucratic organizations, subject, like any employee, to the systems of rules enforced in those organizations;[45] their vision of success may consist of successive promotions up the career ladder of such an organization. Such professionals are not constrained by the expectations of clients; nor are they constrained by the expectations of colleagues except as positions of power within the organization are held by members of the profession. But in gaining this autonomy they have lost autonomy to the bureaucratic systems within which they work.

Implications for Education

Symbols are useful things. They help people and groups organize their lives and embody conceptions of what is good and worth while. They enhance the possibility of purposeful collective action. They make more likely the realization of ideals held by large segments of society.

But symbols have their pathologies. They may become so divorced from reality as to be unattainable. I do not refer here to the discrepancy between what is hoped for and what has so far been attained but, rather, to the kind of disparity that arises when a symbol ignores or distorts large and important parts of reality.

A symbol which becomes so unrealistic may have consequences not intended by its users. For instance, people who accept it as a statement of the ideal may become disillusioned when they discover it is so difficult to bring into reality and give up their attempts to strive for it or become

41. *Ibid.* This informal organization is more fully described in Oswald Hall, "The Informal Organization of the Medical Profession," *Canadian Journal of Economics and Political Science* XII (February 1946), 30–41; and "The Stages of the Medical Career," *American Journal of Sociology* LIII (March 1948), 243–53.

42. Freidson, "Client Control and Medical Practice," *op. cit.*, p. 379.

43. Hall, "Types of Medical Careers," *op. cit.*, p. 248.

44. Freidson, "Client Control and Medical Practice," *op. cit.*, p. 381.

45. The trend toward incorporation of the professions into bureaucratic organizations is discussed in T. H. Marshall, "The Recent History of Professionalism in Relation to Social Structure and Social Policy," *Canadian Journal of Economics and Political Science* V (August 1939), 325–40; A. M. Carr-Saunders, "Metropolitan Conditions and Traditional Professional Relationships," *op. cit.;* and Hughes "The Professions in Society," *op. cit.*

cynical and search for ways to evade the ethical responsibilities it seeks to impose. The symbol may become a useful public relations device which few people take seriously.

If this happens to a symbol, it has ceased to do the job it is expected to do and, in fact, may from the point of view of those concerned with ethics do more harm than good. In my judgment, the symbol of the profession is in danger of undergoing this transformation. As we have seen, it differs from the realities of occupational life in ways that are not random or due to human failing, in ways that cannot be corrected by more effort or better selection of professional candidates. It differs in ways that are structurally chronic, built into the organizations within which professional practice is carried on. The symbol systematically ignores such facts as the failure of professions to monopolize their area of knowledge, the lack of homogeneity within professions, the frequent failure of clients to accept professional judgment, the chronic presence of unethical practitioners as an integrated segment of the professional structure, and the organizational constraints on professional autonomy. A symbol which ignores so many important features of occupational life cannot provide an adequate guide for professional activity.

Professional education tends to build curricula and programs in ways suggested by the symbol and so fails to prepare its students for the world they will have to work in.[46] Educators might perform a great service by working out a symbol more closely related to the realities of work life practitioners confront, a symbol which could provide an intelligible and and workable moral guide in problematic situations.

46. It is my impression that those schools that pay most attention to the realities of the work are apt to be labeled with the invidious term "trade school."

CHAPTER SEVEN

Problems
in the Publication
of Field Studies

The Problem

Publication of field research findings often poses ethical problems. The social scientist learns things about the people he studies that may harm them, if made public, either in fact or in their belief. In what form and under what conditions can he properly publish his findings? What can he do about the possible harm his report may do?

Although many social scientists have faced the problem, it seldom receives any public discussion. We find warnings that one must not violate confidences or bring harm to the people one studies, but seldom a detailed consideration of the circumstances under which harm may be done or of the norms that might guide publication practices.

Let us make our discussion more concrete by referring to a few cases that have been discussed publicly. Most thoroughly discussed, perhaps, is the "Springdale" case, which was the subject of controversy in several successive issues of *Human Organization*.[1] Arthur Vidich and Joseph Bens-

Reprinted by permission from *Reflections on Community Studies*, Arthur J. Vidich, Joseph Bensman, and Maurice R. Stein, eds., pp. 267–284. Copyright © 1964 John Wiley and Sons, Inc.

1. The discussion of the Springdale case began with an editorial, "Freedom and Responsibility in Research: The 'Springdale' Case," in *Human Organization* 17 (Summer 1958), pp. 1–2. This editorial provoked comments by Arthur Vidich and Joseph Bensman, Robert Risley, Raymond E. Ries, and Howard S. Becker, *ibid.* 17 (Winter 1958–1959), pp. 2–7, and by Earl H. Bell and Ure Bronfenbrenner, *ibid.* 18 (Summer 1959), pp. 49–52. A final statement by Vidich appeared in *ibid.* 19 (Spring 1960), pp. 3–4. The book whose effects are discussed is Arthur Vidich and Joseph Bensman, *Small Town in Mass Society* (Princeton, N. J.: Princeton University Press, 1958).

man published a book—*Small Town in Mass Society*—based on Vidich's observations and interviews in a small, upstate New York village. The findings reported in that book were said to be offensive to some of the residents of Springdale; for instance, there were references to individuals who, though their names were disguised, were recognizable by virtue of their positions in the town's social structure. Some townspeople, it is alleged, also found the "tone" of the book offensive. For instance, the authors used the phrase "invisible government" to refer to people who held no official position in the town government but influenced the decisions made by elected officials. The implication of illegitimate usurpation of power may have offended those involved.

Some social scientists felt the authors had gone too far, and had damaged the town's image of itself and betrayed the research bargain other social scientists had made with the townspeople. The authors, on the other hand, felt they were dealing with problems that required discussing the facts they did discuss. They made every effort to disguise people but, when that was impossible to do effectively, felt it necessary to present the material as they did.

In another case John F. Lofland and Robert A. Lejeune[2] had students attend open meetings of Alcoholics Anonymous, posing as alcoholic newcomers to the group. The "agents" dressed in different social-class styles and made various measurements designed to assess the effect of the relation between the social class of the group and that of the newcomer on his initial acceptance in the group. Fred Davis[3] criticized the authors for, among other things, failing to take into account the effect of publication of the article on the attitudes of A. A. toward social science in view of its possible consequences on the A. A. program. (A. A. groups might have refused to cooperate in further studies had the authors reported, for instance, that A. A. groups discriminate on the basis of social class. That their finding led to no such conclusion does not negate Davis' criticism.)

Lofland[4] suggested in reply that the results of the study were in fact not unfavorable to A. A., that it was published in a place where A. A. members would be unlikely to see it, and, therefore, that no harm was actually done. Julius Roth,[5] commenting on this exchange, noted that the problem is not unique. In a certain sense all social science research is secret, just as the fact that observers were present at A. A. meetings was kept secret from the members. He argued that we decide to study some things only after we

2. John F. Lofland and Robert A. Lejeune, "Initial Interaction of Newcomers in Alcoholics Anonymous: A Field Experiment in Class Symbols and Socialization," *Social Problems* 8 (Fall 1960), pp. 102–111.

3. Fred Davis, "Comment," *Social Problems* 8 (Spring 1961), pp. 364–365.

4. John F. Lofland, "Reply to Davis," *ibid.*, pp. 365–367.

5. Julius A. Roth, "Comments on Secret Observation," *Social Problems* 9 (Winter 1962), pp. 283–284.

have been in the field a while and after the initial agreements with people involved have already been negotiated. Thus, even though it is known that the scientist is making a study, the people under observation do not know what he is studying and would perhaps (in many cases certainly would) object and refuse to countenance the research if they knew what it was about.

When one is doing research on a well-defined organization such as a factory, a hospital, or a school, as opposed to some looser organization such as a community or a voluntary association, the problem may arise in slightly different form. The "top management" of the organization will often be given the right to review the social scientist's manuscript prior to publication. William Foote Whyte describes the kinds of difficulties that may arise.

> I encountered such a situation in my research project which led finally to the publication of *Human Relations in the Restaurant Industry*. When members of the sponsoring committee of the National Restaurant Association read the first draft of the proposed book, some of them had strong reservations. In fact, one member wrote that he had understood that one of the purposes of establishing an educational and research program at the University of Chicago was to raise the status of the restaurant industry. This book, he claimed, would have the opposite effect, and therefore he recommended that it should not be published. In this case, the Committee on Human Relations in Industry of that university had a contract guaranteeing the right to publish, and I, as author, was to have the final say in the matter. However, I hoped to make the study useful to the industry, and I undertook to see what changes I could make while at the same time retaining what seemed to me, from a scientific standpoint, the heart of the study. . . . The chief problem seemed to be that I had found the workers not having as high a regard for the industry as the sponsoring committee would have liked. Since this seemed to me an important part of the human relations problem, I could hardly cut it out of the book. I was, however, prepared to go as far as I thought possible to change offensive words and phrases in my own text without altering what seemed to me the essential meaning.[6]

It should be kept in mind that these few published accounts must stand for a considerably larger number of incidents in which the rights of the people studied, from some points of view, have been infringed. The vast majority of such incidents are never reported in print, but are circulated in private conversations and documents. In discussing the problem of publication I am, somewhat ironically, often prevented from being as concrete as I would like to be because I am bound by the fact that many of the cases I know about have been told me in confidence.

6. William Foote Whyte, *Man and Organization: Three Problems in Human Relations in Industry* (Homewood, Ill.: Irwin, 1959), pp. 96–97.

Not much is lost by this omission, however. Whether the institution studied is a school for retarded children, an upper-class preparatory school, a college, a mental hospital, or a business establishment, the story is much the same. The scientist does a study with the cooperation of the people he studies and writes a report that angers at least some of them. He has then to face the problem of whether to change the report or, if he decides not to, whether to ignore or somehow attempt to deal with their anger.

Conditions Affecting Publication

Fichter and Kolb have presented the most systematic consideration of ethical problems in reporting.[7] They begin by suggesting that several conditions, which vary from situation to situation, will affect the problem of reporting. First, the social scientist has multiple loyalties: to those who have allowed or sponsored the study, to the source from which research funds were obtained, to the publisher of the research report, to other social scientists, to the society itself, and to the community or group studied and its individual members. These loyalties and obligations often conflict. Second, the group under study may or may not be in a position to be affected by the published report. A historical study, describing the way of life of a people who never will have access to the research report, poses few problems, whereas the description of a contemporary community or institution poses many. Third, problems arise when the report analyzes behavior related to traditional and sacred values, such as religion and sex, and also when the report deals with private rather than public facts. Fourth, when data are presented in a statistical form, the problem of identifying an individual does not arise as it does when the mode of analysis is more anthropological.

Fichter and Kolb distinguish three kinds of harm that can be done by a sociological research report. It may reveal secrets, violate privacy, or destroy or harm someone's reputation.

Finally, Fichter and Kolb discuss four variables that will affect the social scientist's decision to publish or not to publish. First, his conception of science will affect his action. If he regards social science simply as a game, he must protect the people he has studied at any cost, for his conception of science gives him no warrant or justification for doing anything that might harm them. He will feel a greater urgency if he believes that science can be used to create a better life for people.

The social scientist's decision to publish will also be affected by his determination of the degree of harm that will actually be done to a person or group by the publication of data about them. Fichter and Kolb note that

7. Joseph H. Fichter and William L. Kolb, "Ethical Limitations on Sociological Reporting," *American Sociological Review* 18 (October 1953), pp. 96–97.

there is a difference between imaginary and real harm and that the subjects of studies may fear harm where none is likely. On the other hand, it may be necessary to cause some harm. People, even those studied by social scientists, must take responsibility for their actions; a false sentimentality must not cause the scientist to cover up that responsibility in his report.

Fichter and Kolb further argue that the scientist's decision to publish will be conditioned by the degree to which he regards the people he has studied as fellow members of his own moral community. If a group (they use the examples of Hitler, Stalin, Murder Incorporated, and the Ku Klux Klan) has placed itself outside the moral community, the social scientist can feel free to publish whatever he wants about them without worrying about the harm that may be done. They caution, however, that one should not be too quick to judge another group as being outside the moral community; it is too easy to make the judgment when the group is a disreputable one: homosexuals, drug addicts, unpopular political groups, and so on.

Fichter and Kolb conclude by suggesting that the urgency of society's need for the research will also condition the scientist's decision to publish. Where he believes the information absolutely necessary for the determination of public policy, he may decide that it is a lesser evil to harm some of the people he has studied.

Although the statement of Fichter and Kolb is an admirable attempt to deal with the problem of publication, it does not do justice to the complexities involved. In the remainder of this paper I will first consider the possibility that the relationship between the social scientist and those he studies contains elements of irreducible conflict. I will then discuss the reasons why some reports of social science research do not contain conflict-provoking findings. Finally, I will suggest some possible ways of dealing with the problem.

Before embarking on the main line of my argument, I would like to make clear the limits of the area to which my discussion is meant to apply. I assume that the scientist is not engaged in willful and malicious defamation of character, that his published report has some reasonable scientific purpose, and therefore do not consider those cases in which a scientist might attempt, out of malice, ideological or personal, to destroy the reputation of persons or institutions. I further assume that the scientist is subject to no external constraint, other than that imposed by his relationship to those he has studied, which would hinder him in reporting his results fully and freely. In many cases this assumption is not tenable. Vidich and Bensman argue[8] that a researcher who does his work in the setting of a bureaucratic research

8. Arthur Vidich and Joseph Bensman, "The Springdale Case: Academic Bureaucrats and Sensitive Townspeople," in Arthur J. Vidich *et al.*, *Reflections on Community Studies* (New York: Wiley, 1964), pp. 345–348.

organization of necessity must be unable to report his results freely; he will have too many obligations to the organization to do anything that would harm its interests in the research situation and thus cannot make the kind of report required by the ethic of scientific inquiry. Although I do not share their belief that bureaucratic research organizations necessarily and inevitably restrict scientific freedom, this result certainly occurs frequently. (One should remember, however, that the implied corollary of their proposition—that the individual researcher will be bound only by the ethic of scientific inquiry—is also often untrue. Individual researchers on many occasions have shown themselves to be so bound by organizational or ideological commitments as to be unable to report their results freely.) In any case my argument deals with the researcher who is encumbered only by his own conscience.

The Irreducible Conflict

Fichter and Kolb seem to assume that, except for Hitler, Stalin, and others who are not members of our moral community, there is no irreconcilable conflict between the researcher and those he studies. In some cases he will clearly harm people and will refrain from publication; in others no harm will be done and publication is not problematic. The vast majority of cases will fall between and, as men of good will, the researcher and those he studies will be able to find some common ground for decision.

But this analysis can be true only when there is some consensus about norms and some community of interest between the two parties. In my view that consensus and community of interest do not exist for the sociologist and those he studies.

The impossibility of achieving consensus, and hence the necessity of conflict, stems in part from the difference between the characteristic approach of the social scientist and that of the layman to the analysis of social life. Everett Hughes has often pointed out that the sociological view of the world—abstract, relativistic, and generalizing—necessarily deflates people's view of themselves and their organizations. Sociological analysis has this effect whether it consists of a detailed description of informal behavior or an abstract discussion of theoretical categories. The members of a church, for instance, may be no happier to learn that their behavior exhibits the influence of "pattern variables" than to read a description of their everyday behavior which shows that it differs radically from what they profess on Sunday morning in church. In either case something precious to them is treated as merely an instance of a class.

Consensus cannot be achieved also because organizations and communities are internally differentiated and the interests of subgroups differ. The scientific report that pleases one faction and serves its interests will offend another faction by attacking its interests. Even to say that factions exist may upset the faction in control. What upsets management may be welcomed by the lower ranks, who hope the report will improve their position. Since one cannot achieve consensus with all factions simultaneously, the problem is not to avoid harming people but rather to decide which people to harm.

Trouble occurs primarily, however, because what the social scientist reports is what the people studied would prefer not to know, no matter how obvious or easy it is to discover. Typically, the social scientist offends those he studies by describing deviations, either from some formal or informal rule, or from a strongly held ideal. The deviations reported are things that, according to the ideals of the people under study, should be punished and corrected, but about which, for various reasons that seem compelling to them, nothing can be done. In other words the research report reveals that things are not as they ought to be and that nothing is being done about it. By making his report the social scientist makes the deviation public and may thereby force people to enforce a rule they have allowed to lapse. He blows the whistle both on those who are deviating but not being punished for it and on those who are allowing the deviation to go unpunished.[9] Just as the federal government, by making public the list of persons to whom it has sold a gambling-tax stamp, forces local law-enforcement officials to take action against gamblers whose existence they have always known of, so the social scientist, by calling attention to deviations, forces those in power to take action about things they know to exist but about which they do not want to do anything.

Certain typical forms of blowing the whistle recur in many studies. A study of a therapeutic organization—a mental hospital, a general hospital, a rehabilitation center—may show that many institutional practices are essentially custodial and may in fact be antitherapeutic. A study of a school reveals that the curriculum does not have the intended effect on students, and that many students turn out to be quite different from what the members of the faculty would like them to be. A study of a factory or office discloses that many customary practices are, far from being rational and businesslike, irrational and wasteful. Another typical situation has already been mentioned: a study reveals that members of the lower ranks of an organization dislike their subordinate position.

Nor is this phenomenon peculiar to studies that depend largely on the techniques of anthropological field work, though it is probably most common among them. Any kind of social science research may evoke a hostile

9. I have discussed the role of the person who makes deviation public, the rule enforcer, at some length in *Outsiders: Studies in the Sociology of Deviance* (New York: Free Press of Glencoe, 1963) pp. 155–163.

reaction when it is published. Official statistics put out by communities or organizations can do this. For example, remember the indignation when the 1960 Census revealed that many major cities had lost population, the demands for recounts by Chambers of Commerce, and so on. By simply enumerating the number of inhabitants in a city, and reporting that number publicly, the Bureau of the Census deflated many public-relations dreams and caused a hostile reaction. The statistics on admissions and discharges to hospitals, on salaries and similar matters kept by hospitals and other institutions can similarly be analyzed to reveal great discrepancies, and the revelation can cause much hostile criticism. The results of survey research similarly can cause trouble, as for instance, when a survey of students reveals that they have reactionary political or cultural attitudes. A program of testing can produce the same result by showing that an organization does not recruit people of as high a caliber as it claims, or that a school does not have the effect on its students it supposes it has. Any kind of research, in short, can expose a disparity between reality and some rule or ideal and cause trouble.

That the sociologist, by publishing his findings, blows the whistle on deviance whose existence is not publicly acknowledged may explain why the poor, powerless, and disreputable seldom complain about the studies published about them. They seldom complain, of course, because they are seldom organized enough to do so. Yet I think further reasons for their silence can be found. The deviance of homosexuals or drug addicts is no secret. They have nothing to lose by a further exposure and may believe than an honest account of their lives will counter the stereotypes that have grown up about them. My own studies of dance musicians and marihuana users bear this out.[10] Marihuana users, particularly, urged me to finish my study quickly and publish it so that people could "know the truth" about them.

It may be thought that social science research exposes deviation only when the scientist has an ax to grind, when he is particularly interested in exposing evil. This is not the case. As Vidich and Bensman note:

One of the principal ideas of our book is that the public atmosphere of an organization or a community tends to be optimistic, positive, and geared to the public relations image of the community or the organization. The public mentality veils the dynamics and functional determinants of the group being studied. Any attempt in social analysis at presenting other than public relations rends the veil and must necessarily cause resentment. Moreover, any organization tends to represent a balance of divergent interests held in some kind of equilibrium by the power status of the parties involved. A simple

10. The studies are reported in Becker, *Outsiders, op. cit.,* pp. 41–119.

description of these factors, no matter how stated, will offend some of the groups in question.[11]

Unless the scientist deliberately restricts himself to research on the ideologies and beliefs of the people studied and does not touch on the behavior of the members of the community or organization, he must in some way deal with the disparity between reality and ideal, with the discrepancy between the number of crimes committed and the number of criminals apprehended. A study that purports to deal with social structure thus inevitably will reveal that the organization or community is not all it claims to be, not all it would like to be able to feel itself to be. A good study, therefore, will make somebody angry.

Self-censorship: A Danger

I have just argued that a good study of a community or organization must reflect the irreconcilable conflict between the interests of science and the interests of those studied, and thereby provoke a hostile reaction. Yet many studies conducted by competent scientists do not have this consequence. Under what circumstances will the report of a study fail to provoke conflict? Can such a failure be justified?

In the simplest case, the social scientist may be taken in by those he studies and be kept from seeing the things that would cause conflict were he to report them. Melville Dalton states the problem for studies of industry.

> In no case did I make a formal approach to the top management of any of the firms to get approval or support for the research. Several times I have seen other researchers do this and have watched higher managers set the scene and limit the inquiry to specific areas—outside management proper—as though the problem existed in a vacuum. The findings in some cases were then regarded as "controlled experiments," which in final form made impressive reading. But the smiles and delighted manipulation of researchers by guarded personnel, the assessments made of researchers and their findings, and the frequently trivial areas to which alerted and fearful officers guided the inquiry—all raised questions about who controlled the experiments.[12]

This is probably an uncommon occurrence. Few people social scientists study are sophisticated enough to anticipate or control what the researcher will see. More frequently, the social scientist takes himself in, "goes native," becomes identified with the ideology of the dominant faction in the organi-

11. Vidich and Bensman, "Comment," *op. cit.*
12. Melville Dalton, *Men Who Manage: Fusions of Feeling and Theory in Administration* (New York: Wiley, 1959), p. 275.

zation or community and frames the questions to which his research provides answers so that no one will be hurt. He does not do this deliberately
or with the intent to suppress scientific knowledge. Rather, he unwittingly
chooses problems that are not likely to cause trouble or inconvenience to
those he has found to be such pleasant associates. Herbert Butterfield, the
British historian, puts the point well in his discussion of the dangers of
"official history." He talks of the problems that arise when a government
allows historians access to secret documents.

> A Foreign Secretary once complained that, while he, for his part, was only
> trying to be helpful, Professor Temperley (as one of the editors of the British
> Documents [On the Origins of the War of 1914]) persisted in treating him
> as though he were a hostile Power. Certainly it is possible for the historian
> to be unnecessarily militant, and even a little ungracious in his militancy; but
> what a satisfaction it is to the student if he can be sure that his interests have
> been guarded with the unremitting jealousy! And if we employ a watchdog
> (which is the function the independent historian would be expected to perform
> on our behalf), what an assurance it is to be able to feel that we are served
> by one whom we know to be vigilant and unsleeping! The ideal, in this respect,
> would certainly not be represented by the picture of a Professor Temperley
> and a Foreign Secretary as thick as thieves, each merely thinking the other
> a jolly good fellow; for this historian who is collecting evidence—and par-
> ticularly the historian who pretends as an independent authority to certify
> the documents or verify the claims of the government department—must be as
> jealous and importunate as the cad of a detective who has to find the murderer
> amongst a party of his friends. One of the widest of the general causes of his-
> torical error has been the disposition of a Macaulay to recognize in the case
> of Tory witnesses a need for historical criticism which it did not occur to
> him to have in the same way for the witnesses on his own side. Nothing in
> the whole of historiography is more subtly dangerous than the natural disposi-
> tion to withhold criticism because John Smith belongs to one's own circle
> or because he is a nice man, so that it seems ungracious to try to press him
> on a point too far, or because it does not occur to one that something more
> could be extracted from him by importunate endeavor. In this sense all is
> not lost if our historian-detective even makes himself locally unpopular; for
> (to take an imaginary case) if he communicates to us his judgment that the
> Foreign Office does not burn important papers, the point is not without its
> interest; but we could only attach weight to the judgment if he had gone
> into the matter with all the alertness of an hostile enquirer and with the
> keenly critical view concerning the kind of evidence which could possibly
> authorise a detective to come to such a conclusion. And if an historian were
> to say: "This particular group of documents ought not to be published,
> because it would expose the officials concerned to serious misunderstandings,"
> then we must answer that he has already thrown in his lot with officialdom—
> already he is thinking of their interests rather than ours; for since these

documents, by definition, carry us outside the framework of stories somebody wants to impose on us, they are the very ones that the independent historian must most desire. To be sure, no documents can be published without laying many people open to grievous misunderstanding. In this connection an uncommon significance must attach therefore to the choice of the people who are to be spared. The only way to reduce misunderstanding is to keep up the clamour for more and more of the strategic kinds of evidence. . . .[13]

It is essential for everybody to be aware that the whole problem of "censorship" to-day has been transformed into the phenomenon of "auto-censorship" —a matter to be borne in mind even when the people involved are only indirectly the servants of government, or are attached by no further tie than the enjoyment of privileges that might be taken away. It is even true that where all are "pals" there is no need for censorship, no point where it is necessary to imagine that one man is being overruled by another. And in any case it is possible to conceive of a State in which members of different organizations could control or prevent a revelation with nothing more than a hint or a wink as they casually pass one another amidst the crowd at some tea-party.[14]

Although Butterfield is speaking of the relations of the social scientist to a national government, it takes no great leap of imagination to see the relevance of his discussion to the problem of the sociologist who has studied a community or organization.

Finally, even if he is not deceived in either of the ways so far suggested, the social scientist may deliberately decide to suppress conflict-provoking findings. He may suppress his findings because publication will violate a bargain he has made with those studied. If, for example, he has given the subjects of his study the right to excise offensive portions of his manuscript prior to publication in return for the privilege of making the study, he will feel bound to honor that agreement. Because of the far-reaching consequences such an agreement could have, most social scientists take care to specify, when reaching an agreement with an organization they want to study, that they have the final say as to what will be published, though they often grant representatives of the organization the right to review the manuscript and suggest changes.

The social scientist may also suppress his findings because of an ideological commitment to the maintenance of society as it is now constituted. Shils makes the following case.

Good arguments can be made against continuous publicity about public institutions. It could be claimed that extreme publicity not only breaks the confi-

13. Herbert Butterfield, "Official History: Its Pitfalls and Criteria," in his *History and Human Relations* (London: Collins, 1951), pp. 194–195.
14. *Ibid.,* pp. 197–198.

dentiality which enhances the imaginativeness and reflectiveness necessary for the effective working of institutions but also destroys the respect in which they should, at least tentatively, be held by the citizenry.[15]

He believes that the first of these considerations is probably correct and thus constitutes a legitimate restriction on scientific inquiry, whereas the second, although not entirely groundless ethically, is so unlikely to occur as not to constitute a clear danger.

It is only in the case of deliberate suppression that an argument can be made, for in the other two cases the scientist presumably reports all his findings, the difficulty arising from his failure to make them in the first place. I will discuss the problem of the research bargain in the next section, in the context of possible solutions to the problem of publication. It remains only to consider Shils' argument before concluding that there is no reasonable basis for avoiding conflict over publication by failing to include the items that will provoke conflict.

Shils rests his case on the possibility that the publicity generated by research may interfere with the "effective working of institutions." When this occurs the scientist should restrict his inquiry. We can accept this argument only if we agree that the effective working of institutions as they are presently constituted is an overriding good. Shils, in his disdain for the "populistic" frame of mind that has informed much of American sociology (his way of characterizing the "easy-going irreverence toward authority" and the consequent tendency to social criticism among social scientists), is probably more ready to accept such a proposition than the majority of working social scientists. Furthermore, and I do not know that he would carry his argument so far, the right of public institutions to delude themselves about the character of their actions and the consequences of those actions does not seem to me easily defended.

Possible Solutions

An apparently easy solution to the dilemma of publishing findings and interpretations that may harm those studied is to decide that if a proper bargain has been struck at the beginning of a research relationship no one has any right to complain. If the researcher has agreed to allow those studied to censor his report, he cannot complain when they do. If the people studied have been properly warned, in sufficient and graphic detail, of the conse-

---

15. Edward A. Shils, "Social Inquiry and the Autonomy of the Individual," in Danier Lerner, ed., *Meaning of the Social Sciences* (New York: Meridian Books, 1959), p. 137. I am indebted to William Kornhauser for calling this article to my attention.

quences of a report about them and have still agreed to have a study done, then they cannot complain if the report is not what they would prefer. But the solution, from the point of view of either party, ignores the real problems.

From the scientist's point of view, the problem is only pushed back a step. Instead of asking what findings he should be prepared to publish, we ask what bargain he should be prepared to strike. Considering only his own scientific interests, he should clearly drive the hardest bargain, demanding complete freedom, and should settle for less only when he must in order to gain access to a theoretically important class of institutions that would otherwise be closed to him.

When we look at the problem from the side of those studied, reaching a firm bargain is also only an apparent solution. As Roth pointed out,[16] the people who agree to have a social scientist study them have not had the experience before and do not know what to expect; nor are they aware of the experience of others social scientists have studied. Even if the social scientist has pointed out the possible consequences of a report, the person whose organization or community is to be studied is unlikely to think it will happen to him; he cannot believe this fine fellow, the social scientist with whom he now sees eye to eye, would actually do something to harm him. He thinks the social scientist, being a fine fellow, will abide by the ethics of the group under study, not realizing the force and scope of the scientist's impersonal ethic and, particularly, of the scientific obligation to report findings fully and frankly. He may feel easy, having been assured that no specific item of behavior will be attributed to any particular person, but will he think of the "tone" of the report, said to be offensive to the inhabitants of Springdale?

Making a proper research bargain, then, is no solution to the problem of publication. Indeed, with respect to the question of *what to publish,* I think there is no general solution except as one may be dictated by the individual's conscience. But there are other questions and it is possible to take constructive action on them without prejudicing one's right to publish. The social scientist can warn those studied of the effect of publication and help them prepare for it. When his report is written he can help those concerned to assimilate what it says and adjust to the consequences of being reported on publicly.

It is probably true that the first sociological report on a given kind of institution sits least well, and that succeeding studies are less of a shock to those studied, creating fewer problems both for the researcher and those he studies. The personnel of the first mental hospital or prison studied by

16. Roth, *op. cit.*

sociologists probably took it harder than those of similar institutions studied later. Once the deviations characteristic of a whole class of institutions have been exposed they are no longer secrets peculiar to one. Subsequent reports have less impact. They only affirm that the deviations found in one place also exist elsewhere. Those whose institutions are the subject of later reports can only suffer from having it shown that they have the same faults, a lesser crime than being the only place where such deviations occur. The difference between "In this mental hospital attendants beat patients" and "In this mental hospital *also,* attendants beat patients" may seem small, but the consequences of the difference are large and important.

By having those he studies read earlier reports on their kind of institution or community, the social scientist can lead them to understand that what he reports about them is not unique. By making available to them other studies, which describe similar deviations in other kinds of institutions and communities, he can teach them that the deviations whose exposure they fear are in fact characteristic features of all human organizations and societies. Thus a carefully thought out educational program may help those reported on come to terms with what the scientist reports, and spare both parties unnecessary difficulties.

The program might take the form of a series of seminars or conversations, in which the discussion would move from a consideration of social science in general to studies of similar institutions, culminating in a close analysis of the about-to-be-published report. In analyzing the report the social scientist can point out the two contexts in which publication will have meaning for those it describes.

First, it can affect their relations with other groups outside the institution: the press, the public, national professional organizations, members of other professions, clients, citizens' watchdog groups, and so on. By describing facts about the organization that may be interpreted as deviations by outside groups, the social scientist may endanger the institution's position with them. Second, the publication of descriptions of deviation may add fuel to internal political fires.[17] The social scientist, by discussing the report with those it describes, can help them to face these problems openly and warn them against one-sided interpretations of his data and analyses. For instance, he can help them to see the kinds of interpretations that may be made of his report by outside groups, aid them in assessing the possibility of serious damage (which they are likely to overestimate), and let them test on him possible answers they might make to adverse reaction.

17. The danger of exposure to external publics is most salient in studies of institutions; the danger of exposure of deviation within the group studied is most important in studies of communities.

If he confers with institutional personnel, he will no doubt be present when various people attempt to make use of his work in a selective or distorted way for internal political advantage, when they cite fragments of his conclusions in support of a position they have taken on some institutional or community issue. He can then, at the moment it takes place, correct the distortion or selective citation and force those involved to see the issue in more complete perspective.

In conferring with representatives of the institution or community, the social scientist should keep two things in mind. First, although he should be sensitive to the damage his report might do, he should not simply take complaints and make revisions so that the complaints will cease. Even with his best efforts, the complaints may remain, because an integral part of his analysis has touched on some chronic sore point in the organization; if this is the case, he must publish his report without changing the offending portions. Second, his conferences with representatives of the organization should not simply be attempts to softsoap them into believing that no damage will occur when, in fact, it may. He must keep this possibility alive for them and make them take it seriously; unless he does, he is only postponing the complaints and difficulties to a later time when reactions to the report, within and outside the organization, will bring them out in full strength. In this connection it is useful to make clear to those studied that the preliminary report, if that is what they are given, is slated for publication in some form, even though it may be substantially revised; this fact is sometimes forgotten and many criticisms that would be made if it were clear that the document was intended for publication are not made, with the result that the process must be gone through again when the final version is prepared.

People whose organizations have been studied by social scientists often complain that the report made about them is "pessimistic" or "impractical," and their complaint points to another reason for their anger. Insofar as the report gives the impression that the facts and situations it describes are irremediable, it puts them in the position of being chronic offenders for whom there is no hope. Although some social science reports have such a pessimistic tone, it is more often the case that the report makes clear that there are no easy solutions to the organization's problems. There are solutions, but they are solutions that call for major changes in organizational practice, and for this reason they are likely to be considered impractical. The social scientist can explain that there are no panaceas, no small shifts in practice that will do away with the "evils" his report describes without in any way upsetting existing arrangements, and thus educate those he has studied to the unpleasant truth that they cannot change the things they want to change without causing repercussions in other parts of the organization.[18] By the same token, however, he can point to the directions in which change is possible, even though difficult, and thus relieve them of the oppressive feeling that they have no way out.

A regime of conferring with and educating those studied may seem like an additional and unwelcome job for the social scientist to take on. Is it not difficult enough to do the field work, analyze the data, and prepare a report, without taking on further obligations? Why not finish the work and leave, letting someone else bear the burden of educating the subjects of the study? Although flight may often seem the most attractive alternative, the social scientist should remember that, in the course of working over his report with those it describes, he may get some extremely useful data. For instance, in the course of discussions about the possible effect of the report on various audiences, it is possible to discover new sources of constraint on the actors involved that had not turned up in the original study. One may be told about sources of inhibition of change that are so pervasive as to never have been mentioned until a discussion of change, occasioned by the report, brings them to light. The desire for further data, coupled with simple altruism and the desire to avoid trouble, may prove sufficiently strong motive for an educational effort.

Conclusion

In discussing the several facets of the problem, I have avoided stating any ethical canons. I have relied on those canons implicit in the scientific enterprise in suggesting that the scientist must strive for the freest possible conditions of reporting. Beyond that I have said only that it is a matter of individual conscience. In so restricting my remarks and in discussing the problem largely in technical terms, I have not meant to indicate that one need have no conscience at all, but only that it must remain a matter of individual judgment.

I ought properly, therefore, to express my own judgment. Briefly, it is that one should refrain from publishing items of fact or conclusions that are not necessary to one's argument or that would cause suffering out of proportion to the scientific gain of making them public. This judgment is of course ambiguous. When is something "necessary" to an argument? What is "suffering"? When is an amount of suffering "out of proportion"? Even though the statement as it stands cannot determine a clear line of action for any given situation, I think it does suggest a viable vantage point, an

18. See the discussion of panaceas in Howard S. Becker and Blanche Geer, "Medical Education," in Howard E. Freeman, Leo G. Reeder, and Sol Levine, eds., *Handbook of Medical Sociology* (Englewood Cliffs, N.J.: Prentice-Hall, 1963), pp. 180–184.

appropriate mood, from which decisions can be approached. In particular, it suggests on the one hand that the scientist must be able to give himself good reasons for including potentially harmful material, rather than including it simply because it is "interesting." On the other hand, it guards him against either an overly formal or an overly sentimental view of the harm those he studies may suffer, requiring that it be serious and substantial enough to warrant calling it "suffering." Finally, it insists that he know enough about the situation he has studied to know whether the suffering will in any sense be proportional to gains science may expect from publication of his findings.

The judgment I have expressed is clearly not very original. Nor is it likely that any judgment expressed by a working social scientist would be strikingly original. All the reasonable positions have been stated long ago. The intent of this paper has been to show that a sociological understanding of what we do when we publish potentially harmful materials may help us make the ethical decision that we must, inevitably, make alone.

CHAPTER EIGHT

Whose Side
Are We On?

To have values or not to have values: the question is always with us. When sociologists undertake to study problems that have relevance to the world we live in, they find themselves caught in a crossfire. Some urge them not to take sides, to be neutral and do research that is technically correct and value free. Others tell them their work is shallow and useless if it does not express a deep commitment to a value position.

This dilemma, which seems so painful to so many, actually does not exist, for one of its horns is imaginary. For it to exist, one would have to assume, as some apparently do, that it is indeed possible to do research that is uncontaminated by personal and political sympathies. I propose to argue that it is not possible and, therefore, that the question is not whether we should take sides, since we inevitably will, but rather whose side we are on.

I will begin by considering the problem of taking sides as it arises in the study of deviance. An inspection of this case will soon reveal to us features that appear in sociological research of all kinds. In the greatest variety of subject matter areas and in work done by all the different methods at our disposal, we cannot avoid taking sides, for reasons firmly based in social structure.

We may sometimes feel that studies of deviance exhibit too great a sympathy with the people studied, a sympathy reflected in the research carried out. This feeling, I suspect, is entertained off and on both by those of us who do such research and by those of us who, our work lying in other areas, only read the results. Will the research, we wonder, be distorted by that sym-

Reprinted by permission from *Social Problems*, 14 (Winter 1967), pp. 239–247. Copyright © 1967 The Society for the Study of Social Problems.

pathy? Will it be of use in the construction of scientific theory or in the application of scientific knowledge to the practical problems of society? Or will the bias introduced by taking sides spoil it for those uses?

We seldom make the feeling explicit. Instead, it appears as a lingering worry for sociological readers, who would like to be sure they can trust what they read, and a troublesome area of self-doubt for those who do the research, who would like to be sure that whatever sympathies they feel are not professionally unseemly and will not, in any case, seriously flaw their work. That the worry affects both readers and researchers indicates that it lies deeper than the superficial differences that divide sociological schools of thought, and that its roots must be sought in characteristics of society that affect us all, whatever our methodological or theoretical persuasion.

If the feeling were made explicit, it would take the form of an accusation that the sympathies of the researcher have biased his work and distorted his findings. Before exploring its structural roots, let us consider what the manifest meaning of the charge might be.

It might mean that we have acquired some sympathy with the group we study sufficient to deter us from publishing those of our results which might prove damaging to them. One can imagine a liberal sociologist who set out to disprove some of the common stereotypes held about a minority group. To his dismay, his investigation reveals that some of the stereotypes are unfortunately true. In the interests of justice and liberalism, he might well be tempted, and might even succumb to the temptation to suppress those findings, publishing with scientific candor the other results which confirmed his beliefs.

But this seems not really to be the heart of the charge, because sociologists who study deviance do not typically hide things about the people they study. They are mostly willing to grant that there is something going on that put the deviants in the position they are in, even if they are not willing to grant that it is what the people they studied were originally accused of.

A more likely meaning of the charge, I think, is this. In the course of our work and for who knows what private reasons, we fall into deep sympathy with the people we are studying, so that while the rest of the society views them as unfit in one or another respect for the deference ordinarily accorded a fellow citizen, we believe that they are at least as good as anyone else, more sinned against than sinning. Because of this, we do not give a balanced picture. We focus too much on questions whose answers show that the supposed deviant is morally in the right and the ordinary citizen morally in the wrong. We neglect to ask those questions whose answers would show that the deviant, after all, has done something pretty rotten and, indeed, pretty much deserves what he gets. In consequence, our overall assessment of the problem being studied is one-sided. What we produce is a whitewash of the deviant and a condemnation, if only by implication, of those respectable citizens who, we think, have made the deviant what he is.

It is to this version that I devote the rest of my remarks. I will look first, however, not at the truth or falsity of the charge, but rather at the circumstances in which it is typically made and felt. The sociology of knowledge cautions us to distinguish between the truth of a statement and an assessment of the circumstances under which that statement is made; though we trace an argument to its source in the interests of the person who made it, we have still not proved it false. Recognizing the point and promising to address it eventually, I shall turn to the typical situations in which the accusation of bias arises.

When do we accuse ourselves and our fellow sociologists of bias? I think an inspection of representative instances would show that the accusation arises, in one important class of cases, when the research gives credence, in any serious way, to the perspective of the subordinate group in some hierarchical relationship. In the case of deviance, the hierarchical relationship is a moral one. The superordinate parties in the relationship are those who represent the forces of approved and official morality; the subordinate parties are those who, it is alleged, have violated that morality.

Though deviance is a typical case, it is by no means the only one. Similar situations, and similar feelings that our work is biased, occur in the study of schools, hospitals, asylums and prisons, in the study of physical as well as mental illness, in the study of both "normal" and delinquent youth. In these situations, the superordinate parties are usually the official and professional authorities in charge of some important insitution, while the subordinates are those who make use of the services of that institution. Thus, the police are the superordinates, drug addicts are the subordinates; professors and administrators, principles and teachers, are the superordinates, while students and pupils are the subordinates; physicians are the superordinates, their patients the subordinates.

All of these cases represent one of the typical situations in which researchers accuse themselves and are accused of bias. It is a situation in which, while conflict and tension exist in the hierarchy, the conflict has not become openly political. The conflicting segments or ranks are not organized for conflict; no one attempts to alter the shape of the hierachy. While subordinates may complain about the treatment they receive from those above them, they do not propose to move to a position of equality with them, or to reverse positions in the hierarchy. Thus, no one proposes that addicts should make and enforce laws for policemen, that patients should prescribe for doctors, or that adolescents should give orders to adults. We can call this the *apolitical* case.

In the second case, the accusation of bias is made in a situation that is frankly political. The parties to the hierarchical relationship engage in organized conflict, attempting either to maintain or change existing relations of power and authority. Whereas in the first case subordinates are typically unorganized and thus have, as we shall see, little to fear from a researcher, subordinate parties in a political situation may have much to lose. When the situation is political, the researcher may accuse himself or be accused of bias by someone else when he gives credence to the perspective of either party to the political conflict. I leave the political for later and turn now to the problem of bias in apolitical situations.[1]

We provoke the suspicion that we are biased in favor of the subordinate parties in an apolitical arrangement when we tell the story from their point of view. We may, for instance, investigate their complaints, even though they are subordinates, about the way things are run just as though one ought to give their complaints as much credence as the statements of responsible officials. We provoke the charge when we assume, for the purposes of our research, that subordinates have as much right to be heard as superordinates, that they are as likely to be telling the truth as they see it as superordinates, that what they say about the institution has a right to be investigated and have its truth or falsity established, even though responsible officials assure us that it is unnecessary because the charges are false.

We can use the notion of a *hierarchy of credibility* to understand this phenomenon. In any system of ranked groups, participants take it as given that members of the highest group have the right to define the way things really are. In any organization, no matter what the rest of the organization chart shows, the arrows indicating the flow of information point up, thus demonstrating (at least formally) that those at the top have access to a more complete picture of what is going on than anyone else. Members of lower groups will have incomplete information, and their view of reality will be partial and distorted in consequence. Therefore, from the point of view of a well socialized participant in the system, any tale told by those at the top intrinsically deserves to be regarded as the most credible account obtainable of the organizations' workings. And since, as Summer pointed out, matters of rank and status are contained in the mores,[2] this belief has a moral quality. We are, if we are proper members of the group, morally bound to accept the definition imposed on reality by a superordinate group in preference to the definitions espoused by subordinates. (By analogy, the

1. No situation is necessarily political or apolitical. An apolitical situation can be transformed into a political one by the open rebellion of subordinate ranks, and a political situation can subside into one in which an accommodation has been reached and a new hierarchy been accepted by the participants. The categories, while analytically useful, do not represent a fixed division existing in real life.

2. William Graham Sumner, "Status in the Folkways," *Folkways* (New York: New American Library, 1960), pp. 72–73.

same argument holds for the social classes of a community.) Thus, credibility and the right to be heard are differentially distributed through the
ranks of the system.

As sociologists, we provoke the charge of bias, in ourselves and others,
by refusing to give credence and deference to an established status order,
in which knowledge of truth and the right to be heard are not equally distributed. "Everyone knows" that responsible professionals know more about
things than laymen, that police are more respectable and their words ought
to be taken more seriously than those of the deviants and criminals with
whom they deal. By refusing to accept the hierarchy of credibility, we express disrespect for the entire established order.

We compound our sin and further provoke charges of bias by not giving
immediate attention and "equal time" to the apologies and explanations of
official authority. If, for instance, we are concerned with studying the way
of life inmates in a mental hospital build up for themselves, we will naturally
be concerned with the constraints and conditions created by the actions of
the administrators and physicians who run the hospital. But, unless we also
make the administrators and physicians the object of our study (a possibility
I will consider later), we will not inquire into why those conditions and
constraints are present. We will not give responsible officials a chance to
explain themselves and give their reasons for acting as they do, a chance
to show why the complaints of inmates are not justified.

It is odd that, when we perceive bias, we usually see it in these circumstances. It is odd because it is easily ascertained that a great many more
studies are biased in the direction of the interests of responsible officials
than the other way around. We may accuse an occasional student of medical sociology of having given too much emphasis to the complaints of
patients. But is it not obvious that most medical sociologists look at things
from the point of view of the doctors? A few sociologists may be sufficiently
biased in favor of youth to grant credibility to their account of how the
adult world treats them. But why do we not accuse other sociologists who
study youth of being biased in favor of adults? Most research on youth,
after all, is clearly designed to find out why youth are so troublesome for
adults, rather than asking the equally interesting sociological question:
"Why do adults make so much trouble for youth?" Similarly, we accuse
those who take the complaints of mental patients seriously of bias; what
about those sociologists who only take seriously the complaints of physicians, families and others about mental patients?

Why this disproportion in the direction of accusations of bias? Why do
we more often accuse those who are on the side of subordinates than those
who are on the side of superordinates? Because, when we make the former
accusation, we have, like the well socialized members of our society most

of us are, accepted the hierarchy of credibility and taken over the accusation made by responsible officials.

The reason responsible officials make the accusation so frequently is precisely because they are responsible. They have been entrusted with the care and operation of one or another of our important institutions: schools, hospitals, law enforcement, or whatever. They are the ones who, by virtue of their official position and the authority that goes with it, are in a position to "do something" when things are not what they should be and, similarly, are the ones who will be held to account if they fail to "do something" or if what they do is, for whatever reason, inadequate.

Because they are responsible in this way, officials usually have to lie. That is a gross way of putting it, but not inaccurate. Officials must lie because things are seldom as they ought to be. For a great variety of reasons, well-known to sociologists, institutions are refractory. They do not perform as society would like them to. Hospitals do not cure people; prisons do not rehabilitate prisoners; schools do not educate students. Since they are supposed to, officials develop ways both of denying the failure of the institution to perform as it should and explaining those failures which cannot be hidden. An account of an institution's operation from the point of view of subordinates therefore casts doubt on the official line and may possibly expose it as a lie.[3]

For reasons that are a mirror image of those of officials, subordinates in an apolitical hierarchical relationship have no reason to complain of the bias of sociological research oriented toward the interests of superordinates. Subordinates typically are not organized in such a fashion as to be responsibile for the overall operation of an institution. What happens in a school is credited or debited to the faculty and administrators; they can be identified and held to account. Even though the failure of a school may be the fault of the pupils, they are not so organized that any one of them is responsibile for any failure but his own. If he does well, while others all around him flounder, cheat and steal, that is none of his affair, despite the attempt of honor codes to make it so. As long as the sociological report on his school says that every student there but one is a liar and a cheat, all the students will feel complacent, knowing they are the one exception. More likely, they will never hear of the report at all or, if they do, will reason that they will be gone before long, so what difference does it make? The lack of organization among subordinate members of an institutionalized relationship means that, having no responsibility for the group's welfare, they likewise have no complaints if someone maligns it. The sociologist who favors officialdom will be spared the accusation of bias.

3. I have stated a portion of this argument more briefly in "Problems of Publication of Field Studies," in this volume.

And thus we see why we accuse ourselves of bias only when we take the side of the subordinate. It is because, in a situation that is not openly political, with the major issues defined as arguable, we join responsible officials and the man in the street in an unthinking acceptance of the hierarchy of credibility. We assume with them that the man at the top knows best. We do not realize that there are sides to be taken and that we are taking one of them.

The same reasoning allows us to understand why the researcher has the same worry about the effect of his sympathies on his work as his uninvolved colleague. The hierarchy of credibility is a feature of society whose existence we cannot deny, even if we disagree with its injunction to believe the man at the top. When we acquire sufficient sympathy with subordinates to see things from their perspective, we know that we are flying in the face of what "everyone knows." The knowledge gives us pause and causes us to share, however briefly, the doubt of our colleagues.

When a situation has been defined politically, the second type of case I want to discuss, matters are are quite different. Subordinates have some degree of organization and, with that, spokesmen, their equivalent of responsible officials. Spokesmen, while they cannot actually be held responsible for what members of their group do, make assertions on their behalf and are held responsible for the truth of those assertions. The group engages in political activity designed to change existing hierarchical relationships and the credibility of its spokesmen directly affects its political fortunes. Credibility is not the only influence, but the group can ill-afford having the definition of reality proposed by its spokesmen discredited, for the immediate consequence will be some loss of political power.

Superordinate groups have their spokesmen too, and they are confronted with the same problem: to make statements about reality that are politically effective without being easily discredited. The political fortunes of the superordinate group—its ability to hold the status changes demanded by lower groups to a minimum—do not depend as much on credibility, for the group has other kinds of power available as well.

When we do research in a political situation we are in double jeopardy, for the spokesmen of both involved groups will be sensitive to the implications of our work. Since they propose openly conflicting definitions of reality, our statement of our problem is in itself likely to call into question and make problematic, at least for the purposes of our research, one or the other definition. And our results will do the same.

The hierarchy of credibility operates in a different way in the political situation than it does in the apolitical one. In the political situation, it is precisely one of the things at issue. Since the political struggle calls into question the legitimacy of the existing rank system, it necessarily calls into question at the same time the legitimacy of the associated judgments of credibility. Judgments of who has a right to define the nature of reality that are taken for granted in an apolitical situation become matters of argument.

Oddly enough, we are, I think, less likely to accuse ourselves and one another of bias in a political than in a apolitical situation, for at least two reasons. First, because the hierarchy of credibility has been openly called into question, we are aware that there are at least two sides to the story and so do not think it unseemly to investigate the situation from one or another of the contending points of view. We know, for instance, that we must grasp the perspectives of both the resident of Watts and of the Los Angeles policemen if we are to understand what went on in that outbreak.

Second, it is no secret that most sociologists are politically liberal to one degree or another. Our political preferences dictate the side we will be on and, since those preferences are shared by most of our colleagues, few are ready to throw the first stone or are even aware that stone-throwing is a possibility. We usually take the side of the underdog; we are for Negroes and against Fascists. We do not think anyone biased who does research designed to prove that the former are not as bad as people think or that the latter are worse. In fact, in these circumstances we are quite willing to regard the question of bias as a matter to be dealt with by the use of technical safeguards.

We are thus apt to take sides with equal innocence and lack of thought, though for different reasons, in both apolitical and political situations. In the first, we adopt the commonsense view which awards unquestioned credibility to the responsible official. (This is not to deny that a few of us, because something in our experience has alerted them to the possibility, may question the conventional hierarchy of credibility in the special area of our expertise.) In the second case, we take our politics so for granted that it supplants convention in dictating whose side we will be on. (I do not deny, either, that some few sociologists may deviate politically from their liberal colleagues, either to the right or the left, and thus be more liable to question that convention.)

In any event, even if our colleagues do not accuse us of bias in research in a political situation, the interested parties will. Whether they are foreign politicians who object to studies of how the stability of their government may be maintained in the interest of the United States (as in the *Camelot* affair)[4] or domestic civil rights leaders who object to an analysis of race problems that centers on the alleged deficiencies of the Negro family (as

4. See Irving Louis Horowitz, "The Life and Death of Project Camelot," *Transaction* 3 (Nov./Dec. 1965), pp. 3–7, 44–47.

in the reception given to the Moynihan Report),[5] interested parties are quick to make accusations of bias and distortion. They base the accusation not on failures of technique or method, but on conceptual defects. They accuse the sociologist not of getting false data but of not getting all the data relevant to the problem. They accuse him, in other words, of seeing things from the perspective of only one party to the conflict. But the accusation is likely to be made by interested parties and not by sociologists themselves.

What I have said so far is all sociology of knowledge, suggesting by whom, in what situations and for what reasons sociologists will be accused of bias and distortion. I have not yet addressed the question of the truth of the accusations, of whether our findings are distorted by our sympathy for those we study. I have implied a partial answer, namely, that there is no position from which sociological research can be done that is not biased in one or another way.

We must always look at the matter from someone's point of view. The scientist who proposes to understand society must, as Mead long ago pointed out, get into the situation enough to have a perspective on it. And it is likely that his perspective will be greatly affected by whatever positions are taken by any or all of the other participants in that varied situation. Even if his participation is limited to reading in the field, he will necessarily read the arguments of partisans of one or another side to a relationship and will thus be affected, at least, by having suggested to him what the relevant arguments and issues are. A student of medical sociology may decide that he will take neither the perspective of the patient nor the perspective of the physician, but he will necessarily take a perspective that impinges on the many questions that arise between physicians and patients; no matter what perspective he takes, his work either will take into account the attitude of subordinates, or it will not. If he fails to consider the questions they raise, he will be working on the side of the officials. If he does raise those questions seriously and does find, as he may, that there is some merit in them, he will then expose himself to the outrage of the officials and of all those sociologists who award them the top spot in the hierarchy of credibility. Almost all the topics that sociologists study, at least those that have some relation to the real world around us, are seen by society as morality plays and we shall find ourselves, willy-nilly, taking part in those plays on one side or the other.

There is another possibility. We may, in some cases, take the point of view of some third party not directly implicated in the hierarchy we are investigating. Thus, a Marxist might feel that it is not worth distinguishing

5. See Lee Rainwater and William L. Yancey, "Black Families and the White House," *ibid.* 3 (July/August 1966), pp. 6–11, 48–53.

between Democrats and Republicans, or between big business and big labor, in each case both groups being equally inimical to the interests of the workers. This would indeed make us neutral with respect to the two groups at hand, but would only mean that we had enlarged the scope of the political conflict to include a party not ordinarily brought in whose view the sociologist was taking.

We can never avoid taking sides. So we are left with the question of whether taking sides means that some distortion is introduced into our work so great as to make it useless. Or, less drastically, whether some distortion is introduced that must be taken into account before the results of our work can be used. I do not refer here to feeling that the picture given by the research is not "balanced," the indignation aroused by having a conventionally discredited definition of reality given priority or equality with what "everyone knows," for it is clear that we cannot avoid that. That is the problem of officials, spokesmen and interested parties, not ours. Our problem is to make sure that, whatever point of view we take, our research meets the standards of good scientific work, that our unavoidable sympathies do not render our results invalid.

We might distort our findings, because of our sympathy with one of the parties in the relationship we are studying, by misusing the tools and techniques of our discipline. We might introduce loaded questions into a questionnaire, or act in some way in a field situation such that people would be constrained to tell us only the kind of thing we are already in sympathy with. All of our research techniques are hedged about with precautionary measures designed to guard against these errors. Similarly, though more abstractly, every one of our theories presumably contains a set of directives which exhaustively covers the field we are to study, specifying all the things we are to look at and take into account in our research. By using our theories and techniques impartially, we ought to be able to study all the things that need to be studied in such a way as to get all the facts we require, even though some of the questions that will be raised and some of the facts that will be produced run counter to our biases.

But the question may be precisely this. Given all our techniques of theoretical and technical control, how can we be sure that we will apply them impartially and across the board as they need to be applied? Our textbooks in methodology are no help here. They tell us how to guard against error, but they do not tell us how to make sure that we will use all the safeguards available to us. We can, for a start, try to avoid sentimentality. We are sentimental when we refuse, for whatever reason, to investigate some matter that should properly be regarded as problematic. We are sentimental, especially, when our reason is that we would prefer not to know what is going on, if to know would be to violate some sympathy whose existence we may not even be aware of. Whatever side we are on, we must use our techniques impartially enough that a belief to which we are especially sympathetic could be proved untrue. We must always inspect our work carefully enough to know whether our techniques and theories are open enough to allow that possibility.

Let us consider, finally, what might seem a simple solution to the problems posed. If the difficulty is that we gain sympathy with underdogs by studying them, is it not also true that the superordinates in a hierarchical relationship usually have their own superordinates with whom they must contend? Is it not true that we might study those superordinates or subordinates, presenting their point of view on their relations with their superiors and thus gaining a deeper sympathy with them and avoiding the bias of one-sided identification with those below them? This is appealing, but deceptively so. For it only means that we will get into the same trouble with a new set of officials.

It is true, for instance, that the administrators of a prison are not free to do as they wish, not free to be responsive to the desires of inmates, for instance. If one talks to such an official, he will commonly tell us, in private, that of course the subordinates in the relationship have some right on their side, but they fail to understand that his desire to do better is frustrated by his superiors or by the regulations they have established. Thus, if a prison administrator is angered because we take the complaints of his inmates seriously, we may feel that we can get around that and get a more balanced picture by interviewing him and his associates. If we do, we may then write a report which *his* superiors will respond to with cries of "bias." They, in their turn, will say that we have not presented a balanced picture, because we have not looked at *their* side of it. And we may worry that what they say is true.

The point is obvious. By pursuing this seemingly simple solution, we arrive at a problem of infinite regress. For everyone has someone standing above him who prevents him from doing things just as he likes. If we question the superiors of the prison administrator, a state department of corrections or prisons, they will complain of the governor and the legislature. And if we go to the governor and the legislature, they will complain of lobbyists, party machines, the public and the newspapers. There is no end to it and we can never have a "balanced picture" until we have studied all of society simultaneously. I do not propose to hold my breath until that happy day.

We can, I think, satisfy the demands of our science by always making clear the limits of what we have studied, marking the boundaries beyond which our findings cannot be safely applied. Not just the conventional disclaimer, in which we warn that we have only studied a prison in New York or California and the findings may not hold in the other forty-nine states—which is not a useful procedure anyway, since the findings may very well hold if the conditions are the same elsewhere. I refer to a more sociological disclaimer in which we say, for instance, that we have studied the prison through the eyes of the inmates and not through the eyes of the guards or other involved parties. We warn people, thus, that our study tells us only how things look from that vantage point—what kinds of objects guards are in the prisoners' world—and does not attempt to explain why guards do what they do or to absolve the guards of what may seem, from the prisoners' side, morally unacceptable behavior. This will not protect us from accusations of bias, however, for the guards will still be outraged by the unbalanced picture. If we implicitly accept the conventional hierarchy of credibility, we will feel the sting in that accusation.

It is something of a solution to say that over the years each "one-sided" study will provoke further studies that gradually enlarge our grasp of all the relevant facets of an institution's operation. But that is a long-term solution, and not much help to the individual researcher who has to contend with the anger of officials who feel he has done them wrong, the criticism of those of his colleagues who think he is presenting a one-sided view, and his own worries.

What do we do in the meantime? I suppose the answers are more or less obvious. We take sides as our personal and political commitments dictate, use our theoretical and technical resources to avoid the distortions that might introduce into our work, limit our conclusions carefully, recognize the hierarchy of credibility for what is is, and field as best we can the accusations and doubts that will surely be our fate.

PART II

*Educational
Organizations
and Experiences*

CHAPTER NINE

Social-Class Variations
in the Teacher-Pupil
Relationship

The major problems of workers in the service occupations are likely to be a function of their relationship to their clients or customers, those for whom or on whom the occupational service is performed.[1] Members of such occupations typically have some image of the "ideal" client, and they use this fiction to fashion their conceptions of how their work ought to be performed, and their actual work techniques. To the degree that actual clients approximate this ideal the worker has no "client problem."

In a highly differentiated urban society, however, clients vary greatly, and ordinarily only some fraction of the total of potential clients will be "good" ones. Workers tend to classify clients by the way they vary from this ideal. The fact of client variation from the occupational ideal emphasizes the intimate relation of the institution in which work is carried on to its environing society. If that society does not prepare people to play their client roles in the manner desired by the occupation's members there will be conflicts, and problems for the workers in the performance of their work. One of the major factors affecting the production of suitable clients is the cultural diversity of various social classes in the society. The cultures of particular social-class groups may operate to produce clients who make the worker's position extremely difficult.

Reprinted by permission from *Journal of Educational Sociology*, 25 (April 1952), pp. 451–465. Copyright 1952 American Sociological Association.

1. See Howard S. Becker, "The Professional Dance Musician and His Audience," *American Journal of Sociology* 57 (September 1951), 136–144, for further discussion of this point.

This paper deals with the problem as it appears in the experience of the functionaries of a large urban educational institution, the Chicago public school system, discussing the way teachers in this system observe, classify and react to class-typed differences in the behavior of the children they work with. The material is thus relevant not only to problems of occupational organization but also to the problem of differences in the educational opportunities available to children of various social classes. Warner, Havighurst, and Loeb,[2] and Hollingshead[3] have shown how the schools tend to favor and select out children of the middle classes. Allison Davis has pointed to those factors in the class cultures involved which make lower-class children less and middle-class children more adaptable to the work and behavioral standards of the school.[4] This paper analyzes the way the public school teacher reacts to these cultural differences and, in so doing, perpetuates the discrimination of our educational system against the lower-class child.

The analysis is based on interviews with sixty teachers in the Chicago system.[5] The interviewing was largely unstructured and varied somewhat with each interviewee, according to the difficulty encountered in overcoming teachers' distrust and fear of speaking to outsiders. Despite this resistance, based on anxiety regarding the consequences of being interviewed, I secured material of sufficient validity for the analysis undertaken here through insisting that all general statements of attitude be backed up with concrete descriptions of actual experience. This procedure forced the interviewees to disclose more than they otherwise might have by requiring them to give enough factual material to make their general statements plausible and coherent.

The interviews were oriented around the general question of the problems of being a teacher and were not specifically directed toward discovering feelings about social-class differences among students. Since these differences created some of the teachers' most pressing problems, the interviewees themselves continually brought them up. They typically distinguished three social-class groups with which they, as teachers, came in contact: (1) a bottom stratum, probably equivalent to the lower-lower and parts of the upper-lower class; (2) an upper stratum, probably equivalent to the upper-

2. W. Lloyd Warner, Robert J. Havighurst and Martin B. Loeb, *Who Shall Be Educated?* (New York: Harper & Brothers, 1944).

3. August B. Hollingshead, *Elmtown's Youth: The Impact of Social Class on Adolescents* (New York: John Wiley & Sons, 1949).

4. Allison Davis, *Social-Class Influences upon Learning* (Cambridge, Mass.: Harvard University Press, 1950).

5. The entire research has been reported in Howard S. Becker, "Role and Career Problems of the Chicago Public School Teacher" (Doctoral dissertation, University of Chicago, 1951).

middle class; and (3) a middle stratum, probably equivalent to the lower-middle and parts of the upper-lower class. I will refer to these groups as lower, upper and middle groups, but it should be understood that this terminology refers to the teachers' classification of students and not to the ordinary sociological description.

I will proceed by taking up the three problems that loomed largest in the teachers' discussion of adjustment of their students: (1) the problem of *teaching* itself, (2) the problem of *discipline,* and (3) the problem of the *moral acceptability* of the students. In each case, I focus on the variation in the form of and adjustment to the problem by the characteristics of the children of the various class groups distinguished by teachers.

Teaching

A basic problem in any occupation is that of performing one's given task successfully, and where this involves working with human beings their qualities are a major variable affecting the ease with which the work can be done. The teacher considers that she has done her job adequately when she has brought about an observable change in the children's skills and knowledge which she can attribute to her own efforts:

> Well, I would say that a teacher is successful when she is putting the material across to the children, when she is getting some response from them. I'll tell you something. Teaching is a very rewarding line of work, because you can see those children grow under your hands. You can see the difference in them after you've had them for five months. You can see where they've started and where they've got to. And it's all yours. It really is rewarding in that way, you can see results and know that it's your work that brought those results about.

She feels that she has a better chance of success in this area when her pupils are interested in attending and working hard in school, and are trained at home in such a way that they are bright and quick at school work. Her problems arise in teaching those groups who do not meet these specifications, for then her teaching techniques, tailored to the "perfect" student, are inadequate to cope with the reality, and she is left with a feeling of having failed in performing her basic task.

Davis has described the orientations toward education in general, and schoolwork in particular, of the lower and middle classes:

> Thus, our educational system, which next to the family is the most effective agency in teaching good work habits to middle class people, is largely ineffective and unrealistic with underprivileged groups. Education fails to moti-

vate such workers because our schools and our society both lack *real rewards* to offer underprivileged groups. Neither lower class children or adults will work hard in school or on the job to please the teacher or boss. They are not going to learn to be ambitious, to be conscientious, and to study hard, as if school and work were a fine character-building game, which one plays just for the sake of playing. They can see, indeed, that those who work hard at school usually have families that already have the occupations, homes, and social acceptance that the school holds up as the rewards of education. The underprivileged workers can see also that the chances of their getting enough education to make their attainment of these rewards in the future at all probable is very slight. Since they can win the rewards of prestige and social acceptance in their own slum groups without much education, they do not take very seriously the motivation taught by the school.[6]

As these cultural differences produce variations from the image of the "ideal" student, teachers tend to use class terms in describing the children with whom they work.

They characterize children of the lowest group, from slum areas, as the most difficult group to teach successfully, lacking in interest in school, learning ability, and outside training:

> They don't have the right kind of study habits. They can't seem to apply themselves as well. Of course, it's not their fault; they aren't brought up right. After all, the parents in a neighborhood like that really aren't interested. . . . But, as I say, those children don't learn very quickly. A great many of them don't seem to be really interested in getting an education. I don't think they are. It's hard to get anything done with children like that. They simply don't respond.

They use different terms to describe children of the upper groups:

> In a neighborhood like this there's something about the children, you just feel like you're accomplishing so much more. You throw an idea out and you can see that it takes hold. The children know what you're talking about and they think about it. Then they come in with projects and pictures and additional information, and it just makes you feel good to see it. They go places and see things, and they know what you're talking about. For instance, you might be teaching social studies or geography. . . . You bring something up and a child says, "Oh, my parents took me to see that in the museum."

Children of the middle group arouse ambivalent feelings. While motivated to work hard in school they lack the proper out-of-school training:

6. Allison Davis, "The Motivation of the Underprivileged Worker," in William F. Whyte, ed., *Industry and Society* (New York: McGraw-Hill Book Company, 1947), p. 99.

Well, they're very nice here, very nice. They're not hard to handle. You see, they're taught respect in the home and they're respectful to the teacher. They want to work and do well. . . . Of course, they're not too brilliant. You know what I mean. But they are very nice children and very easy to work with.

In short, the differences between groups make it possible for the teacher to feel successful at her job only with the top group; with the other groups she feels, in greater or lesser measure, that she has failed.

These differences in ability to do school work, as perceived by teachers, have important consequences. They lead, in the first place, to differences in actual teaching techniques. A young high school teacher constrasted the techniques used in "slum" schools with those used in "better" schools:

At S——, there were a lot of guys who were just waiting till they were sixteen so they could get out of school. L——, everybody—well, a very large percentage, I'll say—was going on to secondary school, to college. That certainly made a difference in their classroom work. You had to teach differently at the different schools. For instance, at S——, if you had demonstrations in chemistry they had to be pretty flashy, lots of noise and smoke, before they'd get interested in it. That wasn't necessary at L——. Or at S—— if you were having electricity or something like that you had to get the static electricity machine out and have them all stand around and hold hands so that they'd all get a little jolt.

Further, the teacher feels that where her superiors recognize these differences there will be a corresponding variation in the amount of work she is expected to accomplish. She expects that the amount of work and effort required of her will vary inversely with the social status of her pupils. This teacher compared schools from the extremes of the class range:

So you have to be on your toes and keep up to where you're supposed to be in the course of study. Now, in a school like the D—— [slum school] you're just not expected to complete all that work. It's almost impossible. For instance, in the second grade we're supposed to cover nine spelling words a week. Well, I can do that up here at the K—— ["better" school], they can take nine new words a week. But the best class I ever had at the D—— was only able to achieve six words a week and they had to work pretty hard to get that. So I never finished the year's work in spelling. I couldn't. And I really wasn't expected to.

One result of this situation—in which less is expected of those teachers whose students are more difficult to teach—is that the problem becomes more aggravated in each grade, as the gap between what the children should know and what they actually do know becomes wider and wider. A principal of such a school describes the degeneration there of the teaching problem into a struggle to get a few basic skills across, in a situation where this cumulative effect makes following the normal program of study impossible:

> The children come into our upper grades with very poor reading ability. That means that all the way through our school everybody is concentrating on reading. It's not like at a school like S—— [middle group] where they have science and history and so on. At a school like that they figure that from first to fourth you learn to read and from fifth to eighth you read to learn. You use your reading to learn other material. Well, these children don't reach that second stage while they're with us. We have to plug along getting them to learn to read. Our teachers are pretty well satisfied if the children can read and do simple number work when they leave here. You'll find that they don't think very much of subjects like science, and so on. They haven't got any time for that. They're just trying to get these basic things over. . . . That's why our school is different from one like the S——.

Such consequences of teachers' differential reaction to various class groups obviously operate to further perpetuate those class-cultural characteristics to which they object in the first place.

Discipline

Discipline is the second of the teacher's major problems with her students. Willard Waller pointed to its basis when he wrote that "Teacher and pupil confront each other in the school with an original conflict of desires, and however much that conflict may be reduced in amount, or however much it may be hidden, it still remains."[7] We must recognize that conflict, either actual or potential, is ever present in the teacher-pupil relationship, the teacher attempting to maintain her control against the children's efforts to break it.[8] Teachers feel this conflict even with those children who present least difficulty; a teacher who considered her pupils models of good behavior nevertheless said:

> But there's that tension all the time. Between you and the students. It's hard on your nerves. Teaching is fun, if you enjoy your subject, but it's the discipline that keeps your nerves on edge, you know what I mean? There's

7. Willard Waller, *Sociology of Teaching* (New York: John Wiley & Sons, 1932), p. 197.
8. Although all service occupations tend to have such problems of control over their clients, the problem is undoubtedly aggravated in situations like the school where those upon whom the service is being performed are not there of their own volition, but rather because of the wishes of some other group (the parents, in this case).

always that tension. Sometimes people say, "Oh, you teach school. That's an easy job, just sitting around all day long." They don't know what it's really like. It's hard on your nerves.

The teacher is tense because she fears that she will lose control, defined as some line beyond which she will not allow the children to go. Wherever she may draw this line (and there is considerable variation), the teacher feels that she has a "discipline" problem when the children attempt to push beyond it. The form and intensity of this problem, teachers think, vary from one social-class group to another, as might be expected from Davis' description of class emphases on aggression:

> In general, middle-class aggression is taught to adolescents in the form of social and economic skills which will enable them to compete effectively at that level. . . . In lower-class families, physical aggression is as much a normal, socially approved and socially inculcated type of behavior as it is in frontier communities.[9]

These differences in child training are matched by variation in the teachers' reactions.

Teachers consider children in "slum" schools most difficult to control, being given to unrestrained behavior and physical violence. Our interviews contain many descriptions of such difficulties. Miriam Wagenschein, in a parallel study of the beginning school teacher, gave this summary of the experiences of these younger teachers in lower-class schools:

> The reports which these teachers give of what *can* be done by a group of children are nothing short of amazing. A young white teacher walked into her new classroom and was greeted with the comment, "Another damn white one." Another was "rushed" at her desk by the entire class when she tried to be extremely strict with them. Teachers report having been bitten, tripped, and pushed on the stairs. Another gave an account of a second grader throwing a milk bottle at the teacher and of a first grader having such a temper tantrum that it took the principal and two policemen to get him out of the room. In another school, following a fight on the playground, the principal took thirty-two razor blades from children in a first grade room. Some teachers indicated fear that they might be attacked by irate persons in the neighborhoods in which they teach. Other teachers report that their pupils carry long pieces of glass and have been known to threaten other pupils with them, while others jab each other with hypodermic needles. One boy got angry with his teacher and knocked in the fender of her car.[10]

9. Allison Davis, *Social-Class Influence upon Learning*, pp. 34–35.
10. Miriam Wagenschein, "Reality Shock" (Master's thesis, University of Chicago, 1950), pp. 58 59.

In these schools the teacher must devote a major part of her time to discipline; as one said: "It's just a question of keeping them in line." The emphasis on discipline detracts from the school's primary function of teaching, thus decreasing the educational opportunity available to the children of these schools.

Children of the middle group are thought of as docile, and with them the teacher has least difficulty with discipline:

> Those children were much quieter, easier to work with. When we'd play our little games there was never any commotion. That was a very nice school to work in. Everything was quite nice about it. The children were easy to work with . . .

Children of the upper group are felt hard to handle in some respects, and are often termed "spoiled," "overindulged," or "neurotic"; they do not play the role of the child in the submissive manner teachers consider appropriate. One interviewee, speaking of this group, said:

> I think most teachers prefer not to teach in that type of school. The children are more pampered and, as we say, more inclined to run the school for themselves. The parents are very much at fault. The children are not used to taking orders at home and naturally they won't take them at school either.

Teachers develop methods of dealing with these discipline problems, and the methods tend to vary between social-class groups as do the problems themselves. The basic device used by successful disciplinarians is to establish authority clearly on the first meeting with the class:

> You can't ever let them get the upper hand on you or you're through. So I start out tough. The first day I get a new class in, I let them know who's boss. . . . You've got to start off tough, then you can ease up as you go along. If you start out easy-going, when you try to get tough they'll just look at you and laugh.

Having once established such a relation, teachers believe you must be consistent in your behavior so that the children will continue to respect and obey you:

> I let them know I mean business. That's one thing you must do. Say nothing that you won't follow through on. Some teachers will say anything to keep kids quiet, they'll threaten anything. Then they can't or won't carry out their threats. Naturally, the children won't pay any attention to them after that. You must never say anything that you won't back up.

In the difficult "slum" schools, teachers feel the necessity of stern measures, up to and including physical violence (nominally outlawed):

Technically you're not supposed to lay a hand on a kid. Well, they don't, technically. But there are a lot of ways of handling a kid so that it doesn't show—and then it's the teacher's word against the kid's, so the kid hasn't got a chance. Like dear Mrs.——. She gets mad at a kid, she takes him out in the hall. She gets him stood up against the wall. Then she's got a way of chucking the kid under the chin, only hard, so that it knocks his head back against the wall. It doesn't leave a mark on him. But when he comes back in that room he can hardly see straight, he's so knocked out. It's really rough. There's a lot of little tricks like that that you learn about.

Where such devices are not used, teachers resort to violent verbal punishment, "tongue lashings." All teachers, however, are not emotionally equipped for such behavior and must find other means:

The worst thing I can do is lose my temper and start raving. . . . You've got to believe in that kind of thing in order for it to work. . . . If you don't honestly believe it it shows up and the children know you don't mean it and it doesn't do any good anyway. . . . I try a different approach myself. Whenever they get too rowdy I go to the piano and . . . play something and we have rhythms or something until they sort of settle down. . . . That's what we call "softsoaping" them. It seems to work for me. It's about the only thing I can do.

Some teachers may also call in the parents, a device whose usefulness is limited, since such summons are most frequently ignored. The teacher's disciplinary power in such a school is also limited by her fear of retaliation by the students: "Those fellows are pretty big, and I just think it would take a bigger person than me to handle them. I certainly wouldn't like to try."

Children of the middle group require no strong sanctions, mild reprimands sufficing:

Now the children at Z—— here are quite nice to teach. They're pliable, yes, that's the word, they're pliable. They will go along with you on things and not fight you. You can take them any place and say to them, "I'm counting on you not to disgrace your school. Let's see that Z—— spirit." And they'll behave for you. . . . They can be frightened, they have fear in them. They're pliable, flexible, you can do things with them. They're afraid of their parents and what they'll do to them if they get into trouble at school. And they're afraid of the administration. They're afraid of being sent down to the principal. So that they can be handled.

Children of the upper group often act in a way which may be interpreted as "misbehavior" but which does not represent a conscious attack on the teacher's authority. Many teachers disregard such activity by interpreting it as a natural concomitant of the "brightness" and "intelligence" of such children. Where such an interpretation is not possible the teachers feel hampered by a lack of effective sanctions:

> I try different things like keeping them out of a gym period or a recess period. But that doesn't always work. I have this one little boy who just didn't care when I used those punishments. He said he didn't like the gym anyway. I don't know what I'm going to do with him.

The teacher's power in such schools is further limited because the children can mobilize their influential parents so as to exert a large degree of control over the actions of school personnel.

It should be noted, finally, that discipline problems tend to become less important as the length of the teacher's stay in a particular school makes it possible for her to build a reputation which coerces the children into behaving without attempting any test of strength:[11]

> I have no trouble with the children. Once you establish a reputation and they know what to expect, they respect you and you have no trouble. Of course, that's different for a new teacher, but when you're established that's no problem at all.

Moral Acceptability

Some actions of one's potential clients may offend some deeply felt set of moral standards; these clients are thus morally unacceptable. Teachers find that some of their pupils act in such a way as to violate moral values centered around health and cleanliness, sex and aggression, ambition and work, and the relations of age groups.

Children of the middle group present no problem, being universally described as clean, well dressed, moderate in their behavior, and hard working. Children from the "better" neighborhoods are considered deficient in the important moral traits of politeness and respect for elders:

> Here the children come from wealthy homes. That's not so good either. They're not used to doing work at home. They have maids and servants of all kinds and they're used to having things done for them, instead of doing them themselves. . . . They won't do anything. For instance, if they drop a piece of cloth on the floor, they'll just let it lay, they wouldn't think of bending over to pick it up. That's janitor's work to them. As a matter of fact, one

11. This is part of the process of job adjustment described in detail in Howard S. Becker, "The Career of the Chicago Public School Teacher," in this volume.

of them said to me once: "If I pick that up there wouldn't be any work for the janitor to do." Well it's pretty difficult to deal with children like that.

Further, they are regarded as likely to transgress what the teachers define as moral boundaries in the matter of smoking and drinking; they are particularly shocked that such "nice" children should have such vices.

The "slum" child most deeply offends the teacher's moral sensibilities; in almost every area mentioned above these children, by word, action, or appearance, manage to give teachers the feeling that they are immoral and not respectable. Their physical appearance and condition disgust and depress the middle-class teacher. Even this young woman, whose emancipation from conventional morality is symbolized in her habitual use of the argot of the jazz musician, was horrified by the absence of the toothbrush from the lives of her lower-class students:

> It's just horribly depressing, you know. I mean, it just gets you down. I'll give you an example. A kid complained of a toothache one day. Well, I thought I could take a look and see if I could help him or something so I told him to open his mouth. I almost wigged when I saw his mouth. His teeth were all rotten, every one of them. Just filthy and rotten. Man, I mean, I was really shocked, you know. I said, "Don't you have a toothbrush?" He said no, they were only his baby teeth and Ma said he didn't need a toothbrush for that. So I really got upset and looked in all their mouths. Man, I never saw anything like it. They were all like that, practically. I asked how many had toothbrushes, and about a quarter of them had them. Boy, that's terrible. And I don't dig that crap about baby teeth either, because they start getting molars when they're six, I know that. So I gave them a talking to, but what good does it do? The kid's mouth was just rotten. They never heard of a toothbrush or going to a dentist.

These children, too, are more apt than the other groups to be dishonest in some way that will get them into trouble with law enforcement officials. The early (by middle-class standards) sexual maturity of such children upsets the teacher:

> One thing about these girls is, well, some of them are not very nice girls. One girl in my class I've had two years now. She makes her money on the side as a prostitute. She's had several children. . . . This was a disturbing influence on the rest of the class.

Many teachers reported great shock on finding that words which were innocent to them had obscene meanings for their lower-class students:

> I decided to read them a story one day. I started reading them "Puss in Boots" and they just burst out laughing. I couldn't understand what I had

said that had made them burst out like that. I went back over the story and tried to find out what it might be. I couldn't see anything that would make them laugh. I couldn't see anything at all in the story. Later one of the other teachers asked me what had happened. She was one of the older teachers. I told her that I didn't know; that I was just reading them a story and they thought it was extremely funny. She asked me what story I read them and I told her "Puss in the Boots." She said, "Oh, I should have warned you not to read that one." It seems that Puss means something else to them. It means something awful—I wouldn't even tell you what. It doesn't mean a thing to us.[12]

Warner, Havighurst, and Loeb note that "unless the middle-class values change in America, we must expect the influence of the schools to favor the values of material success, individual striving, thrift, and social mobility."[13] Here again, the "slum" child violates the teacher's moral sense by failing to display these virtues:

Many of these children don't realize the worth of an education. They have no desire to improve themselves. And they don't care much about school and schoolwork as a result. That makes it very difficult to teach them.

That kind of problem is particularly bad in a school like ———. That's not a very privileged school. It's very under-privileged, as a matter of fact. So we have a pretty tough element there, a bunch of bums, I might as well say it. That kind you can't teach at all. They don't want to be there at all, and so you can't do anything with them. And even many of the others—they're simply indifferent to the advantages of education. So they're indifferent, they don't care about their homework.

This behavior of the lower-class child repels the teacher all the more because she finds it incomprehensible; she cannot conceive that any normal human being would act so. This teacher stresses the anxiety aroused in the inexperienced teacher by her inability to provide herself with a rational explanation for her pupils' behavior:

We had one of the girls who just came to the school last year and she used to come and talk to me quite a bit. I know that it was just terrible for her. You know, I don't think she'd ever had anything to do with Negroes before she got there and she was just mystified, didn't know what to do. She was bewildered. She came to me one day almost in tears and said, "But they don't want to learn, they don't even want to learn. Why is that?" Well, she had me there.

12. Interview by Miriam Wagenschein. The lack of common meanings in this situation symbolizes the great cultural and moral distance between teacher and "slum" child.

13. Warner, Havighurst, and Loeb. *op. cit.,* p. 172.

Note that the behavior of the "better" children, even when morally un-acceptable, distresses the teacher less, because she feels that, in this case, she can produce a reasonable explanation for the behavior. An example of such an explanation is the following:

> I mean, they're spoiled, you know. A great many of them are only children. Naturally, they're used to having their own way, and they don't like to be told what to do. Well, if a child is in a room that I'm teaching he's going to be told what to do, that's all there is to it. Or if they're not spoiled that way, they're the second child and they never got the affection the first one did, not that their mother didn't love them, but they didn't get as much affection, so they're not so easy to handle either.

IV

School teachers experience problems in working with their students to the degree that those students fail to exhibit in reality the qualities of the image of the ideal pupil teachers hold. In a stratified urban society many groups, by virtue of their life-style and culture, produce children who do not meet the standards of this image, and who are thus impossible for teachers like these to work with effectively. Programs of action intended to increase the educational opportunities of the under-privileged in our society should take account of the way teachers interpret and react to the cultural traits of this group, and the institutional consequences of their behavior.[14] Such programs might profitably aim at producing teachers who can cope effectively with the problems of teaching this group and not, by their reactions to class differences, perpetuate the existing inequities.

A more general statement of the findings is now in order. Professionals depend on their environing society to provide them with clients who meet the standards of their image of the ideal client. Social class cultures, among other factors, may operate to produce many clients who, in one way or another, fail to meet these specifications and therefore aggravate one or another of the basic problems of the worker-client relation (three were considered in this paper).

In attacking this problem we touch on one of the basic elements of the relation between institutions and society, for the differences between ideal and reality place in high relief the implicit assumptions which insti-tutions, through their functionaries, make about the society around them. All institutions have embedded in them some set of assumptions about the

---

14. One of the important institutional consequences of these class preferences is a constant movement of teachers away from lower-class schools, which prevents these schools from retaining experienced teachers and from maintaining some continuity in teaching and administration.

nature of the society and the individuals with whom they deal, and we must get at these assumptions, and their embodiment in actual social interaction, in order fully to understand these organizations. We can, perhaps, best begin our work on this problem by studying those institutions which, like the school, make assumptions which have high visibility because of their variation from reality.

CHAPTER TEN

The Teacher
in the Authority System
of the Public School

We can think of institutions as forms of collective action which are somewhat firmly established.[1] These forms consist of the organized and related
activities of several socially defined categories of people. In service institutions (like the school) the major categories of people so defined are those
who do the work of the institution, its functionaries, and those for whom
the work is done, its clients. These categories are often subdivided, so that
there may be several categories of functionaries and several varieties of
client.

One aspect of the institutional organization of activity is a division of
authority, a set of shared understandings specifying the amount and kind
of control each kind of person involved in the institution is to have over
others: who is allowed to to do what, and who may give orders to whom.
This authority is subject to stresses and possible change to the degree that
participants ignore the shared understandings and refuse to act on them.
A chronic feature of service institutions is the indifference or ignorance of
the client with regard to the authority system set up by institutional functionaries; this stems from the fact that he looks at the institutions operation
from other perspectives and with other interests.[2] In addition to the prob-

Reprinted by permission from *Journal of Educational Sociology,* 27 (November
1953), pp. 128–141. Copyright 1953 American Sociological Association.

1. Cf. E. C. Hughes, "The Study of Istitutions," *Social Forces* 20 (March 1942),
307–310.
2. See my earlier statement in "The Professional Dance Musician and His Audience," *American Journal of Sociology* 57 (September 1951), 136–144.

lems of authority which arise in the internal life of any organization, the service institution's functionaries must deal with such problems in the client relationship as well. One of their preoccupations tends to be the maintenance of their authority definitions over those of clients, in order to assure a stable and congenial work setting.

This paper deals with the authority problems of the metropolitan public school teacher. I have already described the problems of the teacher in her relations with her pupils,[3] and will here continue that discussion to include the teacher's relations with parents, principals, and other teachers. I consider the following points in connection with each of these relationships: the teacher's conception of her rights and prerogatives, her problems in getting and maintaining acceptance of this conception on the part of others, and the methods used to handle such problems. The picture one should get is that of the teacher striving to maintain what she regards as her legitimate sphere of authority in the fact of possible challenge by others. This analysis of the working authority system of the public school is followed by a discussion which attempts to point up its more general relevance.

Teacher and Parent

The teacher conceives of herself as a professional with specialized training and knowledge in the field of her school activity: teaching and taking care of children. To her, the parent is a person who lacks such background and therefore cannot understand her problems properly. Such a person, as the following quotation shows, is considered to have no legitimate right to interfere with the work of the school in any way:

> One thing, I don't think a parent should try and tell you what to do in your classroom, or interfere in any way with your teaching. I don't think that's right and I would never permit it. After all, I've a special education to fit me to do what I'm doing, and a great deal of them have never had any education at all, to speak of, and even if they did, they certainly haven't had my experience. So I would never let a parent interfere with my teaching.

Hers is the legitimate authority in the classroom and the parent should not interfere with it.

Problems of authority appear whenever parents challenge this conception, and are potentially present whenever parents become involved in the school's operation. They become so involved because the teacher attempts to make use of them to bolster her authority over the child, or because they become aware of some event about which they wish to complain. In either

---

3. Howard S. Becker, "Social-Class Variations in the Teacher-Pupil Relationship," in this volume.

case the teacher fears a possible challenge of her basic assumption that the parent has no legitimate voice with regard to what is done to her child in school.

In the first instance, the teacher may try to secure the parent's help in dealing with a "problem child." But this is always done with an eye to possible consequences for her authority. Thus, teachers avoid this expedient with parents of higher social-class position, who may not only fail to help solve the problem but may actually accuse the teacher of being the source of the problem and defend the child, thus materially weakening the teacher's power over her children:

> You've got these parents who, you know, they don't think that their child could do anything wrong, can't conceive of it. If a teacher has to reprimand their child for something they're up in arms right away, it couldn't be that the child did anything wrong, it must be the teacher. So it's a lot of bother. And the children come from those kind of homes, so you can imagine that they're the same way.

The teacher feels more secure with lower-class parents, whom she considers less likely challengers. But they usually fail to help solve the problem, either ignoring the teacher's requests or responding in a way that increases the problem or is personally distasteful to the teacher.

> [They] have a problem child, but you can't get them to school for love or money. You can send notes home, you can write letters, you can call up, but they just won't come.
> If you send for [the child's] parents, they're liable to beat the child or something. I've seen a mother bring an ironing cord to school and beat her child with it, right in front of me. And, of course, that's not what you want at all.

This tactic, then, is ordinarily dangerous in the sense that the teacher's authority may be undermined by its consequences. Where it is not dangerous, it tends to be useless for strengthening authority over the child. This reinforces the notion that the parent has no place in the school.

Parents may also become involved in the school's operation on their own initiative, when they come to complain about some action of the school's functionaries. Teachers recognize that there are kinds of activity about which parents have a legitimate right to complain, for which they may legitimately be held responsible, although they greatly fear the consequences of the exercise of this right. They recognize, that is, that the community, in giving them a mandate to teach, reserves the right to interfere when that mandate is not acted on in the "proper" manner. As Cooley put it:

The rule of public opinion, then, means for the most part a latent authority which the public will exercise when sufficiently dissatisfied with the specialist who is in charge of a particular function.[4]

Teacher fear that the exercise of this latent authority by parents will be dangerous to them.

One form of fear is that one will be held responsible for any physical harm that befalls the child:

As far as the worst thing that could happen to me here in school, I'd say it would be if something awful happened someplace where I was supposed to be and wasn't. That would be terrible.

This, it is obvious, is more than a concern for the child's welfare. It is also a concern that the teacher not be held responsible for that welfare in such a way as to give the parents cause for complaint, as the following incident makes clear:

I've never had any trouble like that when the children were in my care. Of course, if it happens on the playground or someplace where I'm not there to watch, then it's not my responsibility, you see. . . . My children have had accidents. Last year, two of the little boys got into a fight. They were out on the playground and Ronald gave Nick a little push, you know, and one thing led to another and pretty soon Nick threw a big stone at Ronald and cut the back of his head open. It was terrible to happen, but it wasn't my fault, I wasn't out there when it happened and wasn't supposed to be. . . . Now if it had happened in my room when I was in there or should have been in there, that's different, then I would be responsible and I'd have had something to worry about. That's why I'm always careful when there's something like that might happen. For instance, when we have work with scissors I always am on my toes and keep looking over the whole room in case anything should happen like that.

A similar fear that the parents will exercise their legitimate latent authority arises in the area of teaching competence; the following incident is the kind that provokes such fears:

There was a French teacher—well, there's no question about it, the old man was senile. He was getting near retirement. I think he was sixty-four and had one year to go to retire. The parents began to complain that he couldn't teach. That was true, of course, he couldn't teach any more. He'd just get up in front of his classes and sort of mumble along. Well, the parents came to school and put so much pressure on that they had to get rid of him.

4. Charles Horton Cooley, *Social Organization* (New York: Charles Scribner's Sons, 1927), p. 131.

Teachers fear, in these and similar situations, that intrusion by the parents, even on legitimate grounds, will damage their authority position and make them subject to forms of control that are, for them, illegitimate —control by outsiders. They fear this most with high class groups, who are considered quick to complain and challenge the school's authority. They think such parents organized and militant and, consequently, dangerous. In the lower-class school, on the other hand:

> We don't have any PTA at all. You see, most of the parents work; in most families it's both parents who work. So that there can't be much of a PTA.

These parents are not likely to interfere.

To illustrate the point, one teacher told a story of one of her pupils stabbing another with a scissors, and contrasted the reaction of the lower-class mother with that to be expected from the parents of higher status whose children she now taught:

> I sure expected the Momma to show up, but she never showed. I guess the Negroes are so used to being squelched that they just take it as a matter of course, you know, and never complain about anything. Momma never showed up at all. You take a neighborhood like the one I'm teaching in now, why, my God, they'd be suing the Board of Education and me, and there'd be a court trial and everything.

It is because of dangers like this that movement to a school in such a neighborhood, desirable as it might be for other reasons, is feared.[5]

The school is for the teacher, then, a place in which the entrance of the parent on the scene is always potentially dangerous. People faced with chronic potential danger ordinarily develop some means of handling it should it become "real" rather than "potential," some kind of defense. I consider the more elaborate defenses below. Here I want to point to the existence of devices which teachers develop or grow into which allow them some means of defense in face-to-face interaction with the parent.

These devices operate by building up in the parent's mind an image of herself and of her relation to the teacher which leads her to respect the teacher's authority and subordinate herself to it:

> Quite often the offense is a matter of sassiness or back-talk. . . . So I'll explain to the parent, and tell him that the child has been sassy and disrespectful. And I ask them if they would like to be treated like that if they came to a group of children. . . . I say, "Now I can tell just by looking at you, though

5. See Howard S. Becker, "The Career of the Chicago Public School Teacher," in this volume.

I've never met you before, that you're not the kind of a person who wants this child to grow up to be disrespectful like that. You want the child to grow up mannerly and polite." Well, when I put it to them that way, there's never any argument about it. . . . Of course, I don't mean that I'm not sincere when I say those things, because I most certainly am. But still, they have that effect on those people.

The danger may also be reduced when the teacher, over a period of years, grows into a kind of relationship with the parents of the community which minimizes the possibilities of conflict and challenge:

If you have a teacher who's been in a school twenty years, say, why she's known in that community. Like as not she's had some of the parents as pupils. They know her and they are more willing to help her in handling the children than if they didn't know who she was.

If the teacher works in the same neighborhood that she lives in she may acquire a similar advantage, although there is some evidence that the degree of advantage is a function of the teacher's age. Where she is a middle-aged woman whose neighborhood social life is carried on with those women of similar age who are the parents of her pupils, the relationship gives her a distinct advantage in dealing with those same women in the school situation. If, however, she is a younger woman, parents may regard her as "a kid from the neighborhood" and treat her accordingly, and the danger of her authority being successfully challenged is that much greater.

In short, the teacher wishes to avoid any dispute over her authority with parents and feels this can be accomplished best when the parent gets involved in the school's operation no more than absolutely necessary. The devices described are used to handle the "parent problem" when it arises, but none of them are foolproof and every teacher is aware of the ever-present possibility of a parent intruding and endangering her authority. This constant danger creates a need for defenses and the relations of teacher and principal and of teachers to one another are shaped by this need. The internal organization of the school may be seen as a system of defenses against parental intrusion.

Teacher and Principal

The principal is accepted as the supreme authority in the school:

After all, he's the principal, he is the boss, what he says should go, you know what I mean. . . . He's the principal and he's the authority, and you have to follow his orders. That's all there is to it.

This is true no matter how poorly he fills the position. The office contains the authority, which is legitimated by the same principles of professional education and experience the teacher uses to legitimate her authority over parents.

But this acceptance of superiority has limits. Teachers have a well-developed conception of just how and toward what ends the principal's authority should be used, and conflict arises when he uses it without regard for the teacher's expectations. These expectations are especially clear with regard to the teacher's relationships with parents and pupils, where the principal is expected to act to uphold the teacher's authority no matter what the circumstances. Failure to do this produces dissatisfaction and conflict, for such action by the principal is considered one of the most efficient defenses against attack on authority, whether from parents or pupils.

The principal is expected to "back the teacher up"—support her authority—in all cases of parental "interference." This is, for teachers, one of the major criteria of a "good" principal. In this next quotation the teacher reacts to the failure of a principal to provide this:

> That's another thing the teachers have against her. She really can't be counted on to back you up against a child or a parent. She got one of our teachers most irate with her, and I can't say I blame her. The child was being very difficult and it ended up with a conference with the parent, principal, and teacher. And the principal had the nerve to say to the parent that she couldn't understand the difficulty, none of the other teachers who had the child had ever had any trouble. Well, that was nothing but a damn lie, if you'll excuse me. . . . And everybody knew it was a lie. . . . And the principal knew it too, she must have. And yet she had the nerve to stand there and say that in front of the teacher and the parent. She should never have done that at all, even if it was true she shouldn't have said it. [Interviewer: What was the right thing to do?] Well, naturally, what she should have done is to stand behind the teacher all the way. Otherwise, the teacher loses face with the kids and with the parents and that makes it harder for her to keep order or anything from then on.

This necessity for support is independent of the legitimacy of the teacher's action; she can be punished later, but without parents knowing about it. And the principal should use any means necessary to preserve authority, lying himself or supporting the teacher's lies:

> You could always count on him to back you up. If a parent came to school hollering that a teacher had struck her child, Mr. D—— would handle it. He'd say, "Why, Mrs. So-and-So, I'm sure you must be mistaken. I can't believe that any of our teachers would do a thing like that. Of course, I'll look into the matter and do what's necessary but I'm sure you've made a mistake. You know how children are." And he'd go on like that until he had talked them out of the whole thing.

Of course the teacher would certainly catch it later. He'd call them down to the office and really give them a tongue lashing that they wouldn't forget. But he never failed them when it came to parents.

Not all principals live up to this expectation. Teachers attribute their failure to provide support to cowardice, "liberalism," or an unfortunate ability to see both sides of a question. The witholding of support may also, however, be a deliberate gesture of disapproval and punishment. This undermining of the teacher's authority is one of the most extreme and effective sanctions at the principal's command:

[The teacher had started a class project in which the class, boys and girls, made towels to be given to the parents as Christmas presents.] We were quite well along in our project when in walked this principal one day. And did she give it to me! Boy! She wanted to know what the idea was. I told her it was our Christmas project and that I didn't see anything the matter with it. Well, she fussed and fumed. Finally, she said, "Alright, you may continue. But I warn you if there are any complaints by fathers to the Board downtown about one of our teachers making sissies out of their boys you will have to take the full responsibility for it. I'm not going to take any responsibility for this kind of thing." And out she marched.

Teachers expect the same kind of support and defense in their dealings with pupils, again without regard for the justice of any particular student complaint. If the students find the principal a friendly court of appeal, it is much harder for the teacher to maintain control over them.[6]

The amount of threat to authority, in the form of challenges to classroom control, appears to teachers to be directly related to the principal's strictness. Where he fails to act impressively "tough" the school has a restless atmosphere and control over pupils is difficult to attain. The opposite is true where the children know that the principal will support any action of a teacher.

The children are scared to death of her [the principal]. All she has to do is walk down the hall and let the children hear her footsteps and right away the children would perk up and get very attentive. They're really afraid of her. But it's better that way than the other.

Such a principal can materially minimize the discipline problem, and is especially prized in the lower-class school, where this problem is greatest.

6. Cf. *The Sociology of Georg Simmel,* trans. Kurt Wolff (Glencoe, Ill.: Free Press, 1950), p. 235: "The position of the subordinate in regard to his superordinate is favorable if the latter, in his turn, is subordinate to a still higher authority in which the former finds support."

The principal provides this solid underpinning for the teachers' authority over pupils by daily acts of "toughness," daily reaffirmations of his intention to keep the children "in line." The following quotation contrasts successful and unsuccessful principal activity in this area:

> For instance, let's take a case where a teacher sends a pupil down to the office. . . . When you send a child down to this new principal, he goes down there and he sits on the bench there. . . . Pretty soon, the clerk needs a messenger and she sees this boy sitting there. Well, she sends him running all over the school. That's no punishment as far as he's concerned. Not at all.
>
> The old principal didn't do things that way. If a child was sent down to the office he knew he was in for a rough time and he didn't like it much. Mr. G—— would walk out of his office and look over the children sitting on the bench and I mean he'd look right through them, each of them. You could just see them shiver when he looked at them. Then he'd walk back in the office and they could see him going over papers, writing. Then, he'd send for them, one at a time. And he'd give them a lecture, a real lecture. Then he'd give them some punishment, like writing an essay on good manners and memorizing it so they could come and recite it to him the next day by heart. Well, that was effective. They didn't like being sent to Mr. G——. When you sent someone there that was the end of it. They didn't relish the idea of going there another time. That's the kind of backing up a teacher likes to feel she can count on.

The principal is expected to support all teachers in this way, even the chronic complainers who do not deserve it:

> If the principal's any good he knows that the complaints of a woman like that don't mean anything but he's got to back her just the same. But he knows that when a teacher is down complaining about students twice a week that there's nothing the matter with the students, there's something the matter with her. And he knows that if a teacher comes down once a semester with a student that the kid has probably committed a real crime, really done something bad. And his punishments will vary accordingly.

The teacher's authority is subject to attack by pupils and may be strengthened or weakened depending on which way the principal throws the weight of his authority. Teachers expect the principal to throw it their way, and provide them with a needed defense.

The need for recognition of their independent professional authority informs teachers' conceptions of the principal's supervisory role. It is legitimate for him to give professional criticism, but only in a way that preserves this professional authority. He should give "constructive" rather than "arbitrary" orders, "ask" rather than "snoop." It is the infringement of authority that is the real distinction in these pairs of terms. For example:

You see, a principal ought to give you good supervision. He ought to go around and visit his teachers and see how they're doing—come and sit in the room awhile and then if he has any constructive criticism to make, speak to the teacher about it privately later. Not this nagging bitching that some of them go in for, you know what I mean, but real constructive criticism.

But I've seen some of those bastards that would go so far as to really bawl someone out in public. Now that's a terrible thing to do. They don't care who it's in front of, either. It might be a parent, or it might be other teachers, or it might even be the kids. That's terrible but they actually do it.

Conflict arises when the principal ignores his teachers' need for professional independence and defense against attacks on authority. Both principal and teachers command sanctions which may be used to win such a conflict and establish their definition of the situation: i.e., they have available means for controlling each other's behavior. The principal has, as noted above, the powerful weapon of refusing to support the teacher in crucial situations; but this has the drawback of antagonizing other teachers and, also, is not available to a principal whose trouble with teachers stems from his initial failure to do this.

The principal's administrative functions provide him with his most commonly used sanctions. As administrator he allocates extra work of various kinds, equipment, rooms, and (in the elementary school) pupils to his teachers. In each category, some things are desired by teachers while others are disliked—some rooms are better than others, some equipment newer. By distributing the desired things to a given teacher's disadvantage, the principal can effectively discipline her. Here is a subtle use of such sanctions:

> TEACHER: That woman really used to run the school, too. You had to do just what she said.
> INTERVIEWER: What did she do if you "disobeyed?"
> TEACHER: There were lots of things she could do. She had charge of assigning children to their new rooms when they passed. If she didn't like you she could really make it tough for you. You'd get all the slow children and all the behavior problems, the dregs of the school. After six months of that you'd really know what work meant. She had methods like that.

Such sanctions fail with those few teachers who are either eccentric or determined enough to ignore them. They may also fail in lower-class schools where the teacher does not intend to stay.[7]

The sanctions teachers can apply to a principal who respects or protects their authority are somewhat less direct. They may just ignore him: "After all if the principal gets to be too big a bother, all you have to do is walk in

7. See Becker, "The Career of the Chicago Public School Teacher," *op cit.*

your room and shut the door, and he can't bother you." Another weapon is hardly a weapon at all—making use of the power to request transfer to another school in the system. It achieves its force when many teachers use it, presumably causing higher authorities to question the principal's ability:

> I know of one instance, a principal of that type, practically every teacher in her school asked to leave. Well, you might think that was because of a group that just didn't get along with the new principal. But when three or four sets of teachers go through a school like that, then you know something's wrong.

Finally, the teachers may collectively agree on a line of passive resistance, and just do things their way, without any reference to the principal's desires.

In some cases of extreme conflict the teachers (some of whom may have been located in the school for a longer period than the principal) may use their connections in the community to create sentiment against the principal. Cooperative action of parents and teachers directed toward the principal's superiors is the teachers' ultimate sanction.

The principal, then, is expected to provide a defense against parental interference and student revolt, by supporting and protecting the teacher whenever her authority is challenged. He is expected, in his supervisory role, to respect the teacher's independence. When he does not do these things a conflict may arise. Both parties to the conflict have at their disposal effective means of controlling the other's behavior, so that the ordinary situation is one of compromise (if there is a dispute at all), with sanctions being used only when the agreed-on boundaries are overstepped.

Colleague Relations

Teachers believe they ought to cooperate to defend themselves against authority attacks and to refrain from directly endangering the authority of another teacher. Teachers, like other work groups, develop a sense that they share a similar position and common dangers, and this provides them with a feeling of colleagueship that makes them amenable to influence in these directions by fellow teachers.

Challenging another teacher so as to diminsh her authority is the basic crime:

> For one thing, you must never question another teacher's grade, no matter if you know it's unjustified. That just wouldn't do. There are some teachers that mark unfairly. A girl, or say a boy, will have a four "S" report book and this woman will mark it a "G." . . . Well, I hate to see them get a deal like that, but there's nothing you can do.

Another teacher put it more generally: "For one thing, no teacher should ever disagree with another teacher or contradict her, in front of a pupil." The result for authority vis-a-vis students is feared: "Just let another teacher raise her eyebrow funny, just so they [the children] know, and they don't miss a thing, and their respect for you goes down right away." With regard to authority threats by parents teachers agree that they should not try to cast responsibility for actions which may provoke parental interference on another teacher.

Since teachers work in separate rooms and deal with their own groups of parents and pupils, it is hard for another teacher to get the opportunity to break these rules, even if she were so inclined. This difficulty is increased by an informal rule against entering another teacher's room while she is teaching. Breaches of these rules are rare and, when they do occur, are usually a kind of punishment aimed at a colleague disliked for exceeding the group work quotas or for more personal reasons. However, the danger inherent in such an action—that it may affect your own authority in some way or be employed against you—is so feared that it is seldom used.

In short, teachers can depend on each other to "act right" in authority situations, because of colleague feeling, lack of opportunity to act "wrong," and fear of the consequences of such action.

Discussion

I have presented the teacher as a person who is concerned (among other things) with maintaining what she considers to be her legitimate authority over pupils and parents, with avoiding and defending against challenges from these sources. In her view, the principal and other teachers should help her build a system of defenses against such challenges. Through feelings of colleagueship and the use of various kinds of sanctions, they organize a system of defenses and secrecy oriented toward preventing the intrusion of parents and children into the authority system.

This picture discloses certain points of general relevance for the study of institutional authority systems. In the first place, an institution like the school can be seen as a small, self-contained system of social control. Its functionaries (principal and teachers) are able to control one another; each has some power to influence the others' conduct. This creates a stable and predictable work setting, in which the limits of behavior for every individual are known, and in which one can build a satisfactory authority position of which he can be sure, knowing that he has certain methods of controlling those who ignore his authority.

In contrast the activities of those outside the professional group are not involved in such a network of mutual understanding and control. Parents do not necessarily share the values by which the teacher legitimates her authority. And while parents can apply sanctions to the teacher, the teacher has no means of control she can use in return, in direct retaliation.

To the teacher, then, the parent appears as an unpredictable and uncontrollable element, a force which endangers and may even destroy the existing authority system over which she has some measure of control. For this reason, teachers (and principals who abide by their expectations) carry on an essentially secretive relationship vis-a-vis parents and the community, trying to prevent any event which will give these groups a permanent place of authority in the school situation. The emphasis on never admitting mistakes of school personnel to parents is an attempt to prevent these outsiders (who would not be subject to teacher control) from getting any excuse which might justify their intrusion into and possible destruction of the existing authority system.

This suggests the general proposition that the relations of institutional functionaries to one another are relations of mutual influence and control, and that outsiders are systematically prevented from exerting any authority over the institution's operations because they are not involved in this web of control and would literally be uncontrollable, and destructive of the institutional organization, as the functionaries desire it to be preserved, if they were allowed such authority.[8]

---

8. Cf. Max Weber: "Bureaucratic administration always tends to be an administration of 'secret sessions': in so far as it can, it hides its knowledge and action from criticism . . . the tendency toward secrecy in certain administrative fields follows their material nature: everywhere that the power interests of the domiantion structure toward *the outside* are at stake . . . we find secrecy." H. H. Gerth and C. Wright Mills, eds. and trans., *From Max Weber: Essays in Sociology* (New York: Oxford University Press, 1946), p. 233.

CHAPTER ELEVEN

The Career
of the Chicago
Public School Teacher

The concept of *career* has proved of great use in understanding and analyzing the dynamics of work organizations and the movement and fate of individuals within them. The term refers, to paraphrase Hall, to the patterned series of adjustments made by the individual to the "network of institutions, formal organizations, and informal relationships"[1] in which the work of the occupation is performed. This series of adjustments is typically considered in terms of movement up or down between positions differentiated by their rank in some formal or informal hierarchy of prestige, influence, and income. The literature in the field has devoted itself primarily to an analysis of the types, stages, and contingencies of careers, so conceived, in various occupations.[2] We may refer to such mobility through a hierarchy of ranked positions, if a spatial metaphor be allowed, as the *vertical* aspect of the career.

By focusing our attention on this aspect of career movement, we may tend to overlook what might, in contrast, be called the *horizontal* aspect of

---

Reprinted by permission from *American Journal of Sociology*, 57 (March 1952), pp. 470–477. Copyright 1952 by The University of Chicago Press.

1. Oswald Hall, "The Stages of a Medical Career," *American Journal of Sociology* 53 (March 1948), 327.
2. See Everett C. Hughes, "Institutional Office and the Person," *American Journal of Sociology* 43 (November 1937), 404–413; Hall, *op. cit.*, and "Types of Medical Careers," *American Journal of Sociology* 55 (November 1949), 243–253; and Melville Dalton, "Informal Factors in Career Achievement," *American Journal of Sociology* (March 1951), 407–415.

the career: movement among the positions available at one level of such a hierarchy. We need not assume that occupational positions which share some characteristics because of their similar rank in a formal structure are identical in all respects. They may, in fact, differ widely in the configuration of the occupation's basic problems which they present. That is, all positions at one level of a work hierarchy, while theoretically identical, may not be equally easy or rewarding places in which to work. Given this fact, people tend to move in patterned ways among the possible positions, seeking that situation which affords the most desirable setting in which to meet and grapple with the basic problems of their work. In some occupations more than others, and for some individuals more than others, this kind of career movement assumes greater importance that the vertical variety, sometimes to such an extent that the entire career line consists of movement entirely at one level of a work hierarchy.

The teachers of the Chicago public schools are a group whose careers typically tend toward this latter extreme. Although any educationally qualified teacher can take the examination for the position of principal and attempt ascent through the school system's administrative hierarchy, few make the effort. Most see their careers purely in teaching, in movement among the various schools in the Chicago system.[3] Even those attempting this kind of vertical mobility anticipate a stay of some years in the teacher category and, during that time, see that segment of their career in much the same way. This paper analyzes the nature of this area of career movement among teachers and describes the types of careers found in this group. These, of course, are not the only patterns which we may expect to find in this horizontal plane of career movement. It remains for further research in other occupations to discern other career varieties and the conditions under which each type occurs.

The Chicago School System

The positions open to a particular teacher in the system at a given time appear, in general, quite similar, all having about the same prestige, income, and power attached to them. This is not to deny the existence of variations in income created by the operation of seniority rules or of differences in informal power and prestige based on length of service and length of stay in a given school. The fact remains that, for an individual with a given amount of seniority who is about to begin in a school new to her, all teaching

---

3. The Chicago system has a high enough salary schedule and sufficient security safeguards to be safe as a system in which a person can make his entire career, thus differing from smaller school systems in which the teacher does not expect to spend her whole working life.

positions in the Chicago system are the same with regard to prestige, influence, and income.

Though the available teaching positions in the city schools are similar in formal characteristics, they differ widely in the configuration of the occupation's basic work problems they present. The teacher's career consists of movement among these various schools in search of the most satisfactory position to work in, the position in which the problems are least aggravated and most susceptible of solution. Work problems arise in the teacher's relations with the important categories of people in the structure of the school: children, parents, principal, and other teachers. Her most difficult problems arise in her interaction with her pupils. Teachers feel that the form and degree of the latter problems vary considerably with the social-class background of the students.

Let me summarize the teacher's view of these problems and of their relation to the various social-class groups which might furnish her with students. The interviewees typically distinguished three class groups: (1) a bottom stratum, probably equivalent to the lower-lower and parts of the upper-lower class,[4] and including, for the teacher, all Negroes; (2) and upper stratum, probably equivalent to the upper-middle class; and (3) a middle stratum, probably equivalent to the lower-middle and parts of the upper-lower class. Three major kinds of problems were described as arising in dealings with pupils: (1) the problem of *teaching,* producing some change in the child's skills and knowledge which can be attributed to one's own efforts; (2) the problem of *discipline,* maintaining order and control over the children's activity; and (3) the problem of *moral acceptability,* bringing one's self to bear some traits of the children which one considers immoral and revolting. The teacher believes the lowest group, "slum" children, difficult to teach, uncontrollable and violent in the sphere of discipline, and morally unacceptable on all scores, from physical cleanliness to the spheres of sex and "ambition to get ahead." Children of the upper group, from the "better neighborhoods," were felt to be quick learners and easy to teach but somewhat "spoiled" and difficult to control, and lacking in the important moral traits of politeness and respect for elders. Teachers thought the middle group hard-working but slow to learn, extremely easy to control, and most acceptable on the moral level.

Other important problems arise in interaction with parents, principal, and colleagues and revolve primarily around the issue of authority. Parents of the highest status groups and certain kinds of principals are extremely threatening to the authority the teacher feels basic to the maintenance of

4. The class categories used in this estimate are those used by W. Lloyd Warner and Paul Lunt in *The Social Life of a Modern Community* (New Haven, Conn.: Yale University Press, 1941).

her role; in certain situations colleagues, too, may act in such a way as to diminish her authority.

Thus, positions at the teaching level may be very satisfactory or highly undesirable, depending on the presence or absence of the "right" kind of pupils, parents, principal, and colleagues. Where any of these positions are filled by the "wrong" kind of person, the teacher feels that she is in an unfavorable situation in which to deal with the important problems of her work. Teachers in schools of this kind are dissatisfied and wish to move to schools where "working conditions" will be more satisfactory.

Career movement for the Chicago teacher is, in essence, movement from one school to another, some schools being more and others less satisfactory places in which to work. Such movement is accomplished under the Board of Education's rules governing transfer, which allow a teacher, after serving in a position for more than a year, to request transfer to one of as many as ten other positions. Movement to one of these positions is possible when an opening occurs for which there is no applicant whose request is of longer standing, and transfer takes place upon approval by the principal of the new school.

The career patterns found in this social matrix may not be typical of all career movements of this horizontal type. It is likely that their presence will be limited to occupational organizations which, like the Chicago school system, are impersonal and bureaucratic and in which mobility is accomplished primarily through the manipulation of formal procedures.

Career Patterns

The greatest problems of work occur in lower-class schools and, consequently, most movement in the system results from dissatisfaction with the social-class composition of these school populations. Movement in the system, then, tends to be out from the "slums" to the "better" neighborhoods, primarily because of the characteristics of the pupils. Since there are few or no requests for transfer to "slum" schools, the need for teachers is filled by the assignment to such schools of teachers beginning careers in the Chicago system. Thus, the new teacher typically begins her career in the least desirable kind of school.[5] From this beginning two major types or careers develop.

The first variety of career is characterized by an immediate attempt to

5. Further documentation of this point may be found in Miriam Wagenschein, "Reality Shock" (Master's thesis, University of Chicago, 1951), and in John Winget, "Teacher Interschool Mobility Aspirations: Elementary Teachers, Chicago Public School System, 1947–48." Unpublished Ph.D. dissertation, University of Chicago, 1952.

move to a "better" school in a "better" neighborhood. The majority of interviewees reporting first assignment to a "slum" school had already made or were in the process of making such a transfer. The attitude is well put in this quotation:

When you first get assigned you almost naturally get assigned to one of those poorer schools, because those naturally are among the first to have openings because people are always transferring out of them to other schools. Then you go and request to be transferred to other schools nearer your home or in some nicer neighborhood. Naturally the vacancies don't come as quickly in those schools because people want to stay there once they get there. I think that every teacher strives to get into a nicer neighborhood.

Making a successful move of this kind is contingent on several factors. First, one must have fairly precise knowledge as to which schools are "good" and which are not, so that one may make requests wisely. Without such knowledge, acquired through access to the "grapevine," what appears to be a desirable move may prove to be nothing more than a jump from the frying pan into the fire, as the following teacher's experience indicates:

When I put my name down for the ten schools. I put my name down for one school out around —— ["nice" neighborhood]. I didn't know anything about it, what the principal was like or anything, but it had a short list. Well, I heard later from several people that I had really made a mistake. They had a principal there that was really a terror. She just made it miserable for everyone. . . .

But I was telling you about what happened to me. Or almost did. After I had heard about this principal, I heard that she was down one day to observe me. Well, I was really frightened. If she had taken me I would have been out of luck, I would really have had to stay there a year. But she never showed up in my room. . . . But, whatever it was, I was certainly happy that I didn't have to go there. It just shows that you have to be careful about what school you pick.

Second, one must not be of an ethnic type or have a personal reputation which will cause the principal to use his power of informal rejection. Though a transferee may be rejected through formal bureaucratic procedure, the principal finds it easier and less embarrassing to get the same result through this method, described by a Negro teacher:

All he's got to do is say, "I don't think you'll be very happy at our school." You take the hint. Because if the principal decides you're going to be unhappy, you will be, don't worry. No question about that. He can fix it so that you have every discipline problem in the grade you're teaching right in your room. That's enough to do it right there. So it really doesn't pay to go if you're not wanted. You can fight it if you want, but I'm too old for that kind of thing now.

This destroys the attractive qualities of the school to which transfer was desired and turns choice in a new direction.

Finally, one must be patient enough to wait for the transfer to the "right" school to be consummated, not succumbing to the temptation to transfer to a less desirable but more accessible school:

> When I got assigned to —— [Negro school], for instance, I went right downtown and signed on ten lists in this vicinity. I've lived out here for twenty-five years and I expect to stay here, so I signed for those schools and decided I'd wait ten years if necessary, till I found a vacancy in the vicinity.

The majority of teachers have careers of this type, in which an initial stay in an undesirable "slum" school is followed by manipulation of the transfer system in such a way as to achieve assignment to a more desirable kind of school.

Thirteen interviewees, however, had careers of a different type, characterized by a permanent adjustment to the "slum" school situation. These careers resulted from a process of adjustment to the particular work situation which, while operating in all schools, is seen most clearly where it has such a radical effect on the further development of the career, tying the teacher to a school she would otherwise consider undesirable. The process begins when the teacher, for any of a number of possible reasons, remains in the undesirable school for a number of years. During this stay changes take place in her and in her relations with other members of the school's social structure which make this unsatisfactory school an easier place to work in and change her view of the benefits to be gained by transferring elsewhere. Under the appropriate circumstances, a person's entire career may be spent in one such school.

During this initial stay changes take place in the teacher's skills and attitudes which ease the discomfort of teaching at the "slum" school. First, she learns new teaching and disciplinary techniques which enable her to deal adequately with "slum" children, although they are not suited for use with other social-class groups:

> Technically, you're not supposed to lay a hand on a kid. Well, they don't, technically. But there are a lot of ways of handling a kid so that it doesn't show —and then it's the teacher's word against the kid's so the kid hasn't got a chance. Like dear Mrs. G——. She gets mad at a kid, she takes him out in the hall. She gets him stood up against the wall. Then she's got a way of chucking the kid under the chin, only hard, so that it knocks his head back against the

wall. It doesn't leave a mark on him. But when he comes back in that room he can hardly see straight, he's so knocked out.

Further, the teacher revises her expectations about the amount of material she can teach and learns to be satisfied with a smaller accomplishment; a principal of a "slum" school described such an adjustment on the part of her teachers:

> Our teachers are pretty well satisfied if the children can read and do simple number work when they leave here. . . . They're just trying to get these basic things over. So that if the children go to high school they'll be able to make some kind of showing and keep their heads above water.

She thus acquires a routine of work which is customary, congenial, and predictable; any change would require a drastic change in deep-seated habits.

Finally, she finds for herself explanations for actions of the children which she has previously found revolting and immoral, and these explanations allow her to "understand" the behavior of the children as human, rather than as the activity of lunatics or animals:

> I finally received my permanent assignment at E——. That's that big colored school. Frankly, I wasn't ready for anything like that. I thought I'd go crazy those first few months I was there. I wasn't used to that kind of restlessness and noise. The room was never really quiet at all. There was always a low undertone, a humming, of conversation, whispering, and shoving. . . . I didn't think I would ever be able to stand it. But as I came to understand them, then it seemed different. When I could understand the conditions they were brought up in, the kind of family life and home background that they had, it seemed more natural that they should act that way. And I really kind of got used to it after awhile.

At the same time that these changes are taking place in the teacher's perspectives, she is also gradually being integrated into the network of social relations that make up the school in such a way as to ease the problems associated with the "slum" school. In the first place, the teacher, during a long stay in a school, comes to be accepted by the other teachers as a trustworthy equal and acquires positions of influence and prestige in the informal colleague structure. These changes make it easier for her to maintain her position of authority vis-a-vis children and principal. Any move from the school would mean a loss of such position and its advantages and the need to win colleague acceptance elsewhere.

Second, the problem of discipline eases when the teacher's reputation for firmness begins to do the work of maintaining order for her: "I have no trouble with the children. Once you establish a reputation and they know what to expect, they respect you and you have no trouble. Of course, that's different for a new teacher, but when you're established that's no problem at all."

Finally, problems of maintaining one's authority in relation to parents lessen as one comes to be a "fixture" in the community and builds up stable and enduring relationships with its families: "But, as I say, when you've been in that neighborhood as long as I have everyone knows you, and you've been into half their homes, and there's never any trouble at all."

The "slum" school is thus, if not ideal, at least bearable and predictable for the teacher who has adjusted to it. She has taken the worst the situation has to offer and has learned to get along with it. She is tied to the school by the routine he has developed to suit its requirements and by the relationships she has built up with others in the school organization. These very adjustments cause her, at the same time, to fear a move to any new school, which would necessitate a rebuilding of these relationships and a complete reorganization of her work techniques and routine. The move to a school in a "better" neighborhood is particularly feared, desirable as it seems in the abstract, because the teacher used to the relative freedom of the "slum" school is not sure whether the advantages to be gained in such a move would not be outweighed by the constraint imposed by "interfering" parents and "spoiled" children and by the difficulties to be encountered in integrating into a new school structure. This complete adjustment to a particular work situation thus acts as a brake on further mobility through the system.

Career Dangers

Either of these career patterns results, finally, in the teacher's achieving a position in which she is more or less settled in a work environment she regards as predictable and satisfactory. Once this occurs, her position and career are subject to dangers occasioned by ecological and administrative events which cause radical changes in the incumbents of important positions in the school structure.

Ecological invasion of a neighborhood produces changes in the social-class group from which pupils and parents of a given school are recruited. This, in turn, changes the nature and intensity of the teacher's work problems and upsets the teacher who has been accustomed to working with a higher status group than the one to which she thus falls heir. The total effect is the destruction of what was once a satisfying place to work in, a position from which no move was intended:

> I've been at this school for about twenty years. It was a lovely school when I first went there. . . . Of course, the neighborhood has changed quite

a bit since I've been there. It's not what it used to be.

The neighborhood used to be ninety, ninety-five per cent Jewish. Now I don't think there are over forty per cent Jews. The rest are Greek, Italian, a few Irish, it's pretty mixed now. And the children aren't as nice as they used to be.

Ecological and demographic processes may likewise create a change in the age structure of a population which causes a decrease in the number of teachers needed in a particular school and a consequent loss of the position in that school for the person last added to the staff. The effect of neighborhood invasion may be to turn the career in the direction of adjustment to the new group, while the change in local age structure may turn the career back to the earlier phase, in which transfer to a "nicer" school was sought.

A satisfactory position may also be changed for the worse by a change in principal through transfer or retirement. The departure of a principal may produce changes of such dimension in the school atmosphere as to force teachers to transfer elsewhere. Where the principal has been a major force upholding the teachers' authority in the face of attacks by children and parents, a change can produce a disastrous increase in the problems of discipline and parental interference:

I'm tempted to blame most of it on our new principal. . . . [The old principal] kept excellent order. Now the children don't seem to have the same feeling about this man. They're not afraid of him, they don't respect him. And the discipline in the school has suffered tremendously. The whole school is less orderly now.

This problem is considered most serious when the change takes place in a "slum" school in which the discipline problem has been kept under control primarily through the efforts of a strict principal. Reactions to such an event, and consequent career development, vary in schools in different social-class areas. Such a change in a "slum" school usually produces an immediate and tremendous increase in teacher turnover. A teacher who had been through such an experience estimated that faculty turnover through transfer rose from almost nothing to 60 per cent or more during the year following the change. Where the change takes place in a "nicer," upper-middle-class school, teachers are reluctant to move and give up their hard-won positions, preferring to take a chance on the qualities of the new incumbent. Only if he is particularly unsatisfying are they likely to transfer.

Another fear is that a change in principals will destroy the existing allocation of privilege and influence among the teachers, the new principal failing to respect the informal understandings of the teachers with regard to these matters. The following quotations describe two new principals who acted in this fashion:

> He knows what he wants and he does it. Several of the older teachers have tried to explain a few things to him, but he won't have any part of it. Not that they did it in a domineering way or anything, but he just doesn't like that.

> He's a good hearted man, he really means well, but he simply doesn't know anything about running a school. He gets all mixed up, listens to people he shouldn't pay any attention to. . . . Some people assert themselves and tell him what to do, and he listens to them when he shouldn't.

These statements come from strongly entrenched, "older" teachers who depend greatly for their power on their influence with the principal. Their dissatisfaction with a new principal seldom affects their careers to the point of causing them to move to another school. On the other hand, the coming of a new principal may be to the great advantage of and ardently desired by younger, less influential teachers. The effect of such an event on the career of a young teacher is illustrated in this quotation:

> I was ready to transfer because of the old principal. I just couldn't stand it. But when this new man came in and turned out to be so good, I went downtown and took my name off the transfer list. I want to stay there now . . . Some of those teachers have been there as long as thirty years, you see, and they feel like they really own the place. They want everything done their way. They always had things their way and they were pretty mad when this new principal didn't take to all their ideas.

Any of these events may affect the career, then, in any of several ways, depending on the state of the career at the time the event occurs. The effect of any event must be seen in the context of the type of adjustment made by the individual to the institutional organization in which she works.

Implications

This paper has demonstrated the existence, among Chicago schoolteachers, of a "horizontal" plane of career strivings and movements and has traced the kind of career patterns which occur, at this level, in a public bureaucracy where movement is achieved through manipulation of formal procedures. It suggests that studies of other occupations, in which greater emphasis on vertical movement may obscure the presence and effects of such horizontal mobility, might well direct their attention to such phenomena.

Further research might also explore in detail the relations between the horizontal mobility discussed here and the vertical mobility more prominent in many occupations. Studies in a number of occupations might give us answers to questions like this: To what extent, and under what circumstances, will a person forego actions which might provide him with a better working situation at one level of an occupational hierarchy in the hope of receiving greater rewards through vertical mobility? Hall notes that those doctors who become members of the influential "inner fraternity" undergo a "rigorous system of selection, and a system of prolonged apprenticeship. The participants in the system must be prepared to expect long delays before being rewarded for their loyalty to such a system."[6] We see that the rewards of eventual acceptance into this important group are attractive enough to keep the fledgling doctor who is apprenticed to it from attempting other ways of bettering his position. Turning the problem around, we may ask to what extent a person will give up possible vertical mobility which might interfere with the successful adjustment he has made in terms of horizontal career movement. A suggestion as to the kinds of relationships and processes to be found here comes from the following statement made by a high-school teacher with regard to mobility within the school system:

> That's one reason why a lot of people aren't interested in taking principal's exams. Suppose they pass and their first assignment is to some school like M—— or T——. And it's likely to be at some low-class colored school like that, because people are always dying to get out of schools like that. . . . Those schools are nearly always vacant, so that you have a very good chance of being assigned there when you start in. A lot of people I know will say, "Why should I leave a nice neighborhood like Morgan Park or South Shore or Hyde Park to go down to a school like that?" . . . These guys figure, "I should get mixed up with something like that? I like it better where I am."

Finally, I have explored the phenomenon of adjustment to a particular work situation, the way changes in the individual's perspectives and social relationships acted to tie him to the particular situation and to make it difficult for him to consider movement to another. We may speculate as to the importance and effects of such a process in the vertical mobility prominent in many occupations. One further research problem might be suggested: What are the social mechanisms which function, in occupations where such adjustment is not allowed to remain undisturbed, to bridge the transition between work situations, to break the ties binding the individual to one situation, and to effect a new adjustment elsewhere?

6. Oswald Hall, "The Stages of a Medical Career," *American Journal of Sociology* 53 (March 1948), 334.

The Elements of Identification with an Occupation

One of the major problems to which social psychologists now address themselves is the process of identification and the nature and functioning of identity in conduct. These concepts are of strategic importance in any theory which attempts to relate the self and its workings to an ongoing social structure. As Foote[1] and Strauss[2] have pointed out, individuals identify themselves—answer the question "Who am I?"—with the names and categories current in the groups in which they participate. By applying these labels to themselves they learn who they are and how they ought to behave, acquire a self and a set of perspectives they use to shape their conduct.

It appears theoretically useful to break the concept of identification down into its components, both for comparative purposes and in order to provide finer tools for the analysis of specific problems of social structure and personal development. This paper attempts to provide such a breakdown for one type of identification, that of a man with his work. Its purpose is to discover, by comparing three groups of persons about to enter the work world, some of the threads from which the fabric of occupational identification is woven.

The data were gathered in the course of a study of the genesis of identification with an occupation in students doing graduate work in physiology,

Reprinted by permission from *American Sociological Review,* 21 (June 1956), pp. 341–348. Copyright © 1956 American Sociological Association.

1. Nelson N. Foote, "Identification as the Basis for a Theory of Motivation," *American Sociological Review* 16 (February 1951), pp. 14–22.
2. Anselm L. Strauss, *Mirrors and Masks* (New York: Free Press, 1959).

philosophy, and mechanical engineering. Graduate students were chosen for study not only because they were convenient but, more importantly, because of the central character of graduate school in developing professional identifications. Interviews lasting from one-half to two hours were tape recorded with students ranging from first year in graduate school to those about to receive the Ph.D.[3] While identifications are not so clearly defined in the first year as they become later, the consistency of our findings indicates that the process is already well started at that time.

We conducted our interviews informally, asking questions only to clarify points or to introduce some area in which information was desired that the interviewee had not spontaneously discussed in answer to the initial question: "How did you happen to get into . . . . ?"

Comparison of the three groups suggested four major elements of work identification: (1) occupational title, and associated ideology; (2) commitment to task; (3) commitment to particular organizations or institutional positions; and (4) significance for one's position in the larger society. In what follows we present brief discussions of each of these variables and comparisons of the physiologists, philosophers, and mechanical engineers[4] to illustrate their dimensions and analytic utility. We also include illustrations of the kind of theoretical use to which these concepts might be put.

Occupational Title and Ideology

Kinds of work tend to be named, to become well-defined occupations, and an important part of a person's work-based identity grows out of his relationship to his occupational title. The names carry a great deal of symbolic meaning, which tends to be incorporated into the identity. They specify an area of endeavor belonging to those bearing the name and locate this area in relation to similar kinds of activity in a broader field. They also imply a great deal about the characteristics of their bearers, and these meanings

3. Only men were interviewed, to avoid the complications introduced by sex differences in career patterns and ambitions. Foreign students were excluded to eliminate the difficulty of interpreting information relating to social systems about which we knew little or nothing. Three philosophy students were excluded because they had no serious intentions of doing work in the field but were simply taking courses as a hobby. With these exceptions, we interviewed all the remaining students in philosophy (eleven) and mechanical engineering (twenty-two), and a radomly selected 50 per cent sample of those in physiology (eighteen), a total of fifty-one. The work was done at a large state university which may recruit from lower levels in the class structure. For this reason there may be important differences between our subjects and those studying in the same fields elsewhere.

4. Material on the process by which the identifications we describe as characteristic of each of these groups develop is reported in "The Development of Identification with an Occupation," in this volume.

are often systematized into elaborate ideologies which itemize the qualities, interests, and capabilities of those identified.[5]

These things implied by the occupational title are evaluated and people react to those evaluations. One may reject the specific work area the title specifies, preferring to be identified with some larger field; or he may eagerly claim the specific field, while minimizing the larger area; he may emphasize neither, or both. Similarly, the implicit statements about the person may be proudly claimed, whether these claims are recognized by others or not; or they may be as eagerly avoided, even though others attempt to impute them. The title, with its implications, may thus be an object of attachment or avoidance, and kinds of identification may fruitfully be compared in this regard.

The physiology students[6] feel themselves part of a larger group, devoted to building the edifice of science, and pride themselves on their participation in this endeavor and on the ultimate value of their work to society in the cure and prevention of disease. Nevertheless, they sharply differentiate their work from that of physicians and of other scientists involved in this enterprise. They feel that they make the important scientific discoveries on which medical practice is based, medicine itself being more empirical and superficial; one student put it metaphorically: "We write the music that the doctors play." Another stressed the fact that the scientist is free to pursue questions until he gets a real answer, while the M.D. must of necessity forego following up any particular problem intensively. In contrast to physicians, many saw themselves as men who would devote their lives to meeting the challenge of the unsolved problems of the field. They compare their work with that of other natural scientists—chemists, zoologists, and others—and conclude that theirs is the only science which really studies the problems of the living organism:

> Here you have living organisms, and there are certain rules that these organisms will follow. They don't hold fast; two and two isn't always four. It's up to you to interpret what happens, to be able to meet any emergency which arises. And you're working with something which is living and therefore responds to its environment. Whereas in chemistry, mathematics, there are

5. See, for example, Howard S. Becker, "The Professional Dance Musician in Chicago," *American Journal of Sociology* 57 (September 1951), pp. 136–144; and W. Fred Cottrell, *The Railroader* (Palo Alto: Stanford University Press, 1941).

6. Of the eighteen physiology students interviewed, eleven were fully committed to the field; two were committed to closely allied fields of biological research; three were determined to become physicians; and two still had hopes of becoming physicians, but were well on the way to accepting physiology as an alternative. This discussion of aspects of identification describes all but the five interested in medicine and applies in large measure to the two undecided cases.

certain reactions which occur and you can change them by doing little things but you yourself are the one that is producing these changes whereas in a living tissue, it itself is changing. . . . You're working with something which is alive just as you're alive and it changes and you actually can't control it completely, you just have to be able to work with it.

Others make a similar point in saying that physiology is not "cut and dried," as are the other sciences. In short, these men identify themselves as part of a discipline carrying on a peculiarly valuable kind of work, which no other group can do.

The engineers, like the physiologists, take great pride in their occupational title. Although in a few cases they feel equally identified with the titles of "research scientist" or "teacher," they all share the feeling that it is a good thing to be an engineer. Unlike the physiologists, the majority have no attachment to any particular part of their field; their specialty is the broad area of "technical work." They find the field desirable because of the remarkable skills and abilities engineering training is supposed to produce in them, abilities implied in the occupation's name. With few exceptions, these men are agreed that, as one put it:

All our lives and all through our work we are being trained to think logically and to analyze. And if you can do these two, I don't think anything can stop you.

The ideology tells them that anyone called "engineer" has learned to reason so rationally and effectively that, even though this has been learned only with reference to technical problems, it operates in any line of endeavor, so that the engineer is equipped to solve any kind of problem in any area quickly and efficiently.

The philosophers, in marked contrast, have very little attachment to their occupational title, perhaps because of the august company in which it would place them:

[It's all right to call you a philosopher, isn't it?] Well, I don't know. I do refer to myself every once in a while as a philosopher but I rather hesitate to because when I think of a philosopher I think of somebody like Plato or Aristotle.

The image they have of themselves is that of the "intellectual" whose interests cover the whole range of artistic, scientific, and cultural pursuits. Viewing their earlier specialization in particular fields as "too confining," they turn to philosophy which "does deal . . . with all crucial problems in one way or another."

Frankly, I'm taking the viewpoint of a person who wants to know quite a bit about several things and I never want to give up my catholic interest, catholic meaning of course universal in this sense, and to specialize. Yet I realize that to know very much about anything I have to specialize. Philosophy is the best grab-bag for me. To do something in philosophy I don't have to go terribly deeply into a given discipline and stick with it all my life, so I can shift from one discipline to another. But at the same time to overcome the notion of it being grounded in nothing. Frankly, if somebody asked me what I mean by philosophy it would be very difficult for me to tell them what I mean. I'm just sort of in a big intellectual game and pursuit right now. It happens to go under that name and I think under the aegis of philosophy I'm more able to do this.

In short, they have chosen their occupational title simply as the least undesirable one available, since it will place them in the society's division of labor while allowing them to deal with a broad range of interests ordinarily divided between many specialties.

Commitment to Task

Occupations may also be compared with reference to the degree to which their members feel identified with some specific kind of work. There may be a feeling that only some sharply limited set of work tasks, carried on in a particular way, is proper, all others being excluded, and that one is, among other things, the kind of person who does this kind of work. The opposite attitude may also exist: that there is no kind of task which is impossible. Again, a person may simply be vague on the matter, not really knowing what his work is or how he ought to go about it. The elements of attachment, or lack of it, to a specific set of tasks and ways of handling them, and of a feeling of capability to engage in such activities, thus also play an important part in identification with one's work.

The physiology students exemplify one extreme, identifying closely with a set of specific research tasks and a particular way of going about them. Although task and method may vary from individual to individual, each one has a fairly clearcut notion of what he is about. They see a limited range of problems to which their professional lives will be devoted, and a set of basic techniques in which they take great pride:

> You learn a little more about handling animals, doing regular surgery. After awhile, it becomes automatic. I think the first time I did it it took about twenty-five or thirty minutes. Now I can go into the throat of a dog, sew in the glass tube, isolate the artery there, put a glass tube in it and hook it to a pressure machine and have the whole thing recording in about five minutes.

Beyond this, they are committed to the notion of themselves as persons who do work which is precise, which can be reproduced by other investigators, which is theoretically sound and takes cognizance of existing knowledge available in the discipline's literature. There is no vagueness in this conception; they know what their specific problems are and how they will be handled, and they feel that they are qualified, by virtue of their technical training, to handle this kind of research successfully. They possess a concrete image of their professional future in terms of day-to-day activities which they will perform.

The engineers lie at the opposite pole, having almost no commitment to task—no kinds of work strictly theirs and beyond which they would neither dare nor care to go. Far from having a narrow conception of the engineer's work, eight of our twenty-two interviewees would be quite happy doing any kind of work our industrial system has to offer, as long as it is "interesting" and "challenging." Seven others stipulated simply that it be something technical, while only five consciously limited their work to a particular technical specialty. They are quite ready to forget the specific kinds of work for which they have been trained and take on any kind of job which the title of engineer can win for them. This attitude is expressed in comments like this:

> [Now what did you have in mind, sort of, as a long-term goal in a thing like that?] Well, I think I have the same goal that probably every other kid fresh out of college has, that of going into some type of engineering work. With me, I think it would be production, as I've said. And eventually working up to higher management, I think. That's every young engineer's goal, whether he expresses it or not. [You mean non-engineering. . . .] Eventually ending up, using engineering as just a channel to go into management of some kind.

In addition to this kind of confident assertion that one is able to handle anything that comes up, the lack of commitment to task shows up in the somewhat puzzled statements of younger engineers about what their work really is:

> I really didn't have a good idea of what an engineer does. And I still can't tell you. People asked me, "Well, what does a mechanical engineer do?" and I could give them examples, that's all. I could go on and on and on in the examples, and that pertains to any engineer. All you have to do is just look at the placement records of engineers, and they go into everything.

(Six of the men interviewed included teaching, in combination with either specialized or general technical tasks, among the possible kinds of work for them.)

The philosophers present a third possibility. Lacking both the specific task attachment of the physiologists and the calm assurance of the engineers that all tasks are suitable for them, these students are not quite sure what they should be doing. Realizing that their future probably lies in the university, they accept teaching as a necessary task which is, however, not peculiarly theirs. The following is a typical answer to the question, "What does a philosopher do?"

> I suppose part of a philosopher's job is in telling people how much they don't know: It seems to be so old fashioned now to tell people how much they don't know. I suppose I will be teaching the various branches of philosophy. I'm interested in talking to students. In helping them with reading. In helping them with philosophical problems that come up. I'm sure that they can help me with some fresh ideas I hadn't considered heretofore. I'm interested in just learning as much as I can in my spare time. I might decide at some time to dabble in another profession. I just don't know. I'll never feel that there's any dearth of things to do. I don't know if I can ever categorize them. My job, my source of income, will involve taking so many hours of classes, teaching.

The clearest image of their work tends to center around the notion of continuing to learn and read in all areas of intellectual activity. Beyond this, they see all kinds of possibilities, ranging from semi-scientific research through journalism and artistic activity to such things as politics.

Organization and Institutional Position

An occupational identity tends to specify the kinds of organizations, and positions within them, in which one's future lies, the places in which it is appropriate, desirable, or likely that one will work. A person may see his professional future as tied to one organization, or to a very restricted range of organizations, or he may conceive of himself acting in his occupational role in a great many kinds of institutions. Again, he may feel to tied to one particular kind of institutional position, or find it possible to conceive of holding a large variety of work statuses. These, with the further possibility of vagueness as to these matters, constitute continua along which various kinds of work identification may be located.

Participants in work institutions tend to see themselves in relation to those upon whom their success in these institutions depends. Research has demonstrated the importance of building connections with clients, colleagues, and others in the pursuit of success,[7] and identifications vary in the degree to which they reflect dependence on informal systems of sponsorship, recommendation, and control.

7. See, for example, Oswald Hall, "The Stages of a Medical Career," *American Journal of Sociology* 53 (March 1948), pp. 327–337; and Everett C. Hughes, *French Canada in Transition* (Chicago: University of Chicago Press, 1943), pp. 52–53.

The physiology students see themselves as potential occupants of a few well-defined slots in a highly organized work world. There are only a few places in which they might do their kind of work: universities, where they would teach and do research; research foundations and pharmaceutical companies, where they would do only research; and government agencies, where they would engage in applied research. They do not consider themselves competent to handle positions of any other kind. They are unable to see beyond this narrow conception even to entertain the notion of becoming chairman of a Department of Physiology; this would mean moving out of the expected slot a little too far for comfort, involving as it would unfamiliar duties and responsibilities.

They expect such jobs to become available to them through the workings of a sponsorship system centered around their graduate-school professors. The initial job (the aspect of the career that looms largest at this stage) will come through the professor's contacts, and his recommendations will be of great importance. They feel quite dependent on this personal kind of sponsorship system and see no other way to get established professionally. They expect to progress through the hierarchy of university, industry, or government through careful research, knowledge of the field, and publication of important research.

In contrast, the engineers feel that their future lies somewhere in the country's industrial system, but do not think of any company (no matter what its specialty) or any position as impossible for them. Twelve of the twenty-two interviewees are prepared to work in any kind of industrial organization, while only six limit their possibilities to companies doing work in their technical specialty. (Three of the men expect to become teachers, and one wants to open his own business.) For the majority, any industrial firm in the country represents a possible employer.

Within this range of organizations they expect to compete for a broad range of positions. Of the eighteen who were considering industry, only one would restrict himself to a position involving only his technical specialty. Nine are able to see themselves in any kind of technical position in industry, while eight are confident that they can compete successfully for any position, technical or managerial. Lacking any firm commitment to a particular task and armed with an ideology that stresses their universal ability, they see their futures in ways such as these:

[What kind of job would that be that you would get into eventually?] It would be difficult to say. [Well, what are the possibilities?] Oh, assistant, for instance, a job that I would like to have. If I get back to *X Co.* I think I have a good chance, which would be a tremendous step forward, would be assistant to the general manager, for instance. While this would take me out of the technical field, it would be—It's a tremendous stepping stone, it's a big step forward as far as getting to the administrative end of it. I do not fancy myself as a research engineer who's just going to bury himself in his little office, content to work all his life compiling a set of tables, should we say, to take an illustrative example. A lot of people have done this. Or to investigate the natural laws. I think there's a—I don't fancy myself as doing this. I'd like to get ahead into a position where you are directing things, formulating policies, formulating the lines of the company. Do you follow me?

[Yeah. Yeah. So you could conceivably end up as a general manager?] General manager of the plant, vice president. . . . [The sky's the limit, in other words.] It is. It really is. A good engineer can go anyplace these days.

Only a few feel that their future is in any way tied in with their "connections" with either prospective employers or with sponsors in the academic world. The majority felt quite independent in getting jobs, assuming that in the normal workings of the labor market in an economy becoming more and more "technical" they would be able to command a satisfactory position. This independence is reflected in the language they use to describe job-hunting: They are not "interviewed for a job," but rather "interview companies about jobs." This may, of course, be a temporary phenomenon associated with the present high demand for engineers.

The philosophers again suggest another dimension, having for the greatest part of their time in graduate school no clear notion of where they will work or what position they might hold. They think of themselves as intellectuals, and the term implies no specific relation to the occupational world. Late in their training they begin to realize that their futures are to be made in universities, and primarily as teachers rather than philosophers. By this time teaching, originally viewed as an important function of the philosopher, has become simply a way of earning a living and subsidizing the continuation of their intellectual pursuits. Since the state of the job market may limit opportunities for such positions, they are ready to consider positions involving skills or experience acquired elsewhere. Any position which will allow continued intellectual activity, on or off the job, is considered suitable, even though it may have no relation to the professional organization of philosophy. If they do teach, they feel they are as likely to teach some other intellectual specialty as philosophy; anything within their cultural purview becomes a possible teaching subject.

They are vague about the ways in which jobs become available and professional success is achieved. Only two had a clear notion of the workings of academic sponsorship systems, although several believed that their professors might have some effect on their work future. They tend to be concerned about this, if at all, in a quite offhand manner:

Lately I have begun to think that after all, in part philosophy is a business, so in part business ethics must apply to philosophy—and there are certain things you just have to do. [How about things like publishing, and so on . . .?] Oh, that of course would be in your favor. But that again is something that I haven't thought about, haven't thought about writing any articles for journals. It's certainly . . . when I decided that I should realize that philosophy is partly a business, I also decided that I should think about writing for journals and I should take systematic notes on articles in journals, what kinds of articles are in there, what sort of thing they write about and how they write about it. [But you haven't done much of that yet?] No. It's certainly time to start, I would say.

Social Position

Occupational identities contain an implicit reference to the person's position in the larger society, tending to specify the positions appropriate for a person doing such work or which have become possible for him by virtue of his work. The most frequent reference is, of course, to social-class position and to the opportunities for class mobility opened up or closed off by entrance into the particular occupation. It is also possible for an identification to contain a statement of a particular relation of members of the occupation to the society, quite apart from class considerations.

The physiology students see themselves as achieving a desired move up in the class system. Twelve are men from the lower or lower-middle class who had hoped to become physicians, with the prestige of that profession playing a large role in their choice. This mobility hope has been wrecked on the reef of medical school entrance standards or abandoned during the tedious and trying voyage through "pre-med," and becoming a physiologist represents the salvage. Their parents, desiring to see their sons better themselves, figured importantly in the choice of medicine as a career, and these men remain sensitive to their parents' aspirations for them. Physiology as an occupation will get them some of the prestige and income they desired, although it is second-best; they will never approach the M.D. in these respects.

For four others (in the remaining two cases we did not get sufficient information to make a classification) physiology represents an escape into science from the mobility demands of their well-to-do families. They see physiology as an occupation giving them a respected position without necessitating the competitiveness of medicine or business. They typically want academic positions, while many of the first group favor research positions in the drug industry, which they believe provide larger incomes.

For seventeen of the engineers, success in their profession spells succesful social mobility. Their fathers were skilled or unskilled laborers, farmers, or white-collar workers. Having entered engineering in many instances purely out of interest in "mechanical things," they are pleasantly surprised to find that it enables them to rise significantly (in social class) above their families and childhood friends. For the other five, a career in engineering is a means of continuing their families' solid middle-class status. They all expect to do well financially. At the least, they look forward to a very comfortable living, and eight expressed the desire to make "big money": "You can get your mansion on the hill." Being an engineer is a ticket to financial success and its accompanying social prestige.

The philosophy students' identification of themselves as "intellectuals" carried with it the implication that they are different in important respects from other members of the society. In every case they either consider themselves deviant or recognize that they are so considered by friends and relatives. Most importantly, these men of predominantly lower and lower-middle class origin have renounced the pursuit of class mobility in favor of the intellectual life. They have no concern with material success and tend to be proud of the meagerness of their financial future. They expect that parents and others will be unable to understand these views, and they often break relations with people who would keep these interests before them. In contrast to the physiologists, parental aspirations play no part in the formation of their professional ambitions.

Discussion

The dimensions of work identification detailed above suggest a number of problem areas in which they might be of use in further research. The question immediately arises, for example: To what degree do these dimensions constitute independent variables and to what degree are they functionally or causally related so that they will tend to appear, not randomly, but in relatively stable combinations or syndromes? The identifications of the three groups studied show a considerable degree of inner consistency, suggesting the existence of such relationships. The physiologists exhibit a congruent pattern of commitment to specific and restricted items: only certain limited kinds of tasks, organizational settings, and institutional positions are considered possible and acceptable, while they claim as their own only a small slice of the total pie of science; and these seem to fit naturally with the limited social-class mobility they expect their work to provide for them. One might reasonably assume that these limitations tend to reinforce each other, both psychologically and in movement within social structures. The engineers' identifications are equally consistent in the other direction, with commitments to a broad area of work, a wide range of possible tasks, organizations, and positions, and the expectation of great social mobility. Again, the hypothesis of mutual reinforcement seems appropriate.

While these cases suggest the likelihood of relations of functional interdependence between the elements of identification, that of the philosophers points more to the possibility of causal relationship, since the chief characteristics of their identification—lack of commitment to any organizations or positions, to specific tasks or mobility aspirations—all seem deducible from their basic commitment to the intellectual life as they conceive it. Both detailed genetic studies of the development of identification and cross-sectional studies of the relationship of these attributes seem indicated for the solution of this problem.

The use of such distinctions as these would also provide variables for the intensive analysis of the problem of the development of identification, and for those problems centering around the functioning of identifications in society; for example, the problem of the relation of variation in elements of identification to variation in occupational role behavior, and that of the way the identifications of individuals function within the organizations they work in.

Let us consider, as an instance of the latter class of problem, the way variations in these elements of identification affect the relative ease of an individual's mobility through occupational institutions, keeping in mind the effect which differences in mobility potential have on the organizations these people work in. If, in identifying himself occupationally, an individual exhibits an intense identification with a particular institutional position or a particular set of tasks or with both of these, movement to some other position, or movement which involves a shift in the actual job done, becomes more difficult. The physiologists exemplify this tendency. Tied to their particular research problems and techniques, they cannot envision themselves occupying any but the few positions they know of in which they can pursue these problems in the way they know best. Even the minor move to department chairman worries them. Neither the engineers nor philosophers have any such commitment to task or institutional position, and movement is much more possible, should it become an alternative available to them. The engineers, for example, are ready to move into any kind of position in the country's industrial system, while the philosophers consider with equanimity many kinds of positions involving a variety of skills, as long as they allow for continued intellectual activity. The physiologists' limited view allows them to fit easily into the limited mobility pattern of the university when they actually take their positions in it, just as the engineers' high mobility potential allows them to meet with ease the personnel needs of the expanding industrial economy into which they are moving. In this sense, identifications have functional consequences for institutions.

The Development
of Identification
with an Occupation

One of the most compelling instances of personal change and development
in adult life in our society is the typical growth of an "occupational personality" in the young adult male who, as he matures, takes over an image
of himself as the holder of a particular specialized position in the division
of labor. This paper attempts to specify the processes by which such occupational identifications are internalized by the individual in the course of his
entrance into and passage through a set of training institutions and thus to
provide an example of a mode of analysis suitable for the study of adult
socialization.

We make use of two complementary sets of concepts in dealing with the
development of identification. Changes in institutional participation and the
contingencies on which these depend are analyzed with the notion of career,
which directs attention to typical sequences of movement and to the way
these depend (at least in part) on the evaluative responses of important
persons and groups.[1] The subjective aspects of such movement are treated

Reprinted by permission from *American Journal of Sociology*, 61 (January 1956),
pp. 289–298. Copyright © 1956 by The University of Chicago Press.

1. The concept of career has been treated extensively in the sociological literature.
See particularly H. H. Gerth and C. W. Mills, *From Max Weber: Essays in Sociology*
(New York: Oxford University Press, 1946), chap. iv, "Science as a Vocation"; Oswald
Hall, "The Stages of a Medical Career," *American Journal of Sociology* LIII (March
1948), 327–37, and "Types of Medical Careers," *ibid*. LV (November 1937), 404–13;
Melville Dalton, "Informal Factors in Career Achievement," *American Journal of
Sociology* LVI (March 1951), 407–15; Howard S. Becker, "The Career of the Chicago
Public School Teacher," *American Journal of Sociology* LVII (March 1952), 470–77,
and "Some Contingencies of the Professional Dance Musician's Career," *Human
Organization* XII (Spring 1953), 22–26.

with the concepts of self, identity, and transformation, which direct attention to the way situations present the person with experiences with objects and people out of which may come stabilization of self-conceptions into lasting identities, on the one hand, and their transformation into new identities, on the other.[2]

The analysis is based on the same interviews with graduate students in three fields described in the previous chapter. It proceeds by looking at stages of development, inspecting each case for the way career movements into new situations made possible new experiences, transforming the self-image and thus creating the conditions for further movement.

It is clear that tension may arise where the newly acquired work identity fails to mesh with or to meet the specifications of other strongly held identifications, such as those growing out of participation in the family of orientation. The person finds it expedient to acquire a work identity, since general cultural emphases require some occupational attachment, some answer to the ubiquitous question, "What's your line?" But this may also produce conflict, as the individual is unable to achieve a desired identity, or does not know what to want, and so ends up with an identity in some respects incongruent with his others. We have left consideration of such conflicts for later analysis.[3]

We present descriptions of the types of change which occur in the three groups and the conditions under which they change first, indicating the general type of change illustrated by each and thus the way each training institution operates to produce specific kinds of occupational identities. The physiology students are a group in which originally strong preferences for other fields are transformed by the graduate department into a well-developed identification with physiology. In the case of the philosophers, the experiences provided by their graduate training allow for a kind of moratorium in which a broad and unspecialized intellectual commitment can be maintained, being replaced only partially by a specialized work identification. For the engineers, graduate school serves to maintain a work identity already strongly established in college, little further change taking place.[4]

2. On the self see George Herbert Mead, *Mind, Self, and Society* (Chicago: University of Chicago Press, 1934). On identity see Nelson N. Foote, "Identification as the Basis for a Theory of Motivation," *American Sociological Review* XVI (February 1951), 14–22; and Anselm Strauss, *Mirrors and Masks* (New York: The Free Press, 1959). On transformation see Anselm Strauss, "The Development and Transformation of Monetary Meanings in the Child," *American Sociological Review* XVII (June 1952), 275–86.

3. James Carper and Howard S. Becker, "Conflicts in the Development of Occupational Identification," in this volume.

4. The characteristics of the identities found in these groups are described in Howard S. Becker and James Carper, "The Elements of Occupational Identification," in this volume.

Viewed comparatively, as involving different degrees of change in identity, the three cases serve to locate some general mechanisms through which such change occurs, at least in those occupations whose recruits are trained in graduate schools; they may also be found in less pretentious settings. Taken singly, they exemplify various problems and sequences of development which no doubt have their analogues both within and beyond academic confines. Our discussion, while focused on the three cases at hand, may thus be thought of as raising questions and suggesting answers outside these limits.

The Physiologists

Students typically begin graduate work in physiology without having done their undergraduate work in the field. This is true partly because the department faculty prefers students with a firm background in one of the sciences physiology draws on, such as chemistry or zoölogy, to those who would have to unlearn painfully the half-truths necessarily taught in undergraduate courses. It is true more importantly because these students had not intended to study physiology until shortly before entering graduate school. Twelve of the eighteen had instead fastened their hopes on the medical profession, eight of them turning to physiology only when they were not accepted into medical school. At this point they decide to spend a year in physiology, on the premise that when they *do* enter medical school the training will prove valuable; they do not give up the notion of becoming physicians but see physiology as the best available stopgap. The others have either had an early interest in biological science or acquired such an interest in the course of the premedical program. After receiving the B.S. degree, they feel that real professional success depends on higher degrees, and they enter physiology, perhaps out of an interest developed in undergraduate work, perhaps at the suggestion of an interested teacher.

In any case, no student enters the department irrevocably committed to the notion of becoming a physiologist; most, in fact, are still committed to medicine, and the others feel it quite possible that they may later want to switch fields. Further, they are vague as to the real nature of the field and the kinds of experiences they are likely to have in it, possessing not even the kind of unrealistic picture which may be provided by public stereotypes, such as are attached to other, more well-known occupations like law or medicine. (The absence of such stereotypes or public knowledge of the field is no doubt important in restricting occupational choices in the area to the late college years.) They view their task as students as one of acquiring the vast body of certified knowledge in the field and thus earning good marks and, perhaps, degrees, a perspective created by their undergraduate experience. They are committed through their enrolment as students in the department to at least a year of such activity.

As the year progresses, the student is taught in a new way, with a tremendous stress on the many problems yet to be solved, on the research that needs to be done, and on the essentially problematic character of the "facts" so laboriously acquired as an undergraduate. At first disillusioned, he becomes excited at the thought that all the great work has not been done, that he too may make fundamental and important discoveries, and he begins to realize the value of small, carefully done studies. This interest in the specific problems of the field is enhanced by casual conversations with other students. Likewise, he begins to learn the techniques of research and to acquire a pride in his technical abilities through the evaluations of his instructors and comparisons of his own work with that of others. And, finally, he begins to take over an ideology which identifies physiology for him as the most comprehensive and important of the life-sciences, including medicine.

At the end of the first year the student may again apply for admission to medical school. Those who do and are rejected do not immediately give up all hope but do decide that they might as well continue until they get the Master's degree and perhaps beyond that the Ph.D. As medicine becomes more unattainable, their very real interest in physiology takes on new meaning as they come to consider it as the basis for an alternative career; those whose interests always lay in science begin to realize that unless they remain for a Ph.D. they will be doomed to careers as laboratory technicians.

No later than the end of the second year (and often earlier for those who hold assistantships) the student finds himself spending a great deal of time in the department laboratories, working on his own or his professors' research, and is thrown into continual day-and-night contact with "the clique." This is a loosely organized group of those whose work is centered around the laboratory; in no way exclusive, entrance into it is accomplished simply by being around and is an automatic accompaniment of the laboratory work of the advanced student. Conversations with third- and fourth-year students in this group take place at work and during "coffee breaks," and the student thus becomes integrated into a group whose major concerns are the problems and techniques of physiological research and the job and career prospects of the young physiologist. His interest in the science is reinforced, and he begins to develop specific notions as to the kind of occupational future he might expect as a physiologist, the kinds of jobs available, and the ways one gets them.

These changes are strengthened in the informal apprenticeship in which he now gets involved with professors in the course of beginning his thesis or working on their projects. He is told more of the beauties of physiological research and is often able to model his behavior after that of a professor or of an ideal constructed of the characteristics of several professors, learning through observation of them the kind of tasks which physiologists in fact perform. He learns the facts of their careers and becomes aware of the jobs for which he will qualify as a physiologist in universities, government, and the research departments of pharmaceutical concerns. Frequently, he is deliberately groomed by the professor for some particular kind of job, either because it is felt that he "has what it takes" or because it is felt necessary to point him toward a less difficult job but one which he will be able to handle. (Some students are thus encouraged to take technician jobs after the M.S. rather than try for the Ph.D.)

At the end of the second year the student thinks quite seriously of staying in physiology and can even envision turning down a place in medical school if one materializes (if, indeed, he has even bothered to apply a third time). He feels not only that physiology has something to offer him but that it would be a terrible waste of time to "start over," to give up what he has learned and begin again in a new field. Also, his newly acquired ideology gives him reasons to discount the prestige of the medical profession, a profession he now sees in terms of an invidious comparison between "art" and "science"; this ideology also serves to insulate him against the appeals of other sciences whose importance is deprecated.

All these elements combine to produce an identification with the field of physiology and to lessen identification with other possible work statuses. At some point (for the medically oriented, the point at which they must decide whether to try for medical school again) they become aware of the new identity and accept it, perhaps with the proviso that this acceptance is only temporary and that after the Ph.D. they will again pursue the medical degree. Behavior is now reoriented to what is proper and desirable for the kind of persons they have become. Whereas first-year students cannot understand, for example, the reasons why some of their seniors choose an academic career while others turn to a career in commercial research, the older student has acquired in interaction with teachers and still older students a set of explanations (motives) to be attached to such behavior, and it is with respect to these that he now orients his own behavior. He perceives his own dispositions as one or another of these group-assigned motives and makes his choices accordingly, choosing the academic life if he feels himself more interested in "science," commercial research if he is more interested in "money."

In these later years of graduate work the professors begin to worry about placing the student, who comes himself (a consequence of his new identification) to take the problem seriously. It is probable (although we do not know this) that the seriousness of the student's attachement to his new identity influences the degree to which his teachers work on placing him satisfactorily. Sponsorship activities by professors obligate the student to do well in the position he will be put into, thus further strengthening the new identity as it relates to position in the formal and informal arrangements of the occupational world.

The man who wanted to become a doctor is now the man who is a physiologist. Even in those few cases in which the M.D. is still desired, there is no thought of entering medical practice; rather, it is seen as a necessary preparation for research in human, as well as animal, physiology.

The Engineers

The engineers have made a firm choice of occupation long before reaching graduate school; college and, in some cases, industrial experiences attendant on this choice have produced a very strong identification with engineering. They have acquired a characteristic ideology, centering around the notion of the engineer as a logical thinker, and have internalized the typical motives of the group, primarily "making money" and "getting opportunity for advancement." They expect to spend their careers in the field, with the qualification that they may move, as engineers, into the higher ranks of industrial management; a few older man are teachers of engineering who have found a Ph.D. necessary for further academic promotion. The others either are just out of college or have had a year or two in industry beyond this when they enter graduate school, feeling on the basis of knowledge of the job market (derived from work experience or interviews with employer representatives) that they will be able to command a higher salary if they have additional training or an M.S. degree. The choice of graduate training is thus oriented to a specific and limited goal.

The pattern for the younger group begins with a year of courses devoted to improving one's market price. Many students hold research or teaching assistantships, which do not begin to match financially what they might have had had they left school. The assistantships prevent them from finishing work for the M.S. in one year, and most require a second. But they leave as an open question whether they will continue work for the degree or move on (or back) to the far greater financial rewards of industry, for they will have lost no time by spending the year in school without completing the degree and so feel free to leave without doing so. They tend to reckon the benefits of their graduate work in terms of courses finished and new knowledge gained rather than degrees. New problems and skills interest them only to the extent that they are seen as useful in the pursuit of their basic aims.

In short, this move does not commit them to anything beyond a semester or year of school, which they expect will have immediate practical results; when the results are unsatisfactory, or the immediate goal is achieved, they leave. Most leave at the end of a year, having accomplished their purposes; this is suggested by the fact that, although there are thirteen first-year students, there are none at all in the second year. A few who have comparatively well-paying research jobs stay on, taking a minimal amount of course work. They are interested, although not greatly, in getting a degree; more importantly, they like their jobs and feel that they offer as much in money and in opportunity to meet important people in industry and become known through publication as does an industrial position. So they keep making these short-term commitments year after year without feeling constrained to do so, for it would cost them nothing to leave. When they get the degree, they have become specialists in some particular area, know the people in it, and get jobs as technical experts.

A few others are tempted by the academic life sufficiently to continue as teaching assistants until they finish their Master's work, at which time they may well be offered faculty positions, since engineering schools find it difficult to keep younger faculty, not being able to match the salaries common in industry. They appear during this period to have come to like the relatively relaxed atmosphere of the campus and to have taken over the lower financial and class-mobility goals of academic life, so that industry no longer appears as attractive. And, in any case, if they find that academic life is not so desirable as they had imagined it, they can easily find an industrial position at an appropriate level.

There appears to be little in the way of organized peer relations, perhaps because the conditions of their work do not draw them into touch with one another. The students are typically employed on semiautonomous kinds of projects which do not provide situations in which they might meet and become friendly. It may also be true that the fact that they feel themselves to be in school only temporarily and always have an eye on the outside world mitigates against the development of such groups.

The engineers, then, maintain their basic identification with engineering, simply adding to their abilities during their further schooling in order that they may have a greater range of better jobs available to them as engineers, in industry and possibly in universities. Relations with professors are friendly but not close; where a close relation exists, it is one between younger and older professionals rather than between teacher and student.

The older man's sponsorship is considered helpful but not in any way essential to getting a good job. The students' identification and goals do not change much and can be maintained in school or out.

The Philosophers

The philosophy students typically choose their field of graduate work as being the least bad among a set of undesirable possibilities. Sometime during college, and in some cases even earlier, they have chosen as an important basic identification that of the "intellectual." From the perspective of this identity their task is to be aware of and interested in the whole field of human intellectual endeavor, from science through aesthetics to metaphysics and ethics, to keep an open and inquiring mind, and to avoid the dangers and rigidities of specialization. Philosophy seems to offer the greatest opportunity to maintain such a stance vis-à-vis the world of knowledge.

Although they profess to be uninterested in jobs and financial matters, and do in fact show little apparent interest, they seem to consider a higher degree necessary. Thus the choice of fields is, they feel, forced on them by the organization of universities into departments, in one of which they must take their Ph.D. (They differ in this from intellectuals of earlier periods, who might as easily have gravitated toward the then socially acceptable role of the unattached intellectual.)

They enter graduate work with backgrounds ranging from the natural sciences to the arts and retain interests in these fields along with others they have become aware of since their commitment to the intellectual life. Some made this commitment early enough to escape ever having specialized at all. Their course work can easily cover an equally wide range, so that they are not constrained by departmental requirements to narrow the focus of their intellectual activity and concentrate on some particular specialty. They thus are able to maintain the over-all intellectual identification and avoid being shunted into activities which might have as their consequence the development of a specialized identity.

The formal and informal relationships of faculty and students, and of students with one another, do not operate to make a cohesive group of the department but rather to provide conditions under which little essential change in identification will occur. Student-faculty relations are largely confined to the classroom and office consultations over classwork, and the student sees little and learns little of his professors' professional aims and activities; the professor, likewise, does not come to know students well enough to take a realistically active role in the shaping of their interests, even if he should so desire. Students do not in these circumstances develop any picture of their probable future as philosophers; nor does this trouble them, for they are determined resolutely to avoid the effects of such institutional commitments as jobs. They expect to have them, probably in college teaching, but consider such details unimportant. In the same way, they do not see their teachers at work and thus never learn in the detail that is crucial just what it is that a philosopher does and so do not come to identify themselves with any particular set of tasks.

Their student work does not provide the conditions in which they must come together in continuous association—the equivalent of the physiologist's laboratory is missing—and there is in fact no cohesive student grouping into which younger students are systematically recruited by older ones. Instead, they tend to find their friends scattered through the university, on the basis of those interests which override the boundaries of academic specialties: political and social ethics, art and music, the philosophy of science, and so on. Their primary group participation thus does not channel interest into the confines of a specialized occupational identity but rather reinforces its flowing into areas which cut across the traditional dividing lines between disciplines and academic identities, reinforces their concern with maintaining a "balanced" as opposed to a "specialized" approach to knowledge. If anything, these associations (as well as the professors' example) help them to discover new areas of intellectual activity across which they may spread themselves.

Because philosophy suits the purpose of avoiding specialization so well, the students come increasingly to identify with it as they continue graduate work, viewing it as the academic identity which least constrains their intellectual pursuits; for this reason they do not switch fields as one might expect, given their wide-ranging interests. In addition, like the physiologists, they have after a few years made a sizable investment of time, if nothing else, in a philosophy degree and feel that it would be wasteful to begin again on a degree in another field; they do not question, however, the necessity of getting the degree, as well they might, given their views on jobs and specialization.

As they approach graduation, it becomes clear that they will have to get jobs somewhere and engage in some kind of work. This comes as something of a surprise, for neither faculty nor student associates talk about such things, and the matter has never before been brought forcibly to their attention. Their professors provide relatively little sponsorship, and so they are not constrained to remain in the field because of obligations to such sponsors. Faced with the problem of getting jobs, they do realize that their work futures depend on their identification by others as philosophers, and they tend to accept this fact and incorporate it into their own self-images. In looking for jobs, they become aware of a number of kinds of positions besides that of member of a college philosophy faculty which they might hold; for example, depending on their other interests, they may find it possible to compete for teaching posts in tangential fields such as literature, research jobs as specialists in logic, and so on. They are thus able to maintain a nonspecialized task orientation even upon entering the labor market.

These heavily intellectually oriented students become Ph.D.'s with a less specialized job potential than most but, except in this respect, do not change their basic identification much during their graduate training, rather deepening their commitment to the intellectual life and incorporating consciously more of the implications of this commitment. The attachment to the identity is built from this commitment and from the recognition that their jobs, whatever they may be, will be gotten as a result of their academic work in the field of philosophy.

Discussion

Our analysis suggests the operation of certain specific mechanisms producing changes in identity. These mechanisms, as our introductory statements indicate, consist of ways that participation in organized groups of various kinds affects experience and, through this, self-image. Among the mechanisms operating in the cases under consideration are the development of problem interest and pride in new skills, the acquisition of professional ideology, investment, the internalization of motives, and sponsorship.

Among graduate students changes in participation result from movement into the orbits of three kinds of groups: the informal peer group or student clique, the apprentice relationship with professors, and the formal academic structure of the university, involving courses, grades, credits, and degrees. Each such movement generates characteristic kinds of experiences for the person and consequently creates a potential for change in or development of occupational identification. Comparison of our three cases indicates the conditions under which these mechanisms come into play and the way they produce work identification in three of the areas outlined earlier: attachment to occupational title, task commitment, and commitment to particular work organizations and/or positions in them.

Movement into the academic structure, through matriculation as a graduate student, sets the *investment* mechanism going.[5] Such a move is an investment of an irreplaceable quantum of time in a particular career, and not to follow that career means a loss of the investment. It is a first step up a ladder, and a misstep necessitates a new start and thus a falling-behind in the competition. Such a mechanism works only where general cultural

5. See the discussion by Eli Ginzberg and associates in *Occupational Choice: An Approach to a General Theory* (New York: Columbia University Press, 1951), pp. 193–96.

expectations emphasize age-graded mobility (as they do in this country) and where movement out of the academic structure entirely or into some other specialty would actually prove costly in this respect. The case of the engineers is instructive, for leaving graduate school costs them nothing, and they feel free to leave at any time; they show little change in their occupational identification. The opposite is true of the philosophers and physiologists who, in differing degree, do make this kind of investment. Once in the graduate program, they must continue through until the degree if they are not to lose precious time by having to "start over"; and, once they have the degree, they must remain what they have become in order to cash in on their investment. To the extent that this is true changes take place in their identification, particularly in the area of identification with particular work institutions and positions within them.

Movement into the formal academic structure places the person in classroom contact with men teaching materials new to him and teaching them, owing to the different aims of graduate training, in a quite different way. Matters presented to undergraduates as fact are now interpreted as problematic, as requiring further research, and the person's interest in these problems is aroused. New work techniques are presented, and the student is faced with the challenge of mastering them. Thus constrained by the school situation, perhaps with the opportunity to observe his professors making use of these skills, he acquires them and the interests they presuppose and so becomes associated in the eyes of others with the particular work identity they symbolize. Since his future depends in part on how others identify him, he is pushed in the direction of assuming the identity that goes with his new interests and skills in order that he may satisfactorily meet the expectations of others in the work world. This kind of identification process works best where techniques are highly specialized and there is opportunity to see professors using them and where the graduate program keeps interests clearly pointed in one direction, both being the case with the physiologists and to a smaller degree with the philosophers, whose graduate program does not so direct their interests and who have no techniques to learn and no chance to watch their professors at work. (The engineers simply maintain and deepen previous interests and skills, and there is little change in identification, except in the case of those who become teachers, where the interest aroused by teaching experience is influential.) This mechanism of *development of interest* and *acquisition of skill* thus operates to produce identification in the area of task commitment.

The mechanism of *acquisition of ideology,* which operates to produce commitment to occupational title, appears to be closely related to participation in informal student groups and, secondarily, to classroom and informal participation with teachers. It comes into operation when the person begins to raise questions, or have them raised for him, about the worth of the activity he is engaged in, when he asks himself why he is doing this rather than something else. He looks for answers, finds them in the developed professional ideology he becomes aware of in interaction with older students and professors, and takes them over for his own use. Thus armed, he can say why one should be interested in his field rather than others and why it is the best of all possible pursuits. Both the physiologists and the engineers have this strongly, the former acquiring it in their intensive interaction with students and faculty, the latter having already developed it in their under-graduate work. The philosophers have no such specialized ideology tying them to the field of philosophy and correspondingly little attachment to oc-cupational title, a consequence of the fact that they do not participate in cliques of fellow-philosophers and have relatively little informal interaction with teachers.

The *internalization of motives*,[6] most effective in producing attachment to institutional positions associated with a given work identity, seems to oper-ate primarily in clique and apprenticeship relations. As the person learns about the kinds of positions he may expect after finishing his schooling, he also learns why people want these things. The gossip of the student clique, as well as the talk of his teachers about "placing" him, provides him with a set of reasons for wanting the things which will be available to him and for making choices between them that are relevant to the professional identity he is assuming. He learns to explain and understand the choices and acts of others and thus acquires the means of developing impulses and translating them into socialized action in the sphere of work. Among the groups studied this is clearest for the physiologists, who have the greatest degree of clique interaction and apprenticeship.

The structural functions of the *sponsorship*[7] pattern have been explored in many studies, in which it has been described as a means by which persons low in an occupational hierarchy are recommended by more highly placed persons for better positions; it is seen as functional for the organization in recruiting able and loyal people and for the individual in achieving upward mobility. We wish here to call attention to its social-psychological functions, to the way it operates in the process of change and development in identifi-cation. Sponsorship involves a complex net of responsibilities. The sponsor is responsible to his colleagues for the performance of the person he spon-sors, who is in turn responsible to him for his behavior. When a person is sponsored into a first position in the work world after leaving graduate school, he feels obligated to act as a true member of the occupation and to

6. Foote, *op. cit.*
7. Hall, "The Stages of the Medical Career," *op. cit.*, and Becker, "Some Contin-gencies of the Professional Dance Musician's Career," *op. cit.*

remain within it, because of the trust placed in him by his sponsor. The creation of this obligation solidifies occupational attitudes and loyalties—the individual feels that he must remain what he has become in order not to let down his sponsor—and thus strengthens the identification with occupational title and ideology. The physiologists benefit from a fairly well-operating sponsorship system and exhibit correspondingly strong identification, while the philosophers do not get such energetic sponsorship, operating much more on their own in the search for jobs, and show as a result much weaker identification with their field. The engineers do not, in the state of today's job market in their field, need much sponsorship from their professors, and there is thus little opportunity for the mechanism to operate; there is consequently little change in their identifications in graduate school (except among the teachers, where this may be a factor).

It is through the operation of mechanisms such as those we have described, made up of changes in participation in organized groups and transformations of various aspects of the self-image, that occupational identifications develop and change. Our comparison of the three cases indicates that change in identity, occurring in different degree in each, may be explained by the coming-into-play of these mechanisms and that lack of change results from the failure of such mechanisms to operate because of the absence of the necessary structural conditions and appropriate individual perspectives. This being so, it constitutes in some sense a validation of our original model and suggests that a similar mode of analysis may prove generally useful in the understanding of changes in individual identity in the course of group experience.

Adjustment of Conflicting Expectations in the Development of Identification with an Occupation

Three sets of group expectations[1] influence the development of an individual's social-psychological identification with an occupation: generalized cultural expectations current in the society, specific expectations of the family, and expectations of the occupational group. Cultural expectations direct men in our society to have an occupation, to have one at an appropriate age, and to achieve success in their chosen field. Families elaborate these generalized expectations, setting specific criteria for satisfactory achievement. As the individual becomes involved in and identified with an occupation, he becomes responsive to the particular expectations of his occupational group.

In this paper we explore the problems of adjustment which may appear where these three sets of expectations present contradictions and incompatibilities. The analysis makes use of the interviews with graduate students in physiology, philosophy and mechanical engineering on which the last two chapters were based. Of the three groups, engineers exhibited few problems in the assumption of their occupational roles, while the philosophers and physiologists, in varying degrees and ways, did. We first present short de-

Reprinted by permission from *Social Forces,* 36 (October 1957), pp. 51–56. Copyright © 1957 by The University of North Carolina Press.

1. These three sets of group expectations function clearly in the development of occupational identity in the professions we have studied. Because of particular requirements and conditions of training other group expectations might be important in other occupations.

scriptions of the problems of adjustment and solutions to these which are characteristic of each group, and follow this with a more general discussion which attempts to set up a model in whose terms the forces and processes involved can be analyzed fruitfully.

Engineers

Any problems of adjustment faced by the engineering student in graduate school are solved by the feeling of success he has already achieved, or sees as being just around the corner. He has viewed himself as an engineer since receiving his Bachelor's degree and probably before that time; the knowledge that he can at any time get a highly-paid job supports this view. He comes to graduate school only to broaden the avenues of success already available to him by acquiring more knowledge. At an early age, during his undergraduate training, he has clearly met the formal expectation that he have a profession and it becomes more and more clear that success within this profession can easily be had.

The young engineer has few problems meeting his family's expectations. Most come from the families of skilled workmen; a few have fathers in farming, engineering, business, or small trades. Most indicate that their families wanted them to enter an occupation of higher prestige than the father's, but did not insist on any particular occupation. The choice of engineering met these expectations by placing them (potentially or actually) in positions in industry which can be understood by their parents as positions of prestige and high economic return. All report their parents happy with the choice, some pointing out that their fathers had worked in industrial organizations with engineers, had looked up to them, and thus have a clear image of the worth of this position. In one case where there was some doubt on this point, the interviewee felt that the growing professionalization of engineering would allow him to satisfy his family's more specific desire that he become a "professional man."

The fact that engineers take their place in a rapidly expanding industrial system, and that there are a number of alternative routes upward for them in industry—sales, production, design, management—means that the professional ideology fostering this feeling of inevitable success has some basis in fact. It is, in consequence, extremely effective in minimizing potential conflict over occupational choice.

Physiologists

Of the 18 physiology students 14 had at some time wanted a medical degree, but found it either impossible to get accepted into medical school or the pace is too difficult to continue. This desire, if not originally fostered by parents, is steadfastly maintained by them, and the failure to get into medicine is a failure to meet specific parental expectations. These families tend to be of a kind that can present their desires in a way the individual must take account of, being stable well-knit families in which the fathers play strong male roles; they are not so culturally foreign as to allow the sons to discount their understanding of the occupational world.

All the students who have failed at medicine must find another life's work. Those whose early ambitions carry them as far as applying to medical school are slow to accept this and turn to physiology as a stop-gap measure. This allows them to mark time while making further efforts to enter medical school and yet study something that will be of use in the medical career for which they still strive. As this becomes increasingly unrealistic and they find themselves in need of an alternate career, they turn to physiology (to which they are already partially committed). Still sensitive to their families' specific desires that they achieve social success through a medical career, they find it necessary to justify their new careers, and do this in various ways. They point out, both to themselves and their parents, that they will "still be doctors," albeit Ph.D.'s rather than M.D.'s, and will work in close association with medical men, perhaps teaching in a medical school.

More importantly, they may choose among the alternative careers available to a physiologist in such a way as most nearly to meet their parents' expectations. For example, some consider careers in commercial research because these pay well, hoping thus to approximate the income their parents expected them to achieve as physicians. In fact, the positions they will probably achieve in the academic or research worlds carry more prestige than the positions of their predominantly lower-middle class parents; but the position of physiologist does not seem as good to the parents as that of the M.D., because it is not as easily understood. The parents' own experiences with doctors are more real to them than all of the son's references to Nobel Prize winners and famous professors, none of which convince them that physiology is really as good a thing for their boy.

By the time this problem arises, many have come to accept wholeheartedly the profession's ideology, which spells out in detail the reasons for considering physiology superior to medicine; failing to meet family expectations, they fall back on this ideology as a way of denying the validity of their parents' claims.

Philosophers

Graduate study of philosophy does not represent an occupational commitment for the student, but rather acceptance of a way of life which bars commitment to any specific set of tasks or any particular set of organizational positions. He wishes to remain free to broaden himself intellectually in whatever directions he thinks appropriate, not fully admitting or realizing that he is preparing for a life in academia. To specialize, to have an occupational commitment, is something to be avoided; to strive for success by the standards of society at large is no virtue and may even be conceived as "immoral." These students do not, at this point, feel any compulsion to respond to generalized expectations that they have an occupation, since they accept the view that by the standards of "normal" society they are deviant.

Viewing a Ph.D. degree as the best way to realize these broad intellectual interests, they are forced, on finishing undergraduate work, to choose a specialty. The choice of philosophy makes it apparent for the first time that they are not going to meet the expectations of their parents for, though none of the families had any very specific expectations for their sons' futures, they now realize that they did not want them to become philosophers. Before this choice is made the family can explain away their sons' shifting from subject to subject as a more or less legitimate period of youthful exploration. Once it is made, however, the disparity between the perspectives of parents and child becomes obvious.

But by this time the student is of an age where parental expectations are easily discounted, more easily these students tend to come from families whose desires can be ignored with equanimity. In every case but one, the students came from homes where the parents were foreign born or divorced, where one parent was dead or the father did not play a strong masculine role; there was no functioning group capable of presenting cultural imperatives forcefully. Their parents do not understand what it means to be a philosopher, but this makes little difference and produces few problems of adjustment because there is no effective power to enforce family disapproval.

The study of philosophy represents a definite rejection of conventional occupational expectations buttressed by the ideology current among their fellow students, both in philosophy and other fields in which they have contacts. This ideology specifies the importance of free, wide-ranging intellectual activity, not tied to any specific academic discipline, and finds support both historically and in current academic life.

Discussion

In what follows we present a model of the interaction between family and occupational expectations in the development of an individual's occupational identity. Our case material does not provide proof that the relations discussed are correctly stated, but the model has been built by trying to take account of the several orders of things described in our interviews.

A set of generalized cultural expectations about the relations of an adult male to the work world operates in our society. Occupation is one of the major determinants of social-class position and in other ways as well is one of the important criteria by which individuals are socially identified. At a given age (which varies in different parts of the society) a man is expected to have assumed (or committed himself to the training necessary to assume) a particular occupational role. Such adult responsibilities as marriage require him to have made arrangements guaranteeing the financial independence necessary for adulthood by making such an occupational commitment. With increasing age he is expected to behave "sensibly" and stick with such a choice once made, thus demonstrating his maturity and avoiding the loss of time and training involved in an occupational change. Finally, people generally expect (although this expectation is no doubt violated more frequently than the others) that he will be "successful" (whatever that may mean) at his chosen work and that this success will aid in social-class mobility. Our society confronts adult males with the necessity of satisfying or otherwise adjusting to this set of generalized expectations.

These cultural expectations probably appear most forcefully to the young man in the form of specific expectations of his family, which translate such general dicta into specific and strong imperatives, backed by the family's sanctioning power. These family expectations tend to be specific statements of the more general mobility theme, directing the person to achieve mobility in a particular way, through success in one or a few of occupations. To the degree that these expectations can be met only in one or a few ways, the individual feels his chances of failure to be greater and thus feels under greater pressure.

Families may differ in the specificity of their aspirations for their children and thus in the number of potential mobility routes they see as possibilities.[2] Those with specific notions begin grooming the child for the chosen profession at an early age, forcusing attention on their desires through frequent references to the profession, to relatives and acquaintances in it, and so on. Such focusing constrains the child's choice, causing it to be made earlier.

2. In a study in which parents were asked what information they would consider important about a potential son-in-law, respondents from the lower socio-economic strata mentioned, among other items, whether he had a job and whether he was a good provider, while middle-stratum respondents were more concerned about his specific occupation. The study is reported in William H. Form and Gregory P. Stone, "Urbanism, Anonymity, and Status Symbolism," *American Journal of Sociology* LXII (March 1957), 512.

Constraint of this kind may be ineffective if the family lacks the authority to enforce its decisions on the child. If a son considers his family well-informed about the occupational world, it will have greater authority than one whose perspectives are regarded as limited and unrealistic. If, for example, the father or some other close relative or family friend is a member of the desired profession, the son will regard his family as knowledgeable and its desires will of necessity be taken seriously. Equally, if the child chooses a well-known profession (as the engineering student does) he may agree that, by virtue of general public knowledge, his family is well informed.

In the same way, a family's authority will likely vary with the degree to which it conforms to socially defined patterns of family organization. A family in which the parents are foreign born, poverty stricken, or socially nonconforming may find the son able, through reference to these characteristics, to discount their desires for his future. Similarly, families in which the parents are separated, in which one parent is dead, or in which the father does not play a dominant male role, are not in a position to use the father's traditional sanctioning power in affecting the son's career choices.

Families with expectations of a more general kind allow the youth a much freer range in choosing a career and also allow him to postpont any choice until a later date. He can experiment longer and try out more possibilities, as did the philosophy students in our study. When the choice is finally made, however, it may turn out to be incompatible with the family's expectations; they may have felt, as the philosopher's parents apparently did, that anything their son wanted to do was all right until they found out how far afield he had drifted. But in such cases conflict and the discovery of incompatibility are postponed till a relatively late date.

One of the consequences of such postponement is that by the time difficulties arise the person may be well on the way to commitment to an occupation. Once so committed, he acquires the option of viewing the situation from the perspective of the occupational group, and thus of becoming relatively less sensitive to his family's desires. The philosophers' parents do not realize their sons' deviant aspirations until the sons are well indoctrinated with an intellectual ideology which makes the ultimate break with family easy and painless.

It is not always necessary or possible for an individual to make use of occupational group perspectives in this way. The person who has successfully met parental expectations, as having the engineering students, has no need for an alternative perspective with which to dismiss those expectations. He has no need for answers to parental criticism, for there is no criticism. A person who has committed himself to something his family wanted and failed at it (as have those physiologists who intended to become physicians) finds himself unable to make use of occupational perspectives readily since he himself shares the view of his parents. Still trying to please them and thereby himself, he cannot so easily write off their desires from his new occupational point of view.

Approaching the problem in a different way, let us note that some occupations require very early commitment, while others can be entered later in one's career. One cannot easily decide to become a doctor at the age of 25; 15 or 16 is nearer the proper age to make such a choice. But the decision to become a philosopher can be made at 25 with little difficulty. When an occupation requiring early commitment is chosen, it is typically chosen by the family and individual together; it is not a step that an adolescent makes alone. Such choices may be unrealistic from the point of view of the young man involved. He tends to know less of the realities of the profession he has chosen than a man who makes his choice after he has had more opportunity to explore and observe the work world. This early uninformed choice, in its turn, increases the possibility that he will not be able to meet successfully the problems of his chosen career or that he will find he does not like it after all and would prefer something else. In either case, he will fail to meet his family's expectations and provoke conflict with them.

When the son chooses his father's occupation, the choice is also made early, but is much more likely to be made realistically. As Hall pointed out the boy from a medical family chooses a career about which he knows a good deal at an early age.[3] Further, he will probably be given systematic encouragement and effective assistance in pursuing this career. If tension arises, it is likely to be over the son's failure to take advantage of this assistance, either through his failure to meet professional standards or his discovery that there is something he likes better.

As previously noted, the occupational groups to which these young men become committed have characteristic professional ideologies which specify the kinds of relations proper between members of the occupation and between them and persons who do not belong to the occupational group. These ideologies keep people in the occupation despite tensions produced by incompatible family expectations. Anticipating future difficulties and knotty questions which families are likely to raise, they provide models for action and ready answers to objections. For instance, the philosophers acquire conceptions of the intellectual which explain why he must ignore the pressure of a "middle-class family" and a middle-class culture to settle

3. Oswald Hall, "The Stages of a Medical Career," *American Journal of Sociology* 53 (March 1948), pp. 327–37.

down to a specific occupation. Similarly, the young physiologist learns to believe that his profession is really superior to that of the physician, to believe that, as one of our interviewees put it, "we write the music that the doctor plays" (that is, do the research without which medical diagnosis and treatment would not be possible). This ideology warns them that questions will be raised by the uninformed and provides the answers which make remaining in the profession a reasonable thing.

Such occupational ideologies will become working guides for action only when the person feels them legitimate, ordinarily only when he finds some kind of socially based support for them. Such support can be found in a variety of ways. The physiologists find it in a close-knit clique organization of student life, in which older students continuously indoctrinate younger ones in the same way they are themselves indoctrinated by their professors. They find support in the opinions of those above them in the graduate school and occupational hierarchy. The engineers find their support for an ideology of rapid and inevitable success in their experiences in the work world; the actions and statements of employers, present and potential, bear out the predictions of the ideology. The philosophers find their support in participation in an abstract intellectual "world," an amorphous grouping of those with similar cultural and intellectual interests which finds its concrete expressions in the writings and other productions of its members.

Under what circumstances does one rather than another source of such socially based support become prominent for a given group? Apparently this depends on who else understands one's career problems, and the degree of understanding and sympathy on the part of others whose opinion one considers important. Both the engineers and physiologists consider it important that their parents understand the character of their careers. But the engineer's career, essentially that of an industrial executive, is often discussed and portrayed in popular culture; since parents can be counted on, because of this, to understand, no support is needed from elsewhere. The physiologist, on the other hand, has embarked on a career whose inner workings and peculiar successes and failures are incomprehensible to his parents; if he is to meet successfully the problems his career creates in his relations with them he must find support, as he does, in an actual functioning group of colleagues. The philosopher, like the engineer, does not require such well-organized colleague support because, in his case, the ideology is self-confirming to a very great degree. It formally dismisses the necessity for worrying about parents' expectations on the grounds that they simply do not understand; when their actions bear out this prediction the philosopher is able to turn to the intellectual world freely, unencumbered by worry over his family's feelings.

Conclusion

We often assume that problems of adjustment inevitably arise for persons involved in important steps of their life career: adolescence, marriage, the choice of an occupation, and so on. Because our society is so heterogeneous and lacking in specific rules directing behavior at these points of crisis, the individual is said to be faced with conflicting expectations. Choice between these expectations is viewed as problematic and productive of problems of adjustment.

Our analysis indicates that conflict does not necessarily occur in assuming an occupational identity. When conflict does occur it centers around disparities between parental and occupational expectations. The following elements are importantly involved in the process: the specificity of family desires and the power of the family to make these felt, the character of the commitment and the time at which it is required by particular occupations, the nature of the occupational ideology and the kinds of social support for it, and the timing of appearance of incompatibilities between family and occupational expectations. It is the relationship among these that determines whether or not conflict and the necessity of adjustment will occur.

CHAPTER FIFTEEN

Schools and Systems
of Social Status

In most complex societies, and particularly those organized around the values and institutions of Western culture, schools play an important role in the drama of social mobility. Education being at the same time a symbol of social position and a means by which higher position may be achieved, the amount of access to it is one of the keys to the amount of mobility possible in a society. Research on the American school system has alerted us to some of the ways schools aid or hinder mobility on the part of subordinate groups.[1] In this paper, I compare the American situation with what is known of the educational systems of colonial and underdeveloped areas, with an eye to tracing some of the more general dimensions of this relationship between schools and systems of social stratification.

It must be said immediately that in many areas of the world the whole question of mobility and education may be irrelevant. In the first place, education is not often sufficient in itself to make mobility possible. Other things are needed, and a person who acquires a schooling has only begun to move. How far he gets depends, among other things, on where there is to go. If there are no available positions in the upper strata, as there

Reprinted by permission from *Phylon,* 16 (1955), pp. 159–170. Copyright 1955 by Atlanta University.

1. On the American situation in general, see W. L. Warner, R. J. Havighurst, and M. B. Loeb, *Who Shall Be Educated?* (New York, 1944). I have relied heavily on the studies of the Chicago school system done under the direction of Everett C. Hughes, reported in a number of M. A. and Ph.D. theses at the University of Chicago, as well as in H. S. Becker, "The Career of the Chicago Public Schoolteacher," "Social-Class Variations in the Teacher-Pupil Relationship," and "The Teacher in the Authority System of the Public School," all in this volume.

are not in many colonial societies, no way of earning a living in a properly prestigeful way, schooling does not produce mobility but only frustrates desire; it has no effect on the status system. In such a situation disappointment may be avoided by ignoring the mobility possibility.

This raises another qualification limiting the applicability of our analysis. The degree to which mobility is desired by members of subordinate groups cannot be taken for granted but must be regarded as problematic. To the degree that such groups consider mobility in fact impossible it will not be sought. Equally important, to the degree that a subordinate group maintains a self-sufficient culture and shares only a minimum of common understanding with those above it—to the degree that the society is what M. G. Smith has termed a "plural society"[2]—mobility will be sought only within the group; movement to the culturally alien superordinate group will be neither desired nor pursued. Under these circumstances the school has little effect on systems of status, since mobility between groups, however accomplished, is not an important feature of the society.

Within the limits suggested by these qualifications, i. e., insofar as mobility is considered worth attempting and is aided by exposure to schooling, it becomes pertinent to inquire into how schools affect mobility. In succeeding sections I consider the way school organizations, through their institutional structure, act on the stratification system. (Systems in which openly discriminatory law and practice prevent subordinate groups from gaining access to schooling have not been dealt with, their workings being too obvious to require discussion, although perhaps of major importance in any assessment of the current situation.)

I

Societies vary in degree and kind of cultural heterogeneity, and in the way the school system takes account of these various cultures. In the United States there is, of course, tremendous cultural diversity: ethnic mixture, rural-urban differences and, in the larger cities particularly, well developed social-class subcultures, with characteristic emphases in language, thought, behavior, and values.[3]

2. See his "Social Structure in the British Caribbean about 1820," *Social and Economic Studies,* Vol. 1, no. 4 (August 1953), 55–79; and "Slavery and Emancipation in Two Societies," *ibid.,* Vol. 3, nos. 3 and 4 (December 1954), 239–90.

3. On the differences between lower and middle class behavior and values, see Allison Davis, "The Motivation of the Underprivileged Worker," in *Industry and Society,* ed. by William F. Whyte (New York, 1946), pp. 84–106. On the differences in language and thought, see Leonard Shatzman and Anselm Strauss, "Social Class and Modes of Communication," *American Journal of Sociology* LX (January 1955), 329–38.

Underdeveloped areas, while they do not often exhibit the ethnic variety of the metropolitan centers, tend toward a much more radical gap between the cultures of dominant and subordinate groups. Class cultures in European and American cities, though they differ greatly, grow from the same root. Ethnic differences, while they may be considerable, tend for the most part to be variants of Western European culture. In colonies, established when Europeans migrated and set up governments incorporating the earlier inhabitants of the territory and perhaps other people brought from still elsewhere, the groups may come from two totally different civilizations, as when Europeans met Asians; or Europeans may come into contact with people still living a tribal life, as in Africa. The groups are fewer, the cultures more distinctive, and the distance between much greater.

Not all of these cultures are taken account of and made the basis of practice in the educational institutions that arise in either of these situations. And so the question arises, as Tax put it,[4] "whose cultural tradition it to be transmitted?" In the cities of America and Europe there is ordinarily some basic ethnic tradition which, without argument, becomes the medium and content of educational activity. (There may occasionally be two, as in the case of the French and English in Quebec, or the Flemings and Walloons in Belgium.) Education in this culture is available and those wishing something else for their children must make their own provisions. Of the social-class cultures, that of the middle class (in which most educational personnel have their origin[5]) usually becomes the standard.

In the colonies and underveloped areas, the issue is not so simple. Those at the top waver between wanting everyone else to learn their language and culture, and either of the two opposites of providing no education at all or education more or less within the framework of the native culture. It is easier to rule and to run economic enterprises where native cultures are abandoned for that of the ruling power, for the difficulties in operating Western legal systems and industrial organizations in the midst of an alien culture are tremendous.[6] This implies schools teaching the rulers' culture, in their tongue. On the other hand, the dominant group may take seriously the anthropologists' warning about the consequences of disrupting the subordinate group's culture in this way. They may feel a sympathy for, or be fascinated by, a primitive and exotic way of life. If it is felt that the values of maintaining the native culture ought to be combined with progress of some sort, vernacular schools may be set up; or, if no such combination

4. Sol Tax, "The Education of Underprivileged Peoples in Dependent and Independent Territories," *Journal of Negro Education* XV (Summer 1946), 336–45.
5. Cf. Warner, Havighurst, and Loeb, *op. cit.*
6. On legal systems, see Rene Maunier, *The Sociology of Colonies,* ed. and trans. by E. O. Lorimer (London, 1949), Part III; on industrial systems, see Everett C. and Helen M. Hughes, *Where Peoples Meet* (Glencoe, 1952), Chapter 5.

is sought, the solution may be no schools at all for the subordinate group. This latter possibility is, in effect, what occurs in those places in which a small elite endeavors to retain its position through a monopoly of education, as in Haiti.

The subordinate group may take one of several attitudes toward this question, to the degree that it interests them at all. They may desire education in the culture of the dominant group because of the status advantages with which they know it can equip them. As in Ireland, and more recently in Africa, they may be caught up in a developing nationalism and wish to reject the dominant culture, uniting the institution of the school with their own language and culture. Where the subject people have their own civilization with well-developed schools holding a ritually-sanctioned status in the society, as in India, resistance to Western education may be led by the teachers of these schools, whose jobs and social position would be lost in the change.[7] Because some knowledge of the culture and more especially the language of the ruling power has been essential if one was to better himself, the dominant attitude has usually been a desire for as much education in that area as could be obtained.

The educator faces a real dilemma in such situations, where subordinate groups require training in the dominant culture for social "success." If, on the one hand, teaching proceeds within the cultural and linguistic framework of the dominant group, members of the subordinate group, who have not had the preparation in daily experience presupposed by such an educational program, do not do well. It bears no relation to their daily life, is unfamiliar, difficult to understand, largely meaningless, and can be learned only by rote if at all. This seems to be one of the major problems in Africa,[8] where the African must attempt to acquire a British education, as it is in the cities of the United States, where the lower-class child must try to absorb the teaching of a school oriented to the quite different culture of the middle-class.[9] The problem of motivation is likewise important. As Davis points out, the urban American lower-class child is likely to believe that education will not do him much good, that it is not really worth trying and will not make the effort needed to surmount the obstacles of an unfamiliar culture.[10] (This, of course, is no problem in colonial areas, except to the

7. See J. R. Cunningham, "Education," in L. S. S. O'Malley, *Modern India and the West* (London, 1941), pp. 142–3.

8. T. R. Batten, *Problems of African Development,* Part II (London, 1948), p. 66. See also J. M. van der Kroef's description of a classical case of the effect of this problem on the school's mobility function in Indonesia, both before and after independence from the Dutch had been achieved: "Educational Development and Social Change in Indonesia," *Harvard Educational Review* 24 (Fall 1954), 239–55.

9. Cf. Allison Davis, *Social-Class Influences upon Learning* (Cambridge, 1950), and Kenneth Eells. et al., *Intelligence and Cultural Differences* (Chicago, 1951).

10. Davis, "The Motivation of the Underprivileged Worker," *op. cit.*

extent that compulsory education becomes a reality and students are re-cruited who must be kept in school against their will.) In such situations the child of the subordinate group gets little education; the school may stick determinedly to the alien agenda, but it does not accomplish much. The students learn little that will help them better their social position.

On the other hand, if an attempt is made to adapt the curriculum to the language and culture of the subordinate group, in the hope of increasing the achievement of the school, they are likely to interpret the move as an attempt to prevent them from learning what they need to know and acquir-ing the diplomas they need to get ahead in the world. If, for example, a colonial school is taught in dialect rather than standard English, it may do more teaching; but the students and their families may feel, possibly with some justification, that this only prevents them from learning the language of the dominant group, precisely what they require for success-ful mobility. Attempts to introduce "native" subjects and dialects, to pro-vide education different in any way from what would be given a child of the dominant group, seem an attempt to make sure that the man on the bottom stays there, and may in fact have this consequence, intended or not.[11] For such systems of dual education may easily turn into segregated deadends for the racial or otherwise subordinate groups they are intended to aid. It is for this reason that labor unions in the United States have traditionally opposed plans to build technical secondary schools for work-ing class areas, interpreting this as a move to deny the sons of workers the education they need to rise out of the working class. This even where the ordinary secondary school proceeds in a manner that makes it difficult for the lower-class child to succeed.

In addition, teachers in such areas are likely themselves to be mobile from the subordinate group, one sign of their successful mobility being their ease in the language and cultural ways of the dominant group. They are likely to reject efforts to get them to teach in a language or dialect carry-ing less prestige.[12]

In short, educators in culturally differentiated societies are caught on the horns of this dilemma: to bring education "down" to the level of the subordinate group and thus give something, but not very much, to all or to "maintain standards" and thus aid only the gifted few? In whichever direction they move, they are likely to end by perpetuating the cultural differences between groups, and slowing the mobility flow to the continuing disadvantage of those at the bottom.

(By focusing only on mobility, this kind of argument ignores the im-portance of the school's function as the transmitter of a valued cultural

11. Cf. Arthur Mayhew, *The Education of India* (London, 1926), p. 71.
12. Cf. J. G. Leyburn, *The Haitian People* (New Haven, 1941), p. 279.

heritage. From a different perspective than the rather one-sided one of this paper, one might raise questions about the fate of this important function in school systems faced with these problems.)

II

Not all societies are organized so as easily to accommodate schools fashioned on the Western model. The question of whether a society can support such institutions involves not only the financial problems which everywhere concern educational administrators, but also the questions of the degree to which the society's values mesh with the notion of formal education and the extent to which they can furnish personnel to man the schools.

Although there are many failures of modern Western societies to support fully formal education, these societies do accept the notion of education of all children up to some specified age and pattern social arrangements in such a way as to allow this to go on. In many of the world's underdeveloped areas, on the other hand, particularly those in which subordinate groups are still organized at the tribal level, the very notion of a school is foreign to the accepted way of life. In addition, the child is an economic asset on which the family depends. Schooling, because it ties up a potential worker in non-productive activity, is expensive for them even when it is free. Consequently, attendance is erratic, always at the mercy of family need.

One result of the lack of cultural support of the educational enterprise in either kind of area is that education cannot be really cumulative, cannot progress year by year to new and higher subjects and skills. The teacher can never count on his pupils having already mastered some set of facts or skills just because they have had so-and-so many years of school, and each year tends to become a repetition of the last, devoted to attempting to make sure that everyone has at least mastered the basic skills of reading and writing. At each higher grade level the gap between what should be learned and what actually is learned becomes greater; teaching degenerates into a desperate attempt to instill some minimum amount of learning. Teachers are tempted in such a discouraging situation to take the easy way out, either giving up completely or devoting their efforts only to those few students who will accept them wholeheartedly and are comparatively easy to teach. The teachers' stereotypes about the subordinate group's lack of ability tend to be confirmed by their experience and leads to less effort being expended where more is in fact required, thus increasing the school's failure.

The question of financial support is of course important. Within the limits imposed by the extent of the society's resources—and these are immensely limiting in an area such as Africa where the money is simply not available to do the job—the problem is one of the allocation of funds. How much are people willing to pay to have children educated, particularly where schools are supported through taxation and the person who pays the largest taxes finds himself subsidizing the education of children of the subordinate group? Hughes has suggested that Canadian public education suffers from the reluctance of the smaller group of well-to-do English to so subsidize the education of the poorer and more numerous French Canadians.[13] The same political problems of the allocation of funds, rooted in the relations of status groups, are found in the segregated schools of the southern United States, and in those cities in which residential segregation makes possible selective spending for the education of racial and social-class minorities. Such financial dilemmas tend to be resolved to the disadvantage of subordinate groups.

Finally, there is the question of providing sufficient adequately trained personnel to keep the institution operating. What incentives are available to induce people of the desired kind to become teachers and are they sufficient to do the job? This may be put as a question of career potential. Starting as a teacher, where can one go, and are these prospects attractive enough to those who might enter the profession? In the United States, there are many people with appropriate education. From these, it appears that teachers are drawn largely from the ranks of those of limited ambition, who prefer the relative security of the school teacher's restricted occupational horizon to the risks of occupations which allow for more movement up and down. There are a great many people possessing this combination of limited ambition and higher education, and teachers are recruited in sizeable numbers.

In the underdeveloped areas, on the other hand, anyone who perseveres enough to get the education necessary for teaching wants a greater reward for his effort. And such rewards are often available. In Africa and India, better careers in industry and government were available to English speaking school graduates. Few received the basic education necessary for teacher training; they were ambitious, and passed up teaching for these alternative careers which carried more prestige, paid better, and tended to be nearer the centers of population.[14] This meant, in the first place, a shortage of teachers. Second, when coupled with the inevitable desire of educational authorities to get people with the highest educational qualifications,

---

13. Everett Cherrington Hughes, *French Canada in Transition* (Chicago, 1943), Chapter XI.
14. Cunningham, *op. cit.,* pp. 150, 160; Batten, *op. cit.,* pp. 43–7; The Nuffield Foundation and the Colonial Office, *African Education: A Study of Educational Policy and Practice in British Tropical Africa* (Oxford, 1953), p. 37.

it meant that teachers tended to be those who had failed in a try for the bigger prizes. "There has been (in India) a tendency to prefer 'failed matriculates' ready for the sake of a living to face work and surroundings with which they are out of sympathy, to less advanced, but more appropriate candidates."[15] A system which thus almost deliberately selects disgruntled failures for its teachers is bound not to get the greatest amount of teaching enthusiasm, which may be more important than a degree.

It may be taken for granted that where teachers are difficult to recruit, those groups they dislike teaching—the subordinate ones—will get something less than their share. Any system faced with a real shortage of teachers, therefore, will operate to reduce the possibility of upward mobility for these groups. It is only where an institutional system has been devised that will recruit successfully that this tendency is reversed. It is clear that different kinds of incentives and potential careers than those made available by the bureaucratic seniority systems of the older countries must be utilized in the underdeveloped areas if recruitment is to be successful.

III

Individual schools are linked, formally or otherwise, into systems, within whose boundaries teachers move from school to school in search of whatever satisfactions they happen to seek in their work. The teacher's career consists of a series of such movements between schools in the system, each of these constituting a stage in the career.[16] Looking at such a system at any given moment, we see a distribution of teachers at various stages of their careers among the schools making up the system. Systems tend to breed distinctive career patterns and this distribution of teachers of various kinds is not random. The question can thus be raised: what kinds of teachers do schools of various types tend to get?

The first point to be noted is that all schools in such a system do not look alike to the teacher. They differ in the kind of children they have as pupils, in the salaries they pay, in location, and so on. Some schools are very attractive to the teacher, places at which she would like very much to teach, while others are thought of as places to be avoided if possible. It may be, as in Chicago, that lower-class and Negro children are considered hardest to teach and most difficult to handle, so that schools containing them are avoided.[17] It may be, as in many places in the United States, that

15. Mayhew, *op. cit., p.* 250.
16. On careers, see Everett C. Hughes, "Institutional Office and the Person," *American Journal of Sociology* XLIII (November 1937), 404–13; and Oswald Hall, "The Stages of a Medical Career," *ibid.* LIII (March 1948), 327–36.
17. Becker, "The Career of the Chicago Public School Teacher," *op. cit.*

the teacher attempts to work her way out of the poorer paying, socially constraining rural hinterland into the nearest big city; Kansas City exemplifies this.[18] In underdeveloped areas, generally, living conditions, salaries, prestige, and ease of teaching, all combine to draw teachers toward the centers of population and away from the "backwoods" areas. For any of the reasons suggested, it is typically the schools handling children of subordinate groups which are least desired, and teachers' careers tend to be structured in terms of movement away from such schools.

Career movements tend to take this pattern, no matter what the arrangements by which movement occurs. In Chicago, teachers may request transfers to other schools, and will be moved as soon as there is a vacancy for which their request is of longest standing; this is essentially an arrangement by which seniority gets one the desired job. The record of these requests, when mapped, shows a tremendous movement away from the slums toward the middle-class areas. The same pattern may be seen in those informal rural-urban systems, like that of Kansas City, in which one moves by acquiring experience and bargaining successfully for the more desired jobs. In general, those teachers who have what the system wants—experience, teaching ability, whatever it may be—have most choice of position, and this leads to the pattern described.

Such a pattern of movement means that the less desirable schools, those teachers want to avoid, get something less than an equal share of teaching talent. At the least, it typically means that they do not get the experienced teachers, for experience is almost always a ticket to a better job whether through the workings of a seniority system or though the greater bargaining power it provides in bidding for jobs. In Chicago, many lower-class Negro schools are staffed almost entirely by teachers fresh from training school, the only ones who cannot choose their assignments; as soon as they build up enough seniority to move, they go, to be replaced by a new batch of beginners. More generally, it is probably true that, whatever the qualities a school system wishes to reward in its teachers, those qualities can be effectively rewarded only by assignment to the more desired schools, so that disadvantaged groups, who require the most skilled and experienced teaching, get the opposite and something less than an equal chance to an education.

There is very little information on problems of this order in underdeveloped areas. It seems likely that this picture holds for the West Indies, and for Africa—the poor, the rural folk, those most backward being taught by teachers who, through lack of experience or ability, cannot get positions in the cities. It would be most revealing to see studies made of the aspira-

18. See Warren A. Peterson, "Career Phases and Interage Relationships." Unpublished Ph.D. dissertation, University of Chicago, 1956.

tions and careers of teachers in such societies, with special emphasis on the fate of enthusiasm and ability in these systems. Is it true here too that careers move in such a way that students of the dominant groups get the best teaching, and vice versa, with the obvious consequences for the mobility chances of the subordinate group?

Such tendencies get reinforced, after they have been operating any length of time, in a way that makes them very difficult to change. The teachers who have been fortunate enough to locate in what are commonly considered the "more desirable" schools come to consider these positions their inalienable property. They feel that they have "served their time" (suggestive phrase!) and are now enjoying a well-earned reward. Others look forward to an equal reward when they too have served their time in the less desirable places; careers are built around this expectation. Any attempt to remove teachers from these schools and put them in places where their skills are more needed is looked on with great disfavor, as though the terms of contract were being broken; it may even be regarded as a species of punishment. (It is said that such transfers were used as disciplinary measures in the Chicago schools at one time, in much the same way policemen are punished by being assigned a beat in the "sticks.") There are hints of this tendency in Africa. The group reporting on educational problems in East and Central Africa mentions a similar "uneasiness in the teaching profession at the arbitrariness with which teachers and especially heads of schools are transferred from one school to another. . . . Instances were encountered in which a head of a school was transferred to a backward school as soon as his energy had produced an obvious improvement in his present school."[19] A transfer is arbitrary only when it violates some established expectation, and it appears that such expectations have already begun to form.

IV

Institutions try to become self-contained systems of power and to protect themselves against interference from the outside. Institutions are the means by which society delegates particular functions to specialized groups, always retaining the right to examine and pass judgment on that group's performance. Institutional functionaries feel that they understand the problems involved better than any layman and dislike any potential or actual interference, wanting to be left free to run things in their own way. Consequently, they erect defensive barriers designed to keep outsiders on the

19. The Nuffield Foundation and the Colonial Office, *op. cit.*, p. 117.

outside and prevent the surrounding society from directly affecting the institution's operation.

Schools share this tendency. Teachers and administrators find most satisfaction in their work, and feel they do their best work, when laymen do not interfere. They erect barriers of secrecy and mutual defense. The development of such defenses probably proceeds in relation to the perceived possibility of effective attack from the outside. The independence of the schools from such interference has an important, though by no means always the same, effect on the way the schools affect social mobility patterns.

Educational institutions differ greatly in the degree to which they are likely to be attacked, and in the success of their defense of their autonomy. The Chicago situation presents a fully developed case. These schools are very likely to be attacked at almost any time by the parents of their pupils, for not doing their job well enough or in the right way, for using improper disciplinary measures, and so on. They have developed, quite informally, an amazingly strong self-protective code. No principal or teacher ought ever to admit that anyone on the school staff has done anything wrong, even if this necessitates open lying, for to admit such a thing would be to admit the parents into the power structure of the school. The fact that anything has gone wrong is a closely kept secret. Parents and other outsiders are allowed to see the schools in action only when there is plenty of warning and a "show" of some kind has been prepared for them.[20] In systems oriented more toward examination systems of one kind or another, the possibility of attack may produce in addition an emphasis on demonstrable results—a high proportion of passes, for instance—even when this must be achieved by using rote learning methods in preference to more substantial kinds of education.

Such a system does not work equally well with all kinds of people. In Chicago, it works to perfection with lower-class parents who are easily intimidated by middle-class institutions. But it does not work well at all with the middle-class parent, who knows how to make trouble for the school and will do so without compunction if not satisfied.

Along with these two possibilities—that attacks will be successfully defended against, or that defense will fail—is a third: that there is no danger of attack and no need of defense. This may be the case in some of the newer colonies in which the parents are relatively unable to assess the school's work and deal with educational authorities. (It is always possible, however,

---

20. Summarized from Becker, "The Teacher in the Authority System . . . ," *op. cit.*, and from material in the Ph.D. thesis of Harold MacDowell, "The Principal's Role in a Metropolitan School System," (University of Chicago, 1954).

that groups from outside the society whose opinion carries weight will play the role that parents do elsewhere). It is likely, in colonial situations, that such attacks as are made will be focused more on quantitative concerns— numbers of schools and teachers, etc.—and that the brunt of any attack will be borne not by the teacher but by those administrative officers in charge of running the whole system.

In any case, whether by protective arrangements or through freedom from attack, the schools may gain for themselves an almost free hand, so that the teachers can pursue their real purpose relatively unhampered. In a system like Chicago's, particularly in lower-class areas, the teacher's primary aim is just to get along and not have too much trouble; educational standards come second. It is only where the institutional defenses are breached, as they are in middle-class areas, that this can be avoided and educational standards maintained. One of the elements preventing the lower class from receiving the full benefits of education in a class society is its lack of organization and effectiveness in pushing teachers to do better work. Where, on the other hand, the public demands quantity rather than quality, as may be the case in Africa, a determined teaching group able to withstand attack may actually provide more lasting benefit to underprivileged groups.

Again, such a public may be effective in forcing the schools to give out symbols of achievement whether or not there has been any achievement in fact; this is probably particularly the case in status-conscious underdeveloped societies, where the certificate or degree is almost a passport to higher position; see for example, Tugwell's description of the University of Puerto Rico where, at one time, students demanded and got, from a vulnerable faculty, degrees without accomplishment.[21] These can be hollow victories for the native group where, as in Africa and India, some real learning—at least, of a new language—must occur, where the symbols of accomplishment without the fact do no good.

The results of the educator's effort to run his enterprise in his own way, with no interference from outside, is thus quite important for the kind of education the child receives and the amount of social mobility made possible. The specific effect in any situation depends on three variables: the desires of parents and others who may possibly wish to have a voice in the school's operation; the desires of teachers and educational administrators; and the way the conflict over control of the schools is resolved, either to make them more responsive to outside pressure or to preserve for them effective autonomy.

21. Rexford G. Tugwell, *The Stricken Land* (New York, 1947), p. 109.

V

The schools, then, function importantly in the operation of the system of status and social class of the societies in which they exist. Where a society contains disadvantaged groups, education is one of the possible means of mobility for them just as it is one of the means by which members of the dominant group maintain their status. Education can provide a sizeable amount of opportunity for disadvantaged groups, if all groups have an equal chance to get an education.

It has been the concern of this paper to point out the way the ordinary operation of educational institutions, quite apart from deliberately discriminatory measures, tends to cut down the amount of mobility opportunity the schools provide. In solving such problems as the recruitment and distribution of personnel, the defense of institutional autonomy, etc., the schools, organized around one of the sub-cultures of a heterogeneous society, tend to operate in such a way that members of subordinate groups of differing culture do not get their fair share of educational opportunity, and thus of opportunity for social mobility.

If it is true that the schools have this conservative effect in general, it is of great importance, both theoretically and practically, to search for and investigate systematically such situations as that which existed, for example, in various cities of the United States at various times, in which the schools functioned in the opposite direction, becoming great channels of mobility for large groups. More research is needed on cases of this kind in order to bring out more fully the basic forces at work in orienting educational institutions toward one or another of these modes of relation to status systems.

CHAPTER SIXTEEN

Noncollege
Youth

When we talk of education, we ordinarily refer to the conventional institutions in which it is carried on: elementary schools, secondary schools, colleges and universities, graduate and professional schools. But this a narrow and class-biased view. It allows us to talk only about some of the things people learn and some of the places they learn them. For many people, conventional schools are not the only places in which learning occurs. We need, therefore, to ask more general questions, of which questions about conventional educational institutions are special cases. What do people learn as they grow up in our society? Where do they learn it? What do they want to learn? What must they learn if they are to achieve certain things in life? What opportunities have they for learning the things they need to know?

Rather than trying to answer all these questions for all kinds of learning, I will restrict myself to the kind of learning necessary for, to put it colloquially, "making out" in adult life. I will be concerned with the years after high school, the years in which adolescent boys and girls become adult men and women. I will be concerned with what it means, in a public way, to grow up in our society: how one learns the things and acquires the skills needed both to become and to feel oneself to be a mature adult. Social class differences influence this process and, because we know more about the middle class than the lower class in this regard, I will adopt the strategy

Reprinted by permission from *The Public Library and the City*, pp. 46–64. Copyright © 1965 M.I.T. Press.

The first section of this paper was originally published as "What Do They Really Learn in College?" *Trans-action*, I (May 1964), pp. 14–17.

of summarizing some of what we know about the middle class and then speculating about what may be true of the lower class.

Our society distinguishes many categories of people according to age. Following anthropological usage, we can call these categories age-grades. For each age-grade, people have some sense of what is characteristic and appropriate for a member of it to do and be. These conceptions are held both by others and by members of the age-grade itself. To move into the next higher age-grade successfully one must convince others and oneself that he is entitled to make the move. The conviction is established by showing that one has the appropriate skills and knowledge.

I will be concerned to show that most of what the middle-class youth needs to know can be learned in college, while some of the things the lower-class youth needs to know are not ordinarily taught him by the institutions with which he comes in contact. Indeed, after surveying the educational institutions, conventional and otherwise, with which lower-class postadoles-cents come into contact, I will conclude that there are a number of things that need to be done which no institutions are now doing.

Those Who Go to College: The Middle Class

Most middle-class boys and girls graduate from high school and go on to college. Many, perhaps most, college-goers learn in college precisely what they need to know to get along as adults in a middle-class world. The middle-class worlds of business and the professions demand a number of specific skills and abilities, and the experience of college is such as to provide college students with training in precisely those skills and abilities. I shall discuss a number of the demands made by the adult middle-class world, indicating in each case how the world of the college is organized to provide relevant training. Most of what I will talk about is not convention-ally regarded as an important part of the college curriculum; nevertheless, these are matters which are important for college students while they are in school and afterwards. They know it and act accordingly.[1]

INDEPENDENCE FROM HOME

Ours is one of the most mobile societies ever known. People move fre-quently and they move great distances. Unlike nomadic groups, they do

1. I rely here on research carried out by Blanche Geer, Everett C. Hughes and myself at the University of Kansas. See *Making the Grade: The Academic Side of College Life* (New York: John Wiley and Sons, 1968), for a report on one aspect of our findings. See also Blanche Geer, "Student Government, The Fraternity System, and the University Administration," *Journal of the Asociations of Deans and Admin-istrators of Student Affairs* 3 (July 1965), pp. 17–21.

not move together, taking their families and communities with them. They move because opportunity beckons elsewhere and it beckons to individuals, not groups. (It is sometimes the case, however, that people, moving individually, will gravitate to the same areas of their new community, so that some semblance of the old can be restored in a new place. I am told that Los Angeles contains many such colonies of people of a particular ethnic background and from the same home town who have somehow reformed in a cluster in some area of the city.)[2]

Moving for the sake of opportunity is very common in the middle class. As more and more people enter itinerant professions or go to work for one of the national organizations which ships its men around from city to city, more and more members of the middle class find themselves as young adults leaving their homes, neighborhoods, and families behind and setting out for new territory. Friends, instead of being furnished almost automatically by family connections and neighborhood contiguity, must be made without that help. To make the break from family and community requires an independence of spirit that does not come naturally.

Going away to college provides a rehearsal for the real thing, an opportunity to be away from home and friends, to make a new life among strangers, while still retaining the possibilities and affiliation with the old. In the dormitory, and even more in the fraternity and sorority, one finds himself on his own but at the same time surrounded by strangers who may become friends. One has the experience of learning to shift for oneself, of making friends among strangers.

Further, all the little chores that one's family performed now have to be taken care of in some other way. One gets one's own meals, takes care of one's own room, makes one's own bed, cleans one's own clothes. These are small things but, until one has learned to do them, things which may be difficult. They are a kind of training for the passage from home, whether it is geographical or simply the making of a new home upon marriage. Going to college provides the opportunity for this kind of playing at moving away from home for good and prepares the youngster for the world he will have to live in.

DATING, MARRIAGE, AND POISE

We normally expect young people to achieve some kind of workable relationship with members of the opposite sex, to learn how to get along with them, and eventually to choose or be chosen for marriage. For the middle-class youth, the problem is complicated by the requirement of the adult

2. I am indebted for this point to Santo F. Camilleri.

work world into which he will move that he choose a wife who will be "culturally adequate" for the circles in which his business or profession will require him to move. He must acquire the ability to attract and marry the kind of woman who can run a proper house for him and entertain for him. This means, of course, that women must learn how to perform these functions in an adequate middle-class way. It means that both men and women must learn the kind of manners, poise, and cultural skills necessary to move in such a world and to attract such a mate.

Again, the college (and particularly the large state university) provides the proper kind of training. Although it is not a standard part of the curriculum, training in manners, poise, and cultural skills is given in a wide variety of places on the campus. Fraternities and sororities specialize in it. Pledges are taught in formal classes how to introduce themselves to strangers, how to ask for a date or accept one, how to behave on a date, how to handle silverware at a formal dinner, and so on. (The necessity for this training is obvious if one watches incoming freshmen during Orientation Week. The people who prepare dinners for these students know that, in order to avoid embarrassment, they had better not serve any strange dishes which require more than rudimentary skill with silver.) Formal training is reinforced by constant practice. A stranger who walks into a fraternity house finds himself assaulted by a stream of young men rushing up to introduce themselves, fearing that if they do not one of the active members will punish them.

The dating system and the round of formal and informal social functions provided by both the Greek system and the university proper afford a fine training ground for meeting the opposite sex and finding a proper mate. Some students are required to have a certain minimum number of dates per month; most students feel some vague pressure to date, even when they find it anxiety-provoking. By participating in a round of parties and social functions, students learn the kind of manners and poise necessary for the social life of the country club or civic organization, skills that will stand them in good stead in their later middle-class lives.

Many, though by no means all, students receive training in dealing socially with "important people." Fraternities, dormitories, and other kinds of student groups make a practice of inviting important people, both campus personages and visitors, to meet with them. Students may have experience interacting with the governor of the state, the chancellor of the university, national political figures, or important visitors from overseas.

Two qualifications are necessary. First, many students learn manners, poise, and similar skills long before they reach college. Some have gone to good preparatory schools and many receive similar training in their own homes. Second, not everyone who goes to college acquires social skills. Some colleges are not set up with the array of organizations characteristic of the University of Kansas. And not all Kansas students receive this training. The ones who are most likely to receive it are those who belong to fraternities and sororities and those who are active in the world of extra-curricular activities. Students not in these categories often receive a good deal of social training too, but it is among them that one finds students who slip through without it.

WORK SKILLS

The middle-class occupational world demands a number of generalized work skills from its recruits. They must, first of all, acquire skills for their prospective occupations which the university is set up to teach. It may be that they need to learn the analytic techniques of chemistry or engineering; they may need to learn the skills of reading, writing, and the use of a library. Whatever it is, the university has courses which teach them some of the knowledge and techniques necessary to hold a job. (We must not overdo this. Many businesses, industries, and professional and graduate schools feel that the undergraduate college cannot, or at least does not, teach the required skills in the proper way. They prefer to train their recruits from scratch. To this end, many firms have in-service training programs which provide the specific knowledge recruits need.)

More important than the specific knowledge and techniques necessary for entrance into an occupation is a more generalized kind of work skill, one that in older days was referred to as "stick-to-itive-ness." The recruit to the middle-class occupational world must have the ability to see a job through from beginning to end, to start a project and keep his attention and energy focused on it until it is completed. The ability to get things done does not come naturally to young people; it is a hard-won skill. In acquiring it, the middle-class youth must learn to defer immediate gratifications for those that are longer in coming, to give up the pleasures of the moment for the larger rewards that await a big job well done. Most students have not had to learn this in high school, where the parade of daily requirements and assignments places the emphasis on receiving the immediate gratification of having done a particular day's job well. For many students, it is only when one reaches college that one is required to plan ahead in units of four or five months, keeping attention focused on the long-range goal of passing the course without the constant prodding of the daily assignment. (This is not to deny that many colleges, particularly in the freshman and sophomore years, mimic the pattern of daily assignments typical of the high school.) In learning to organize himself well enough to get a good grade in a college course, in learning to keep his mind on one job that long, the college student learns the middle-class skill of getting things done, so important in business and industry.

Finally, the middle-class world demands of those who enter it that they be able to juggle several things at once, that they be able to handle several jobs at one time, keeping them straight as they successfully finish all of them. One must learn to manage his time successfully and not fritter it away in actions that produce no reward. At least some college students get magnificent training in how to budget time and energy. The kind of student, of whom there are many, who does well in his courses and at the same time is, let us say, a high-ranking officer in several campus-wide organizations and an officer of his fraternity or dormitory, learns that he cannot waste his time if he is to achieve anything. He learns to set aside particular times for studying and to allow nothing to intervene; he learns to handle organizational matters with dispatch; he learns to give up or strictly ration the joys of watching television and drinking beer with the boys. He learns, in short, how to have a time for everything and to do everything in its time.

ORGANIZATIONAL SKILLS

The typical middle-class career now takes place in a bureaucratized organization. Even the professions, which used to be the stronghold of the individual practitioner, increasingly center their activities in an organization rather than a professional office. The doctor spends most of his time in and is most responsive to the social controls of the bureaucratically-organized hospital, rather than centering his practice in his own office. The recruit to the middle-class occupational world requires, if he is to operate successfully in it, the ability to get along in organization and bureaucracy. If the rules and constraints of large organizations frighten or anger him, he will not be able to achieve what he wants nor will he be an effective member of the organization. Among the specific things an effective member of a large organization must know and be able to do we can include the following: He must be willing and able to take the consequences for his own actions, to see ahead far enough to realize the effect of his actions on others and the organization. He must have some skill in manipulating other people, in getting them to do what he wants without the use of force or coercion; he must learn to be persuasive. He must have the ability to compromise, to give up some of what he wants in order to gain the rest; he must not be a narrow-minded fanatic, who either has his way or has none at all. And he must, finally, be knowledgeable and skillful in manipulating the rules and impersonal procedures of bureaucratic organizations to his own advantage, rather than being stymied and buffaloed by them.

The network of extracurricular organizations characteristic of the large state university provides a perfect setting in which to learn these skills. The student can participate in student politics, either as an active candidate or as a behind-the-scenes organizer. He can become an officer of one of the organizations that helps run campus activities. He can work on the student newspaper. He may be an officer of his fraternity or dormitory. A large number of students have experiences in one or more such organizations during their four years in college.

Melville Dalton, tracing the antecedents of successful industrial managerial careers, argues that experience in extracurricular campus life is a perfect background for success in industry:

> Taking a part in campus politics gives the student an experience he may not get outside of college, at his age, short of entering professional politics. He tries his hand at helping select and elect officers, and may himself serve, His part in the intro- and inter-organizational struggles is educational. He learns to move in and out of cliques and organizations with minimum friction. . . .
>
> He becomes sensitive to intangibles, and learns to live with the elusive and ambiguous. This unofficial training teaches him to get in his own claims and gracefully escape those of others that he must. He learns to appear sophisticated and to adjust quickly to endless new situations and personalities.[3]

Our observations at the University of Kansas corroborate Dalton's findings. Let me point out some additional sources of experience, important for the recruit to the middle-class occupational world, which Dalton does not mention. Many officers of campus organizations find themselves exercising responsibility for large amounts of money; they may administer budgets running as high as $50,000 a year. Some of them administer programs of activity in which it is necessary to coordinate the efforts of several hundred or more of their fellow students. You have only to think, for an example, of the effort and organization necessary for the traditional Homecoming Weekend at any big university. Some students even have the experience of discovering that the important people with whom they come in contact have feet of clay. As they deal with officers of the university in the course of their organizational work, they may be asked to do things they regard as improper. A typical case, which occurs in many universities, arises when some university officer attempts to prevent the student newspaper from publishing matter he believes harmful to the university. The student reporters and editors discover, in such a situation, that university officials are,

3. Melville Dalton, *Men Who Manage: Fusions of Feeling and Theory in Administration* (New York: John Wiley & Sons, 1959), pp. 166–167.

after all, only human too; it is a shocking and educational discovery for a nineteen-year-old to make.

MOTIVATION

The recruit to the middle-class world must, finally, learn to attach his own desires to the requirements of the organizations he joins. He must learn to have what we might call *institutional motivation*.[4] He must learn to want things simply and only because the institution in which he participates says these are the things to want. This linking of personal and institutional desire occurs in a paradigmatic way in college. The student learns that he requires, at the least, a degree and that he must do whatever it is the college asks of him in order to get that degree. This attachment to the long-range goal furnishes him with the motivation to continue in classes that bore or confound him, to meet requirements that seem to him foolish or childish. The college student learns to want to surmount the obstacles posed for him by the college, simply because the college has put them there. He learns to regard mastery of these external obstacles as marks of his own ability and maturity and, because he interprets the obstacles that way, sees his success in college as a sign of his own personal worth. The ability to link institutional and personal desires is probably an important prerequistite for occupational success in adult life.

I have just alluded to the major process by which the prospective recruit to the middle-class occupational world acquires the skills he does in college. In large part through participation in the college community, the student comes to define himself as the kind of person who ought to have these skills. He pins his self-respect and his sense of personal worth on acquiring them. He feels that he will have properly become an adult only when he has all these qualities and skills. He directs his effort and organizes his life in such a way as to achieve them and thus prove to himself and others that he has grown up.

Those Who Do Not Go to College: The Lower Class

Our problem is somewhat more complicated in considering the lower class, for two reasons. First, we know much less about lower-class youth than we do about those who go to college. Second, the lower classes must be divided into those who are mobile or potentially mobile—those who want to become

4. The sociological theory of motivation employed here is explicated in C. Wright Mills, "Situated Actions and Vocabularies of Motive," in Irving Louis Horowitz, ed., *Power, Politics and People: The Collected Essays of C. Wright Mills* (New York: Oxford University Press, 1963), pp. 439–452.

middle-class, who share the aspirations of those born to the middle class— and those who are not. We can simplify our problem somewhat by leaving the mobile members of the lower class out of consideration, assuming that they need the same things the person born into the middle class does. We can assume further that at least some of them will get to college and with luck will have the same kind of experiences as the middle-class youth and achieve the same things. These assumptions, of course, are questionable and conceal many important and interesting problems. I make them only so that we can leave these problems in abeyance and turn to the more clear-cut case of the nonmobile lower-class youth who does not go to college. What does he need to know? Where does he learn it, if he does learn it?

We realize immediately that we do not know what constitutes the definition of maturity or growing up in the lower class. We do not know what goal of adulthood motivates lower-class youth—what they are striving for and what they see as the signs of successfully moving into the adult age-grade.

Since we have little solid data to go on, I have had to approach the problem in a roundabout way. There are many studies available of occupations into which lower-class youth move. By looking at these studies, I am able to speculate about the possible demands on the lower-class youths as he moves into the work world. I will compare the demands for skills and knowledge likely to be made on the lower-class youth with those made on the middle-class youth. In some respects, the demands are similar while in others, of course, they are quite different. I will then go on to consider the institutions in which lower-class youth may or may not receive the kind of education they need.

Lower-class youth move around a good deal, though probably not as much as middle-class youth. Insofar as they move less, they need less the training in independence from kin and community the college provides for the middle-class youth. In addition, other institutions may give them this training prior to their entrance into the work world. In particular, a hitch in the armed services may be functionally equivalent in this respect to college, though no doubt more traumatic. Similarly, since work and family tend to be kept quite separate from one another in the lower class, the need for elaborate training in getting along with the opposite sex and in poise in social situations is clearly not so important for the lower-class youth. It makes little difference in his adjustment to the adult world whether he knows which fork to use or not, whether he knows how to introduce himself to people or not. The training the college youth receives in these social skills does not come to the lower-class youth, but then he does not need it very much.

Clearly, any lower-class youth will be better off for having some marketable skills than otherwise. It cannot hurt him to know something for which there is a demand, something for which the demand is expressed in a good salary. You are better off if you know how to weld or run an IBM machine than if you do not; you are better off to know how to set hair or type and take shorthand than not. The desire for technical training among lower-class youth (reflected in their patronage of the trade schools that abound in any urban area) indicates that members of the lower class recognize this fact and are willing to do something about it. The substantial number of lower-class recruits to such subprofessional specialties as practical nursing testifies to the same thing.

It is not so clear, however, that lower-class youth need the qualities of sticking with the job until it is done or the ability to budget their time and energy wisely. Insofar as his work tends to be relatively simply organized, consisting of one or a few tasks rather than a large number, the lower-class young adult will have little problem allocating his time and energy. His job ends when the whistle blows at the end of the day, rather than spilling over into after-work hours as does the work of the young professional person or businessman. Nor, since his work consists of a number of tasks of relatively short duration, need he have the ability to stick to a job that lasts over a long time until it is done. No doubt it is a good thing to have these skills, no matter what kind of work you do, but some kinds of work are so organized as to make them necessary and to reward those who have them and punish those who do not, while other kinds of work are not so organized. The work of lower-class adults puts no great premium on getting things done and there is no good reason why members of the lower class cannot do without these skills. They do not need the training provided the middle-class youth by his experiences with the college curriculum.

When we come to the skills of manipulating other people so they will act in ways you want them to and of manipulating the rules and regulations of bureaucratic organizations, whatever the career aspirations of the lower-class youth, it is clear that these are important skills for him to have. Whether in the world of work or in other areas of their lives, members of the lower class constantly bump up against the world of impersonal bureaucracy. Their failure to understand it, how it works, and how its workings may be turned to their advantage, may cost them dearly. Herbert Gans, discussing the world of the Italian residents of the West End of Boston, notes some of the characteristics of their culture which made it difficult or impossible for them to deal effectively with government when their area was slated to be torn up for urban redevelopment.

Gans describes the West Enders as lacking in the skills of, indeed being characterologically unsuited for, the kind of interpersonal manipulation necessary for effective social action. They feared that anyone who attempted to lead them in any collective action was only out for himself and were afraid to follow him. Would-be leaders had no skill in coercing support; they were unable to overcome the fear of others that their interest was self-interest. Similarly, the world of impersonal bureaucracy was a mystery. They interpreted it in ways that made it impossible to act effectively. Gans speaks of

> . . . the West Ender's inability to recognize the existence of object-oriented bureaucracies. The idea that individual officials follow rules and regulations based not on personal morality but on the concept of efficiency, order, administrative hierarchy, and the like, is difficult to accept. For example, when the redevelopment agency initiated its procedures for taking title to the West End properties and for relocating people and demolishing houses, West Enders refused to believe that these procedures were based on local and Federal regulations. They saw them only as individuals, and individually motivated, acts. Taking title to the land was described as a land grab to benefit the redeveloper. Relocation was explained in terms of the desire of the redeveloper and his governmental partners to push West Enders out of their homes as quickly as possible, so that the new buildings could be put up. The protest of redevelopment officials that they were only following standard operating procedures went unheeded.[5]

An extreme example of the kind of trouble a lower-class person can get into because he does not understand the workings of bureaucracy appears in the story told by Rocky Graziano of his war with the United States Army. Graziano, inducted into the army, refuses to get up in the morning, make his bed, or do any of the other things required of recruits. Since he is stronger and tougher than the people giving him orders, he sees no reason why he should obey them. Finally, he is taken to see the captain, who tells him that he is going to be taught a lesson and have some of the New York knocked out of him.

> So I said, "Listen, you bum, you may be a captain and all that, but you don't impress me so hot. If you think you're tough, come on outside and I'll fight you."
> "Soldier, are you crazy?" he says.
> "Maybe I'm crazy, but at least I ain't yellow," I say. Maybe that will draw the son-of-a-bitch outside.
> He made a quick move out of his chair. My instinct tells me he's coming at me right there in the office. I hauled back and let him have a good fast right

5. Herbert J. Gans, *The Urban Villagers: Group and Class in the Life of Italian-Americans* (New York: Free Press of Glencoe, 1962), p. 165.

on the jaw. Baroom! He crashes back across his desk, slides off the corner of the desk and onto the floor. I guess he was only reaching for the phone to call the MPs to come and get me. Well, my mistake.[6]

Naturally, Graziano ended up in the stockade and eventually in Fort Leavenworth. Middle-class boys may not have liked the army any better than Graziano did, but they knew enough about its workings to avoid his kind of trouble with it.

The inability of members of the lower class to manipulate people and organizations undoubtedly costs them dearly, and in many other ways than the two I have just given examples of. In their run-ins with police, landlords, unions, factories, and retail merchants, their inability to understand the workings of an impersonal institutional order is an expensive luxury.[7] Their inability to manipulate people so that they can cooperate in the achievement of some common goal makes it difficult for them to fight against the people and agencies who exploit and harm them. It may well be one of the chief sources of difficulty in "making out" in life.

Insofar as lower-class youth do want technical training, because of the increased income it will bring, their lack of motivation is a serious weakness. I do not mean that they lack the desire to get the training, but rather that they lack the focus on long-range goals that will give them the push necessary to get through a course of technical training. Obviously, I overstate the case here, because many lower-class youth do finish such programs of training. But they are, perhaps, less vulnerable to the implanting of institutional motivation. Or it may be that the institutions in which they participate are not capable of implanting such motivation.

Lower-class youth do need to learn that their actions have consequences and that they are responsible for those consequences. In many kinds of lower-class work, the man who is unwilling or unable to understand and accept the consequences of what he does may be penalized. For instance, Ray Gold has shown that even the occupant of such a lowly position as janitor has serious responsibilities which he cannot take lightly. In sorting the garbage put out by his tenants, he discovers a good many of their secrets: he knows, for instance, which tenants are not paying their bills, by finding unopened letters in the garbage, and he has the responsibilty of keeping this information to himself. Similarly, if he fails to take proper care of the mechanical equipment in a building, he may flood the building or

6. Rocky Graziano (with Rowland Barber), *Somebody Up There Likes Me* (New York: Pocket Books, 1956), p. 187.

7. *See* David Caplovitz, *The Poor Pay More* (New York: Free Press of Glencoe, 1963).

cause the boiler to blow up, with resulting damage to life and property. Janitors come to take these responsibilities very seriously.[8]

In the same way, the young man who becomes a dance musician learns that he must take seriously the contracts he makes, even though these are made in an offhand verbal way. If he fails to show up for a job he has contracted to play, he will find himself in serious trouble with the band leader and the union as well as the employer. The young man who has not learned to take this kind of responsibility seriously, who does not recognize that his failures will have undesirable consequences, can find himself in a great deal of trouble.[9]

I have till now ignored the question of whether there are skills other than those desirable for life in the middle class which the lower-class person needs to learn. I have ignored it largely because I do not know the answer to it. We can speculate, however, that the conditions of lower-class life may be different enough from those of middle-class life that there are such necessary skills. For instance, physical violence is much more common in lower-class areas and families than it is in the middle class. The lower-class person certainly needs to know either how to avoid violence when it occurs or how to handle it. In the same way, lower-class occupations tend to be much more responsive to general economic conditions. Therefore, the lower-class person faces a chancier economic prospect and must be prepared to put up with violent fluctuations in income. His life is more unstable.

We can also raise the question of whether learning some middle-class skills may not be a disadvantage for many aspects of lower-class life. To have learned to take seriously certain kinds of middle-class manners and styles of dress and speech would seriously unsuit one for many kinds of factory and office work.

The Institutions of Lower-Class Education: Trade Schools and Others

A great variety of institutions exists to give training to lower-class youth. They include trade schools of many kinds (secretarial, technical, and so on), subprofessional training programs (as for practical nurses, masseuses, and medical and dental technicians), apprenticeships such as are found in many unionized trades, in-service training programs, schools in the armed forces, and, finally, the experiences of those who simply go to work in a

8. Ray Gold, "Janitors Versus Tenants: A Status-Income Dilemma," *American Journal of Sociology* Vol. 57 (March 1952), pp. 486–493.

9. *See* Howard S. Becker, *Outsiders: Studies in the Sociology of Deviance* (New York: Free Press of Glencoe, 1963), pp. 101–119.

small shop or factory and acquire a set of skills in what is not nominally an educational institution.

I have argued that what lower-class youth most need to get from their educational experiences is, on the one hand, some set of salable skills and, on the other hand, the ability to recognize and reckon with the consequences of their actions. It might also be that these educational experiences could help with other problems, such as meeting an appropriate mate. How are these educational organizations set up? What can they teach? What are the problems of education in such circumstances? Again, I do not know the answers to these questions. My colleagues and I are now studying precisely these kinds of educational organizations. Till those studies are completed and digested, I can only speculate about what is likely to be true about them. In what follows, I will speak mainly of the trade school and not consider the somewhat different problems of apprenticeships and the other varieties of educational institutions just mentioned.

Trade schools tend to be one-sex schools. Just as the occupational world is divided into those jobs considered proper for men and those considered proper for women, so the trade school (unlike the college, which offers a generalized training for many kinds of jobs) is ordinarily limited to one or the other sex. Men go to welding school; women go to secretarial school. Men study to be tree surgeons; women study to be airline hostesses. The trade school offers none of the vast opportunity for mingling casually with members of the opposite sex that the residential college does. The maturity achieved in the area of relations with the opposite sex by those who do not go to college is achieved outside the confines of any educational institution.

Typically, too, the trade school does not have the vast network of extracurricular organizations that characterizes the residential college. There is no equivalent training ground in which the youngster who does not go to college can get experience in dealing with the world of organizations. There are no offices for him to hold, no responsibilities for him to exercise, no political situations in which he can learn to maneuver and can acquire the kind of flexibility Dalton speaks of. Whatever experience of this kind the person who does not go to college acquires, he gets somewhere else than in school.

Whatever the noncollege youth learns in a trade school, then, he learns in the encounter with his teachers. Presumably, he acquires those skills the school is set up to teach. But does he also have the experience, characteristically undergone by the college students, of having to learn something in order to earn some future reward? The college student, as I have said, has institutional motivation. He may not care about chemistry, history, or English literature, but he does care about passing his courses successfully, because he wants to graduate. He wants to graduate because the degree will open many doors, both occupational and social, for him in the world he moves into.

But what can the person who goes to a trade school expect as a consequence of learning what the school has to offer? First of all, he can probably expect something much more limited than the college student. The training he gets will open only a few doors, will get him a job in the specialty he is trained in, but no more. Conversely, he does not stand to lose very much if he does not do well. If he does not graduate from welding school he won't be able to be a welder, but he will still be able to do a great many other things, for failure in welding school makes no record that will harm him in any other area. Therefore, it is likely that the trade school student is interested in his studies only insofar as he expects what he learns to be useful. The apparatus of courses and requirements which gives structure and organization to the life of the college student does not exist for him. He may not even care very much whether he continues or not. The educational institutions themselves provide none of the reinforcement and support for continuing along the line of educational activity he has begun that is provided for the college student.

There is one important exception to this. Many schools prepare a person for state-required examinations necessary for a license to practice a trade. The person who studies to be a masseuse or beauty operator, for instance, must pass an examination set by a state board. This can provide some motivation for continuing in the course even though the student finds it dull. Nevertheless, as I have said, if he fails or drops out he loses nothing but the tuition already invested. This being the case, the trade school student probably does not have the experience the college student does of having to meet a set of requirements in order to achieve some desired consequence. He does not have to "meet his responsibilities" as the college student does and does not have that kind of experience which we have seen is undoubtedly useful even in lower-class work and community life.

On the other hand, precisely because he is interested in the subject matter and not in more abstract goals, the trade school student may have a problem not characteristically faced by college students. He may be concerned, because he is interested mainly in the utility of the knowledge he is getting, about getting the maximum amount of knowledge out of his teacher. When we consider that trade schools are profit-making organizations, it seems a possibility that teachers tend to string out the presentation of substantive material so as to spread it over a longer period of time and get more tuition.

What student culture there is in trade schools and similar places remains to be discovered. It may well be, however, that the common problem most students in them have to face is precisely the problem of forcing the teacher to teach them more than he wants to. (Interestingly, we found this same kind of perspective among medical students, who felt that teachers were holding back on "practical" knowledge.[10] And indeed they were, since they considered "practical" knoweldge to be worthless unless one understood its theoretical basis. The perspective of trying to get the teacher to "give" more may, perhaps, arise whenever the student is greatly concerned with knowledge enough in a particular area after he gets out of school.)[11]

10. *See* Howard S. Becker, Blanche Geer, Everett C. Hughes, and Anselm L. Strauss, *Boys in White: Student Culture in Medical School* (Chicago: University of Chicago Press, 1961), *passim*.

11. Since this paper was written, the study of trade schools (mentioned as being planned) has taken place, conducted jointly by myself and Blanche Geer of Northeastern University, with the aid of several colleagues. The results are reported in Blanche Geer, editor, *Learning to Work* (Chicago: Aldine Publishing Co.), forthcoming.

PART III

The Processes
of Personal Change

Careers, Personality
and Adult Socialization

In contradistinction to other disciplines, the sociological approach to the study of personality and personality change views the person as a member of a social structure. Usually the emphasis is upon some cross-section in his life: on the way he fills his status, on the consequent conflicts in role and his dilemmas. When the focus is more developmental, then concepts like career carry the import of movement through structures. Much writing on career, of course, pertains more to patterned sequences of passage than to the persons. A fairly comprehensive statement about careers as related both to institutions and to persons would be useful in furthering research. We shall restrict our discussion to careers in work organizations and occupations, for purposes of economy.[1]

Career Flow

Organizations built around some particular kind of work or situation at work tend to be characterized by recurring patterns of tension and of problems. Thus in occupations whose central feature is performance of a service for outside clients, one chronic source of tension is the effort of members to control their work life themselves while in contact with outsiders. In

Reprinted by permission from *American Journal of Sociology*, 62 (November 1956), pp. 253–263. Copyright © 1956 by The University of Chicago Press.

1. Everett C. Hughes, of the University of Chicago, has undoubtedly done more than any other sociologist in this country to focus attention and research on occupational careers. Several of our illustrations will be drawn from work done under his direction, and our own thinking owes much to his writing and conversation.

production organizations somewhat similar tensions arise from the workers' efforts to maintain relative autonomy over job conditions.

Whatever the typical problems of an occupation, the pattern of associated problems will vary with one's position. Some positions will be easier, some more difficult; some will afford more prestige, some less; some will pay better than others. In general, the personnel move from less to more desirable positions, and the flow is usually, but not necessarily, related to age. The pure case is the bureaucracy as described by Mannheim, in which seniority and an age-related increase in skill and responsibility automatically push men in the desired direction and within a single organization.[2]

An ideally simple model of flow up through an organization is something like the following: recruits enter at the bottom in positions of least prestige and move up through the ranks as they gain in age, skill, and experience. Allowing for some attrition due to death, sickness, and dismissal or resignation, all remain in the organization until retirement. Most would advance to top ranks. A few reach the summit of administration. Yet even in bureaucracies, which perhaps come closest to this model the very highest posts often go not to those who have come up through the ranks but to "irregulars"—people with certain kinds of experiences or qualifications not necessarily acquired by long years of official service. In other ways, too, the model is oversimple: posts at any rank may be filled from the outside; people get "frozen" at various levels and do not rise. Moreover, career movements may be not only up but down or sideways, as in moving from one department to another at approximately the same rank.

The flow of personnel through an organization should be seen, also, as a number of streams; that is, there may be several routes to the posts of high prestige and responsibility. These may be thought of as escalators. An institution invests time, money, and energy in the training of its recruits and members which it cannot afford to let go to waste. Hence just being on the spot often means that one is bound to advance. In some careers, even a small gain in experience gives one a great advantage over the beginner. The mere fact of advancing age or of having been through certain kinds of situations or training saves many an employee from languishing in lower positions. This is what the phrase "seasoning" refers to—the acquiring of requisite knowledge and skills, skills that cannot always be clearly specified even by those who have them. However, the escalator will carry one from opportunities as well as to them. After a certain amount of time and money have been spent upon one's education for the job, it is not always easy to get off one escalator and on another. Immediate superiors will block transfer. Sponsors will reproach one for disloyalty. Sometimes a man's special training and experience will be thought to have spoiled him for a particular post.

2. Karl Mannheim, *Essays on the Sociology of Kowledge,* ed. Paul Kecskemeti (New York: Oxford University Press, 1953), pp. 247–49.

Recruitment and Replacement

Recruitment is typically regarded as occurring only at the beginning of a career, where the occupationally uncommitted are bid for, or as something which happens only when there is deliberate effort to get people to commit themselves. But establishments must recruit for all positions; whenever personnel are needed, they must be found and often trained. Many higher positions, as in bureaucracies, appear to recruit automatically from aspirants at next lower levels. This is only appearance: the recruitment mechanisms are standardized and work well. Professors, for example, are drawn regularly from lower ranks, and the system works passably in most academic fields. But in schools of engineering young instructors are likely to be drained off into industry and not be on hand for promotion. Recruitment is never really automatic but depends upon developing in the recruit certain occupational or organizational commitments which correspond to regularized career routes.

Positions in organizations are being vacated continually through death and retirement, promotion and demotion. Replacements may be drawn from the outside ("an outside man") or from within the organization. Most often positions are filled by someone promoted from below or shifted from another department without gaining in prestige. When career routes are well laid out, higher positions are routinely filled from aspirants at the next lower level. However, in most organizations many career routes are not so rigidly laid out: a man may jump from one career over to another to fill the organization's need. When this happens, the "insider-outsider" may be envied by those who have come up by the more orthodox routes; and his associates on his original route may regard him as a turncoat. This may be true even if he is not the first to have made the change, as in the jump from scholar to dean or doctor to hospital administrator. Even when replacement from outside the organization is routine for certain positions, friction may result if the newcomer has come up by an irregular route—as when a college president is chosen from outside the usual circle of feeding occupations. A candidate whose background is too irregular is likely to be eliminated unless just this irregularity makes him particularly valuable. The advantage of "new blood" versus "inbreeding" may be the justification. A good sponsor can widen the limits within which the new kind of candidate is judged, by asking that certain of his qualities be weighed against others; as Hall says, "the question is not whether the applicant possesses a specific trait . . . but whether these traits can be assimilated by the specific institutions."[3]

Even when fairly regular routes are followed, the speed of advancement may not be rigidly prescribed. Irregularity may be due in part to unexpected

3. Oswald Hall, "The Stages in a Medical Career," *American Journal of Sociology* LIII (March 1948), 332.

needs for replacement because a number of older men retire in quick succession or because an older man leaves and a younger one happens to be conveniently present. On the other hand, in some career lines there may be room for a certain amount of manipulation of "the system." One such method is to remain physically mobile, especially early in the career, thus taking advantage of several institutions' vacancies.

The Limits of Replacement and Recruitment

Not all positions within an organization recruit from an equally wide range. Aside from the fact that different occupations may be represented in one establishment, some positions require training so specific that recruits can be drawn only from particular schools or firms. Certain positions are merely way stations and recruit only from aspirants directly below. Some may draw only from the outside, and the orbit is always relevant to both careers and organization. One important question, then, about any organization is the limits within which positions recruit incumbents. Another is the limits of the recruitment in relation to certain variables—age of the organization, its relations with clients, type of generalized work functions, and the like.

One can also identify crucial contingencies for careers in preoccupational life by noting the general or probable limits within which recruiting is carried on and the forces by which they are maintained. For example, it is clear that a position can be filled, at least at first, only from among those who know of it. Thus physiologists cannot be recruited during high school, for scarcely any youngster then knows what a physiologist is or does. By the same token, however, there are at least generally formulated notions of the "artist," so that recruitment into the world of art often begins in high school.[4] This is paradoxical, since the steps and paths later in the artist's career are less definite than in the physiologist's The range and diffusion of a public stereotype are crucial in determining the number and variety of young people from whom a particular occupation can recruit, and the unequal distribution of information about careers limits occupations possibilities.

There are problems attending the systematic restrictions of recruiting. Some kinds of persons, for occupationally irrelevant reasons (formally, anyway), may not be considered for some positions at all. Medical schools restrict recruiting in this way: openly, on grounds of "personality assessments," and covertly on ethnicity. Italians, Jews, and Negroes who do become doctors face differential recruitment into the formal and informal

4. Cf. Strauss's unpublished studies of careers in art and Howard S. Becker and James Carper, "The Development of Identification with an Occupation," in this volume.

hierarchies of influence, power, and prestige in the medical world. Similar mechanisms operate at the top and bottom of industrial organizations.[5]

Another problem is that of "waste." Some recruits in institutions which recruit pretty widely do not remain. Public caseworkers in cities are recruited from holders of Bachelor's degrees, but most do not remain caseworkers. From the welfare agency's point of view this is waste. From other perspectives this is not waste, for they may exploit the job and its opportunities for private ends. Many who attend school while supposedly visiting clients may be able to transfer to new escalators because of the acquisition, for instance, of a Master's degree. Others actually build up small businesses during this "free time." The only permanent recruits, those who do not constitute waste, are those who fail at such endeavors.[6] Unless an organization actually finds useful a constant turnover of some sector of its personnel, it is faced with the problem of creating organizational loyalties and—at higher levels anyhow—satisfactory careers or the illusion of them, within the organization.

Training and Schools

Schooling occurs most conspicuously during the early stages of a career and is an essential part of getting people committed to careers and prepared to fill positions. Both processes may, or may not, be going on simultaneously. However, movement from one kind of job or position or another virtually always necessitates some sort of learning—sometimes before and sometimes on the job, sometimes through informal channels and sometimes at school. This means that schools may exist within the framework of an organization. In-service training is not only for jobs on lower levels but also for higher positions. Universities and special schools are attended by students who are not merely preparing for careers but getting degrees or taking special courses in order to move faster and higher. In some routes there is virtual blockage of mobility because the top of the ladder is not very high; in order to rise higher, one must return to school to prepare for ascending by another route. Thus the registered nurse may have to return to school to become a nursing educator, administrator, or even supervisor. Sometimes the aspi-

5. Cf. Hall, *op. cit.*; David Solomon, "Career Contingencies of Chicago Physicians" (unpublished Ph.D. thesis, University of Chicago, 1952); Everett C. Hughes, *French Canada in Transition* (Chicago: University of Chicago Press, 1943), pp. 52–53; Melville Dalton, "Informal Factors in Career Achievement," *American Journal of Sociology* LVI (March 1951), 407–15; and Orvis Collins, "Ethnic Behavior in Industry: Sponsorship and Rejection in a New England Factory," *American Journal of Sociology* LI (January 1946), 293–98.

6. Cf. unpublished M.A. report of Earl Bogdanoff and Arnold Glass, "The Sociology of the Public Case Worker in an Urban Area" (University of Chicago, 1954).

rant may study on his own, and this may be effective unless he must present a diploma to prove he deserves promotion.

The more subtle connections are between promotion and informal training. Certain positions preclude the acquiring of certain skills or information, but others foster it. It is possible to freeze a man at given levels or to move him faster, unbeknownst to him. Thus a sponsor, anticipating a need for certain requirements in his candidate, may arrange for critical experiences to come his way. Medical students are aware that if they obtain internships in certain kinds of hospitals they will be exposed to certain kinds of learning: the proper internship is crucial to many kinds of medical careers. But learning may depend upon circumstances which the candidate cannot control and of which he may not even be aware. Thus Goldstein has pointed out that nurses learn more from doctors at hospitals not attached to a medical school; elsewhere the medical students become the beneficiaries of the doctors' teaching.[7] Quite often who teaches whom and what is connected with matters of convenience as well as with prestige. It is said, for instance, that registered nurses are jealous of their prerogatives and will not transmit certain skills to practical nurses. Nevertheless, the nurse is often happy to allow her aides to relieve her of certain other jobs and will pass along the necessary skills; and the doctor in his turn may do the same with his nurses.

The connection between informal learning and group allegiance should not be minimized. Until a newcomer has been accepted, he will not be taught crucial trade secrets. Conversely, such learning may block mobility, since to be mobile is to abandon standards, violate friendships, and even injure one's self-regard. Within some training institutions students are exposed to different and sometimes antithetical work ideologies—as with commercial and fine artists—which results in sharp and sometimes lasting internal conflicts of loyalty.

Roy's work on industrial organization furnishes a subtle instance of secrecy and loyalty in training.[8] The workers in Roy's machine shop refused to enlighten him concerning ways of making money on difficult piecework jobs until given evidence that he could be trusted in undercover skirmishes with management. Such systematic withholding of training may mean that an individual can qualify for promotion by performance only by shifting group loyalties, and that disqualifies him in some other sense. Training hinders as well as helps. It may incapacitate one for certain duties as well as train him for them. Roy's discussion of the managerial "logic of efficiency" makes this clear: workers, not trained in this logic, tend to see short

7. Rhoda Goldstein, "The Professional Nurse in the Hospital Bureaucracy" (unpublished Ph.D. thesis, University of Chicago, 1954).

8. Donald Roy, "Quota Restriction and Goldbricking in a Machine Shop," *American Journal of Sociology* LVII (March 1952), 427–42.

cuts to higher production more quickly than managers, who think in terms of sentimental dogmas of efficiency.[9]

Certain transmittable skills, information, and qualties facilitate movement, and it behooves the candidate to discover and distinguish what is genuinely relevant in his training. The student of careers must also be sensitized to discover what training is essential or highly important to the passage from one status to another.

Recruiting for Undesirable Positions

A most difficult kind of recruiting is for positions which no one wants. Ordinary incentives do not work, for these are positions without prestige, without future, without financial reward. Yet they are filled. How, and by whom? Most obviously, they are filled by failures (the crews of gandy dancers who repair railroad tracks are made up of skid-row bums), to whom they are almost the only means of survival. Most positions filled by failures are not openly regarded as such; special rhetorics deal with misfortune and make their ignominious fate more palatable for the failures themselves and those around them.[10]

Of course, failure is a matter of perspective. Many positions represent failure to some but not to others. For the middle-class white, becoming a caseworker in a public welfare agency may mean failure; but for the Negro from the lower-middle class the job may be a real prize. The permanent positions in such agencies tend to be occupied by whites who have failed to reach anything better and, in larger numbers, by Negroes who have succeeded in arriving this far.[11] Likewise, some recruitment into generally undesirable jobs is from the ranks of the disaffected who care little for generally accepted values. The jazz musicians who play in Chicago's Clark Street dives make little money, endure bad working conditions, but desire the freedom to play as they could not in better paying places.[12]

Recruits to undesirable positions also come from the ranks of the transients, who, because they feel that they are on their way to something different and better, can afford temporarily to do something *infra dig*. Many organizations rely primarily on transients—such are the taxi companies and some of the mail-order houses. Among the permanent incumbents of undesirable positions are those, also, who came in temporarily

9. Donald Roy, "Efficiency and the 'Fix': Informal Intergroup Relations in a Piecework Machine Shop," *American Journal of Sociology* LX (November 1954), 255–66.

10. Cf. Erving Goffman, "On Cooling the Mark Out: Some Aspects of Adaptation to Failure," *Psychiatry* XV (November 1952), 451–63.

11. Bogdanoff and Glass, *op. cit.*

12. Howard S. Becker, "The Professional Dance Musician and His Audience," *American Journal of Sociology* LVII (September 1951), 136–44.

but whose brighter prospects did not materialize; they thus fall into the "failure" group.

Still another group is typified by the taxi dancer, whose career Cressey has described. The taxi dancer starts at the top, from which the only movement possible is down or out. She enters the profession young and good-looking and draws the best customers in the house, but, as age and hard work take their toll, she ends with the worst clients or becomes a street-walker.[13] Here the worst positions are filled by individuals who start high and so are committed to a career that ends badly—a more common pattern of life, probably, than is generally recognized.

Within business and industrial organizations, not everyone who attempts to move upward succeeds. Men are assigned to positions prematurely, sponsors drop protégés, and miscalculations are made about the abilities of promising persons. Problems for the organization arise from those contingencies. Incompetent persons must be moved into positions where they cannot do serious damage, others of limited ability can still be useful if wisely placed. Aside from outright firing, various methods of "cooling out" the failures can be adopted, among them honorific promotion, banishment "to the sticks," shunting to other departments, frank demotion, bribing out of the organization, and down-grading through departmental mergers. The use of particular methods is related to the structure of the organization; and these, in turn, have consequences both for the failure and for the organization.[14]

Attachment and Severance

Leaders of organizations sometimes complain that their personnel will not take responsibility or that some men (the wrong ones) are too ambitious. This complaint reflects a dual problem which confronts every organization. Since all positions must be filled, some men must be properly motivated to take certain positions and stay in them for a period, while others must be motivated to move onward and generally upward. The American emphasis on mobility should not lead us to assume that everyone wants to rise to the highest levels or to rise quickly. Aside from this, both formal mechanisms and informal influences bind incumbents, at least temporarily, to certain positions. Even the ambitious may be willing to remain in a given post, provided that it offers important contacts or the chance to learn certain skills and undergo certain experiences. Part of the bargain in staying

13. Paul G. Cressey, *The Taxi-Dance Hall* (Chicago: University of Chicago Press, 1932), pp. 84–106.

14. Norman Martin and Anselm Strauss, "Patterns of Mobility within Industrial Organizations," *Journal of Business* XXIX (April 1956), 101–10.

in given positions is the promise that they lead somewhere. When career lines are fairly regularly laid out, positions lead definitely somewhere and at a regulated pace. One of the less obvious functions of the sponsor is to alert his favorites to the sequence and its timing, rendering them more ready to accept undesirable assignments and to refrain from champing at the bit when it might be awkward for the organization.

To certain jobs, in the course of time, come such honor and glory that the incumbents will be satisfied to remain there permanently, giving up aspirations to move upward. This is particularly true when allegiance to colleagues, built on informal relations and conflict with other ranks, is intense and runs counter to allegiance to the institution. But individuals are also attached to positions by virtue of having done particularly well at them; they often take great satisfaction in their competence at certain techniques and develop self-conceptions around them.

All this makes the world of organizations go around, but it also poses certain problems, both institutional and personal. The stability of institutions is predicated upon the proper preparation of aspirants for the next steps and upon institutional aid in transmuting motives and allegiances. While it is convenient to have some personnel relatively immobile, others must be induced to cut previous ties, to balance rewards in favor of moving, and even to take risks for long-run gains. If we do not reat mobility as normal, and thus regard attachment to a position as abnormal, we are then free to ask how individuals are induced to move along. It is done by devices such as sponsorship, by planned sequences of positions and skills, sometimes tied to age; by rewards, monetary and otherwise, and negatively, by ridicule and the denial or responsibility to the lower ranks. There is, of course, many a slip in the inducing of mobility. Chicago public school teachers illustrate this point. They move from schools in the slums to middle-class neighborhoods. The few who prefer to remain in the tougher slum schools have settled in too snugly to feel capable of facing the risks of moving to "better" schools.[15] Their deviant course illuminates the more usual patterns of the Chicago teacher's career.

Timing in Status Passage

Even when paths in a career are regular and smooth, there always arise problems of pacing and timing. While, ideally, successors and predecessors should move in and out of offices at equal speeds, they do not and cannot. Those asked to move on or along or upward may be willing but must make actual and symbolic preparations; meanwhile, the successor waits impa-

15. Howard S. Becker, "The Career of the Chicago Public Schoolteacher," in this volume.

tiently. Transition periods are a necessity, for a man often invests heavily of himself in a position, comes to possess it as it possesses him, and suffers in leaving it. If the full ritual of leavetaking is not allowed, the man may not pass fully into his new status. On the other hand, the institution has devices to make him forget, to plunge him into the new office, to woo and win him with the new gratifications, and, at the same time, to force him to abandon the old. When each status is conceived as the logical and temporal extension of the one previous, then severance is not so disturbing. Nevertheless, if a man must face his old associates in unaccustomed roles, problems of loyalty arise. Hence a period of tolerance after formal admission to the new status is almost a necessity. It is rationalized in phrases like "it take time" and "we all make mistakes when starting, until . . . ."

But, on the other hand, those new to office may be too zealous. They often commit the indelicate error of taking too literally their formal promotion or certification, when actually intervening steps must be traversed before the attainment of full prerogatives. The passage may involve trials and tests of loyalty, as well as the simple accumulation of information and skill. The overeager are kept in line by various controlling devices: a new assistant professor discovers that it will be "just a little while" before the curriculum can be rearranged so that he can teach his favorite courses. Even a new superior has to face the resentment or the cautiousness of established personnel and may, if sensitive, pace his "moving in on them" until he has passed unspoken tests.

When subordinates are raised to the ranks of their superiors, an especially delicate situation is created. Equality is neither created by that official act, nor, even if it were, can it come about without a certain awkwardness. Patterns of response must be rearranged by both parties, and strong self-control must be exerted so that acts are appropriate. Slips are inevitable, for, although the new status may be fully granted, the proper identities may at times be forgotten, to everyone's embarassment. Eventually, the former subordinate may come to command or take precedence over someone to whom he once looked for advice and guidance. When colleagues who were formerly sponsors and sponsored disagree over some important issue, recrimination may become overt and betrayal explicit. It is understandable why those who have been promoted often prefer, or are advised, to take office in another organization, however much they may wish to remain at home.

Multiple Routes and Switching

Theoretically, a man may leave one escalator and board another, instead of following the regular route. Such switching is most visible during the schooling, or preoccupational, phases of careers. Frequently students change their line of endeavor but remain roughly within the same field; this is one way for less desirable and less well-known specialties to obtain recruits. Certain kinds of training, such as the legal, provide bases for moving early and easily into a wide variety of careers. In all careers, there doubtless are some points at which switching to another career is relatively easy. In general, while commitment to a given career automatically closes paths, the skills and information thereby acquired open up other routes and new goals. One may not, of course, perceive the alternatives or may dismiss them as risky or otherwise undesirable.

When a number of persons have changed escalators at about the same stage in their careers, then there is the beginning of a new career. This is one way by which career lines become instituted. Sometimes the innovation occurs at the top ranks of older careers; when all honors are exhausted, the incumbent himself may look for new worlds to conquer. Or he may seem like a good risk to an organization looking for personnel with interestingly different qualifications. Such new phases of career are much more than honorific and may indeed be an essential inducement to what becomes pioneering.

Excitement and dangers are intimately tied up with switching careers. For example, some careers are fairly specific in goal but diffuse in operational means: the "fine artist" may be committed to artistic ideals but seize upon whatever jobs are at hand to help him toward creative goals. When he takes a job in order to live, he thereby risks committing himself to an alternative occupational career; and artists and writers do, indeed, get weaned away from the exercise of their art in just this way. Some people never set foot on a work escalator but move from low job to low job. Often they seek better conditions of work or a little more money rather than chances to climb institutional or occupational ladders. Many offers of opportunities to rise are spurned by part-time or slightly committed recruits, often because the latter are engaged in pursuing alternative routes while holding the job, perhaps a full-time one providing means of livelihood. This has important and, no doubt, subtle effects upon institutional functioning. When careers are in danger of being brought to an abrupt end—as with airplane pilots—then, before retirement, other kinds of careers may be prepared for or entered. This precaution is very necessary. When generalized mobility is an aim, specific routes may be chosen for convenience' sake. One is careful not to develop the usual motivation and allegiances. This enables one to get off an escalator and to move over to another with a minimum of psychological strain.

Considerable switching takes place within a single institution or a single occupational world and is rationalized in institutional and occupational terms, both by the candidates and by their colleagues. A significant consequence of this, undoubtedly, is subtle psychological strain, since the new positions and those preceding are both somewhat alike and difficult.

Climactic Periods

Even well-worn routes have stretches of maximum opportunity and danger. The critical passage in some careers lies near the beginning. This is especially so when the occupation or institution strongly controls recruitment; once chosen, prestige and deference automatically accrue. In another kind of career the critical time comes at the end and sometimes very abruptly. In occupations which depend upon great physical skill, the later phases of a career are especially hazardous. It is also requisite in some careers that one choose the proper successor to carry on, lest one's own work be partly in vain. The symbolic last step of moving out may be quite as important as any that preceded it.

Appropriate or strategic timing is called for, to meet opportunity and danger, but the timing becomes vital at different periods in different kinds of careers. A few, such as the careers of virtuoso musical performers, begin so early in life that the opportunity to engage in music may have passed long before they learn of it. Some of the more subtle judgments of timing are required when a person wishes to shift from one escalator to another. Richard Wohl, of the University of Chicago, in an unpublished paper has suggested that modeling is a step which women may take in preparation for upward mobility through marriage; but models may marry before they know the ropes, and so marry too low; or they may marry too long after their prime, and so marry less well than they might. Doubtless organizations and occupations profit from mistakes of strategic timing, both to recruit and then to retain their members.

During the most crucial periods of any career, a man suffers greater psychological stress than during other periods. This is perhaps less so if he is not aware of his opportunities and dangers—for then the contingencies are over before they can be grasped or coped with: but probably it is more usual to be aware, or to be made so by colleagues and seniors, of the nature of imminent or current crisis. Fortunately, together with such definitions there exist rationales to guide action. The character of the critical junctures and the ways in which they are handled may irrevocably decide a man's fate.

Interdependence of Careers

Institutions, at any given moment, contain people at different stages in their careers. Some have already "arrived," others are still on their way up, still others just entering. Movements and changes at each level are in various ways dependent on those occurring at other levels.

Such interdependence is to be found in the phenomenon of sponsorship, where individuals move up in a work organization through the activities of older and more-well-established men. Hall[16] has given a classic description of sponsorship in medicine. The younger doctor of the proper class and acceptable ethnic origin is absorbed, on the recommendation of a member, into the informal "inner fraternity" which controls hospital appointments and which is influential in the formation and maintenance of a clientele. The perpetuation of this coterie depends on a steady flow of suitable recruits. As the members age, retire, or die off, those who remain face a problem of recruiting younger men to do the less honorific and remunerative work, such as clinical work, that their group performs. Otherwise they themselves must do work inappropriate to their position or give place to others who covet their power and influence.

To the individual in the inner fraternity, a protégé eases the transition into retirement. The younger man gradually assumes the load which the sponsor can no longer comfortable carry, allowing the older man to retire gracefully, without that sudden cutting-down of work which frightens away patients, who leap to the conclusion that he is too old to perform capably.

In general, this is the problem of retiring with honor, of leaving a life's work with a sense that one will be missed. The demand may arise that a great man's work be carried on, although it may no longer be considered important or desirable by his successors. If the old man's prestige is great enough, the men below may have to orient themselves and their work as he suggests, for fear of offending him or of profaning his heritage. The identities of the younger men are thus shaped by the older man's passage from the pinnacle to retirement.

This interdependence of career may cross occupational lines within organizations, as in the case of the young physician who receives a significant part of his training from the older and more experienced nurses in the hospital; and those at the same level in an institution are equally involved in one another's identities. Sometimes budding careers within work worlds are interdependent in quite unsuspected ways. Consider the younger painter or craftsman who must make his initial successes in enterprises founded by equally young art dealers, who, because they run their galleries on a shoestring, can afford the frivolity of exhibiting the works of an unknown. The very ability to take such risks provides the dealer a possible opportunity to discover a genius.

One way of uncovering the interdependence of careers is to ask: Who

16. Hall, *op. cit.*

are the important *others* at various stages of the career, the persons significantly involved in the formation of one's own identity? These will vary with stages; at one point one's agemates are crucial, perhaps as competitors, while at another the actions of superiors are the most important. The interlocking of careers results in influential images of similarity and contrariety. In so far as the significant others shift and vary by the phases of a career, identities change in patterned and not altogether unpredictable ways.

The Changing Work World

The occupations and organizations within which careers are made change in structure and direction of activity, expand or contract, transform purposes. Old functions and positions disappear, and new ones arise. These constitute potential locations for a new and sometimes wide range of people, for they are not encrusted with traditions and customs concerning their incumbents. They open up new kinds of careers to persons making their work lives within the institution and thus the possibility of variation in long-established types of career. An individual once clearly destined for a particular position suddenly finds himself confronted with an option; what was once a settled matter has split into a set of alternatives between which he must now choose. Different identities emerge as people in the organization take cognizance of this novel set of facts. The positions turn into recognized social entities, and some persons begin to reorient their ambitions. The gradual emergence of a new specialty typically creates this kind of situation within occupations.

Such occupational and institutional changes, of course, present opportunity for both success and failure. The enterprising grasp eagerly at new openings, making the most of them or attempting to; while others sit tight as long as they can. During such times the complexities of one's career are further compounded by what is happening to others with whom he is significantly involved. The ordinary lines of sponsorship in institutions are weakened or broken because those in positions to sponsor are occupied with matters more immediately germane to their own careers. Lower ranks feel the consequences of unusual pressures generated in the ranks above. People become peculiarly vulnerable to unaccustomed demands for loyalty and alliance which spring from the unforseen changes in the organization. Paths to mobility become indistinct and less fixed, which has an effect on personal commitments and identities. Less able to tie themselves tightly to any one career, because such careers do not present themselves as clearly, men become more experimental and open-minded or more worried and apprehensive.

Careers and Personal Identity

A frame of reference for studying careers is, at the same time, a frame for studying personal identities. Freudian and other psychiatric formulations of personality development probably overstress childhood experiences. Their systematic accounts end more or less with adolescence, later events being regarded as the elaboration of, or variations on, earlier occurrences. Yet central to any account of adult identity is the relation of change in identity to change in social position; for it is characteristic of adult life to afford and force frequent and momentous passages from status to status. Hence members of structures that change, riders on escalators that carry them up, along, and down, to unexpected places and to novel experiences even when in some sense foreseen, must gain, maintain, and regain a sense of personal identity. Identity "is never gained nor maintained once and for all."[17] Stabilities in the organization of behavior and of self-regard are inextricably dependent upon stabilities of social structure. Likewise, change ("development") is shaped by those patterned transactions which accompany career movement. The crises and turning points of life are not entirely institutionalized, but their occurrence and the terms which define and help to solve them are illuminated when seen in the context of career lines. In so far as some populations do not have careers in the sense that professional and business people have them, then the focus of attention ought still to be positional passage, but with domestic, age, and other escalators to the forefront. This done, it may turn out that the model sketched here must undergo revision.

---

17. Erik H. Erikson, *Childhood and Society* (New York: W. W. Norton & Co., 1950), p. 57.

CHAPTER EIGHTEEN

Notes
on the Concept
of Commitment

The term "commitment" enjoys an increasing vogue in sociological discussion. Sociologists use it in analyses of both individual and organizational behavior. They use it as a descriptive concept to mark out forms of action characteristic of particular kinds of people or groups. They use it as an independent variable to account for certain kinds of behavior of individuals and groups. They use it in analyses of a wide variety of phenomena: power, religion, occupational recruitment, bureaucratic behavior, political behavior, and so on.[1]

In spite of its widespread use, the appearance of the concept of commitment in sociological literature has a curious feature the reader with an eye for trivia will have noticed. In articles studded with citations to previous literature on such familiar concepts as power or social class, commitment emerges unscathed by so much as a single reference. This suggests what is in fact the case: there has been little formal analysis of the concept of

Reprinted by permission from *American Journal of Sociology*, 66 (July 1960), pp. 32–40. Copyright © 1960 by The University of Chicago Press.

1. See the following examples: E. Abramson *et al.*, "Social Power and Commitment: A Theoretical Statement," *American Sociological Review* XXIII (February 1958), 15–22; Howard S. Becker and James Carper, "The Elements of Identification with an Occupation," in this volume; Bryan R. Wilson, "An Analysis of Sect Development," *American Sociological Review* XXIV (January 1959), 3–15; Philip Selznick, *TVA and the Grass Roots* (Berkeley: University of California Press, 1953); and Irving Howe and Lewis Coser, *The American Communist Party: A Critical History, 1919–57* (Boston: Beacon Press, 1957).

commitment and little attempt to integrate it explicitly with current sociological theory. Instead, it has been treated as a primitive concept, introduced where the need is felt without explanation or examination of its character or credentials. As is often the case with unanalyzed concepts used in an *ad hoc* fashion, the term has been made to cover a wide range of common-sense meanings, with predictable ambiguities.

In what follows, I consider the uses to which the concept of commitment has been put and the possible reasons for its increasing popularity, indicate the nature of one of the social mechanisms to which the term implicitly refers, and develop a rudimentary theory of the social processes and conditions involved in the operation of this mechanism. Because the term has been used to express a varied assortment of ideas, it is fruitless to speculate on its "real" meaning. I have instead chosen one of the several images evoked by "commitment" and tried to make its meaning clearer. In doing so, I will unavoidably short-change those for whom the term evokes other of the associated images more strongly. The ultimate remedy for this injustice will be a classification and clarification of the whole family of images involved in the idea of commitment.[2]

Sociologists typically make use of the concept of commitment when they are trying to account for the fact that people engage in *consistent lines of activity*.[3] Howe and Coser, for instance, seek to explain the behavior of the follower of the Communist party line in this fashion: "The Stalinist did not commit himself to the use of Marxism; he committed himself to the claims of the Party that it 'possessed' Marxism."[4] By this they mean that the Stalinist did not undertake always to use Marxist styles of thought but that he did undertake always to honor the party's claim that it knew what the Marxist truth was. In short, they explain a man's persistent support of the shifting party line by referring to a commitment on his part to the belief that the party represented the source of correct Marxist knowledge.

The concept of commitment enjoys use in studies of occupational careers. We can explain the fact that men ordinarily settle down to a career in a limited field, and do not change jobs and careers with the alacrity of the proverbial economic man under changing market conditions, by referring to a process whereby they become committed to a particular occupation.

2. Such a classification and clarification are not attempted here. For a pioneer effort see Gregory P. Stone, "Clothing and Social Relations: A Study of Appearance in the Context of Community Life" (unpublished Ph.D. dissertation, Department of Sociology, University of Chicago, 1959). I have also confined myself to consideration of the concept as it applies to individual behavior, though it often appears in analyses of the behavior of organizations.

3. Cf. Nelson N. Foote, "Concept and Method in the Study of Human Development," in *Emerging Problems in Social Psychology,* ed. Muzafer Sherif and M. O. Wilson (Norman, Okla.: Institute of Group Relations, 1957), pp. 29–53.

4. *Op. cit.,* p. 521.

James Carper and I found that graduate students in physiology originally wanted to become physicians but eventually developed commitments to the field of physiology such that they were no longer interested in the medical degree they had earlier desired so much.[5]

In these examples, and others that might be cited, commitment is used to explain what I have already called "consistent behavior." What are the characteristics of this kind of behavior, for which commitment seems so useful an explanatory variable?

To begin with, it persists over some period of time. The person continues to follow the party line; he remains in the same occupation. But the notion of a consistent line of activity implies more than this, for we often think of complexes of quite diverse kinds of activities as consistent. In fact, the examples just cited conceal a great diversity of activity. The Stalinist may engage in diametrically opposed lines of activity as the party line shifts. A person remaining in the same occupation may engage in many kinds of activity in the course of his career. The diverse activities have in common the fact that they are seen by the actor as activities which, whatever their external diversity, serve him in pursuit of the same goal. Finally, the notion of consistent lines of activity seems to imply a rejection by the actor of feasible alternatives. He sees several alternative courses open to him, each having something to commend it, but chooses one which best serves his purposes.

It is one of the central problems of social science, of course, to account for consistency, so defined, in human behavior. Many explanations have been forthcoming, but none has remained unscarred by critical attack. The volume of criticism suggests that sociologists are still looking for an unexceptionable explanation of consistent behavior. At the risk of doing violence, by reason of brevity, to some complex arguments, let me summarize these explanations and the criticisms that have been made of them.

Some of the most clearly sociological explanations (in the sense of being based most firmly in the process of social interaction) have been theories built around the related concepts of social sanction and social control. These theories propose that people act consistently because activity of some particular kind is regarded as right and proper in their society or social group and because deviations from this standard are punished. People act consistently, therefore, because it is morally wrong, practically inexpedient, or both, to do otherwise.

Such a theory, however, has still to explain consistently deviant behavior. Deviance is often explained by a circular process: a person who initially commits a minor infraction is increasingly alienated from normal society,

5. Howard S. Becker and James Carper, "The Development of Identification with an Occupation," in this volume.

therefore commits increasingly serious infractions, and so on.[6] Alternatively, it is explained as the result of a process of differential association:[7] the deviant has associated more with people who think his deviant act is proper than he has with those of the majority which thinks it is wrong. Again, deviance is explained by reference to a conflict between cultural goals which all members of the society value and a sharp restriction of institutionally legitimate means for achieving them;[8] this explanation, though, accounts only for the genesis of deviance and deals with the question of consistency only by assuming continuous presentation to the individual of the conflict. Serious objections have been raised as to the validity or area of applicability of all these theories; none constitutes a complete explanation of consistently deviant behavior.[19]

The second problem associated with theories based on the concept of social control, the fact that people obey social rules even when no sanctions would follow an infraction, has been dealt with by positing the internalization of a generalized other which constitutes the hidden audience that enforces the rules. This theory is quite generally accepted by sociologists but is just as generally criticized because it offers no reasonable explanation of how people choose one from among the many audiences they can mentally summon to observe any given act.

Other efforts to explain consistent lines of activity also meet criticism. Such activity is sometimes explained by the presumed existence of universally accepted cultural values which inform and constrain behavior. Thus a society is characterized by, let us say, a stress on the value of affective neutrality or the value of achievement; therefore, it is argued, people will consistently choose in any situation that alternative which allows expression of this value. Put another way, individuals will choose alternatives which are consistent with and logically deducible from such a basic value position. Such a theory has difficulty, first of all, in specifying what the basic values of a society are; those theorists who hold that modern society is characteristically ridden with value conflicts might claim such difficulty

6. Talcott Parsons, *The Social System* (Glencoe, Ill.: Free Press, 1951), pp. 249–325.

7. Albert K. Cohen, Alfred R. Lindesmith, and Karl F. Schuessler (eds.), *The Sutherland Papers* (Bloomington: Indiana University Press, 1956), pp. 7–29.

8. Robert K. Merton, *Social Theory and Social Structure* (Glencoe, Ill.: Free Press, 1957), pp. 131–60.

9. For some questions about the Parsons and Merton approaches see Albert K. Cohen, "The Study of Social Disorganization and Deviant Behavior," in *Sociology Today: Problems and Prospects,* ed. Robert K. Merton, Leonard Broom, and Leonard S. Cottrell, Jr. (New York: Basic Books, 1959), pp. 461–74. For Sutherland's own critique of the theory of differential association see Cohen, Lindesmith, and Schuessler (eds.), *op. cit.,* pp. 30–41. See also Foote, *op. cit.,* p. 35.

will be chronic. Second, such a theory does not explain the process by which values, so conceived, affect behavior. It is not likely, for instance, that people make logical deductions from value premises and act on them.

Explanations of consistent behavior are sometimes imported from psychology or psychoanalysis. They refer consistency of behavior to a stable structure of personal needs. They predicate that individuals have stable needs and consistently act so as to maximize the possibility of satisfying them. This kind of scheme is widely used in sociology, either alone or in eclectic combination. But the explanation of behavior by reference to needs not directly observable and, indeed, often inferred from the presence of the behavior they are supposed to explain often causes sociologists to feel queasy about employing it.

In short, many sociologists are dissatisfied with current explanations of consistent human behavior. In my view, use of the concept of commitment in current sociology constitutes an attempt to solve the problem of explaining consistent human behavior in a sociological way without the flaws often attributed to the theories just reviewed. The concept hints at a theory which would do this, but it only hints; it does not deliver the theory full blown. Such a theory would contain a definition of the nature of acts or states of commitment. It would specify the conditions under which commitments come into being. It would indicate the consequences for behavior of acts or states of commitment. In the remainder of this paper I consider some of these points, not attempting to construct such a theory entire, but giving a first approximation of answers to these questions.

In writing of these questions, I have deliberately narrowed the referent of "commitment" to one specific social-psychological mechanism, one of the mechanisms hinted at in the term. It should be clear that this mechanism is not offered as the only possible explanation of consistent human behavior. The present analysis simply undertakes to clarify the nature of one of a family of related mechanisms operating to produce this result.

II

What kind of explanation of consistent human behavior lies implicit in the concept of commitment? Clearly, the person is envisioned as having acted in such at way ("made a commitment") or being in such a state ("being committed") that he will now follow a consistent course. But, as the term is ordinarily used, the nature of this act or state of commitment is not specified; it appears to be regarded as either self-explanatory or intuitively understandable. If we use the concept in this way, the proposition that commitment produces consistent lines of activity is tautological, for commitment, whatever our intuitions about its independent existence, is in fact synonymous with the committed behavior it is supposed to explain. It is a hypothesized event or condition whose occurrence is inferred from the fact that people act as though they were committed. Used in this way, the concept has the same flaws as those psychological theories which explain behavior by referring to some unobserved state of the actor's psyche, this state deduced from the occurrence of the event it is supposed to explain.

To avoid this tautological sin, we must specify the characteristics of "being committed" independent of the behavior commitment will serve to explain. Schelling, in his analysis of the process of bargaining,[10] furnishes a hypothetical example whose analysis may help us arrive at a characterization of the elements of one of the mechanisms that might be called "commitment." Suppose that you are bargaining to buy a house; you offer sixteen thousand dollars, but the seller insists on twenty thousand. Now suppose that you offer your antagonist in the barganing certified proof that you have bet a third party five thousand dollars that you will not pay more than sixteen thousand dollars for the house. Your opponent must admit defeat because you would lose money by raising your bid; you have committed yourself to pay no more than you originally offered.

This commitment has been achieved by making a *side bet*. The committed person has acted in such a way as to involve other interests of his, originally extraneous to the action he is engaged in, directly in that action. By his own actions prior to the final bargaining session he has staked something of value to him, something originally unrelated to his present line of action, on being consistent in his present behavior. The consequences of inconsistency will be so expensive that inconsistency in his bargaining stance is no longer a feasible alternative.

The major elements of commitment present themselves in this example. First, the individual is in a position in which his decision with regard to some particular line of action has consequences for other interests and activities not necessarily related to it.[11] Second, he has placed himself in that position by his own prior actions. A third element is present, though so obvious as not to be apparent: the committed person must be aware that he has made the side bet and must recognize that his decision in this case will have ramifications beyond it. The element of recognition of the interest created by one's prior action is a necessary component of commitment because, even though one has such an interest, he will not act to

10. Thomas C. Schelling, "An Essay on Bargaining," *American Economic Review* XLVI (June 1956), 281–306.

11. So far, the definition of commitment proposed here parallels that of Abramson *et al.* (*op. cit.*, p. 16): "*Committed* lines are those lines of action the actor feels obligated to pursue by force of penalty . . . . Committed lines . . . are sequences of action with penalties and costs so arranged as to guarantee their selection."

implement it (will not act so as to win his side bet) unless he realizes it is necessary.

Note that in this example commitment can be specified independent of the consistent activity which is its consequence. The side bet not to pay more and the additional interest this creates in sticking to the original offered price occur independent of the fact of refusing to pay more. Were we to interview this clever bargainer before the final bargaining session, he presumably would tell us that he understood his interests could now be served only by paying no more.

Thus, whenever we propose commitment as an explanation of consistency in behavior, we must have independent observations of the major components in such a proposition: (1) prior actions of the person staking some originally extraneous interest on his following a consistent line of activity; (2) a recognition by him of the involvement of this originally extraneous interest in his present activity; and (3) the resulting consistent line of activity.

We cannot, of course, often expect social life to be of the classic simplicity of this economic example. Rather, interests, side bets and acts of commitment, and consequent behavior will seem confounded and irremediably mixed, and it will require considerable ingenuity to devise appropriate indices with which to sort them out. But the economic example shows us the skeleton we can look for beneath the flesh of more complicated social processes.

III

If we confined our use of commitment to those cases where individuals have deliberately made side bets, we would seldom bring it into our analyses of social phenomena. What interests us is the possibility of using it to explain situations where a person finds that his involvement in social organization has, in effect, made side bets for him and thus constrained his future activity. This occurs in several ways.

A person sometimes finds that he has made side bets constraining his present activity because the existence of *generalized cultural expectations* provides penalties for those who violate them. One such expectation operates in the area of work. People feel that a man ought not to change his job too often and that one who does is erratic and untrustworthy. Two months after taking a job a man is offered a job he regards as much superior but finds that he has, on the side, bet his reputation for trustworthiness on not moving again for a period of a year and regretfully turns the job down. His decision about the new job is constrained by his having moved two months prior and his knowledge that, however attractive the new job, the penalty in the form of a reputation for being erratic and unstable will be severe if he takes it. The existence of generalized cultural expectations about the behavior of responsible adult males has combined with his recent move to stake his personal reputation, nominally extraneous to the decision about the new job, on that decision.

A person often finds that side bets have been made for him by the operation of *impersonal bureaucratic arrangements*. To take a single instance, a man who wishes to leave his current job may find that, because of the rules governing the firm's pension fund, he is unable to leave without losing a considerable sum of money he has in that fund. Any decision about the new job involves a financial side bet the pension fund has placed for him by its rules.

The situation of the Chicago schoolteacher presents a somewhat more complicated system of side bets made by the operation of bureaucratic arrangements. Teachers prefer to teach middle-class children. To do so, they must be assigned to a school containing such children. Teachers can request assignment to as many as ten different schools; assignments are made, as openings occur, to the teacher whose request for a given school is of longest standing. New teachers are assigned to schools for which there are no requests, the lower-class schools teachers like least. The desirable schools have the longest list of requests outsanding, while less desirable schools have correspondingly shorter lists. The teacher in the lower-class school who desires to transfer must, in picking out the ten schools she will request, take into account the side bets the operation of the bureaucratic transfer system has made for her. The most important such bet has to do with time. If she selects one of the most desirable schools, she finds that she has lost a bet about the time it will take her to get out of her present position, for it takes a long time to reach the top of the list for one of these schools. She can instead choose a less desirable school (but better than her present situation) into which she can move more quickly, thus winning the side bet on time. This system of bets constraining her transfer requests has been made in advance by the bureaucratic rules governing requests for transfer.[12]

One might ask in what sense the person's prior actions have made a side bet in these two instances. How has he, by his own act, placed himself in a position where his decision on a new job or request for transfer involves these other considerations? Is it not rather the case that he has had no part in it, being constrained by forces entirely outside himself? We can without sophistry, I think, locate the crucial action which has created the commitment in the person's acquiescence to the system, in his agreeing to

12. For a fuller account of the operation of this system see Howard S. Becker, "The Career of the Chicago Public Schoolteacher," in this volume.

work under the bureaucratic rules in force. By doing this, he has placed all the bets which are given in the structure of that system, even though he does not become aware of it until faced with an important decision.

Side bets constraining behavior also come into existence through the process of *individual adjustment to social positions.* A person may so alter his patterns of activity in the process of conforming to the requirements for one social position that he unfits himself for other positions he might have access to. In so doing, he has staked the ease of performance in the position on remaining where he is. To return to our earlier example, some Chicago schoolteachers chose to remain in a lower-class school for the lengthy period necessary to reach the top of the list for a very desirable middle-class school. When the opportunity to make the move came, they found that they no longer desired to move because they had so adjusted their style of teaching to the problems of dealing with lower-class children that they could not contemplate the radical changes necessary to teach middle-class children. They had, for instance, learned to discipline children in ways objectionable to middle-class parents and become accustomed to teaching standards too low for a middle-class school.[13] They had, in short, bet the ease of performance of their job on remaining where they were and in this sense were committed to stay.

Goffman's analysis of *face-to-face interaction*[14] suggests another way side bets are made through the operation of social processes. He notes that persons present to their fellows in any sequence of interaction an image of themselves they may or may not be able to live up to. Having once claimed to be a certain kind of person, they find it necessary to act, so far as possible, in an appropriate way. If one claims implicitly, in presenting himself to others, to be truthful, he cannot allow himself to be caught in a lie and is in this way committed to truth-telling. Goffman points out that the rules governing face-to-face interaction are such that others will ordinarily help one preserve the front he has put forward ("safe face"). Nevertheless, a person will often find his activity constrained by the kind of front he has earlier presented in interaction; he finds he has bet his appearance as a responsible participant in interaction on continuing a line of activity congruent with that front.

This review of the social mechanisms through which persons make side bets extraneous to a particular line of activity that nevertheless later constrain that activity is not exhaustive. It serves only to point the direction for empirical study of side-bet mechanisms, in the course of which a more definitive classification might be made.

13. *Ibid.*
14. Erving Goffman, "On Face-Work," *Psychiatry* XVIII (August 1955), 213–31.

IV

As some of our examples indicate, commitments are not necessarily made conciously and deliberately. Some commitments do result from conscious decisions, but others arise crescively; the person becomes aware that he is committed only at some point of change and seems to have made the commitment without realizing it. By examining cases of both kinds, we may get some hints toward a theory of the genesis of commitments.

Such a theory might start with the observation that the commitment made without realization that it is being made—what might be termed the "commitment by default"—arises through a series of acts no one of which is crucial but which, taken together, constitute for the actor a series of side bets of such magnitude that he finds himself unwilling to lose them. Each of the trivial acts in such a series is, so to speak, a small brick in a wall which eventually grows to such a height the person can no longer climb it. The ordinary routines of living—the daily recurring events of everyday life—stake increasingly more valuable things on continuing a consistent line of behavior, although the person hardly realizes this is happening. It is only when some event changes the situation so as to endanger those side bets that the person understands what he will lose if he changes his line of activity. The person who contributes a small amount of each paycheck to a nontransferable pension fund which eventually becomes sizable provides an apposite illustration of this process; he might willingly lose any single contribution but not the total accumulated over a period of years.

If this is the case with commitment by default, we might conjecture that it is also true of commitments resulting from conscious decisions. Decisions do not of themselves result in consistent lines of action, for they are frequently changed. But some decisions do produce consistent behavior. We can perhaps account for this variety of outcomes of decisions by the proposition that only those decisions bolstered by the making of sizable side bets will produce consistent behavior. Decisions not supported by such side bets will lack staying power, crumpling in the face of opposition or fading away to be replaced by other essentially meaningless decisions until a commitment based on side bets stabilizes behavior.[15]

We might also note that a consistent line of activity will often be based on more than one kind of side bet; several kinds of things valuable to the

15. The preceding paragraphs are adapted from Howard S. Becker, "The Implications of Research on Occupational Careers for a Model of Household Decision Making," in *Consumer Behavior,* Vol. IV: *Models of Household Decision Making,* ed. Nelson Foote (New York: New York University Press, 1961) pp. 239–254.

person may be staked on a particular line of activity. For instance, the man who hesitates to take a new job may be deterred by a complex of side bets: the financial loss connected with a pension fund he would lose if he moved; the loss of seniority and "connections" in his present firm which promise quick advance if he stays; the loss of ease in doing his work because of his success in adjusting to the particular conditions of his present job; the loss of ease in domestic living consequent on having to move his household; and so on.

V

For a complete understanding of a person's commitments we need one more element: an analysis of the system of values or, perhaps better, valuables with which bets can be made in the world he lives in. What kinds of things are conventionally wanted, what losses feared? What are the good things of life whose continued enjoyment can be staked on continuing to follow a consistent line of action?

Some systems of value permeate an entire society. To recur to Schelling's example of the canny house-buyer, economic commitments are possible only within the confines of a system of property, money, and exchange. A side bet of five thousand dollars has meaning only where money is conventionally valued.

However, it is important to recognize that many sets of valuable things have value only within subcultural groups in a society and that many side bets producing commitment are made within systems of value of limited provenience. Regional, ethnic, and social class subcultures all provide raw material for side bets peculiar to those sharing in the culture, as do the variants of these related to differing age and sex statuses. A middle-class girl can find herself committed to a consistently chaste line of behavior by the sizable side bet of her reputation that middle-class culture attaches to virginity for females. A girl who is a member of a social class where virginity is less valued could not be committed in this way; and, except for a few puritanical enclaves in our society, boys cannot acquire commitments of this kind at all, for male virginity has little value, and no side bet of any magnitude could be made with it.[16]

More limited subcultures, such as those associated with occupational groups or political parties, also provide sets of valuables with which side bets can be made. These esoteric systems of value must be discovered if the commitments of group members are to be understood. For instance, the professional dance musician achieves job security by becoming known as a

16. I hasten to say that this illustration is hypothetical; I do not know the facts of the differential distribution of evaluations of chastity.

dependable man to a large group of employing bandleaders and to an even larger group of musicians who are not leaders but will recommend him for jobs they hear about. The dependable man is, among other things, a man who will take any job offered him unless he is already engaged; by doing this, he shows that he will not let a leader who needs a vital man down. His reputation for not letting leaders down has economic value to him, for leaders who believe in that reputation will keep him working. When he is offered a job that he does not, for whatever reason, want, he finds himself committed to taking it anyway; by failing to do so, he would lose the reputation for dependability and the consequent steady supply of jobs the value system of the music business has bet for him on his consistency in always taking whatever job is offered.[17]

In short, to understand commitments fully, we must discover the systems of value within which the mechanisms and processes described earlier operate. By so doing, we understand not only how side bets are made but the kind of counters with which they can be made; in fact, it is likely that we cannot fully penetrate the former without understanding the latter.

VI

The conception of commitment I have been proposing has certain disadvantages for empirical and theoretical work. In the first place, many of the difficulties faced in using other theories remain unresolved. People often have conflicting commitments, and the theory proposed here offers no answer to the question of how people choose between the commitments they have acquired when such conflicts are activated. Problems like this do not magically disappear on the introduction of a new concept.

Furthermore, the limited conception of commitment I have suggested covers a limited area. Many kinds of consistent behavior will probably prove unexplainable in its terms. This is as it should be, for analytic precision comes through the breaking-down of global categories into more limited and homogenous classificatory types. However, the concept of commitment has been made to cover such a wide range of phenomena in ordinary discourse that confusion may arise from trying to limit its use. This difficulty should be met by clarifying analytically the several mechanisms that have been subsumed under commitment, the conditions under which they operate, and the ways they may be distinguished from one another.[18]

17. An earlier and somewhat different account of dance musicians' job security can be found in Howard S. Becker, "Some Contingencies of the Professional Dance Musician's Career," *Human Organization* XII (Spring 1953), 22–26.

18. See Stone, *op. cit.,* and Erving Goffman, *Encounters* (Indianapolis: Bobbs-Merrill Co., 1961) pp. 85–152.

It seems convenient to retain "commitment" to refer to the specific mechanism of constraint of behavior through previously placed side bets and use such terms as "involvement," "attachment," "vocation," "obligation," and so on, to refer to related but distinguishable phenomena. Unfortunately, we cannot make our concepts precise and at the same time keep the full range of evocative meaning they have acquired in ordinary discourse.

These disadvantages, serious as they are, must be weighed against the advantages that use of the concept confers. First, the idea of the side bet allows us to specify the elements of commitment independently of the consistent line of behavior they are used to account for and thus avoid tautology. Though it may not always be easy to find empirical indicators of the side bets constraining people's activity, side bets and consistent activity are thus able to avoid a common difficulty in the use of the concepts.

Beyond this, the conception of commitment I have sketched gives us the theoretical tools for assimilating the common-sense notion that people often follow lines of activity for reasons quite extraneous to the activity itself. While we are all aware of this fact, we have no conceptual language which allows us to put this insight to work in our research and theory. The concept of commitment furnishes the requisite terms. In addition, it outlines the mechanisms by which past actions link extraneous interests to a line of activity.

Personal Change
in Adult Life

People often exhibit marked change—in their attitudes, beliefs, behavior and style of interaction—as they move through youth and adulthood. Many social scientists, and others interested in explaining human behavior, think that human beings are governed by deep and relatively unchanging components of the personality or self, so that important changes at late stages in the life cycle are veiwed as anomalies that need to be explained away. They may trace the roots of behavior to personality components formed in early childhood—needs, defenses, identifications, and the like—and interpret change in adulthood as simply a variation on an already established theme. Or they may, more sociologically, see the sources of everyday behavior in values established in the society, inculcated in the young during childhood, and maintained thereafter by constraints built into major communal institutions. Like the personality theorists, those who use values as a major explanatory variable see change in adulthood as essentially superficial, a new expression of an unchanging underlying system of values. In either case, the scientist wishes to concern himself with basic processes that will explain lasting trends in individual behavior.

Both these approaches err by taking for granted that the only way we can arrive at generalized explanations of human behavior is by finding some unchanging components in the self or personality. They err as well in making the prior assumption that human beings are essentially unchanging, that changes which affect only such "superficial" phenomena as behavior without affecting deeper components of the person are trivial and unimportant.

Reprinted by permission from *Sociometry*, 27 (March 1964), pp. 40–53. Copyright © 1964 American Sociological Association.

There are good reasons to deny these assumptions. Brim, for instance, has argued persuasively that there are no "deep" personality characteristics, traits of character which persist across any and all situations and social roles.[1] In any case, it is clearly a useful strategy to explore the theoretical possibilities opened up by considering what might be true if we look in other directions for generalizeable explanations of human behavior.

A good many studies now available suggest that an appropriate area in which further explanations might be sought is that of social structure and its patterned effects on human experience. Two of these seem of special importance, and I devote most of what I have to say to them. The process of *situational adjustment,* in which individuals take on the characteristics required by the situations they participate in, provides an entering wedge into the problem of change. It shows us one example of an explanation which can deal with superficial and immediate changes in behavior and at the same time allow us to make generalized theories about the processes involved. The process of *commitment,* in which externally unrelated interests of the person become linked in such a way as to constrain future behavior, suggests an aproach to the problem of personal stability in the face of changing situations. Before dealing with these processes, however, I will consider a problem of definition which reveals a further influence of social structure, this time an influence on the very terms in which problems of socialization are cast.

The Eye of The Beholder

Many of the changes alleged to take place in adults do not take place at all. Or, rather, a change occurs but an optical illusion causes the outside observer to see it as a change quite different in kind and magnitude from what it really is. The observer (a layman or a social scientist looking at the phenomenon from a layman's point of view), through a semantic transformation, turns an observable change into something quite different.

Take, for example, the commonly asserted proposition that the professional education of physicians stifles their native idealism and turns it into a profound professional cynicism.[2] Educated laymen believe this, and sci-

1. Orville G. Brim, Jr., "Personality as Role-Learning," in Ira Iscoe and Harold Stevenson, editors, *Personality Development in Children;* (Austin: University of Texas Press, 1960), pp. 127–59.
2. This problem is discussed at greater length in Howard S. Becker and Blanche Geer, "The Fate of Idealism in Medical School," *American Sociological Review* 23 (Feb. 1958), pp. 50–56, and in Howard S. Becker, Blanche Geer, Everett C. Hughes, and Anselm L. Strauss, *Boys in White: Student Culture in Medical School* (Chicago: University of Chicago Press, 1961), pp. 419–33.

entific studies have been carried out to test the proposition.[3] Observed changes in the behavior of fledgling physicians attest to its truth. Doctors are in fact inclined to speak with little reverence of the human body; they appear to be and probably are to a large extent unmoved in the emotional way a layman would be by human death; their standards are not as high as the layman thinks they ought to be, their desire for wealth stronger than it ought to be.

People describe these changes with reference to an unanalyzed conception of idealism and cynicism. It would not be unfair to describe the conception as the perspective of a disgruntled patient, who feels that the doctor he has to deal with is thinking about other things than the patient's welfare. The perspective of the disgruntled patient itself draws on some very general lay conceptions which suggest that those who deal with the unpleasant and the unclean—in this case, with death and disease—must of necessity by cynical, since "normal people" prefer what is pleasant and clean and find the unclean repulsive.

In service occupations, however, the practitioners who perform the service typically have a perspective quite different from the clients, patients or customers for whom they perform it.[4] They understand the techniques used by professionals, the reasons for their use in one case and not in another, the contingencies of the work situation and of work careers which affect a man's judgment and behavior, and the occupational ethos and culture which guide him. The client understands nothing of this. In an effort to make sense of his experience with those who serve him, he may resort to the folk notions I have already mentioned, reasoning that people who constantly deal with what decent people avoid may be contaminated: some of the dirt rubs off. The client is never sure that the practitioner has his best interests at heart and tends to suspect the worst.

But why should we assess and evaluate the change that takes place in the doctor as he goes through professional school from the point of view of his patient? Suppose we look at it instead from the characteristic perspective of the medical profession. If we do this, we find (as we would find if we studied the views of almost any occupation toward the institutions which train people for entrance into them) that medical schools are typically regarded as too idealistic. They train students to practice in ways that are not

3. See Leonard D. Eron, "Effect of Medical Education on Medical Students," *Journal of Medical Education* 10 (Oct. 1955), pp. 559–66; and Richard Christie and Robert K. Merton, "Procedures for the Sociological Study of the Values Climate of Medical Schools," *ibid.* 33 (1958), Part II, pp. 125–53.

4. See, for a discussion of this point, Howard S. Becker, *Outsiders: Studies in the Sociology of Deviance,* (New York: The Free Press, 1963), pp. 82 ff.; and Everett C. Hughes, *Men and their Work,* (New York: The Free Press, 1958), *passim.*

"practical," suited to an ideal world but not to the world we live in. They teach students to order more laboratory tests than patients will pay for, to ignore the patient's requests for "new" drugs or "popular" treatments,[5] but do not teach students what to do when the waiting room holds more patients than can be seen during one's office hours. Similarly, people often complain of schools of education that they train prospective teachers in techniques that are not adapted to the situation the teacher will really have to deal with; they idealistically assume that the teacher can accomplish ends which in fact cannot be gained in the situations she will face. They do not tell the teacher how to teach a fifteen-year-old fifth grader, nor do they tell her what to do when she discovers a pupil carrying a switchblade knife.

It is a paradox. In one view, professional training makes physicians less idealistic, in the other, more idealistic. Where does the truth lie? I have already noted that many of the changes seen as signs of increasing cynicism in the young physician do in fact take place. It can equally be demonstrated that the changes which make him seem too idealistic also take place. The medical students we studied at the University of Kansas expected, when they graduated, to practice in ways that would be regarded as hopelessly idealistic by many, if not most, medical practitioners. They proposed to see no more than 20 patients a day; they proposed never to treat a disease without having first made a firm diagnosis. These beliefs, inculcated by a demanding faculty, are just the opposite of the cynicism supposed to afflict the new physician.[6]

The lesson we should learn from this is that personality changes are often present only in the eye of the beholder. Changes do take place in people, but the uninformed outsider interprets the change wrongly. Just as doctors acquire new perspectives and ideas as a result of their medical training, any adult may acquire new perspectives and ideas. But it would be a mistake to assume that these changes represent the kind of fundamental changes suggested by such polar terms as "idealism" and "cynicism." We learn less by studying the students who are alleged to have lost their idealism than we do by studying those who claim they have become cynical.

Even so, adults do change. But we must make sure, not only by our own observation but also by careful analysis of the terms we use to describe what we see, that the changes we try to explain do in fact take place. Parenthetically, an interesting possibility of transfering concepts from the study of adults to the study of socialization of children lies in defining the character of the changes that take place as children develop. Is it too farfetched to say that the definitions ordinarily used are excessively parochial in that they are all arrived at from the adult point of view? What

5. See Eliot Freidson, *Patients' Views of Medical Practice* (New York: Russell Sage Foundation, 1961), pp. 200–202.

6. Becker *et al.*, *Boys in White, op. cit.*, pp. 426–8.

would our theories look like if we made a greater effort to capture the child's point of view? What does he think is happening to him? How does his conception of the process differ from that of the adults who bring him up and those who study his growing up?

Situational Adjustment

One of the most common mechanisms in the development of the person in adulthood is the process of situational adjustment. This is a very gross conception, which requires analytic elaboration it has not yet received. But the major outlines are clear. The person, as he moves in and out of a variety of social situations, learns the requirements of continuing in each situation and of success in it. If he has a strong desire to continue, the ability to assess accurately what is required, and can deliver the required performance, the individual turns himself into the kind of person the situation demands.

Broadly considered, this is much the same as Brim's notion of learning adult roles. One learns to be a doctor or a policeman, learns the definitions of the statuses involved and the appropriate behavior with respect to them. But the notion of situational adjustment is more flexible than that of adult role learning. It allows us to deal with smaller units and make a finer analysis. We construct the process of learning an adult role by analyzing sequences of smaller and more numerous situational adjustments. We should have in our minds the picture of a person trying to meet the expectations he encounters in immediate face-to-face situations: doing well in today's chemistry class, managing to be poised and mature on tonight's date, surmounting the small crises of the moment. Sequences and combinations of small units of adjustment produce the larger units of role learning.

If we view situational adjustment as a major process of personal development, we must look to the character of the situation for the explanation of why people change as they do. We ask what there is in the situation that requires the person to act in a certain way or to hold certain beliefs. We do not ask what there is in him that requires the action or belief. All we need to know of the person is that for some reason or another he desires to continue his participation in the situaiton or to do well in it. From this we can deduce that he will do what he can to do what is necessary in that situation. Our further analysis must adjust itself to the character of the situation.

Thus, for example, in our study of college undergraduates,[7] we find that they typically share a strong desire to get high grades. Students work very hard to get grades and consider them very important, both for their immediate consequences and as indicators of their own personal ability and worth.

7. See Howard S. Becker, Blanche Geer, and Everett C. Hughes, *Making the Grade: The Academic Side of College Life* (New York: John Wiley and Sons, 1968).

We need not look very deeply into the student to see the reason for his emphasis on grades. The social structure of the campus coerces students to believe that grades are important because, in fact, they are important. You cannot join a fraternity or sorority if your grades do not meet a certain minimum standard. You cannot compete for high office in important campus organizations if your grades are not high enough. As many as one-fourth of the students may not be able to remain in school if they do not raise their grades in the next semester. For those who are failing, low grades do not simply mean blocked acces to the highest campus honors. Low grades, for these unfortunates, mean that every available moment must be spent studying, that the time the average student spends dating, playing, drinking beer or generally goofing off must be given over to the constant effort to stay in school. Grades are the currency with which the economy of campus social life operates. Only the well-to-do can afford the luxuries; the poor work as hard as they can to eke out a marginal existence.

The perspectives a person acquires as a result of situational adjustments are no more stable than the situation itself or his participation in it. Situations occur in institutions: stable institutions provide stable situations in which little change takes place. When the institutions themselves change, the situations they provide for their participants shift and necessitate development of new patterns of belief and action. When, for instance, a university decides to up-grade its academic program and begins to require more and different kinds of work from its students, they must adjust to the new contingencies with which the change confronts them.

Similarly, if an individual moves in and out of given situations, is a transient rather than a long-term participant, his perspectives will shift with his movement. Wheeler has shown that prisoners become more "prisonized" the longer they are in prison; they are more likely to make decisions on the basis of criminal than of law-abiding values. But he has also shown that if you analyze prisoners' responses by time still to be served, they become more law-abiding the nearer they aproach release.[8] This may be interpreted as a situational shift. The prisoner is frequently sorry that he has been caught and is in a mood to give up crime; he tends to respect law-abiding values. But when he enters prison he enters an institution which, in its lower reaches, is dominated by men wedded to criminal values. Studies of prisons have shown that the most influential prisoners tend to have stable criminal orientations and that inmate society is dominated by these perspectives.[9] In order

8. Stanton Wheeler, "Socialization in Correctional Communities," *American Sociological Review* 26 (Oct. 1961), pp. 697–72.

9. See Donald R. Cressey, editor, *The Prison: Studies in Institutional Organization and Change* (New York: Holt, Rinehart & Winston, 1961); and Richard A. Cloward et al., *Theoretical Studies in Social Organization of the Prison* (New York: Social Science Research Council, 1960).

to "make out" in prison, the new inmate discovers that he must make his peace with this criminally oriented social structure, and he does. As he approaches release, however, he realizes that he is going back into a world dominated by people who respect the law and that the criminal values which stand him in such good stead in prison society will not work as well outside. He thereupon begins to shed the criminal values appropriate to the prison and renew his attachment to the law-abiding values of the outside world.

We discovered the same process in the medical school, where students gave up a naive idealistic approach to the problems of medicine for an approach that was specifically oriented toward getting through school. As they approached the end of their schooling, they relinquished their attachment to these school-specific values and once more returned to their concern with problems that would arise in the outer world, albeit with a new and more professional approach than they would have been capable of before.

We find a similar change in college students, when we observe them in the Spring of their last college year. They look back over the four years of school and wonder why they have not spent their time better, wonder if college has been what they wanted. This concern reflects their preoccupation, while in school, with the pursuit of values that are valuable primarily within the confines of the collegiate community: grades, office in campus organizations, and the like. (Even though they justify their pursuit of these ends in part on the basis of their utility in the outside world, students are not sure that the pursuit of other ends, less valued on the campus, might not have even more usefulness for the future.) Now that they are leaving for the adult community, in which other things will be valuable, they find it hard to understand their past concerns as they try, retrospectively, to assess the experience they have just been through.

Situational adjustment is very frequently not an individual process at all, but a collective one. That is, we are not confronted with one person undergoing change, but with an entire cohort, a "class" of people, who enter the institution and go through its socializing program together. This is most clearly the case in those institutions which typically deal with "batches" of people.[10] Schools are perhaps the best example, taking in a class of students each year or semester who typically go through the entire training program as a unit, leaving together at the end of their training.

But situational adjustment may have a collective character even where people are not processed in groups. The individual enters the institution alone, or with a small group, but joins a larger group there already, who

10. See Erving Goffman's use of this idea in *Asylums: Essays on the Social Situation of Mental Patients and Other Inmates* (Garden City: Doubleday and Company, 1961), pp. 6 and *passim*.

stand ready to tell him how it is and what he should do, and he will be followed by others for whom he will perform the same good turn.[11] In institutions where people are acted upon in groups by socializing agents, much of the change that takes place—the motivation for it and the perceived desirability of different modes of change—cannot be traced to the predilections of the individual. It is, instead, a function of the interpretive response made by the entire group, the consensus the group reaches with respect to its problems.

The guidelines for our analysis can be found in Sumner's analysis of the development of folkways.[12] A group finds itself sharing a common situation and common problems. Various members of the group experiment with possible solutions to those problems and report their experiences to their fellows. In the course of their collective discussion, the members of the group arrive at a definition of the situation, its problems and possibilities, and develop consensus as to the most appropriate and efficient ways of behaving. This consensus thenceforth constrains the activities of individual members of the group, who will probably act on it, given the opportunity.

The collective character of socialization processes has a profound effect on their consequences. Because the solutions the group reaches have, for the individual being socialized, the character of "what everyone knows to be true," he tends to accept them. Random variation in responses that might arise from differences in prior experiences is drastically reduced. Medical students, for instance, began their training with a variety of perspectives on how one ought to approach academic assignments. The pressure generated by their inability to handle the tremendous amount of work given them in the first year anatomy course forced them to adopt collectively one of the many possible solutions to the problem, that of orienting their studying to learning what the faculty was likely to ask about on examinations. (Where the situation does not coerce a completely collective response, variation due to differences in background and experience remains. Irwin and Cressey[13] argue that the behavior of prisoners, both in prison and after release, varies depending on whether the convict was previously a member of the criminal underworld.)

In addition, where the response to problematic situations is collective,

11. See Anselm L. Strauss, *Mirrors and Masks: The Search for Identity* (New York: The Free Press, 1959); and Howard S. Becker and Anselm L. Strauss, "Careers, Personality and Adult Socialization," in this volume.

12. William Graham Sumner, *Folkways* (Boston: Ginn and Co., 1907). See also Albert K. Cohen, *Delinquent Boys: The Culture of a Gang,* (New York: The Free Press, 1955); and Richard A. Cloward and Lloyd E. Ohlin, *Delinquency and Opportunity: A Theory of Delinquent Gangs,* (New York: The Free Press, 1960).

13. John Irwin and Donald R. Cressey, "Thieves, Convicts and the Inmate Culture," *Social Problems* 10 (Fall 1962), pp. 142–55. See also Howard S. Becker and Blanche Geer, "Latent Culture: A Note on the Theory of Latent Social Roles," *Administrative Science Quarterly* 5 (Sept. 1960), pp. 304–13.

members of the group involved develop group loyalties that become part of the environment they must adjust to. Industrial workers are taught by their colleagues to restrict production in order that an entire work group may not be held to the higher production standard one or two people might be able to manage.[14] Medical students, similarly, find that they will only make it harder for others, and eventually for themselves, if they work too hard and "produce" too much.[15]

One major consequence of the collective character of situational adjustment, a result of the factors just mentioned, is that the group being socialized is able to deviate much more from the standards set by those doing the socializing than would be possible for an individual. Where an individual might feel that his deviant response was idiosyncratic, and thus be open to persuasion to change it, the member of a group knows that there are many who think and act just as he does and is therefore more resistant to pressure and propaganda. A person being socialized alone, likewise, is freer to change his ways than one who is constrained by his loyalties to fellow trainees.

If we use situational adjustment as an explanation for changes in persons during adulthood, the most interesting cases for analysis are the negative cases, those instances in which people do not adjust appropriately to the norms implicit or explicit in the situation. For not everyone adjusts to the kind of major situational forces I have been discussing. Some prison inmates never take on criminal values; some college students fail to adopt campus values and therefore do not put forth their full effort in the pursuit of grades. In large part, cases in which it appears that people are not adjusting to situational pressures are cases in which closer analysis reveals that the situation is actually not the same for everyone involved in the institution. A job in the library may effectively remove the prisoner from the control of more criminally oriented prisoners; *his* situation does not constrain him to adopt criminal values. The political rewards owed a student's living group may require a campus organization to give him an office his grade point average would otherwise make it difficult for him to obtain.

More generally, subgroups in an institution will often have somewhat different life situations. College, for instance, is clearly one thing for men, another for women; one thing for members of fraternities and sororities, another for independents. We only rarely find an institution as monolithic as the medical school, in which the environment is, especially during the first two years, exactly alike for everyone. So we must make sure that we have discovered the effective environment of those whose personal development we want to understand.

Even after removing the variation in personal change due to variation in

---

14. Donald Roy, "Quota Restriction and Goldbricking in a Machine Shop," *American Journal of Sociology* 57 (Mar. 1952), pp. 427–42.
15. Becker *et al., Boys in White,* pp. 297–312.

the situation, we will find a few cases in which people sturdily resist situational pressures. Here we can expect to find a corresponding weakness in the desire to remain in the situation or to do well in it, or a determination to remain in the situation only on one's terms or as long as one can get what one wants out of it. Many institutions have enough leeway built into them for a clever and determined operator to survive without much adjustment.

Commitment

The process of situational adjustment allows us to account for the changes people undergo as they move through various situations in their adult life. But we also know that people exhibit some consistency as they move from situation to situation. Their behavior is not infinitely mutable, they are not infinitely flexible. How can we account for the consistency we observe?

Social scientists have increasingly turned to the concept of commitment for an explanation of personal consistency in situations which offer conflicting directives. The term has been used to describe a great variety of social-psychological mechanisms, such a variety that it has no stable meaning. Nevertheless, I think we can isolate at least one process referred to by the term commitment, a process which will help explain a great deal of behavioral consistency.[16]

Briefly, we say a person is committed when we observe him pursuing a consistent line of activity in a sequence of varied situations. Consistent activity persists over time. Further, even though the actor may engage in a variety of disparate acts, he sees them as essentially consistent; from his point of view they serve him in pursuit of the same goal. Finally, it is a distinguishing mark of commitment that the actor rejects other situationally feasible alternatives, choosing from among the available courses of action that which best suits his purpose. In so doing, he often ignores the principle of situational adjustment, pursuing his consistent line of activity in the face of a short-term loss.

The process of commitment consists in the linking of previously extraneous and irrelevant lines of action and sets of rewards to a particular line of action under study. If, for instance, a person refuses to change jobs, even though the new job would offer him a higher salary and better working conditions, we should suspect that his decision is a result of commitment, that other sets of rewards than income and working conditions have become attached to his present job so that it would be too painful for him to change. He may have a large pension at stake, which he will lose if he moves; he may dread the cost of making new friends and learning how to get along with new

16. Howard S. Becker, "Notes on the Concept of Commitment," in this volume.

working associates; he may feel that he will get a reputation for being flighty and erratic if he leaves his present job. In each instance, formerly extraneous interests have become linked to keeping his present job. I have elsewhere described this process metaphorically as the making of side-bets.

> The committed person has acted in such a way as to involve other interests of his, originally extraneous to the action he is engaged in, directly in that action. By his own actions . . . he has staked something of value to him, something originally unrelated to his present line of action, on being consistent in his present behavior. The consequences of inconsistency will be so expensive that inconsistency . . . is no longer a feasible alternative.[17]

A person may make side-bets producing commitments consciously and deliberately or he may acquire them or have them made for him almost without his knowledge, becoming aware that he is committed only when he faces a difficult decision. Side-bets and commitments of the latter type, made by default, arise from the operation of generalized cultural expectations, from the operation of impersonal bureaucratic arrangements, from the process of individual adjustment to social positions, and through the need to save face.

One way of looking at the process of becoming an adult is to view it as a process of gradually acquiring, through the operation of all these mechanisms, a variety of commitments which constrain one to follow a consistent pattern of behavior in many areas of life. Choosing an occupation, getting a job, starting a family—all these may be seen as events which produce lasting commitments and constrain the person's behavior. Careful study might show that the operation of the process of commitment accounts for the well-known fact that juvenile delinquents seldom become adult criminals, but rather turn into respectable, conventional, law-abiding lower-class citizens. It may be that the erratic behavior of the juvenile delinquent is erratic precisely because the boy has not yet taken any actions which commit him more or less permanently to a given line of endeavor.

Viewing commitment as a set of side-bets encourages us to inquire into the kind of currency with which bets are made in the situation under analysis. What things are valuable enough to make side-bets that matter with? What kinds of counters are used in the game under analysis? Very little research has been done on this problem, but I suspect that erratic behavior and "random" change in adult life result from situations which do not permit people to become committed because they deny to them the means, the chips, with which to make side-bets of any importance.

Members of medical faculties complain, for instance, that students' behavior toward patients is erratic. They do not exhibit the continued interest

17. *Ibid.*

in or devotion to the patient's welfare supposed to characterize the practicing physician. They leave the hospital at five o'clock, even though a patient assigned to them is in critical condition. Their interest in a surgical patient disappears when the academic schedule sends them to a medical ward and a new set of student duties. The reason for students' lack of interest and devotion becomes clear when we consider their frequent complaint that they are not allowed to exercise medical responsibility, to make crucial decisions or carry out important procedures. Their behavior toward patients can be less constrained than that of a practicing physician precisely because they are never allowed to be in a position where they can make a mistake that matters. No patient's life or welfare depends on them; they need not persist in any particular pattern of activity since deviation costs nothing.[18]

The condition of being unable to make important side-bets and thus commit oneself may be more widespread than we think. Indeed, it may well be that the age at which it becomes possible to make lasting and important side-bets is gradually inching up. People cannot become committed to a consistent line of activity until later in life. As divorce becomes more frequent, for instance, the ability to make a lasting commitment by getting married becomes increasingly rare. In studying the possibilities of commitment afforded by social structures, we discover some of the limits to consistent behavior in adult life.

(It might be useful to apply similar concepts in studies of child socialization. It is likely, for instance, that children can seldom commit themselves. Our society, particularly, does not give them the means with which to make substantial side-bets, nor does it think it appropriate for children to make committing side-bets. We view childhood and youth as a time when a person can make mistakes that do not count. Therefore, we would expect children's behavior to be flexible and changeable, as in fact it seems to be.)

Situational adjustment and commitment are closely related, but by no means identical, processes. Situational adjustment produces change; the person shifts his behavior with each shift in the situation. Commitment produces stability; the person subordinates immediate situational interests to goals that lie outside the situation. But a stable situation can evoke a well-adjusted pattern of behavior which itself becomes valuable to the person, one of the counters that has meaning in the game he is playing. He can become committed to preserving the adjustment.

We find another such complementary relationship between the two when we consider the length of time one is conventionally expected to spend in a situation, either by oneself or by others, and the degree to which the present situation is seen as having definite connections to important situations

18. Becker *et al.*, *Boys in White, op. cit.*, pp. 254–273.

anticipated at some later stage of development. If one sees that his present situation is temporary and that later situations will demand something different, the process of adjustment will promote change. If one thinks of the present situation as likely to go on for a long time, he may resist what appear to him temporary situational changes because the strength of the adjustment has committed him to maintaining it. This relationship requires a fuller analysis than I have given it here.

Conclusion

The processes we have considered indicate that social structure creates the conditions for both change and stability in adult life. The structural characteristics of institutions and organizations provide the framework of the situations in which experience dictates the expediency of change. Similarly, they provide the counters with which side-bets can be made and the links between lines of activity out of which commitment grows. Together, they enable us to arrive at general explanations of personal development in adult life without requiring us to posit unvarying characteristics of the person, either elements of personality or of "value structure."

A structural explanation of personal change has important implications for attempts to deliberately mold human behavior. In particular, it suggests that we need not try to develop deep and lasting interests, be they values or personality traits, in order to produce the behavior we want. It is enough to create situations which will coerce people into behaving as we want them to and then to create the conditions under which other rewards will become linked to continuing this behavior. A final medical example will make the point. We can agree, perhaps, that surgeons ought not to operate unless there is a real need to do so; the problem of "unnecessary surgery" has received a great deal of attention both within and outside the medical profession. We might achieve our end by inculcating this rule as a basic value during medical training; or we might use personality tests to select as surgeons only those men whose own needs would lead them to exercise caution. In fact, this problem is approaching solution through a structural innovation: the hospital tissue committee, which examines all tissue removed at surgery and disciplines those surgeons who too frequently remove healthy tissue. Surgeons, whatever their values or personalities, soon learn to be careful when faced with the alternative of exposure or discipline.

CHAPTER TWENTY

The Self
and Adult
Socialization

Everyone knows what the self is. It seems to avoid nicely that brace of faults, one or the other of which afflict most concepts of social science. It is not merely a lay term, togged up with a new polysyllabic definition that conceals all the ambiguities of the original, though not very well. Nor is it totally esoteric, a barbarous neologism whose relation to anything known to ordinary men is questionable. (The concept of criminal, as social scientists habitually use it, nicely illustrates the first difficulty. Examples of the second can be found in any sociology textbook.)

The notion of the self avoids these troubles. It is not a term that plays a role in ordinary discourse so that it acquires emotional overtones or gets involved in questions that give rise to argument. On the other hand, it is not totally foreign. We immediately have an intuitive apprehension of the direction in which the concept points, a general idea of the kind of thing it must be. When a social scientist speaks of the self we feel, with some relief, that for a change we know what he is talking about.

He is talking, of course, about the essential core of the individual, the part that calls itself "I," the part that feels, thinks and originates action. Or is he? For despite the seeming clarity of the concept, people do not seem to agree on what they mean by it. This should not be surprising because, in fact, no concept can be defined in isolation. Any concept is, explicitly or implicitly, part of a theoretical system and derives its true meaning from its place in that system, from its relation to the other concepts of which the system is constructed. So the self means one thing in a sociologist's theory and another in a psychologist's, one thing (even among sociological theories) in a structural-functional theory and another in a theory based on symbolic interaction. When we accept the term intuitively we gloss over the differences it hides, differences due to the differing theoretical systems in which it has been embedded. Intuition conceals the disagreement we find when we explore the implications of the word.

In what follows I will approach the concept of self by suggesting the meaning it takes on in the framework of a theory of symbolic interaction, a theory that has long been of major importance in sociology. Of necessity, I will have to say a good deal about the symbolic character of human interaction, the nature of individual action, and the meaning of society before I can begin to speak of the self. But, having done so, I will then be able to proceed directly to the question of changes in the self during the years after childhood, a topic that has in the past few years become popular under the title "adult socialization."

Symbolic Interaction

The theory of symbolic interaction achieved for a time a commanding position in American sociology. Its dominance arose from the presence of George Herbert Mead at the University of Chicago at the very time that sociology was establishing its first American beachhead there. Mead was a philosopher who developed a theory of society and the self as interdependent parts of the same process, a theory that became integral to the tradition of sociological research that grew up a little later around the figure of Robert E. Park. Mead's theory of symbolic interaction (as it has lately come to be called) provided, with assists from Dewey and Cooley, the basic imagery sociologists used in their work.[1]

Other sources of theoretical support for sociology eventually grew up to dispute the Chicago School. But Mead's theory still seems to me to provide a representation of the character of social life and individual action that is unsurpassed for its fidelity to the nature of society as we experience it.[2]

The theory of symbolic interaction takes as its central problem this question: How is it possible for collective human action to occur? How can

1. See George Herbert Mead, *Mind, Self and Society* (Chicago: University of Chicago Press, 1934); John Dewey, *Human Nature and Conduct* (New York: Holt, Rinehart & Winston, 1930); and Charles Horton Cooley, *Human Nature and the Social Order* (New York: Charles Scribner's Sons), 1902.

2. See the explication in Herbert Blumer, "Sociological Implications of the Thought of George Herbert Mead," *American Journal of Sociology* 71 (March 1966), 535–544.

people come together in lines of action that mesh with one another in something we can call a collective act? By collective act we should understand not simply cooperative activities, in which people consciously strive to achieve some common goal, but any activity involving two or more people in which individual lines of activity come to have some kind of unity and coherence with one another. In a collective act, to smuggle part of the answer into the definition, individual lines of action are *adjusted* to one another. What I do represents an attempt on my part to come to terms with what you and others have done, to so organize my action that you in turn will be able to respond to it in some meaningful way. Playing a string quartet embodies this notion of mutual adjustment of several individual lines of action. But so do less cooperative activities, such as arguing or fighting, for even in them we mutually take account of what each other does.

By asking how such collective actions are possible, the theory of symbolic interaction marks out a distinctive subject matter and gives a distinctive cast to the study of society. For we may, without exaggeration, regard all of society and it component organizations and institutions as collective acts, as organizations of mutually adjusted lines of individual activity, admittedly of great complexity. A city, a neighborhood, a factory, a church, a family—in each of these many people combine what they do to create a more-or-less recurring pattern of interaction. By focusing on the phenomenon of mutual adjustment, the theory rises two kinds of questions: first, what patterns of mutual adjustment exist, how do they arise and change, and how do they affect the experience of individuals? Second, how is it possible for people to adjust their actions to those of others in such a way as to make collective acts possible? Having raised the question of how collective action is possible, it answers briefly by referring to the phenomenon of mutual adjustment and then asks how that is possible.

The second question concerns us here. Mead, and those who have followed him, explained the mutual adjustment of individual lines of activity by invoking a connected set of conceptions: meaning, symbols, taking the role of the other, society and the self. Actions come to have meaning in a human sense when the person attributes to them the quality of foreshadowing certain other actions that will follow them. The meaning is the as yet uncompleted portion of the total line of activity. Actions become significant symbols when both the actor and those who are interacting with him attribute to them the same meaning. The existence of significant symbols allows the actor to adjust his activities to those of others by anticipating their response to what he does and reorganizing his act so as to take account of what they are likely to do if he does that. What we do when we play chess—think to ourselves, "If I move here, he'll move there, so I'd better not do that"—is a useful model, although it suggests a more self-conscious process than is ordinarily at work.

The actor, in short, inspects the meaning his action will have for others, assesses its utility in the light of the actions that meaning will provoke in others, and may change the direction of his activity in such a way as to make the anticipated response more nearly what he would like. Each of the actors in a situation does the same. By so doing they arrive at mutually understood symbols and lines of collective action that mesh with one another and thus make society, in the large and in the small, possible. The process of anticipating the response of others in the situation is usually referred to as taking the role of the other.

Our conception of the self arises in this context. Clearly the actions of a person will vary greatly depending on the others whose role he takes. He learns over time from the people he ordinarily associates with certain kinds of meanings to attribute to actions, both his own and theirs. He incorporates into his own activity certain regularized expectations of what his acts will mean, and regularized ways of checking and reorganizing what he does. He takes, in addition to the role of particular others, what Mead referred to as the role of the generalized other, that is, the role of the organization of people in which he is implicated. In Mead's favorite example, the pitcher on a baseball team not only takes into accout what the batter is going to do in response to his next pitch, but also what the catcher, the infielders, and outfielders are going to do as well. Similarly, Strauss[3] has argued that when we use money we are taking into account, as a generalized other, the actions of all those who we know to be involved in handling money and giving monetary value to things: storekeepers, bosses, workers, bankers, and the government.

The self consists, from one point of view, of all the roles we are prepared to take in formulating our own line of action, both the roles of individuals and of generalized others. From another and complementary view, the self is best conceived as a process in which the roles of others are taken and made use of in organizing our own activities. The processual view has the virtue of reminding us that the self is not static, but rather changes as thoses we interact with change, either by being replaced by others or by themselves acting differently, presumably in response to still other changes in those they interact with.

I have presented a complicated theory in a very summary fashion. The reader who is interested in pursuing it further may be interested in Mead's

---

3. Anselm L. Strauss, "The Development and Transformation of Monetary Meanings in the Child," *American Sociological Review* 17 (June 1952), 275–286.

own writings, admittedly difficult, or may be satisfied with any of a number of good critical accounts already available.[4]

Adult Socialization

The current interest in adult socialization arose out of an attempt to generalize research in a great variety of fields on the changes that take place in people as they move through various institutional settings. Thus, some social psychologists had undertaken studies of the effects of participation in college life on college students; did the participation change them in any way? Others, out of an interest in the professions, had begun to explore the professional training of doctors, lawyers, nurses, and others. Still others, interested in medical sociology and social influences on mental health, had investigated the impact of mental hospitals and other kinds of hospitals on patients. Criminologists concerned themselves with the effects of a stay in prison on convicts, largely from a practical interest in how we might deal with problems of recidivism.

As workers in these different areas strove to find the general rubric under which all these studies might be subsumed and out of which might come propositions that were more abstract and more powerful, they were influenced by a desire common to most sociologists. They wanted to counter the common assumption that the important influences on a person's behavior occur in childhood, that nothing of much importance happens after that, observable changes being merely rearrangements of already existing elements in the personality. Since the term "socialization" had conventionally been applied to the formation of the personality in childhood, it seemed natural to indicate the belief that all change did not end with adolescence by speaking of "adult socialization," thus indicating that the same processes operated throughout the life cycle.[5]

The process of change indicated by the term can easily, and fruitfully, be conceptualized as a matter of change in the self. Our ways of thinking about our world and acting in it, arising as they do out of the responses of others we have internalized and now use to organize our own behavior prospectively, will change as the others with whom we interact change themselves or are replaced. These changes are precisely the ones students

4. See, for example, George J. McCall and J. L. Simmons, *Identities and Interactions* (New York: The Free Press, 1966).
5. Some of the major discussions of this theme include Orville G. Brim and Stanton Wheeler, *Socialization After Childhood* (New York: John Wiley and Sons, 1966); Howard S. Becker and Anselm L. Strauss, "Careers, Personality and Adult Socialization," in this volume; Anselm L. Strauss, *Mirrors and Masks* (New York: Free Press, 1959); and Robert K. Merton, Patricia Kendall, and George Reader, eds., *The Student Physician* (Cambridge, Mass.: Harvard University Press, 1957).

of adult socialization have concerned themselves with, though they have not always used the language of symbolic interaction or the self.

Two central questions have occupied students of adult socialization, each of them generating interesting lines of research and theorizing. The first directs itself outward, into the social context of personal change: What kinds of changes take place under the impact of different kinds of social structures? To put it in somewhat more interactionist terms, and spell out the process involved a little more fully, what kinds of situations do the socializing institutions place their new recruits in, what kinds of responses and expectations do recruits find in those situations, and to what extent and in what ways are these incorporated into the self? The second question, somewhat less studied, turns our attention inward: What kinds of mechanisms operate to produce the changes we observe in adults? I will take these up in order.

SOCIAL STRUCTURE

The study of adult socialization began, naturally enough, with studies of people who were participants in institutions deliberately designed to produce changes in adults. The research was often evaluative in character, designed to find out whether these institutions actually produced the changes they were supposed to produce. Had students of professional schools, at the end of their training, developed the appropriate skills and attitudes? Did prisoners lose their antisocial character and become potentially law-abiding citizens? The studies done usually disappointed the administrators of the institutions studied, for they generally revealed that the desired results were not being achieved. This disappointment led to an inquiry into exactly what was going on, in the hope of discovering how these malfunctions could be avoided. Later inquiries were more complex, went beyond asking simply whether or not the institution achieved its purpose, began to raise more interesting questions, and produced some important discoveries.

One discovery was that the processes of change involved were more complicated than changing in a way that was not officially approved. Wheeler discovered, for instance, in a study of criminal attitudes among convicts, that their attitudes became more "antisocial" the longer they were in prison —until the date of their release approached. Then, confronted with the prospect of returning to civilian society, they rapidly shed the criminal orientation that the impact of prison had fostered in them. The curve of "criminalization," rather than being a straight line slanting up, was U-shaped. This indicated that one had to take seriously the obvious possibility

6. Stanton Wheeler, "Socialization in Corrrectional Communities," *American Sociological Review* 26 (October 1961), 697–712.

that the curve of institutional influence might take any of a number of forms, each to be discovered by research rather than being taken for granted.

A second, and equally obvious, discovery was that to speak of "the institution" as producing change was a vast oversimplification. Institutions do not operate so monolithically. In order to understand the changes that took place one had to look at the structure of the institution in detail—at the particular relationships, both formal and informal, among all the participants, and at the kinds of recurring situations that arose among them. Thus, Stanton and Schwartz were able to show that mental patients responded dramatically to quarrels that took place between staff members of a mental hospital. A staff member might decide, against the opinion of others, that a particular patient would respond to intensive treatment. The staff member's intramural quarrel would lead him to invest vast amounts of time and effort on the patient and thereby produce radical improvement in the patient. But this investment also drove him out on a limb vis-à-vis his colleagues, and when he discovered his precarious situation, he clambered back to safety. The patient then returned to his original condition or, perhaps, to a worse one.[7]

A third discovery, one that could easily have been predicted from early studies in industrial sociology, was that the people the institution was trying to socialize did not respond to its efforts as individuals, but might, given the opportunity, respond as an organized group. Thus, my colleagues and I, when we studied the socializing effects of a medical school, found it necessary to speak of *student culture*.[8] By this term we referred to the meanings and understandings generated in interaction among students, the perspectives they developed and acted on in confronting the problems set for them by the school, its authorities, and curriculum. The importance of this observation is that the school's impact does not strike the individual student, with his own unique feelings and emotions, directly. Rather, it is mediated by the interpretations given him by the culture he participates in, a culture which allows him to discount and circumvent some of the efforts of his teachers.

A fourth discovery was that the world beyond the socializing institution played an important part in the socializing process, affecting the amount of impact it had either positively or negatively. This is apparent in the earlier prison example, where the experience of prison actually produced a change

7. Alfred Stanton and Morris Schwartz, *The Mental Hospital* (New York: Basic Books, 1954), pp. 301–365.

8. Howard S. Becker, Blanche Geer, Everett C. Hughes and Anselm L. Strauss, *Boys in White: Student Culture in Medical School* (Chicago: University of Chicago Press, 1961).

in attitudes in a direction opposite to what was desired, this trend being overcome when the prospect of leaving the prison for the larger world loomed ahead. It was, in fact, only during the period when the influence of the outside world was minimized that prison had an influence. Similarly, Davis and Olesen and their colleagues have shown that the professional training of nurses is deeply marked by the nursing school's inability to shut out external influences, in the form of generalized cultural expectations that the girls will soon marry and never become practicing professionals.[9]

As a consequence of these discoveries and rediscoveries, we can now look at the effects of socializing institutions with something of a model in mind. We know that the changes they produce in the self are likely to be complicated and many-faceted, the course in every case needing to be traced out empirically rather than assumed; we know that we must have detailed knowledge of the pattern of social relations within the socializing organization, as these impinge on the person being changed; we understand that we must see the process of socialization as at least potentially a collective experience, undergone by a group acting in and interpreting their world together, rather than as individuals; and we realize that we cannot ignore the influence of extraorganizational social groups. This gives us a framework for organizing research and a set of central concerns, each of which can be elaborated in specialized investigations.

As an example of the kind of elaboration possible, consider the question of the culture that grows up among those being socialized. (I give as an example student culture, but it is important to realize that we may similarly have convict culture, patient culture, or a culture of any group confronted with the problem of having attempts made to influence their selves.) Such a culture may or may not develop, depending on the conditions of interaction among those being socialized. In the extreme case, if people cannot communicate they cannot develop a culture (though studies of prisons have shown that people are remarkably ingenious in devising methods of communication in unpromising circumstances). Less extremely, the kind of communication possible and the paths along which it can move will determine the degree and kind of culture that arise.[10]

This leads to analysis of how socializing institutions handle their recruits, as these affect communication possibilities. Wheeler has suggested two dimensions of prime analytic importance. An institution may take recruits in cohorts, as most schools do when they admit a freshman class each fall, or it may take them in individually, as prisons and hospitals

9. Fred Davis and Virginia L. Olesen, "Initiation into a Women's Profession," *Sociometry* 26 (March 1963), 89–101.
10. Howard S. Becker and Blanche Geer, "Latent Culture: A Note on the Theory of Latent Social Roles," *Administrative Science Quarterly* 5 (September 1960), 304–313.

usually do. In the first instance, the recruits will face similar problems simultaneously, which maximizes the need for communication. In the second, each person will face his own problems alone; his fellows will either already have dealt with it and thus no longer be interested or will not be there yet and thus have no awareness of the problem, both tending to make communication more difficult.

The second dimension suggested by Wheeler distinguishes disjunctive from serial forms of socialization. In the first, one cohort or individual is released from the institution before another enters, so that communication is possible only outside the institution's walls; thus, delinquents might tell one another about the juvenile home before they enter it. In the second, several cohorts or individuals are present simultaneously, allowing the culture to be passed on rather than being developed anew, as happens when various perspectives on college life are passed on from one class to the next. Wheeler's analysis explores the consequences for the self of the various combinations of these dimensions that can arise.[11]

Let me conclude our exploration of the effects of social structure by making the essential jump from the socializing institution, which may be taken as an extreme case, to social organizations generally, any of which can be analyzed as though it, in effect, were attempting to socialize its participants. That is, any social organization, of whatever size or complexity, has effects on the selves of those who are involved in its workings. By taking these effects as the object of our attention and viewing every organization, whatever its stated intentions, as a socializing organiaztion, we can see how society is perpetually engaged in changing the selves of its members. For every part of society constantly confronts people with new situations and unexpected contingencies, with new others whose role they must take, with new demands and responses to be incorporated into the generalized other. The self, as I remarked earlier, is constantly changing and, in this sense, the label "adult socialization" is a misnomer, suggesting as it does that the process occurs only occasionally and then only in special places.

Take the processes involved in the use of addictive and intoxicating drugs as an example. Throughout the history of any individual's experience with such drugs, society will confront him with situations that produce appreciable changes in the self. His initial willingness to experiment with drugs that are legally and morally forbidden comes about, typically, after he has begun to participate in circles where drugs are regarded as morally appropriate, as much less dangerous than popularly believed, and as productive of desirable kinds of experience.

When the person first takes any drug, the subjective experience he has will itself be a consequence of the anticipated responses he has learned to

11. Brim and Wheeler, *op. cit.*

expect as a result of his interaction with more experienced users, responses he has incorporated into his self. For example, the novice marihuana user usually experiences nothing at all when he first uses the drug. It is only when other users have pointed out to him subtle variations in how he feels, in how things look and sound to him, that he is willing to credit the drug with having had any effect on him at all.[12] Similarly, Lindesmith has shown that people can be habituated to opiate drugs without becoming addicted, so long as no one points out to them the connection between the withdrawal distress they feel and the actual cessation of drug use. It is only when the withdrawal symptoms are interpreted as indicating a need for another shot, an interpretation often furnished by other users, and the shot taken with the predicted relief following, that the process of addiction is set in motion.[13] When a drug-using culture exists, this process operates smoothly. When it does not, as appears to be presently true with respect to LSD-25, people are likely to have a great variety of symptoms, especially anxiety reactions, triggered by their surprise at unexpected effects (because they have not been forecast by participants in such a culture), which may lead to diagnoses of drug-induced psychosis.[14] Finally, drastic changes in the self may occur as changes in the user's social relations, incident to his drug use, take place. On the one hand, his use may involve him more and more deeply (though it will not necessarily do so) in participation with other users and deviants, whose responses, growing out of a shared culture, will lead him to see himself as one of them and to act more like them and less like any of the other social beings he might be. (This process seems most marked among opiate users, as it is among some homosexuals, and much less marked with users of marihuana.) On the other hand, the use of drugs may bring the person to the attention of authorities (mainly the police) who will brand him as deviant and treat him accordingly, thus inducing a conception of himself as the victim of uninformed outsiders. In either case, he is likely to come out of the process a more confirmed deviant than he entered. (Such processes, of course, do not always run the full course; we particularly need studies of the contingencies of social structure and interaction that lead away from the formation of deviant selves.)[15]

To repeat, this extended example serves simply as an instance of the utility of regarding all of society as a socializing mechanism which operates

12. Howard S. Becker, "Becoming a Marihuana User," *American Journal of Sociology* LIX (November 1953), pp. 235–242.

13. Alfred R. Lindesmith, *Addiction and Opiates* (Chicago: Aldine Publishing Co., 1968).

14. Howard S. Becker, "History, Culture and Subjective Experience: An Exploration of the Social Bases of Drug-Induced Experiences," in this volume.

15 See the discussion in Howard S. Becker, *Outsiders: Studies in the Sociology of Deviance* (New York: The Free Press, 1963), pp. 25–39.

throughout a person's life, creating changes in his self and his behavior. We can just as well view families, occupations, work places, and neighborhoods in this fashion as we can deviant groups and legal authorities. All studies of social organizations of any kind are thus simultaneously studies of adult socialization.

MECHANISMS OF CHANGE

The second major area of research and theorizing in the study of adult socialization, less thoroughly explored than that of social structure, consists of the mechanisms by which participation in social organizations produces change. To introduce the topic, let me first mention that, in the view I have been presenting, stability in the self is taken to be just as problematic as change, so that we shall be looking at mechanisms that operate in both directions.

The general explanations of both stability and change in the self have been hinted at already in the discussion of interactionist theory and require only a slight elaboration. The person, as he participates in social interaction, constantly takes the roles of others, viewing what he does and is about to do from their viewpoint, imputing to his own actions the meaning he anticipates others will impute to them, and appraising the worth of the course on which he has embarked on accordingly. One important implication of this view is that people are not free to act as their inner dispositions (however we may conceptualize them) dictate. Instead, they act as they are constrained to by the actions of their coparticipants. To cite an obvious example, we use grammatical forms and words in accord with how others will understand them, knowing that if we become inventive and make up our own we will not be understood. The example indicates the limits of the proposition: It applies only when the actor wishes to continue interaction and have what he does be intelligible to others, or when he wishes to deceive them in some predictable way. But most social behavior meets this criterion and we need not concern ourselves with those rare instances in which communication is not desired.

The overall mechanism of change in the self, therefore, consists of the continual changes that occur in the person's notions of how others are likely to respond to his actions and the meanings he imputes to his own actions by virtue of the imputations others have made earlier. In his effort to continue interaction, to communicate, the person is continually confronted with his own wrong guesses on this score and thus with the need to revise the roles of others he has incorporated into his self.

This points the way to one specific mechanism of change, which has been called situational adjustment.[16] As the person moves into a new situation,

16. Howard S. Becker, "Personal Change in Adult Life," in this volume.

he discovers that, just because it is new, it contains some unexpected contingencies. Everything does not work out as he expects. People respond to him in unanticipated ways, leading him to appraise what he is doing afresh. He gradually discovers "how things are done here," incorporates these new anticipations of the responses of others into his self and thus adjusts to the situation. He can then continue to act without further change in the self until he is precipitated into a new situation or until the situaion changes beneath his feet.

The convicts studied by Wheeler provide an interesting example of this process. When they first enter prison they are ready to believe that crime does not pay. If it did, would they be there? But they enter an organization which is actually run by other prisoners. While prison administrators make rules and set policy, while guards attempt to enforce those rules and policies, the details of daily life come largely under the surveillance and control of the convicts' shadow government, to which prison officials largely abandon these tasks in return for peace and quiet in the institution. Convict culture is dominated by criminal values, by beliefs such as that crime does pay and that one should never snitch on a fellow inmate. To get along with the other prisoners, to play any meaningful part in what goes on and thus influence the conditions of one's own life, it is necessary to act in ways that are congruent with these beliefs and perspectives. Therefore, the longer one is in prison, the more "criminal" one's perspective.

By the same token, when one is about to leave the prison, it suddenly becomes clear that the world outside is, after all, not the prison and that it does not operate with the criminal perspectives that make collective action possible inside prison walls. The convict realizes that what works inside will probably not work outside, that his adjustment to prison ways will not enable him to interact easily with the people he will meet once he is out. In anticipation of the change in situation, he begins once again to adjust his self, changing it to incorporate the new responses of others he anticipates.[17] (Wheeler did not study what happened to inmates once released. It may well be that the repsonses of other people include some the prisoners did not anticipate, so that they begin to move once more toward a criminal perspective.)

Situational adjustment is not very complicated, as explanatory mechanisms go. But it seems to explain a great deal of what can be observed of change and stability in the self. The self changes when situations change and remains relatively stable when they do not. Some aspects of the self, however, display great stability over a variety of situational pressures and this easily observable fact points to the need for other explanatory mecha-

17. Wheeler, *op. cit.*

nisms. One which is congruent with the position taken here is the mechanism of commitment.[18]

A person is committed whenever he realizes that it will cost him more to change his line of behavior than it will to continue to act in a way that is consistent with his past actions, and that this state of affairs has come about through some prior action of his own. So committed, he will resist pressures to adjust to new situations that push him in a contrary direction, perhaps moving out of those situations where that is possible or else attempting to change the situation so that he can continue in the direction of his commitment.

A simple example of commitment is a man who is offered a new job but, on calculating its advantages and disadvantages, decides that the cost of taking the new job—in loss of seniority and pension rights, in having to learn a new set of ropes, and so on—makes it prohibitive. The trick in understanding commitment is to grasp the full range of things that have sufficient value to be included in the calculation. In analyzing occupational commitments, Geer[19] has suggested the following as the minimal list of valuables by which people can be committed: specialized training, which can only be used in the particular occupation; generalized social prestige, which would be lost if one left the occupation; loss of face following an exhibition of being unable to continue at one's chosen work; perquisites of the job to which one has become accustomed; rewarding personal involvements with clients or coworkers; promotional opportunities and other career possibilities; successful situational adjustment to one's present way of doing things; and prestige among colleagues. We can discover how people are committed only by finding out from them which things have sufficient value for their loss to constitute a constraint.

The list above of committing valuables indicates clearly the importance of social structure for the commitment process. Commitment can only occur when there are things present in the environment which are valuable enough that their loss constitutes a real loss. But objects acquire that kind of value only through the operation of a social organization, which both embodies the consensus that ascribes major value to them and creates the structural conditions under which they achieve the necessary attribute of scarcity. If you can get a certain valuable anywhere and with great ease, it is no longer very valuable; but if the social structure makes it scarce, allowing it to be gained in only a few ways that are structurally guarded, it takes on greater value.

18. The concept is explored at greater length in Howard S. Becker, "Notes on the Concept of Commitment," in this volume.
19. Blanche Geer, "Occupational Commitment and the Teaching Profession," *The School Review* 74 (Spring 1966), pp. 31–47.

Commitment and situational adjustment are clearly of great importance, and each is congruent with a symbolic interactionist approach to the self and adult socialization. Other mechanisms have yet to be discovered and explored. We might speculate, for instance, that involvement will be another such mechanism. People sometimes create a new and at least temporarily stable self by becoming deeply engrossed in a particular activity or group of people, becoming involved in the sense that they no longer take into account the responses of a large number of people with whom they actually interact.

Just as in the case of commitment, one of the crucial questions in the analysis of involvements is how organizations are constructed so as to allow the mechanism to come into play. What kinds of special arrangements allow a person to become so involved in an object, activity, or group that he becomes insensitive to the expectations of others to whom we might equally, on the basis of propinquity and frequency of interaction, expect him to be responsive? Selznick's analysis of the "fanaticism" of grass roots recruits to the TVA suggests the direction such analyses might take.[20] Their fanaticism consisted in always acting with the interests of their local community, and especially its businessmen, in mind, and systematically ignoring the considerations of national interest and bureaucratic constraint put forward by national TVA officials, both in Washington and in the field. They were able to maintain such a consistently one-sided perspective, which caused other agency officials to label them "fanatics," because all of their personal interests were bound up in the local community to which they knew they would return. They had no career or other interests in the national agency, so that the arguments and pleas of other officials (which took for granted that everyone had motives like theirs, actually unique to those who did have long term interests in the agency) meant nothing to them.

Generalizing from this case, we can look for the mechanism of involvement to operate whenever people are insulated from the opinions of others who, on the basis of common sense, we would expect to exert influence on them. Those others may be family members, as when an adolescent becomes so involved with his peers that he loses interest in what his parents think about his activities. They may be work associates, as in the TVA case. They may be such community representatives as the police, as when we speak of drug addicts being obsessed or totally involved in the activities surrounding drug use. Or we may have in mind some generalized conception of "public opinion," as when we wonder how people can do things that "everyone knows" are bizarre or unusual, such as being a nudist.

20. Philip Selznick, *TVA and the Grass Roots* (Berkeley: University of California Press, 1953), pp. 210–213.

The structural conditions that produce such involvements consist of social arrangements which effectively isolate people from other opinion, which allow them to ignore the expectations of some of those with whom they interact. Physical isolation is the most obvious example: religious sects often attempt to move away from the rest of society, as the Mormons once did, thus protecting their members from the necessity of shaping their behavior in the light of the scandalized responses of others. People may also be isolated, as the grass roots fanatics in TVA were, in an organizational sense; though they interact with others, their organizational positions and interests are so different as to preclude the development of any sense of community or common fate. More subtly, a person may be taught by the members of a group he has joined how to discount the opinions of those he once took seriously. Drug users learn to do this, and so do young people who enter an occupation their parents disapprove. Or, to conclude this preliminary and incomplete catalogue, they may have an experience commonly defined in one way or another, as setting them apart from others: a serious illness, a religious conversion, an emotional trauma. In every case, the crucial fact is that the person's social relationships—whom he comes into contact with and what they expect of him—become patterned in a way that allows him to dismiss certain categories of people from the self process.

I have briefly indicated the nature of a few mechanisms of change in the self: situational adjustment, through which much of the day-to-day variation in behavior can be explained; commitment, through which the development of long-term interests arises; and involvement, a process of shutting out of potential influences. Much work, empirical and theoretical, remains to be done.

Conclusion

Work in the field of adult socialization has made several contributions to the study of personality. It is one of the developments that is helping to turn the theory of symbolic interaction, by filling it out with research and the differentiated network of propositions research brings with its findings, from a programmatic scheme into a usable scientific tool. By doing this, it also begins to make available to students of personality, by providing the necessary concepts, much of the rich body of data sociologists have accumulated. It has, finally, introduced all of us to some areas of society that had not heretofore been studied and in so doing enriched our understanding both of society and of the great variety of influences which play on the continual development of the self.

PART IV

Deviance

CHAPTER TWENTY-ONE

History, Culture
and Subjective Experience:
An Exploration of
the Social Bases
of Drug-Induced Experiences

In 1938, Albert Hoffman discovered the peculiar effects of lysergic acid diethylamide (LSD-25) on the mind. He synthesized the drugs in 1943 and, following the end of World War II, it came into use in psychiatry, both as a method of simulating psychosis for clinical study and as a means of therapy.[1] In the early 1960's, Timothy Leary, Richard Alpert and others began using it with normal subjects as a means of "consciousness expansion." Their work received a great deal of publicity, particularly after a dispute with Harvard authorities over its potential danger. Simultaneously, LSD-25 became available on the underground market and, although no one has accurate figures, the number of people who have used or continue to use it is clearly very large.

The publicity continues and a great controversy now surrounds LSD use. At one extreme, Leary considers its use so beneficial that he has founded a

Reprinted by permission from *Journal of Health and Social Behavior,* 8 (September 1967), pp. 163–176. Copyright © 1967 American Sociological Association.

1. See "D-lysergic Acid Diethylamide—LSD," *Sandoz Excerpta* 1 (1955), pp. 1–2, quoted in Sanford M. Unger, "Mescaline, LSD, Psilocybin and Personality Change," in David Solomon, editor, *LSD: The Consciousness-Expanding Drug* (New York: Berkley Publishing Corp., 1966), p. 206.

new religion in which it is the major sacrament. At the other extreme, psychiatrists, police and journalists allege that LSD is extremely dangerous, that it produces psychosis, and that persons under its influence are likely to commit actions dangerous to themselves and others that they would not otherwise have committed. Opponents of the drug have persuaded the Congress and some state legislatures to classify it as a narcotic or dangerous drug and to attach penal sanctions to its sale, possession, or use.

In spite of the great interest in the drug, I think it is fair to say that the evidence of its danger is by no means decisive.[2] If the drug does prove to be the cause of a bona fide psychosis, it will be the only case in which anyone can state with authority that they have found *the* unique cause of any such phenomenon; a similar statement applies to causes of crime and suicide. Whatever the ultimate findings of pharmacologists and others now studying the drug, sociologists are unlikely to accept such an asocial and unicausal explanation of any form of complex social behavior. But if we refuse to accept the explanations of others we are obligated to provide one of our own. In what follows, I consider the reports of LSD-induced psychoses and try to relate them to what is known of the social psychology and sociology of drug use. By this means I hope to add both to our understanding of the current controversy over LSD and to our general knowledge of the social character of drug use.

In particular, I will make use of a comparison between LSD use and marihuana use, suggested by the early history of marihuana in this country. That history contains the same reports of "psychotic episodes" now current with respect to LSD. But reports of such episodes disappeared at the same time as the number of marihuana users increased greatly. This suggests the utility of considering the historical dimension of drug use.

2. On this point, to which I return later, the major references are: Sydney Cohen, "Lysergic Acid Diethylamide: Side Effects and Complications," *Journal of Nervous and Mental Diseases* 130 (January 1960), pp. 30–40; Sydney Cohen and Keith S. Ditman, "Prolonged Adverse Reactions to Lysergic Acid Diethylamide," *Archives of General Psychiatry* 8 (1963), pp. 475–480; Sydney Cohen and Keith S. Ditman, "Complications Associated with Lysergic Acid Diethylamide (LSD-25)," *Journal of the American Medical Association* 181 (July 14, 1962), pp. 161–162; William A. Frosch, Edwin S. Robins and Marvin Stern, "Untoward Reactions to Lysergic Acid Diethylamide (LSD) Resulting in Hospitalization," *New England Journal of Medicine* 273 (December 2, 1965), pp. 1235–1239; A. Hoffer, "D-Lysergic Acid Diethylamide (LSD): A Review of its Present Status," *Clinical Pharmacology and Therapeutics* 6 (March 1965), pp. 183–255; S. H. Rosenthal, "Persistent Hallucinosis Following Repeated Administration of Hallucinogenic Drugs," *American Journal of Psychiatry* 121 (1964), pp. 238–244; and J. Thomas Ungerleider, Duke D. Fischer and Marielle Fuller, "The Dangers of LSD: Analysis of Seven Months' Experience in a University Hospital's Psychiatric Service," *Journal of the American Medical Association,* 197 (August 8, 1966), pp. 389–392.

I must add a cautionary disclaimer. I have not examined thoroughly the literature on LSD, which increases at an alarming rate.[3] What I have to say about it is necessarily speculative with respect to its effects; what I have to say about the conditions under which it is used is also speculative, but is based in part on interviews with a few users. I present no documented conclusions, but do hope that the perspective outlined may help orient research toward generalizations that will fit into the corpus of sociological and social psychological theory on related matters.

The Subjective Effects of Drugs

The physiological effects of drugs can be ascertained by standard techniques of physiological and pharmacological research. Scientists measure and have explanations for the actions of many drugs on such observable indices as the heart and respiratory rates, the level of various chemicals in the blood, and the secretion of enzymes and hormones. In contrast, the subjective changes produced by a drug can be ascertained only by asking the subject, in one way or another, how he feels. (To be sure, one can measure the drug's effect on certain measures of psychological functioning—the ability to perform some standardized task, such as placing pegs in a board or remembering nonsense syllables—but this does not tell us what the drug experience is like.)[4]

We take medically prescribed drugs because we believe they will cure or control a disease from which we are suffering; the subjective effects they produce are either ignored or defined as noxious side effects. But some people take some drugs precisely because they want to experience these subjective effects; they take them, to put it colloquially, because they want to get "high." These recreationally used drugs have become the focus of sociological research because the goal of an artificially induced change in consciousness seems to many immoral, and those who so believe have been able to transform their belief into law. Drug users thus come to sociological attention as lawbreakers, and the problems typically investigated have to do with explaining their lawbreaking.

Nevertheless, some sociologists, anthropologists and social psychologists have investigated the problem of drug-induced subjective experience in its

3. Hoffer's review of this literature, for which he disclaims completeness, cites 411 references (Hoffer, *op. cit.*).

4. See, for instance: New York City Mayor's Committee on Marihuana, *The Marihuana Problem in the City of New York* (Lancaster: Jaques Cattell Press, 1944), pp. 69–77; and C. Knight Aldrich, "The Effect of a Synthetic Marihuana-Like Compound on Musical Talent as Measured by the Seashore Test," *Public Health Reports* 59 (1944), pp. 431–433.

own right. Taking their findings together, the following conclusions seem justified.[5] First, many drugs, including those used to produce changes in subjective experience, have a great variety of effects and the user may single out
many of them, one of them, or none of them as definite experiences he is
undergoing. He may be totally unaware of some of the drug's effects, even
when they are physiologically gross, although in general the grosser the
effects the harder they are to ignore. When he does perceive the effects, he
may not attribute them to drug use but dismiss them as due to some other
cause, such as fatigue or a cold. Marihuana users, for example, may not
even be aware of the drug's effects when they first use it, even though it is
obvious to others that they experiencing them.[6]

Second, and in consequence, the effects of the same drug may be experienced quite differently by different people or by the same people at different
times. Even if physiologically observable effects are substantially the same
in all members of the species, individuals can vary widely in those to which
they choose to pay attention. Thus, Aberle remarks on the quite different
experiences Indians and experimental subjects have with peyote[7] and Blum
reports a wide variety of experiences with LSD, depending on the circumstances under which it was taken.[8]

Third, since recreational users take drugs in order to achieve some subjective state not ordinarily available to them, it follows that they will expect and
be most likely to experience those effects which produce a deviation from
conventional perceptions and interpretations of internal and external experience. Thus, distortions in perception of time and space and shifts in

5. I rely largely on the following reports: Howard S. Becker, *Outsiders* (New York:
The Free Press, 1963), pp. 41–58 (marihuana); Alfred R. Lindesmith, *Opiate Addiction*
(Bloomington: Principia Press, 1947) (opiates); Richard Blum and associates, *Utopiates*
(New York: Atherton Press, 1964) (LSD); Ralph Metzner, George Litwin and Gunther
M. Weil, "The Relation of Expectation and Mood to Psilocybin Reactions: A Ques-
tionnaire Study," *Psychedelic Review* No. 5, 1965, pp. 3–39 (psilocybin); David F.
Aberle, *The Peyote Religion Among the Navaho* (Chicago: Aldine Publishing Co.,
1966), pp. 5–11 (peyote); Stanley Schacter and Jerome E. Singer, "Cognitive, Social and
Physiological Determinants of Emotional State," *Psychological Review* 69 (September
1962), pp. 379–399 (adrenalin); and Vincent Nowlis and Helen H. Nowlis, "The
Description and Analysis of Mood," *Annals of the New York Academy of Science* 65
(1956), pp. 345–355 (benzedrine, seconal and dramamine).
  Schacter and Singer propose a similar approach to mine to the study of drug experiences, stressing the importance of the label the person attaches to the experience
he is having.
  6. Becker, *op. cit.*
  7. Aberle, *op. cit.*, and Anthony F. C. Wallace, "Cultural Determinants of Response
to Hallucinatory Experience," *Archives of General Psychiatry* 1 (July 1959), pp. 58–69
(especially Table 2 on p. 62). Wallace argues that ". . . . both the subjective feeling tone
and the specific content of the hallucination are heavily influenced by . . . . the
cultural milieu in which the hallucination, and particularly the voluntary hallucination, takes place." (P. 62.)
  8. Blum *et al., op. cit.*, p. 42.

judgements of the importance and meaning of ordinary events constitute the most common reported effects.

Fourth, any of a great variety of effects may be singled out by the user as desirable or pleasurable, as the effects for which he has taken the drug. Even effects which seem to the uninitiated to be uncomfortable, unpleasant or frightening—perceptual distortions or visual and auditory hallucinations —can be defined by users as a goal to be sought.[9]

Fifth, how a person experiences the effects of a drug depends greatly on the way others define those effects for him.[10] The total effect of a drug is likely to be a melange of differing physical and psychological sensations. If others whom the user believes to be knowledgeable single out certain effects as characteristics and dismiss others, he is likely to notice those they single out as characteristic of his own experience. If they define certain effects as transitory, he is likely to believe that those effects will go away. All this supposes, of course, that the definition offered the user can be validated in his own experience, that something contained in the drug-induced melange of sensations corresponds to it.

Such a conception of the character of the drug experience has its roots, obviously, in Mead's theory of the self and the relation of objects to the self.[11] In that theory, objects (including the self) have meaning for the person only as he imputes that meaning to them in the course of his interaction with them. The meaning is not given in the object, but is lodged there as the person acquires a conception of the kind of action that can be taken with, toward, by and for it. Meanings arise in the course of social interaction, deriving their character from the consensus participants develop about the object in question. The findings of research on the character of drug-induced experience are therefore predictable from Mead's theory.

Drug Psychoses

The scientific literature and, even more, the popular press frequently state that recreational drug use produces a psychosis. The nature of "psychosis" is seldom defined, as though it were intuitively clear. Writers usually seem to mean a mental disturbance of some unspecified kind, involving auditory and visual hallucinations, an inability to control one's stream of thought, and a tendency to engage in socially inappropriate behavior, either because one has lost the sense that it is inappropriate or because one cannot stop

9. See the case cited in Becker, *op. cit.,* pp. 55–56.
10. The studies cited in footnote 5, *supra,* generally make this point.
11. See George Herbert Mead, *Mind, Self and Society* (Chicago: University of Chicago Press, 1934), and Herbert Blumer, "Sociological Implications of the Thought of George Herbert Mead," *American Journal of Sociology* 71 (March 1966), pp. 535–544.

oneself. In addition, and perhaps most important, psychosis is thought to be a state that will last long beyond the specific event that provoked it. However it occurred, it is thought to make a more-or-less permanent change in the psyche and this, after all, is why we usually think of it as such a bad thing. Overindulgence in alcohol produces many of the symptoms cited but this frightens no one because we understand that they will soon go away.

Verified reports of drug-induced psychoses are scarcer than one might think.[12] Nevertheless, let us assume that these reports have not been fabricated, but represent an interpretation by the reporter of something that really happened. In the light of the findings just cited, what kind of event can we imagine to have occurred that might have been interpreted as a "psychotic episode"? (I use the word "imagine" advisedly, for the available case reports usually do not furnish sufficient material to allow us to do more than imagine what might have happened.)

The most likely sequence of events is this. The inexperienced user has certain unusual subjective experiences, which he may or may not attribute to having taken the drug. He may find his perception of space distorted, so that he has difficulty climbing a flight of stairs. He may find his train of thought so confused that he is unable to carry on a normal conversation and hears himself making totally inappropriate remarks. He may see or hear things in a way that he suspects is quite different from the way others see and hear them.

Whether or not he attributes what is happening to the drug, the experiences are likely to be upsetting. One of the ways we know that we are normal human beings is that our perceptual world, on the evidence available to us, seems to be pretty much the same as other people's. We see and hear the same things, make the same kind of sense out of them and, where perceptions differ, can explain the difference by a difference in situation or perspective.[13] We may take for granted that the inexperienced drug user, though he wanted to get "high," did not expect an experience so radical as to call into question that common sense set of assumptions.

In any society whose culture contains notions of sanity and insanity, the person who finds his subjective state altered in the way described may think

12. See the studies cited in footnote 2, *supra,* and the following reports of marihuana psychoses: Walter Bromberg, "Marihuana: A Psychiatric Study," *Journal of the Medical Association* 113 (July 1, 1939), pp. 4–12; Howard C. Curtis, "Psychosis Following the Use of Marihuana with Report of Cases," *Journal of the Kansas Medical Society* 40 (1939), pp. 515–517; and Marjorie Nesbitt, "Psychosis Due to Exogenous Poisons," *Illinois Medical Journal* 77 (1940), 278–281.

13. See Alfred Schutz, *Collected Papers,* vols. I and II (The Hague: Martinus Nijhoff, 1962 and 1964), and Harold Garfinkel, "A Conception of and Experiments with 'Trust' as a Condition of Stable Concerted Actions," in O. J. Harvey, editor, *Motivation and Social Interaction* (New York: Ronald Press Co., 1963), pp. 187–238.

he has become insane. We learn at a young age that a person who "acts funny," "sees things," "hears things," or has other bizarre and unusual experiences may have become "crazy," "nuts," "loony" or a host of other synonyms.[14] When a drug user identifies some of these untoward events occurring in his own experience, he may decide that he merits one of those titles—that he has lost his grip on reality, his control of himself, and has in fact "gone crazy." The interpretation implies the corollary that the change is irreversible or, at least, that things are not going to be changed back very easily. The drug experience, perhaps originally intended as a momentary entertainment, now looms as a momentous event which will disrupt one's life, possibly permanently. Faced with this conclusion, the person develops a full-blown anxiety attack, but it is an anxiety caused by his reaction to the drug experience rather than a direct consequence of drug use itself. (In this conection, it is interesting that, in the published reports of LSD psychoses, acute anxiety attacks appear as the largest category of untoward reactions.)[15]

It is perhaps easier to grasp what this must feel like if we imagine that, having taken several social drinks at a party, we were suddenly to see varicolored snakes peering out at us from behind the furniture. We would instantly recognize this as a sign of delirium tremens, and would no doubt become severely anxious at the prospect of having developed such a serious mental illness. Some such panic is likely to grip the reactional user of drugs who interprets his experience as a sign of insanity.

Though I have put the argument with respect to the inexperienced user, long-time users of recreational drugs sometimes have similar experiences. They may experiment with a higher dosage than they are used to and experience effects unlike anything they have known before. This can easily occur when using drugs purchased in the illicit market, where quality may vary greatly, so that the user inadvertently gets more than he can handle.

The scientific literature does not report any verified cases of people acting on their distorted perceptions so as to harm themselves and others, but such cases have been reported in the press. Press reports of drug-related events are very unreliable, but it may be the users have, for instance, stepped out

14. See Thomas J. Scheff, *Being Mentally Ill: A Sociological Theory* (Chicago: Aldine Publishing Co., 1966).

15. See Frosch *et al., op. cit.,* Cohen and Ditman, "Prolonged Adverse Reactions . . . ," *op cit.,* and Ungerleider *et al., op. cit.* It is not always easy to make a judgment, due to the scanty presentation of the material, and some of the reactions I count as anxiety are placed in these sources under different headings. Bromberg, *op. cit.,* makes a good case that practically all adverse reactions to marihuana can be traced to this kind of anxiety, and I think it likely that the same reasoning could be applied to the LSD reports, so that such reactions as "hallucination," "depression" and "confused" (to use Ungerleider's categories) are probably reactions to anxiety.

of a second story window, deluded by the drug into thinking it only a few feet to the ground.[16] If such cases have occurred, they too may be interpreted as examples of psychosis, but a different mechanism than the one just discussed would be involved. The person, presumably, would have failed to make the necessary correction for the drug-induced distortion, a correction, however, that experienced users assert can be made. Thus, a novice marihuana user will find it difficult to drive while "high," but experienced users have no difficulty. Similarly, novices find it difficult to manage their relations with people who are not also under the influence of drugs, but experienced users can control their thinking and actions so as to behave appropriately.[17] Although it is commonly assumed that a person under the influence of LSD must avoid ordinary social situations for 12 or more hours, I have been told[18] of at least one user who takes the drug and then goes to work; she explained that once you learn "how to handle it" (i.e., make the necessary corrections for distortions caused by the drug) there is no problem.

In short, the most likely interpretation we can make of the drug-induced psychoses reported is that they are either severe anxiety reactions to an event interpreted and experienced as insanity, or failures by the user to correct, in carrying out some ordinary action, for the perceptual distortions caused by the drug. If the interpretation is correct, then untoward mental effects produced by drugs depend in some part on the physiological action, but to a much larger degree find their origin in the definitions and conceptions the user applies to that action. These can vary with the individual's personal makeup, a possibility psychiatrists are most alive to, or with the groups he participates in, the trail I shall pursue here.

The Influence of Drug-Using Cultures

While there are no reliable figures, it is obvious that a very large number of people use recreational drugs, primarily marihuana and LSD. From the previous analysis one might suppose that, therefore, a great many people would have disquieting symptoms and, given the ubiquity in our society of the concept of insanity, that many would decide they had gone crazy and

16. Although LSD is often said to provoke suicide, there is very little evidence of this. Cohen, *op. cit.,* after surveying 44 investigators who had used LSD with over 5,000 patients, says that the few cases reported all occurred among extremely disturbed patients who might have done it anyway; Hoffer, *op cit.,* remarks that the number is so low that it might be argued that LSD actually lowers the rate among mental patients. Ungerleider reports that 10 of 70 cases were suicidal or suicide attempts, but gives no further data.

17. See Becker, *op. cit.,* pp. 66–72.

18. By David Oppenheim.

thus have a drug-induced anxiety attack. But very few such reactions occur. Although there must be more than are reported in the professional literature, it is unlikely that drugs have this effect in any large number of cases. If they did there would necessarily be many more verified accounts than are presently available. Since the psychotic reaction stems from a definition of the drug-induced experience, the explanation of this paradox must lie in the availability of competing definitions of the subjective states produced by drugs.

Competing definitions come to the user from other users who, to his knowledge, have had sufficient experience with the drug to speak with authority. He knows that the drug does not produce permanent disabling damage in all cases, for he can see that these other users do not suffer from it. The question, of course, remains whether it may not produce damage in some cases and whether his is one of them, no matter how rare.

When someone experiences disturbing effects, other users typically assure him that the change in his subjective experience is neither rare nor dangerous. They have seen similar reactions before, and may even have experienced them themselves with no lasting harm. In any event, they have some folk knowledge about how to handle the problem.

They may, for instance, know of an antidote for the frightening effects; thus, marihuana users, confronted with someone who has gotten "too high," encourage him to eat, an apparently effective countermeasure.[19] They talk reassuringly about their own experiences, "normalizing" the frightening symptom by treating it, mater-of-factly, as temporary. They maintain surveillance over the affected person, preventing any physically or socially dangerous activity. They may, for instance, keep him from driving or from making a public display that will bring him to the attention of the police or others who would disapprove of his drug use. They show him how to allow for the perceptual distortion the drug causes and teach him how to manage interaction with nonusers.

They redefine the experience he is having as desirable rather than frightening, as the end for which the drug is taken.[20] What they tell him carries conviction, because he can see that it is not some idiosyncratic belief but is instead culturally shared. It is what "everyone" who uses the drug knows. In all these ways, experienced users prevent the episode from having lasting

19. Cf. the New York City Mayor's Committee on Marihuana, *op. cit.,* p. 13: "The smoker determines for himself the point of being 'high,' and is over-conscious of preventing himself from becoming 'too high.' This fear of being 'too high' must be associated with some form of anxiety which causes the smoker, should he accidentally reach that point, immediately to institute measures so that he can 'come down.' It has been found that the use of beverages such as beer, or a sweet soda pop, is an effective measure. A cold shower will also have the effect of bringing the person 'down.'"

20. *Ibid.,* and Becker, *op. cit.*

effects and reassure the novice that whatever he feels will come to a timely and harmless end.

The anxious novice thus has an alternative to defining his experience as "going crazy." He may redefine the event immediately or, having been watched over by others throughout the anxiety attack, decide that it was not so bad after all and not fear its reoccurrence. He "learns" that his original definition was "incorrect" and that the alternative offered by other users more nearly describes what he has experienced.

Available knowledge does not tell us how often this mechanism comes into play or how effective it is in preventing untoward psychological reactions; no research has been addressed to this point. In the case of marihuana, at least, the paucity of reported cases of permanent damage coupled with the undoubted increase in use suggests that it may be an effective mechanism.

For such a mechanism to operate, a number of conditions must be met. First, the drug must not produce, quite apart from the user's interpretations, permanent damage to the mind. No amount of social redefinition can undo the damage done by toxic alcohols, or the effects of a lethal dose of an opiate or barbituate. This analysis, therefore, does not apply to drugs known to have such effects.

Second, users of the drug must share a set of understandings—a culture —which includes, in addition to material on how to obtain and ingest the drug, definitions of the typical effects, the typical course of the experience, the permanence of the effects, and a description of methods for dealing with someone who suffers an anxiety attack because of drug use or attempts to act on the basis or distorted perceptions. Users should have available to them, largely through face-to-face participation with other users but possibly in such other ways as reading as well, the definitions contained in that culture, which they can apply in place of the common-sense definitions available to the inexperienced man in the street.

Third, the drug should ordinarily be used in group settings, where other users can present the definitions of the drug-using culture to the person whose inner experience is so unusual as to provoke use of the common-sense category of insanity. Drugs for which technology and custom promote group use should produce a lower incidence of "psychotic episodes."

The last two conditions suggest, as is the case, that marihuana, surrounded by an elaborate culture and ordinarily used in group settings, should produce few "psychotic" episodes.[21] At the same time, they suggest the prediction that drugs which have not spawned a culture and are ordinarily used

---

21. I discuss the evidence on this point below.

in private, such as barbiturates, will produce more such episodes. I suggest possible research along these lines below.

Non-User Interpretations

A user suffering from drug-induced anxiety may also come into contact with non-users who will offer him definitions, depending on their own perspectives and experiences, that may validate the diagnosis of "going crazy" and thus prolong the episode, possibly producing relatively permanent disability. These non-users include family members and police, but most important among them are psychiatrists and psychiatrically oriented physicians. (Remember that when we speak of reported cases of psychosis, the report is ordinarily made by a physician, though police may also use the term in reporting a case to the press.)

Medical knowledge about the recreational use of drugs is spotty. Little research has been done, and its results are not at the fingertips of physicians who do not specialize in the area. (In the case of LSD, of course, there has been a good deal of research, but its conclusions are not clear and, in any case, have not yet been spread throughout the profession.) Psychiatrists are not anxious to treat drug users, so few of them have accumulated any clinical experience with the phenomenon. Nevertheless, a user who develops severe and uncontrollable anxiety will probably be brought, if he is brought anywhere, to a physician for treatment. Most probably, he will be brought to a psychiatric hospital, if one is available; if not, to a hospital emergency room, where a psychiatric resident will be called once the connection with drugs is established, or to a private psychiatrist.[22]

Physicians, confronted with a case of drug-induced anxiety and lacking specific knowledge of its character or proper treatment, rely on a kind of generalized diagnosis. They reason that people probably do not use drugs unless they are suffering from a severe underlying personality disturbance; that use of the drug may allow repressed conflicts to come into the open where they will prove unmanageable; that the drug in this way provokes a true psychosis; and, therefore, that the patient confronting them is psychotic. Furthermore, even thought the effects of the drug wear off, the psychosis may not, for the repressed psychological problems it has brought to the surface may not recede as it is metabolized and excreted from the body.

22. It may be that a disproportionate number of cases will be brought to certain facilities. Ungerleider *et al., op. cit.,* say (p. 392): "A larger number of admissions, both relative and real, than in other facilities in the Los Angeles area suggests the prevalence of a rumor that 'UCLA takes care of acid heads,' as several of our patients have told us."

Given such a diagnosis, the physician knows what to do. He hospitalizes the patient for observation and prepares, where possible, for long-term therapy designed to repair the damage done to the psychic defenses or to deal with the conflict unmasked by the drug. Both hospitalization and therapy are likely to reinforce the definition of the drug experience as insanity, for in both the patient will be required to "understand" that he is mentally ill as a precondition for return to the world.[23]

The physician, then, does *not* treat the anxiety attack as a localized phenomenon, to be treated in a symptomatic way, but as an outbreak of a serious disease heretofore hidden. He may thus prolong the serious effects beyond the time they might have lasted had the user instead come into contact with other users. This analysis, of course, is frankly speculative; what is required is study of the way physicians treat cases of the kind described and, especially, comparative study of the effects of treatment of drug-induced anxiety attacks by physicians and by drug users.

Another category of non-users deserves mention. Literary men and journalists publicize definitions of drug experiences, either of their own invention or those borrowed from users, psychiatrists or police. (Some members of this category use drugs themselves, so it may be a little confusing to classfy them as non-users; in any case, the definitions are provided outside the ordinary channels of communication in the drug-using world.) The definitions of literary men—novelists, essayists and poets—grow out of a long professional tradition, beginning with De Quincey's *Confessions,* and are likely to be colored by that tradition. Literary descriptions dwell on the fantasy component of the experience, on its cosmic and ineffable character, and on the threat of madness.[24] Such widely available definitions furnish some of the substance out of which a user may develop his own definition, in the absence of definitions from the drug-using culture.

Journalists use any of a number of approaches conventional in their craft; what they write is greatly influenced by their own professional needs. They must write about "news," about events which have occurred recently and require reporting and interpretation. Furthermore, they need "sources," persons to whom authoritative statements can be attributed. Both needs dispose them to reproduce the line taken by law enforcement officials and physicians, for news is often made by the passage of a law or by a public statement in the wake of an alarming event, such as a bizarre murder or suicide. So journalistic reports frequently dwell on the theme of madness or

23. See Thomas Szasz, *The Myth of Mental Illness* (New York: Paul B. Hoeber, Inc., 1961).

24. For a classic in the genre, see Fitzhugh Ludlow, *The Hasheesh Eater* (New York: Harper and Brothers, 1857). A more modern example is Alan Harrington, "A Visit to Inner Space," in Solomon, *op. cit.,* pp. 72–102.

suicide, a tendency intensified by the newsman's desire to tell a dramatic story.[25] Some journalists, of course, will take the other side in the argument, but even then, because they argue against the theme of madness, the emphasis on that theme is maintained. Public discussion of drug use thus tends to strengthen those stereotypes that would lead users who suffer disturbing effects to interpret their experience as "going crazy."

An Historical Dimension

A number of variables, then, affect the character of drug-induced experiences. It remains to show that the experiences themselves are likely to vary according to when they occur in the history of use of a given drug in a society. In particular, it seems likely that the experience of acute anxiety caused by drug use will so vary.

Consider the following sequence of possible events, which may be regarded as a natural history of the assimilation of an intoxicating drug by a society. Someone in the society discovers, rediscovers or invents a drug which has the properties described earlier. The ability of the drug to alter subjective experience in desirable ways becomes known to increasing numbers of people, and the drug itself simultaneously becomes available, along with the information needed to make its use effective. Use increases, but users do not have a sufficient amount of experience with the drug to form a stable conception of it as an object. They do not know what it can do to the mind, have no firm idea of the variety of effects it can produce, and are not sure how permanent or dangerous the effects are. They do not know if the effects can be controlled or how. No drug-using culture exists, and there is thus no authoritative alternative with which to counter the possible definition, when and if it comes to mind, of the drug experience as madness. "Psychotic episodes" occur frequently.

But individuals accumulate experience with the drug and communicate their experiences to one another. Consensus develops about the drug's objective effects, their duration, proper dosages, predictable dangers and how they may be avoided; all these points become matters of common knowledge, validated by their acceptance in a world of users. A culture exists. When a user experiences bewildering or frightening effects, he has available to him an authoritative alternative to the lay notion that he has gone mad. Every time he uses cultural conceptions to interpret drug experiences and control his response to them, he strengthens his belief that the culture is indeed a reliable source of knowledge. "Psychotic episodes" occur less

25. Examples are J. Kobler, "Don't Fool Around with LSD," *Saturday Evening Post* 236 (November 2, 1963), pp. 30–32, and Noah Gordon, "The Hallucinogenic Drug Cult," *The Reporter* 29 (August 15, 1963), pp. 35–43.

frequently in proportion to the growth of the culture to cover the range of possible effects and its spread to a greater proportion of users. Novice users, to whom the effects are most unfamiliar and who therefore might be expected to suffer most from drug-induced anxiety, learn the culture from older users in casual conversation and in more serious teaching sessions and are thus protected from the dangers of "panicking" or "flipping out."

The incidence of "psychoses," then, is a function of the stage of development of a drug-using culture. Individual experience varies with historical stages and the kinds of cultural and social organization associated with them.

Is this model a useful guide to reality? The only drug for which there is sufficient evidence to attempt an evaluation is marihuana; even there the evidence is equivocal, but it is consistent with the model. On this interpretation, the early history of marihuana use in the United States should be marked by reports of marihuana-induced psychoses. In the absence of a fully formed drug-using culture, some users would experience disquieting symptoms and have no alternative to the idea that they were losing their minds. They would turn up at psychiatric facilities in acute states of anxiety and doctors, eliciting a history of marihuana use, would interpret the episode as a psychotic breakdown. When, however, the culture reached full flower and spread throughout the user population, the number of psychoses should have dropped even though (as a variety of evidence suggests) the number of users increased greatly. Using the definitions made available by the culture, users who had unexpectedly severe symptoms could interpret them in such a way as to reduce or control anxiety and would thus no longer come to the attention of those likely to report them as cases of psychosis.

Marihuana first came into use in the United States in the 1920's and early '30's, and all reports of psychosis associated with its use date from approximately that period.[26] A search of both *Psychological Abstracts* and the *Cumulative Index Medicus* (and its predecessors, the *Current List of Medical Literature* and the *Quarterly Index Medicus)* revealed no cases after 1940. The disappearance of reports of psychosis thus fits the model. It is, of course, a shaky index, for it depends as much on the reporting habits of physicians as on the true incidence of cases, but it is the only thing available.

The psychoses described also fit the model, insofar as there is any clear indication of a drug-induced effect. (The murder, suicide and death in an automobile accident reported by Curtis, for instance, are equivocal in this respect; in no case is any connection with marihuana use demonstrated other than that the people involved used it.)[27] The best evidence comes from the 31 cases reported by Bromberg. Where the detail given allows judgment, it appears that all but one stemmed from the person's inability to deal with

26. Bromberg, *op. cit.,* Curtis, *op. cit.,* and Nesbitt, *op. cit.*
27. Curtis, *op cit.*

either the perceptual distortion caused by the drug or with the panic at the thought of losing one's mind it created.[28] Bromberg's own interpretation supports this:

> In occasional instances, and these are the cases which are apt to come to medical attention, the anxiety with regard to death, insanity, bodily deformity and bodily dissolution is startling. The patient is tense, nervous, frightened; a state of panic may develop. Often suicide or assaultive acts are the result [of the panic]. The anxiety state is so common . . . that it can be considered a part of the intoxication syndrome.[29]
>
> The inner relationship between cannabis [marihuana] and the onset of a functional psychotic state is not always clear. The inner reaction to somatic sensation seems vital. Such reactions consisted of panic states which disappeared as soon as the stimulus (effects of the drug) faded.[30]

Even though Bromberg distinguishes between pure panic reactions and those in which some underlying mental disturbance was present (the "functional psychotic state" he refers to), he finds, as our model leads us to expect, that the episode is provoked by the user's interpretation of the drug effects in terms other than those contained in the drug-using culture.

The evidence cited is extremely scanty. We do not know the role of elements of the drug-using culture in any of these cases or whether the decrease in incidence is a true one. But we are not likely to do any better and, in the absence of conflicting evidence, it seems justified to take the model as an accurate representation of the history of marihuana use in the United States.

The final question, then, is whether the model can be used to interpret current reports of LSD-induced psychosis. Are these episodes the consequence of an early stage in the development of an LSD-using culture? Will the number of episodes decrease while the number of users rises, as the model leads us to predict?

LSD

We cannot predict the history of LSD by direct analogy to the history of marihuana, for a number of important conditions may vary. We must first ask whether the drug has, apart from the definitions users impose on their experience, any demonstrated causal relation to psychosis. There is a great deal of controversy on this point, and any reading of the evidence must be tentative. My own opinion is that LSD has essentially the same charac-

28. See Table 1 in Bromberg, *op. cit.*, pp. 6–7.
29. *Ibid.*, p. 5.
30. *Ibid.*, pp. 7–8.

teristics as those described in the first part of this paper; its effects may be more powerful than those of other drugs that have been studied, but they too are subject to differing interpretations by users,[31] so that the mechanisms I have described can come into play.

The cases reported in the literature are, like those reported for marihuana, mostly panic reactions to the drug experience, occasioned by the user's interpretation that he has lost his mind, or further disturbance among people already quite disturbed.[32] There are no cases of permanent derangement directly traceable to the drug, with one puzzling exception (puzzling to those who report it as well as to me). In a few cases the visual and auditory distortions produced by the drug reoccur weeks or months after it was last ingested; this sometimes produces severe upset among those who experience it. Observers are at a loss to explain the phenomenon, except for Rosenthal, who proposes that the drug may have a specific effect on the nerve pathways involved in vision; but this theory, should it prove correct, is a long way from dealing with questions of possible psychosis.[33]

The whole question is confused by the extraordinary assertions about the effects of LSD made by both proponents and opponents of its use. Both sides agree that it has a very strong effect on the mind, disagreeing only as to whether this powerful effect is benign or malignant. Leary, for example, argues that we must "go out of our minds in order to use our heads,"[34] and that this can be accomplished by using LSD. Opponents[35] agree that it can drive you out of your mind, but do not share Leary's view that this is a desirable goal. In any case, we need not accept the premise simply because both parties to the controversy do.

Let us assume then, in the absence of more definitive evidence, that the drug does not in itself produce lasting derangement, that such psychotic episodes as are now reported are largely a result of panic at the possible meaning of the experience, that users who "freak out" do so because they fear they have permanently damaged their minds. Is there an LSD-using culture? In what stage of development is it? Are the reported episodes of psychosis congruent with what our model would predict, given that stage of development?

Here again my discussion must be speculative, for no serious study of this culture is yet available.[36] It appears likely, however, that such a culture is in an early stage of development. Several conceptions of the drug and

31. Blum *et al., op. cit.*, p. 42.
32. See footnote 2, *supra*.
33. Rosenthal, *op. cit.*
34. Timothy Leary, "Introduction" to Solomon, *op. cit.*, p. 13.
35. Frosch *et al., op. cit.* and Ungerleider *et al., op. cit.*
36. The book by Blum *et al., op. cit.*, attempts this, but leaves many important questions untouched.

its possible effects exist, but no stable consensus has arisen. Radio, television and the popular press present a variety of interpretations, many of them contradictory. There is widespread disagreement, even among users, about possible dangers. Some certainly believe that use (or injudicious use) can lead to severe mental difficulty.

At the same time, my preliminary inquiries and observations hinted at the development (or at least the beginnings) of a culture similar to that surrounding marihuana use. Users with some experience discuss their symptoms and translate from one idiosyncratic description into another, developing a common conception of effects as they talk. The notion that a "bad trip" can be brought to a speedy conclusion by taking thorazine by mouth (or, when immediate action is required, intravenously) has spread. Users are also beginning to develop a set of safeguards against committing irrational acts while under the drug's influence. Many feel, for instance, that one should take one's "trip" in the company of experienced users who are not under the drug's influence at the time; they will be able to see you through bad times and restrain you when necessary. A conception of the appropriate dose is rapidly becoming common knowledge. Users understand that they may have to "sit up with" people who have panicked as a result of the drug's effects, and they talk of techniques that have proved useful in this enterprise.[37] All this suggests that a common conception of the drug is developing which will eventually see it defined as pleasurable and desirable, with possible untoward effects that can however be controlled.

Insofar as this emergent culture spreads so that most or all users share the belief that LSD does not cause insanity, and the other understandings just listed, the incidence of "psychoses" should drop markedly or disappear. Just as with marihuana, the interpretation of the experience as one likely to produce madness will disappear and, having other definitions available to use in coping with the experience, users will treat the experience as self-limiting and not as a cause for panic.

The technology of LSD use, however, has features which will work in the opposite direction. In the first place, it is very easily taken; one need learn no special technique (as one must with marihuana) to produce the characteristic effects, for a sugar cube can be swallowed without instruction. This means that anyone who gets hold of the drug can take it in a setting where there are no experienced users around to redefine frightening effects and "normalize" them. He may also have acquired the drug without acquiring any of the pres-

37. Ungerleider *et al.,* deny the efficacy of these techniques (pp. 391–392): "How do we know that persons taking LSD in a relaxed friendly environment with an experienced guide or 'sitter' will have serious side effects? We have no statistical data to answer this, but our impression (from our weekly group sessions) is that bad experiences were common with or without sitters and with or without 'the right environment.' This does not minimize the importance of suggestion in the LSD experience."

ently developing cultural understandings so that, when frightening effects occur, he is left with nothing but current lay conceptions as plausible definitions. In this connection, it is important that a large amount of the published material by journalists and literary men places heavy emphasis on the dangers of psychosis.[38] It is also important that various medical facilities have become alerted to the possibility of patients (particularly college students and teenagers) coming in with LSD-induced psychoses. All these factors will tend to increase the incidence of "psychotic episodes," perhaps sufficiently to offset the dampening effect of the developing culture.

A second feature of LSD which works in the opposite direction is that it can be administered to someone without his knowledge, since it is colorless, tasteless and odorless. (This possibility is recognized in recent state legislation which specifies *knowing* use as a crime; no such distinction has been found necessary in laws about marihuana, heroin, peyote or similar drugs.) It is reported, for instance, that LSD has been put in a party punchbowl, so that large numbers of people have suffered substantial changes in their subjective experience without even knowing they had been given a drug that might account for the change. Under such circumstances, the tendency to interpret the experience as a sudden attack of insanity might be very strong.[39] If LSD continues to be available on the underground market without much difficulty, such events are likely to continue to occur. (A few apocalyptic types speak of introducing LSD into a city water supply—not at all impossible, since a small amount will affect enormous quantities of water—and thus "turning a whole city on." This might provoke a vast number of "psychoses," should it ever happen.)

In addition to these technological features, many of the new users of LSD, unlike the users of most illicit recreational drugs, will be people who, in addition to never having used any drug to alter their subjective experience before, will have had little or nothing to do with others who have used drugs in that way. LSD, after all, was introduced into the United States under very reputable auspices and has had testimonials from many reputable and conventional persons. In addition, there has been a great deal of favorable publicity to accompany the less favorable—the possibility that the drug can

38. For journalistic accounts, see Kobler, *op. cit.;* Gordon, *op. cit.;* R. Coughlan, "Chemical Mind-Changers," *Life* 54 (March 15, 1963); and H. Asher, "They Split My Personality," *Saturday Review* 46 (June 1, 1963), pp. 39–43. See also two recent novels in which LSD plays a major role: B. H. Friedman, *Yarborough* (New York: Knopf, 1964); and Alan Harrington, *The Secret Swingers* (New York: World Publishing Co., 1966).

39. Cf. Cohen and Ditman, "Complications. . . .," *op cit.,* p. 161: "Accidental ingestion of the drug by individuals who are unaware of its nature has already occurred. This represents a maximally stressful event because the perceptual and ideational distortions then occur without the saving knowledge that they were drug induced and temporary."

do good as well as harm has been spread in a fashion that never occurred with marihuana. Finally, LSD has appeared at a time when the mores governing illicit drug use among young people seem to be changing radically, so that youth no longer reject drugs out of hand. Those who try LSD may thus not even have had the preliminary instruction in being "high" that most novice marihuana users have before first using it. They will, consequently, be even less prepared for the experience they have. (This suggests the prediction that marihuana users who experiment with LSD will show fewer untoward reactions than those who have had no such experience.)[40]

These features of the drug make it difficult to predict the number of mental upsets likely to be "caused" by LSD. If use grows, the number of people exposed to the possibility will grow. As an LSD-using culture develops, the proportion of those exposed who interpret their experience as one of insanity will decrease. But people may use the drug without being indoctrinated with the new cultural definitions either because of the ease with which the drug can be taken or because it has been given to them without their knowledge, in which case the number of episodes will rise. The actual figure will be a vector made up of these several components.

A Note on the Opiates

The opiate drugs present an interesting paradox. In the drugs we have been considering, the development of a drug-using culture causes a decrease in rates of morbidity associated with drug use, for greater knowledge of the true character of the drug's effects lessens the likelihood that users will respond to those effects with uncontrolled anxiety. In the case of opiates, however, the greater one's knowledge of the drug's effects, the more likely it is that one will suffer its worst effect, addiction. As Lindesmith has shown,[41] one can only be addicted when he experiences physiological withdrawal symptoms, recognizes them as due to a need for drugs, and relieves them by taking another dose. The crucial step of recognition is most likely to occur when the user participates in a culture in which the signs of withdrawal are interpreted for what they are. When a person is ignorant of the nature of withdrawal sickness, and has some other cause to which he can attribute his discomfort (such as a medical problem), he may misinterpret the symptoms and thus escape addiction, as some of Lindesmith's cases demonstrate.[42]

This example makes clear how important the actual physiology of the drug response is in the model I have developed. The culture contains inter-

---

40. Negative evidence is found in Ungerleider *et al.*, *op. cit.* Twenty-five of their 70 cases had previously used marihuana.
41. Lindesmith, *op. cit.*
42. *Ibid.*, cases 3, 5 & 6 (pp. 68–69, 71, 72).

pretations of the drug experience, but these must be congruent with the drug's actual effects. Where the effects are varied and ambiguous, as with marihuana and LSD, a great variety of interpretations is possible. Where the effects are clear and unmistakable, as with opiates, the culture is limited in the possible interpretations it can provide. Where the cultural interpretation is so constrained, and the effect to be interpreted leads, in its most likely interpretation, to morbidity, the spread of a drug-using culture will increase morbidity rates.

Conclusion

The preceding analysis, to repeat, is supported at only a few points by available research; most of what has been said is speculative. The theory, however, gains credibility in several ways. Many of its features follow directly from a Meadian social psychology and the general plausibility of that scheme lends it weight. Furthermore, it is consistent with much of what social scientists have discovered about the nature of drug-induced experiences. In addition, the theory makes sense of some commonly reported and otherwise inexplicable phenomena, such as variations in the number of "psychotic" episodes attributable to recreational drug use. Finally, and much the least important, it is in accord with my haphazard and informal observations of LSD use.

The theory also has the virtue of suggesting a number of specific lines of research. With respect to the emerging "social problem" of LSD use, it marks out the following areas for investigation: the relation between social settings of use, the definitions of the drug's effects available to the user, and the subjective experiences produced by the drug; the mechanisms by which an LSD-using culture arises and spreads; the difference in experiences of participants and non-participants in that culture; the influence of each of the several factors described on the number of harmful effects attributable to the drug; and the typical response of physicians to LSD-induced anxiety states and the effect of that response as compared to the response made by experienced drug culture participants.

The theory indicates useful lines of research with respect to other common drugs as well. Large numbers of people take tranquilizers, barbiturates and amphetamines. Some frankly take them for "kicks" and are participants in drug-using cultures build around those drugs, while others are respectable middleclass citizens who probably do not participate in any "hip" user culture. Do these "square" users have some shared cultural understandings of their own with respect to use of these drugs? What are the differential effects of the drugs—both on subjective experience and on rates of morbidity associated with drug use—among the two classes of users? How do physicians handle the pathological effects of these drugs, with which they are relatively familiar, as compared to their handling of drugs which are only available illicitly?

The theory may have implications for the study of drugs not ordinarily used recreationally as well. Some drugs used in ordinary medical practice (such as the adrenocortical steroids) are said to carry a risk of provoking psychosis. It may be that this danger arises when the drug produces changes in subjective experience which the user does not anticipate, does not connect with the drug, and thus interprets as signs of insanity. Should the physician confirm this by diagnosing a "drug psychosis," a vicious circle of increasing validation of the diagnosis may ensue. The theory suggests that the physician using such drugs might do well to inquire carefully into the feelings that produce such anxiety reactions, interpret them to the patient as common, transient and essentially harmless side effects, and see whether such action would not control the phenomenon. Drugs that have been incriminated in this fashion would make good subjects for research designed to explore some of the premises of the argument made here.

The sociologist may find most interesting the postulated connection between historical stages in the development of a culture and the nature of individual subjective experience. Similar linkages might be discovered in the study of political and religious movements. For example, at what stages in the development of such movements are individuals likely to experience euphoric and ecstatic feelings? How are these related to shifts in the culture and organization of social relations within the movement? The three-way link between history, culture and social organization, and the person's subjective state may point the way to a better understanding than we now have of the social bases of individual experience.

CHAPTER TWENTY-TWO

Conventional Crime: Rationalizations and Punishment

Edwin Sutherland, some twenty-five years ago, denounced academic criminologists for their failure to take theoretical account of the crimes committed by members of the white collar classes.[1] His complaint was duly acknowledged, argued over, and effectively forgotten in the years that followed. Sutherland did not look widely enough for his examples, and he may have trained his big theoretical guns on the wrong target; yet there was much substance to his charges and they are as valid today as when he first made them. Criminologists still devote their greatest efforts to such minor areas as juvenile delinquency and drug addiction. They continue, with a few distinguished exceptions, to ignore phenomena that are by many criteria more important: anti-trust violations, gambling, employee theft, and a host of other infractions.

I include in conventional crime all activities that could, if prosecutors so wished, lead to prosecution under the criminal law. That is why I speak of *crime*. I use the qualifying adjective "conventional" because the kinds of crimes with which I am concerned are seldom subject to public criminal sanction. The people who commit them are not prosecuted under the criminal law, nor do they expect to be. In fact, no one, save an occasional reformer or crusading journalist, expects them to be prosecuted.

Conventional crime, so defined, is taken for granted by the community.

Reprinted from *Orthopsychiatry and the Law,* Morton Leavitt and Ben Rubinstein, eds., pp. 199–212, by permission of the Wayne State University Press. Copyright © 1968 Wayne State University Press.

1. Edwin H. Sutherland, *White Collar Crime* (New York, 1949).

The institutions in which it is carried on are essential parts of the community and nation, not abnormalities or evils people would abolish if they could. Conventional criminal activities frequently are regarded as normal and appropriate; it is, of course, understood that one who engages in them may be subject to criminal action, but since this happens so seldom, this threat has only the reality of a fairy tale.

Kinds of Conventional Crime

Let us distinguish between two major kinds of conventional crime. Many kinds of crime attain conventional status because, although they are criminal acts, they are not policed by the ordinary enforcement agencies of the community. Other crimes lie within the province of the regular police, but for one reason or another do not, in the ordinary run of events, have criminal sanctions applied to them.

A recent study of shoplifting illustrates the first type.[2] Cameron inspected the records of department store detectives to discover the number and characteristics of shoplifters apprehended. She found that few of these shoplifters are professional thieves stealing to resell the merchandise. Most are amateurs stealing for their own use. Hardly any of the apprehended shoplifters can be classified as kleptomaniacs; Cameron deduces this from the interesting fact that a shoplifter, once picked up, rarely repeats her crime. Most important, only a small proportion of those seized by store detectives are turned over to the city police and taken to court. Within this group are a disproportionate number of Negroes and juveniles; the average white woman engaging in shoplifting stands little chance of having criminal sanctions applied to her. Shoplifting allows her to indulge in luxuries she could not otherwise afford and tends to become a routine part of her "consumer" activities.

A similar example may be found in Dalton's discussion of employee theft in industrial plants and retail concerns.[3] Estimates place the amount of employee theft in the billions of dollars annually. But action against employees who steal is taken by private police employed by the companies rather than by official governmental agents who could use criminal sanctions. Dalton makes clear that significant amounts of employee theft may, in a certain sense, not be theft at all. Legally theft, such stealing is often carried on with the tacit approval of superiors in the organization and constitutes what Dalton refers to as an "informal reward." A superior will often want a subordinate to do something for him personally or for the company which the subordinate cannot reasonably be officially required to do; if he does what is wanted, he is rewarded by being allowed

2. Mary Owen Cameron, *The Booster and the Snitch* (New York, 1964).
3. Melville Dalton, *Men Who Manage* (New York, 1959), pp. 194–217.

to steal. Of course, not all employee theft has this character; some of it is very much like shoplifting undertaken from the "inside." In any case, here again we have numbers of people doing a large amount of stealing, with no criminal action resulting.[4]

A final example also comes from industrial plants. Gerver and Bensman describe the illegal use of the "tap," a gimmick used by aircraft workers to correct errors made in the placement of nuts and bolts in, for instance, airplane wings.[5] The use of the tap to rethread misplaced bolts speeds up the work but also weakens the structure on which it is employed. This practice is forbidden by employers and, where the government is the contracting party, by the government as well; in this case, the enforcement of the rule is often policed by government inspectors. Practically all workers in the plant conspire to maintain the routine use of the tap. Superiors demand that the work be finished and shipped out, indicating that the tap can be used, but at the same time telling them not to use the tap. The worker soon learns which message he is supposed to hear. It seems obvious, from the account given, that many fewer airplanes would have been built during the war if not for the workers' persistent use of taps. Although the practice was "illegal," it was carried on with impunity; it, too, may be regarded as an instance of conventional crime.

The second large category of conventional crimes consists of those within the province of police agencies, of which gambling is a good illustration. Although estimates of the amount of money annually changing hands in gambling are open to doubt, it is clearly a multi-billion dollar business. In a recent year, over six million dollars was paid for federal licenses to operate slot machines. It is further clear that gambling is accepted as a somewhat shady part of the business world. Gamblers are not gangsters and are rarely conceived or represented as such except by congressional committees and cynical journalists.[6] One could name similar examples at length: the operations of call girls, especially as they are made use of by businessmen; black market activities during the war;[7] professional misconduct;[8] and anti-trust violations and similar sharp practices of the kind

4. Gerald D. Robin, in his unpublished dissertation, "Employees as Offenders: A Sociological Analysis of Occupational Crime" (University of Pennsylvania, 1965), analyzes theft from several department store chains, indicating that at most a third of those apprehended are ever tried for their crime (p. 167).

5. Joseph Bensman and Israel Gerver, "Crime and Punishment in the Factory," *American Sociological Review* 28 (1963): 588–98.

6. Daniel Bell, *The End of Ideology* (New York, 1960), pp. 115–58.

7. Marshall B. Clinard, *The Black Market: A Study of White Collar Crime* (New York, 1952).

8. Charles Winick, "Physician Narcotic Addicts," *Social Problems* 9 (Fall 1961): 174–86; Kenneth J. Reichstein, "Ambulance Chasing: A Case Study of Deviation and Control within the Legal Profession," ibid, 13 (Summer 1965):3–17; Earl R. Quinney, "Occupational Structure and Criminal Behavior: Prescription Violation by Retail Pharmacists," ibid 11 (Fall 1963): 179–85.

described by Sutherland and more recently brought to attention in the price-fixing case in the electrical industry.[9]

In all these instances, it is striking and characteristic that the people engaging in these activities are perfectly cognizant of the criminal nature of their actions, but also know perfectly well that these activities can probably be continued with no threat of punishment. There may be many informal sanctions—a known abortionist may not be welcomed into the inner fraternity of medicine—but the criminal sanctions which might be applied to them are extremely rare.

Distinguishing Characteristics

We can locate the conditions under which a crime will take on the conventional character I have just described by looking at two dimensions which can be used to analyze any kind of crime: the character of the rationalizations used to justify the "criminal" act, and the perceived or actual likelihood of punishment.

RATIONALIZATIONS

Undeniably, people prefer to have a moral justification for what they do, a reason which vindicates their actions and which would be accepted by other reasonable persons if all circumstances were made public. To whom are these justifications available and among what circle of people can they be safely used?[10]

At one extreme are the private and idiosyncratic rationalizations. The person may believe that he has been wronged, even though other people do not recognize the wrong, and that he is entitled to revenge, although others do not recognize the right. Or he may believe that, while the act is wrong, he cannot help himself because he is in the grip of an uncontrollable force. In both cases, while the rationalization exists, it gets no support from the surrounding social group; only the possibility that others might recognize the justification as reasonable allows the actor to expiate his behavior.

At the other extreme are rationalizations and justifications so widespread and commonly known that they are almost universally applicable. While not everyone holds to them, they remain within the range of what any "normal" member of the society would recognize as rational and sensible, even though an individual may perceive flaws in the argument and reject it personally. Such a justification might be a phrasing of our con-

9. John G. Fuller, *The Gentlemen Conspirators* (New York, 1962).
10. Gresham M. Sykes and David Matza, "Techniques of Neutralization: A Theory of Delinquency," *American Sociological Review* 22 (December 1959).

stitutional law—an appeal to the right of free speech, for instance. Or it might be an item of folklore—"It's all right to steal from a big company, they'll never miss it, and besides they cheat, too."[11] Although they generally do not steal on this basis, most people see some logic in so justifying an act of shoplifting. Similarly, people in general are increasingly willing to excuse marijuana smoking on the ground that "It doesn't hurt anyone and it's really no one's business if I want to do it."

Between these extremes lie those justifications which make sense only within a subcultural group. We may usefully distinguish two types: justifications which have their locus in criminal groups and those which are found in non-criminal groups (such as ethnic, occupational, or social class enclaves). An example of the first might be the con man's maxim: "You can't cheat an honest man," rationalizing that the con game cheats only those who are essentially dishonest.[12] An example of the second type of justification might be the code of honor brought by the southern migrant to the northern city, in which an insult to one's mother becomes sufficient excuse for mayhem. In both cases, the rationale can only be used among those who share the actor's code—in the one case, self-consciously criminal; in the other, unintentionally so.

LIKELIHOOD OF PUNISHMENT

The likelihood of being punished for a criminal act varies greatly, depending upon a number of factors. While I cannot consider all of them, I will discuss several that are particularly relevant to the understanding of conventional crime.

1. Some crimes occur too frequently for the police, given their resources and the other items on their agenda, to take any action. The character of the crime makes the cost of detection and apprehension so high in relation to the loss involved that the society is unwilling to pay for more efficient policing. The police do apprehend criminals who have committed the act, but they catch very few of all those who practice it. The probability of any given offender being apprehended is almost as small as the likelihood of being struck by lightning. Under these circumstances the impact of the law is capricious, always possible but never likely. Marijuana use probably exemplifies this situation. No accurate count of the number of marijuana users in the U.S. exists, but a variety of evidence suggests that it is much larger than the number apprehended.[13]

11. Erwin C. Smigel, "Public Attitudes toward 'Chiseling' with Special Reference to Unemployment Compensation," ibid. 18 (February 1953): 59–67.

12. David Maurer, *The Big Con* (Indianapolis, 1940).

13. Howard S. Becker, *Outsiders* (New York, 1963), pp. 59–78; Alfred R. Lindesmith, *The Addict and the Law* (Bloomington, 1965), pp. 222–42.

2. In some kinds of property crimes, the persons victimized want more to recover what has been stolen than to see the criminal punished. Shoplifting and employee theft are of this character. Department stores much prefer to get the merchandise back and generally have no wish to indict the offenders. Prosecution will ordinarily be waived if the thief makes restitution. Even if the probability of being caught is high, the chance of being brought to trial is very low.

3. Some criminals are able to protect themselves against the consequences of their crime. The classic case is the professional thief or con man who, before committing the crime, arranges for legal aid, pays for protection through a professional "fixer," and is ordinarily able to delay the legal process until the complainants give up.[14] But "protection" can take other forms; if a person holds a high enough position in an organization, others are afraid or unwilling to make a move against him. A high-ranking officer of an industrial firm who appropriates company-owned material for his own use is less likely to become the object of prosecution than lower ranked employees. In general, the higher one's rank, the less likely one is to be punished for a wide range of crimes.

4. Those charged with enforcing the law may share the beliefs rationalizing the offense with those committing it and fail to proceed against offenders on this basis; they may agree with the marijuana smoker that use of the drug is essentially harmless; they may share the conviction that a big department store can stand being robbed once in a while. Insofar as they do, the probability of the culprit being punished decreases. In this sense, the degree of harm to the society conventionally imputed to a crime is directly related to the likelihood of being punished.

The Perspective and Situation of the Conventional Criminal

Conventional crime characteristically occurs when 1) rationalizations for committing the act in question are widely shared among otherwise conventional people, and 2) when the likelihood of punishment, for any of the reasons just suggested, is small. By what mechanisms does the conventional criminal come to engage in the illegal act? What else characterizes his perspective? How is his crime integrated into the rest of his activities and into community organization?

If he feels his action is justified, the conventional criminal will be restrained from carrying it out only by the thought of possible punishment. Of course, we must recognize that rationalizations are not always effective. Cameron describes convincingly how the shoplifter's rationalizations break

14. Chic Conwell and Edwin H. Sutherland, *The Professional Thief* (Chicago, 1937).

down when she is confronted by a store detective who persuades her that she has, after all, committed a crime. Nonetheless, the actor usually can maintain his rationalizations sufficiently to justify the act; if these justifications are weakened by challenge from respectable authority before he commits the act, he will probably not carry it out.

If only the thought of punishment restrains the conventional criminal (and in this he presumably does not differ from his professional counterpart), how does he envision this threat? I suggest that he plays the odds.[15] He calculates the probable payoff and measures it against the possibility of capture. If, as the previous discussion indicates, the likelihood of punishment is small, he will decide to go ahead with the act.

The conventional criminal probably calculates the chances of being caught as very low, even when they are not that small. Because punishment is rare, the chance of any person being aware of the few cases in which an offender has been caught is small. This is less true of those crimes (such as marijuana use) for which apprehension is accompanied by a great hue and cry. But it is very true of a great many crimes in which apprehension (because it is done by private agencies, as in the case of shoplifting or employee theft) is never made public. Thus, the actor's personal experience tells him there is little danger.

It is probably characteristic of conventional crimes that, as the initial commission depends heavily upon calculating the odds against being caught, once an offender has been apprehended he is likely to give up that form of conventional crime. Cameron reports that amateur shoplifters seldom continue after they have been caught (even though they may have stolen frequently before). There is little evidence on this point, and some research is in order. Are, for instance, doctors convicted of malpractice less likely following conviction to engage in those activities which prompted the suit?[16]

We can now turn to the problem of integrating conventional crime with both the lives of conventional people and conventional institutions. People who commit these crimes do not expect to be viewed or treated as criminals. Therefore, their crime never assumes for them the importance that it does for someone running the risk of imprisonment. Their "criminal" activities are not, for them, the one overriding fact about themselves which they must never forget, which they must always consider, no matter what they plan to do. Crime is, instead, just another one of their many activities, exciting and daring for some, routine and commonplace for others. How different it must be to be a professional burglar who, as he goes about his

15. James F. Short and Fred L. Strodtbeck, *Group Process and Gang Delinquency* (Chicago, 1965), pp. 248–64.
16. Richard D. Schwartz and Jerome H. Skolnick, "Two Studies of Stigma," in Howard S. Becker (ed.), *The Other Side* (New York, 1964), pp. 103–17.

business, knows that he may end the night in jail; a professional gambler expects, at the close of the day's activities, to go about his normal business like any other citizen.

Because the criminal act carries with it no feared consequences, because the actor does not conceive of himself as a criminal and does not think of his activity as criminal, it is possible for conventional crime to be functionally integrated into or interdependent with the more "normal" aspects of the person's life. He depends on the rewards of his criminal activity just as he depends on the rewards of his conventional activity. His long-range plans include quite naturally the idea that his criminal activity will place him in command of certain resources he would not otherwise have.

Because conventional criminal activity plays such an important and taken-for-granted role in the lives of many people, it rarely becomes the subject of attack by enforcement agencies. Of course, the argument is circular here: conventional crime exists because it is not attacked by law enforcement agencies, and it is not attacked by law enforcement agencies because it is conventional. But the circularity, I think, does not detract from the argument. We need not establish which came first, although that might be done by historical studies. Once the pattern is established, it is self-perpetuating.

Instead of being the object of attack, conventional criminality is seen, even by those who neither engage in nor profit from it, as part of the social structure, no more likely to disappear than schools or subways. Like the institutions that contain it and allow its continued existence, conventional criminality is characteristic of contemporary life; either one makes use of the institutions and the crime, or one doesn't, as seems appropriate. Think, for instance, of the institution of the bootlegger in a "dry" state. Everyone knows bootleggers exist, though some disapprove both of them and the drinking they make possible; everybody knows that it is against the law, but no one does anything about it; some people use the bootlegger's services, others do not. Bootlegging is simply a different kind of retail business. Nevertheless, conventionally criminal activities remain criminal, no matter how well accepted; and this fact is universally known. How do communities maintain criminal activities they have legally prohibited? One way is described by Charles Warriner in his study of a small town which was officially dry and, like so many dry towns, unofficially very wet.[17] Citizens drank with their shades pulled, feeling or pretending that they were the few who did so, in every other way respecting and maintaining the public fiction that drinking was wrong. Most people in the town publicly supported prohibition; privately, they continued to drink.

17. Charles Warriner, "The Nature and Functions of Official Morality," *American Journal of Sociology* 64 (1958): 165–68.

Another way of integrating conventional criminality into the structure of the community is described by Hughes as the "dirty work" syndrome.[18] Discussing the role of the SS in the concentration camps in Nazi Germany, Hughes argues that the SS had considerable underground support by the populace. While disagreeing with the methods employed, many Germans supported the SS in the belief that something had to be done about the "Jewish problem." They both had their cake and ate it; the SS did for them what they wanted done, and they neither admitted nor took responsibility for the action. Hughes describes this organization of deviance as a moral division of labor, allowing some people to be moral because an "immoral" group does what the moralists want done and what they would otherwise have to do for themselves. The relevance of this concept to such phenomena as gambling and prostitution is clear.

Implications

I am not interested in exposing the seamy side of American life, worthy as that enterprise might be. Nor do I share Sutherland's concern with criticizing etiological theories of crime. He used his data on white collar crime to show that criminologists, in theorizing about the causes of crime, based their theories on a biased sample of lawbreakers. Most of the criminals included in crime statistics were lower-class people who broke laws prohibiting burglary, rape, murder, and similar crimes. The middle-class or wealthy people who violated the anti-trust laws, who gave their customers short weight, who issued fraudulent advertising—none of these, even though they had violated the criminal law, were prosecuted under its provisions and none of them appeared in crime statistics. As such theories of crime ignored white collar criminals, they arrived at fallacious conclusions about the correlates of crime, particularly in the areas of class and race. Criminologists fooled themselves with theories attributing the etiology of crime to factors related to class or ethnicity or such associated phenomena as broken homes; they might have avoided these mistakes by including in their thinking the white collar criminal.

Sutherland's argument is relevant, but remains a minor issue in relation to a larger consideration of conventional crime. Etiology was never as important a question as Sutherland felt it to be; we can, however, understand his concern by recognizing the almost exclusive emphasis put on this problem by earlier criminologists.

A more interesting implication of the material on conventional crime concerns our image of the criminal. In traditional criminological thought,

18. Everett C. Hughes, "Good People and Dirty Work," in *The Other Side*, pp. 23–36.

he is someone "different," an individual whose behavior requires a special kind of explanation not needed for the ordinary law-abiding citizen. He may be neurotic, or suffering from anomie, or any of a dozen other diseases of causal significance. With few exceptions (Matza's recent book on delinquency is one[19]), students of crime do not attempt to explicate the criminal's behavior in the same way they explain normal behavior. If one were to attempt this, the mechanisms involved would be the same for the normal person and the criminal, differing only in the circumstances under which they operate.

Consider the mechanisms suggested by the phenomenon of conventional crime. We view the actor as rational, within the limits of his information and abilities. He decides what he wants and goes after it, taking into account alternative paths open to him for gaining it. He may decide that the cost of his goal is too high and either abandon it or substitute another. If the odds are good enough, he may decide to take a chance and risk detection. This kind of calculating, rational behavior is the same for both criminal and conventional citizens. What varies are the opportunities available to achieve their goals, the kind of goals they value and strive for, the methods of calculation they learn, and the awareness they build up of the possible costs of illegal activity.

This picture of the human actor contradicts much of what is usually taken for granted by social scientists. But the amount and variety of conventional crime in the United States, the degree to which it is integrated into the lives of so many citizens and so many organizations, convinces me that this is the only picture of man which offers a sufficient explanation. When we see how easily values as basic to our society as those surrounding property rights are ignored, we can no longer think of man as governed by fundamental values which he attempts to put into practice in particular situations. We cannot imagine man a victim of uncontrollable compulsive urges when we see how easily he gives them up once he has been punished for putting them into practice.

These facts about conventional crime also have implications for our conception of society, both on the factual and the theoretical levels. I find it difficult now, after contemplating the findings of the studies I have mentioned, to be content with textbook depictions of American society which delineate our major institutions without, somehow, describing any of these phenomena. Are they talking about the same country? And when I read discussions of the way American values inform and shape American instutions, I wonder again if we are talking about the same country, because the values discussed would not produce the behavior embodied in con-

19. David Matza, *Delinquency and Drift* (New York, 1964).

ventional crime. Nor would one guess from these descriptions of American society that American institutions have, built into them, the kind of conventional deviance they contain.

(Of course, it would be foolish to pretend that social scientists have been blind to these things. A number of people have called attention to corruption and graft in municipal government,[20] and how these practices function in urban society. Dalton, Roy, and Tumin, among others,[21] give us straightforward and realistic accounts of the operations of American business and industry).

If we take this view of crime and its role in society, what then do we make of those crimes on which criminologists spend most of their time? This kind of crime can be seen as a special case of the *law-breaking act,* a larger category which includes the conventional crimes I have discussed. The criminologist's "crime" is the sub-class of law-breaking acts against which criminal sanctions are invoked, no matter how crudely or spottily. Its practitioners are relatively (but only relatively) unintegrated with the rest of society and so are (again relatively) easy to attack and to study. It is no accident that when academicians talk of crime they usually mean drug addicts and juvenile delinquents and not corporate price-fixers.[22]

20. Eric L. McKitrick, "The Study of Corruption," *Political Science Quarterly* 72 (1957): 502–14; Robert K. Merton, *Social Theory and Social Structure* (New York, 1957). pp. 72–81; William F. Whyte, *Street Corner Society* (Chicago, 1955), pp. 111–252.

21. Donald Roy, "Efficiency and the 'Fix': Informal Intergroup Relations in a Piecework Machine Shop," *American Journal of Sociology* 60 (November 1954): 255–66; Melvin Tumin, "Business as a Social System," *Behavioral Science,* 9 (April 1964): 120–30.

22. This entire essay owes much to the thinking of Edwin M. Lemert; see especially his "Social Structure, Social Control, and Deviation," in Marshall B. Clinard (ed.), *Anomie and Deviant Behavior* (New York, 1964), pp. 57–97.

CHAPTER TWENTY-THREE

Deviance
and Deviates

What is interesting about deviance is not what it is, but what people think it is. To be sure, there are such things as drug addiction and homosexuality, and they pose interesting problems for the physiologist, the biochemist and the psychologist. But interesting scientific problems do not create public concern. The still unexplained physiological mechanisms that produce heroin addiction do not generate newspaper headlines. What arouses the government, the press and the public is the crime attributed to addicts, the fear of attack by a drug-crazed kid on a lonely street, even though addicts engage mainly in shoplifting and other kinds of petty theft; the stories of high school students using marijuana, though there is no evidence that marijuana will harm them as much as the alcohol their parents allow them to drink; the fear even, for some, that the Chinese Communists are using narcotics to weaken the will of the American people.

Deviance, in general, as opposed to concrete forms of behavior like drug use or homosexuality, is a creation of the public imagination. The act of injecting heroin into a vein is not inherently deviant. If a nurse gives a patient drugs under a doctor's orders, it is perfectly proper. It is when it is done in a way that is not publicly defined as proper that it becomes deviant. The act's deviant character lies in the way it is defined in the public mind.

The public definition of an act as deviant has, of course, drastic consequences for the person who commits it. Under one definition, he may continue to live as an ordinary citizen. Under another definition, he may become a hounded criminal. A consideration of deviance in America over the

From *The State of the Nation,* edited by David Boroff. © 1965 by The Nation Centennial, Inc. Published by Prentice-Hall, Inc., Englewood Cliffs, New Jersey.

last one hundred years must inevitably focus on what people have thought of deviance and how public thinking about it has changed, and must interpret what deviants do as a reaction to the way society reacts to them.

We have had drug addicts for a long time. Before the turn of the century, as a number of early studies show, many older people were addicted to patent medicines that were liberally laced with opium. Women helped themselves through menopause with the aid of opiates, and men and women alike alleviated their minor ills with such remedies. They came to depend on their "medicine" and were addicts without knowing it. We also had more self-conscious addicts: jockeys, gamblers, pimps, whores and others in the "sporting life," who smoked opium and became addicted.

Prostitution is, of course, the oldest profession. But prostitutes in earlier times were fallen women, fenced off (in red-light districts) from more respectable people.

Homosexuality is one of the oldest vices. Homosexual literature delights in naming the famous homosexuals of early times, from Nero to the present. But it seems likely that homosexual activity in an earlier day was usually practiced as a secret vice by those who lived in the conventional world.

The examples indicate the range of possibilities, in an earlier period, in the relations between respectable people and those they considered deviant. People who engaged in practices thought to be morally repellent either did not know that they were "doing wrong," like the patent medicine addicts; knew what they were doing, but did it secretly and despised themselves for it, as they would have been despised by others if their sin were known; or lived in a separate part of society, like the sporting world, segregated and isolated from the conventional society.

Have things changed? Yes and no. The same relationships can be observed today between some kinds of deviants and the rest of society. Large numbers of people are addicted to sleeping pills and tranquilizers; since the public has not yet been persuaded that these are dangerous drugs, they do not think of themselves, and are not thought of, as deviant. Yet the observation I heard attributed to a Kansas City tavern owner—"Everybody who doesn't drink takes pills"—becomes more true every day.

The practitioners of secret vices are still around, though the catalogue of vices involved has been enlarged. There are still secret addicts and "closet queens" who hide their homosexuality. There are, in addition, secret transvestites, secret devotees of sadomasochistic thrills, secret fetishists, and others whose kicks are mailed to them in plain brown envelopes with no return address.

But the analogue of the old red-light district, in which the deviant lived walled off from a society that might otherwise be contaminated by contact with him, is harder to find. Prostitutes inhabit most of the public places people go to for entertainment—bars, night clubs and hotels—at every level of society. Their way of life is not so different from that of other people as to mark them off as a special breed. It is difficult to think of any class of deviants so segregated and marked today.

Though some of the relations between deviants and respectable society characteristic of an earlier era can still be found, much has changed. Not only are deviants less segregated, but they have come, in increasing measure, to take a different view of themselves and of how they ought to be treated by others.

One component of the change is an increasing tolerance of deviance by respectable society. The deviant is no longer branded as a sinner whose consignment to hell is a foregone conclusion. Instead, ordinary people are willing to see extenuating circumstances that might account for the deviance, are willing to believe that deviants can be reformed, and are increasingly unwillingly to take harsh punitive action toward deviants. Public beliefs have changed in this way, in part, because high court decisions have made it more difficult for the police to "roust" deviants in what used to be their customary fashion. Police habitually control deviance not only by actually convicting people of crimes on the basis of evidence, but rather by harassing them with illegal and quasi-legal arrests that deviants are not disposed to fight because they cannot come into court with clean hands. But increasingly strict judicial interpretations of the search and seizure rule, and other decisions affecting civil rights in the area of vice and obscenity, have handcuffed the police so that these means are less available to them. (They have not, of course, given up completely; the nationwide harassment of Lenny Bruce, in clear contravention of Supreme Court decisions on obscenity, is a case in point.)

With the gradual lessening of police harassment, other influences have been at work. The rise of dime-store psychoanalysis—the easy explanation of deviant or odd behavior as the product of childhood traumas that might have happened to anyone—has helped the public to absolve deviants of responsibility for what they do. And, perhaps more important, it has helped deviants themselves to decide that what they do, right or wrong, is not their fault and, indeed, that it might not even be wrong. It is unlikely that any deviant believes this so completely that he never has a qualm about his deviant acts, but it provides the moral basis on which he can demand to be let alone.

Finally, various kinds of popular philosophical positions—the Eastern philosophies, psychological doctrines of self-development, and so on—have brought some people to see the means of salvation in what were formerly thought to be deviant practices. In particular, the use of drugs—both old-fashioned marijuana and heroin and such newer discoveries as peyote and

LSD—has been seen as a way of expanding the consciousness and achieving higher levels of human experience. From this point of view, what ordinary people think deviant is not deviant at all; it is all a mistake and they need to be enlightened if they are capable of it and fought against if they attempt to interfere with one's own enlightenment.

In any case, for any or all of these reasons, deviants have become more self-conscious, more organized, more willing to fight with conventional society than ever before. They are more open in their deviance, prouder of what they are and less willing to be treated as others want to treat them without having some voice in the matter.

Homosexuals have organized what can only be called "defense groups," very much on the model of such ethnic defense organizations as the Anti-Defamation League or the NAACP. The Mattachine Society (for male homosexuals) and the Daughters of Bilitis (for Lesbians) have branches in several large cities and publish magazines (*The Mattachine Review* and *The Ladder*); they hold annual conventions at which panels of experts and members discuss the biological, psychological, sociological and legal problems of homosexuality. Their magazines are filled with discussions of famous homosexuals in history, of civil rights cases and decisions involving them or applicable to their problem, and other matters justifying their right to be homosexual.

When I addressed a Lesbian group not long ago, I was surprised (a sign of how much I accepted conventional stereotypes) at how much the group looked like a middle-class women's club having a meeting to decide how to run the next charity bazaar. Since they were conventionally dressed, not in the least "butchy," I found myself amused by the disparity between my conception of them and the reality. But I stopped smiling when I realized the aggressiveness and courage it took to identify oneself publicly as the officer of a Lesbian organization and the risk these women were taking in doing so.

Homosexual organizations have won support from "straight" scientists, psychologists, lawyers and, most recently, the clergy. A group of San Francisco clergymen sponsored a homosexual New Year's Eve dance, a gesture deliberately designed to make the affair publicly respectable. Though the police had not bothered a Halloween dance at the Hilton (to which the guests came "in drag," to the great delight of news photographers), they saw a threat in this legitimately sponsored affair and moved in, taking pictures of everyone there. Lawyers, on hand to protest such maneuvers, were the only ones arrested. But the police, undoubtedly motivated by a wish to "keep them in their place," will not prevent homosexual defense groups from winning further allies in the respectable world and pressing their fight for equal rights. The militancy of the homosexual organizations has provoked a frightened warning from a committee of the New York Academy of Medicine.

Another version of the new self-conscious deviant organization is found in Synanon, a self-help organization of heroin addicts now more or less permanently settled in several places around the country, from Santa Monica and Marin County in the West to Westport in the East. The characteristic feature of Synanon is not that it thinks addicts ought to be allowed to take drugs in peace, even though many experts feel this the most efficient and humane solution to the drug problem, but that it thinks addicts ought to break the habit with the help of ex-addicts rather than being cured forcibly by police or psychiatrists. With merciless discipline, Synanon forces the addicts who join to toe the line or get out. Since no professional group has very much success curing addicts, Synanon (whose successes are not yet reliably measured, if indeed there is any reliable measure) stands on solid ground when it demands that its members be given the right to help themselves. It has, of course, provoked strong reactions from many professionals in the drug-cure field, who cannot believe that any good can come of ex-addicts associating with one another. On the other hand, it has won strong support from many legislators and a few of the professionals who have had an opportunity to inspect its establishments.

Synanon is a grim operation. Not so the short-lived International Foundation for Internal Freedom (IFIF), headed by Timothy Leary and Richard Alpert, the psychologists who left Harvard after an extended battle over whether their experimental use of LSD and other psychedelic (mind-expanding) drugs with students was a proper professional activity. IFIF, in contrast to Synanon and the homosexual groups, is a frankly utopian organization. It looks forward to a radically changed society, in which people will see through the games of life they now play in deadly earnest—the family game, the work game, etc.—and, freed by the use of LSD, live in happier forms of human association, realizing at last the as yet untapped resources of the human mind and spirit.

Leary and Alpert attempted to found a colony embodying these ideas in Zihuatanejo, but the Mexican government drove them out. They are now giving seminars and lectures designed to let others in on the good news, and Leary has just published a book, based on the *Tibetan Book of the Dead,* of ritual and instruction to be used to enhance the LSD experience. They have had a fair amount of success, most of it with well-educated people, including many engineers and "hard" scientists, who seem especially drawn by the appeal of new kinds of mystical experience. Their success has been clouded, however, by the hostility with which officialdom greets them everywhere from Massachusetts to Mexico.

The LSD movement (if it is really big enough to merit being called a movement) differs from the organizations of drug addicts and homosexuals in being composed of people who were not, prior to their involvement with LSD, deviant in any sense. But all three groups exemplify the increasing militancy, organization and self-consciousness of deviant worlds and their growing unwillingness to let respectable society have its own way with them unchallenged.

A sense of what this might lead to (if every group engaged in deviant practices became self-consciously aggressive) comes from the recent lighthearted attempt in San Francisco to have marijuana legalized. One man staged a "puff-in" at the Hall of Justice, lighting up a marijuana cigarette in front of police officers so that he could become a test case. A local attorney has become interested in testing the legality of the law. A group of forty or fifty paraded around Union Square every Sunday for a month (some of the paraders were mothers pushing baby carriages) carrying signs advocating legalization. And when President Johnson spoke, during the campaign, in front of St. Peter and Paul's Church in North Beach, scattered among the "LBJ All the Way" signs that greeted him were a few that said, "Make Marijuana Legal."

Perhaps more interesting than the organization of deviant groups, though much harder to document, is the possibility that practices and beliefs formerly labeled deviant have spread to broad segments of the "normal" population. This possibility first became known to the public, I think, with the publication of the Kinsey Report, which reported surprisingly high percentages of men who had engaged in various abnormal forms of sex behavior. Although substantial questions have been raised about Kinsey's sampling and techniques, the figures were so much higher than anyone had suspected that it is a worthwhile hypothesis that there is a lot more deviance around than meets the eye and that Americans, while not advertising the fact, are by no means as straitlaced as we had thought.

With the Kinsey findings to point the way, a good deal more evidence, most of it quite impressionistic, can be cited in favor of such conclusions. As a simple example, note the mammoth sales of works like *Candy, Fanny Hill* and the *Tropics,* which had been smuggled in from France as pornography only a few years ago. Once the legal restraints were removed, there turned out to be a good many pornography fans around.

Other evidence is not hard to come by. Not long ago, police discovered that some sixty high school students in Woodside, an affluent suburb of San Francisco, were smoking marijuana supplied by a recent graduate. Similar stories could no doubt be told about hundreds of other communities. Marijuana use is not confined to Negroes, Puerto Ricans, musicians and show people. I know of no profession which does not have at least a few members who are at least occasional marijuana users. As an example, far out enough to make the point, one user I know was first offered marijuana by a clergyman, who himself saw nothing wrong with it, though he made sure that his congregation did not find out his views. (Perhaps because I have studied marijuana use and published on the subject, similar cases are constantly brought to my attention.)

Somewhat less direct evidence comes from a survey recently conducted by Paul Verden and Harold Hodges in Santa Clara County. They asked people a number of questions designed to measure "cultural orthodoxy," the tendency to be conservative in areas ranging from political and economic attitudes to attitudes toward sex. The results are somewhat surprising. There are a great many more people who are culturally unorthodox than one might have expected. In addition, the unorthodox are scattered uniformly through all the social classes of the community. In other words, that kind of deviance —and let us grant that asking people whether or not they agree with a number of unorthodox statements is at best a weak measure of actual deviant practice—is not the monopoly of any group in the community. People of all kinds, rich and poor, feel restive under the constraints of our Victorian public morality.

Given the growing underground of practicing deviants and adherents to the culturally unorthodox, what can we make of our official morality? Why does it receive overwhelming public support, even though many, probably a growing number, no longer believe in it or allow it to restrain their activity? The most likely answer is, of course, that official morality— preached by leading public figures, embodied in laws and enforced sporadically by police—is a political product. Politicians make laws embodying its precepts, or refuse to repeal laws which embody them, because organized pressure groups make that a wise course. Those in favor of a more relaxed official morality seldom organize in a way that makes them politically effective, although ministers, physicians or lawyers may occasionally act on their behalf, as when a New York county medical society issued a report advocating less punitive narcotics laws.

Public morality must, of course, keep itself in some sort of relation to "the times," to the slow drift of opinion and practice in the country. If it gets too far out of step, it creates the kind of situation we had during Prohibition; and public leaders do not care for the widespread disrespect for law such a situation engenders and soon put an end to it. But as long as some sizable and politically influential group demands a particular official morality, state legislatures and others are likely to bow to the demand, even if the consequence is simply a public affirmation of a way of life many no longer follow. If the laws embodying the morality are not enforced too strictly and if deviants do not mind being somewhat secretive in their activities, an accommodation can be worked out more or less to everyone's satisfaction.

But our public morality may have gotten too far out of step. Recent reports on college students indicate that a vast number of college girls, whatever their private beliefs and whatever their practice, simply no longer believe in chastity, virginity and the sexual double standard that once was the American way. Whether they "do" or "don't" they do not feel that they can successfully argue—either with the boys who pursue them or with other girls—that premarital intercourse is wrong in and of itself. In the same way, it seems likely that the general public is now prepared to accept revisions of our extremely punitive laws on homosexuality and addiction.

It is hard to say what things will be like if the trend toward relaxation of older standards of morality continues. We can get a clue, perhaps, from a look at the "swingers" of Los Angeles. Los Angeles is probably the most unorganized city in the country. It has a vast number of new migrants every year, no well-organized elites to absorb and tame the newcomers (as does the San Francisco Bay Area, which also has a large in-migration), and nearly perpetual summer. With none of the constraints that might be imposed by tightly organized neighborhoods, the presence of extended families close by, or even by a seasonal change that would get people off the beach, new kinds of manners and morals seem to have grown up.

A long-time resident of the Los Angeles beach communities told me the following tale. When he moved into a house already inhabited by three other bachelors, one of them handed him a pack of calling cards that had just a phone number, the number of the house phone, printed on them. He was told to hand the cards out to likely girls wherever he met them—on the beach, in bars, in department stores, wherever—and wait for the response. And, just as he had been told, within a week the phone started ringing and never stopped. Girls who couldn't even remember who had given them the card, girls he had thought attractive but unlikely to be intrigued, old ones, young ones—they all called and they all wanted to go to bed. Neither he nor his housemates have ever wanted for companionship.

While few Angelenos are so enterprising as to have cards printed up, and while such a story is a slim basis for generalization, a community where such a gimmick will work must surely be something new in American life. Though no one has really done a thorough investigation of the matter, the casualness about sex indicated by the story is said to permeate large segments of Los

Angeles society. (This in a town whose police harass Lenny Bruce as efficiently and conscientiously as those of more puritanical eastern cities!)

David Boroff suggested that sex is the politics of the sixties, and I think he was right, though perhaps not in the sense he meant. Sex of the Los Angeles variety, drugs (both the hipster's marijuana and the more intellectual drugs like LSD), and other varieties of exotic behavior may well come to be thought of as inalienable rights, not to be interfered with by either the police or self-appointed censors of family, neighborhood or community. Whether proponents take the low road of quiet evasion of existing moralities (like the quiet coteries of marijuana users found everywhere) or the high road of principled defiance (best exemplified by Leary and Alpert's open conflict with their Harvard colleagues), they will contribute to a growing tension between themselves and those who are not ready to countenance the new ways.

The newly organized deviant groups are making use of the potential for revolutionary change contained in our cultural emphasis on egalitarianism and our legal emphasis on due process. Our institutions can, when they are spurred into action by determined men, protect minorities of whatever kind from the restraints of cultural tradition and local prejudice. The civil rights movement has shown that. The techniques, legal and extra-legal, used by opponents of racial segregation, will probably be used more and more frequently by deviant groups in the years ahead. Recent events in Berkeley have shown that political freedoms and less conventional freedoms go hand in hand; the same powers use the same means to stifle both. As the indivisible nature of freedom becomes clear, even those who do not engage in forbidden activities will be drawn into the battle, just as physicians, lawyers and ministers have already been drawn into the fight for more humane and rational treatment of addicts and homosexuals. The seeds of independence planted in 1776 will yet bear some strange fruit.

Name Index

Subject Index